Lecture Notes in Computer Science

Edited by G. Goos, J. Hartmanis and J. van

Advisory Board: W. Brauer   D. Gries   J. Stoer

Springer
Berlin
Heidelberg
New York
Barcelona
Budapest
Hong Kong
London
Milan
Paris
Santa Clara
Singapore
Tokyo

Otto Spaniol   Claudia Linnhoff-Popien
Bernd Meyer   (Eds.)

Trends in Distributed Systems

CORBA and Beyond

International Workshop TreDS '96
Aachen, Germany, October 1-2, 1996
Proceedings

Springer

Series Editors

Gerhard Goos, Karlsruhe University, Germany

Juris Hartmanis, Cornell University, NY, USA

Jan van Leeuwen, Utrecht University, The Netherlands

Volume Editors

Otto Spaniol
Claudia Linnhoff-Popien
Bernd Meyer
RWTH Aachen, Institute for Computer Science IV
Ahornstr. 55, D-52056 Aachen, Germany
E-mail: spaniol@informatik.rwth-aachen.de

Cataloging-in-Publication data applied for

Die Deutsche Bibliothek - CIP-Einheitsaufnahme

Trends in distributed systems : CORBA and beyond ;
proceedings / International Workshop TreDS '96, Aachen,
Germany, October 1996. Otto Spaniol ... (ed.). - Berlin ;
Heidelberg ; New York ; Barcelona ; Budapest ; Hong Kong ;
London ; Milan ; Paris ; Santa Clara ; Singapore ; Tokyo :
Springer, 1996
  (Lecture notes in computer science ; Vol. 1161)
  ISBN 3-540-61842-2
NE: Spaniol, Otto [Hrsg.]; International Workshop TreDS <1996,
  Aachen>; GT

CR Subject Classification (1991): C.2.4, D.3.2, D.4.2-3, D.1.3, H.2.4, D.4.7,
D.2.7, H.4.3, H.5.1

ISSN 0302-9743
ISBN 3-540-61842-2 Springer-Verlag Berlin Heidelberg New York

© Springer-Verlag Berlin Heidelberg 1996
Printed in Germany

Typesetting: Camera-ready by author
SPIN 10549755   06/3142 – 5 4 3 2 1 0   Printed on acid-free paper

Preface

Distributed Systems are becoming more and more important. The increasing complexity of modern information systems enforces software reuse supported by object-oriented techniques. Existing computer systems from different computer vendors are integrated through middleware, bridging heterogeneity within large computer networks. This approach has several advantages. On the one hand users can retain their familiar environment, on the other hand the functionality of the information system is enhanced as more services can be made available.

The Object Management Group have devoted considerable resources to the development of object-oriented standard interfaces. In particular, this consortium considers aspects like reusability of software components, interoperability, portability, and the integration of proprietary software. As a result of these efforts the Common Object Request Broker Architecture (CORBA) has been developed, and has been integrated into numerous products from different companies, including amongst others Orbix by IONA, SUN Network Enabled Objects (NEO), IBM Distributed System Object Model (DSOM), DCE Object Broker, HP Distributed Smalltalk, and HP ORB+. These CORBA implementations are of increasing importance and form the central point of our workshop.

TreDS'96 has been organized to bring together researchers from industry and universities as well as users who are developing additional facilities for distributed system products, new methodologies, tools, and concepts. Beyond CORBA, the workshop focuses on interoperability problems, formal methods, CORBA Services, and related approaches and their applications.

A total of 51 papers were submitted for TreDS'96, from which 20 papers have been selected for publication in the proceedings. In addition, some more papers have been selected for presentation in two industrial and two short paper sessions. The overall quality of the submissions was impressive, not least demonstrating the prominence of Distributed Systems. The programme committee did an excellent job; each paper was reviewed by up to five referees, leaving each member with about 10 papers, to be reviewed to a very tight schedule.

The workshop is supported by the Aachen University of Technology, the European Commission, DG III/F, the German Association of Computer Science (Gesellschaft für Informatik), and by several industrial organisations, to whom we are especially grateful.

Aachen, August 1996   Otto Spaniol
                                          Claudia Linnhoff-Popien
                                                     Bernd Meyer

Programme Committee

S. Abeck, Germany

B. Butscher, Germany

O. Drobnik, Germany

R. Friedrich, USA

K. Geihs, Germany

R. Gotzhein, Germany

B. Haverkort, Germany

D. Hogrefe, Switzerland

K. Irmscher, Germany

H. Krumm, Germany

M. Leclerc, Germany·

G. Leduc, Belgium

C. Linnhoff-Popien, Germany

B. Meyer, Germany

C. Mittasch, Germany

E. Najm, France

K. Raymond, Australia

G. Saake, Germany

A. Schill, Germany

G. Schürmann, Germany

O. Spaniol, Germany

R. Soley, USA

V. Tschammer, Germany

Referees (in addition to all PC members)

Jürgen Berghoff

Henrik Bohnenkamp

Andy Bond

Roland Büschkes

Martin Chilvers

Stefan Conrad

Christian Cseh

Keith Duddy

Reza Fars

Andreas Fasbender

Arnaud Fevrier

Steffen Geschke

Holger Gründer

Kai Jakobs

Raschid Karabek

Dogan Kesdogan

Andreas Köppel

Henner Krabbe

Axel Küpper

Maria Lekkou

Anselm Lingnau

Torsten Lodderstedt

Christian Mayerl

Jens Meggers

Christian Mönch

Ralf Muhlberger

Alexander Ost

Anthony S. Park

Stephan Paschke

Arno Puder

Herwart Pusch

Ulrich Quernheim

Andry Rakotonirainy

Tim Redhead

Peter Reichl

Kai-Uwe Sattler

Peter Schoo

Marko Schuba

Kerstin Schwarz

Michael Semrau

Kai Sommerfeld

Linda Strick

Dirk Thißen

Dirk Trossen

Can Türker

Andreas Vogel

Wolfgang Wunderlich

Michael Zapf

Contents

Quality of Service
in Distributed Multimedia Systems

Sape J. Mullender and Paul Sijben

University of Twente, Faculty of Computer Science, Enschede, The Netherlands
{mullender,sijben}@cs.utwente.nl

Abstract. The Unix operating system made a vital contribution to information technology by introducing the notion of composing complicated applications out of simple ones by means of pipes and shell scripts. One day, this will also be possible with multimedia applications. Before this can happen, however, operating systems must support multimedia in as general a way as Unix now supports 'ordinary' applications. Particularly, attention must be paid to allowing the operating-system service to degrade gracefully under heavy loads.

This paper presents the Quality-of-Service architecture of the Huygens project. This architecture provides the mechanisms that allow applications to adapt the level of their service to the resources the operating system can make available.

1 Introduction

If one defines a multimedia system to be a computer system that allows applications to adequately process text, graphics, images, sound and vision and convert between these media, then most systems advertised with 'multimedia' among the adjectives do not deserve that qualification for one of two reasons. The first and most common reason is that they do not or they hardly allow processing the time-dependent media of audio and video. The second, more subtle, reason is that they do not allow *applications* to process audio and video, but leave it to the operating system instead.

Delivering the real-time performance necessary to capture, transport and render audio and video on time is much easier to do in the bowels of an operating system than it is for an application. The operating system merely has to assign a higher priority to its internal real-time processes than to the (non-real-time) applications. The price paid here, however, is lack of flexibility: the only multimedia processing possible is that built into the operating system and the multimedia load that can be placed on the system is fixed *a priori*.

Multimedia applications are starting to play an important rôle as a vehicle for improving the quality of interpersonal communication over long distances. As a result, it is essential that operating systems support *distributed* multimedia applications.

Multimedia may be expected to be the next quantum leap in making information processing accessible to the layman: having to control computer systems through keyboards and mice is not a natural way to do business and providing instant feedback to mouse commands only in the form of an hourglass-shaped mouse icon, while taking a highly variable amount of time for the real work is, for the uninitiated, completely bewildering.

Multimedia, therefore, should not merely be about adding audio and video to computers, it should just as much be about designing human interfaces on human reaction-time scales. Having made transatlantic phone calls via satellite links, one realizes just how much the modified timing — a satellite link adds a quarter second to the end-to-end communication latency — throws one off.

The issues in designing operating system architectures for the support of distributed multimedia applications are thus providing low-latency communication and processing, and predictable real-time behaviour for unpredictable multimedia loads placed on the system.

This is, in a nutshell, the goal of the University of Twente Huygens project: the design of an architecture for distributed multimedia systems. The remainder of this paper describes our research of operating-system support mechanisms for distributed multimedia applications and presents the Huygens Quality-of-Service scheduling architecture.

The Huygens project is closely linked to the Pegasus Esprit projects[1] [LMM94] which investigates multimedia support on a broader scale: new operating-system structures, multimedia data storage, multimedia local and long-haul networking, and Quality of Service.

2   The Nature of Multimedia

From the viewpoint of an operating-system designer, multimedia support is about handling time-dependent media. The most prominent examples of such media are digital audio and video, but sensor data, such as the output of an ILS[2] in an aircraft are often time dependent too. A frequently used technical term for time-dependent media is *continuous media*.

We may consider it an attractive property of multimedia systems if they support *ad hoc* compositions of 'multimedia building blocks' into multimedia applications. Consider, for instance, how a teleconferencing application, a multimedia-document player, and a multimedia recording application can be combined to record the reactions of the participants in a multimedia conference to playing a multimedia document.

When the sum of the resources requested by the applications exceeds what the operating system can offer, then things become interesting. Since the applications have real-time requirements, *virtualizing* resources in the way of time-sharing

---

[1] The Pegasus Project is a project, initially of the Universities of Twente and Cambridge, now also of the University of Glasgow, the Swedish Institute of Computer Science, and APM Ltd., supported by the European Communities' ESPRIT Programme through BRA project 6586 (1992 – 1995) and LTR project *21917* (1996 – 1999).

[2] Instrument Landing System

systems is not possible. The only way for applications to cohabit on a host is by making certain that the resources consumed by them do no exceed the available.

This is where multimedia systems essentially differ from real-time systems: real-time behaviour has to be maintained even in a *'resource-overload* situation'. The basic technique is, confusingly, alluded to using the term *Quality-of-Service*, or *QoS*. The idea is that applications adjust the quality of the service they provide to the types and amounts of resources available. Over a narrow-band network, a tele-conferencing application will thus display fewer video channels of lower resolution than over a broad-band network.

The big challenges in multimedia system design are, first, to design multimedia applications that can indeed adapt to a wide range of resource offerings and that maximize their QoS under a given resource allocation, second, to design the operating system such that the amount of resources available to actual multimedia processing is maximized and that the amounts needed for the allocation itself is minimized, and, third, to define algorithms and mechanism for allocating resources to a set of applications — or even users — competing for them.

3 Quality of Service

Applications can adapt to the resources available by adjusting the quality of the service they provide. When there are ample resources, applications can give a high quality of service, when resources are scarce, applications can provide only limited quality of service.

Such adaptation by applications is, of course, limited. At the high-quality end of an application's spectrum, a point will be reached where the supply of more resources can no longer be used to improve quality. At the low-quality end of the spectrum, a point is reached where any further reduction of resources renders an application useless. In multimedia applications with no QoS adaptation, the ends of the spectrum coincide [DHH+93,EA95].

Both ends of the spectrum give rise to observations. At the high end, it must be noted that a point can be reached where pure *continuous*-media applications do not run better or faster when more CPU bandwidth or network bandwidth is made available to them. Traditional applications usually do run better in that they return results more quickly. Multimedia system design, therefore, is not simply about performance optimization — enough resources is usually enough.

At the low end of the spectrum, we find that there is a lower limit on the amount of resources needed by an application to do something useful. If those resources cannot be found, it is better not to start the application at all. Before making such a decision, however, it is a good idea to see if running applications can reduce their QoS to make room for the newcomer.

Multimedia applications can adapt their resource consumption to what can be allocated in basically three ways. (1) They can change their functionality; e.g., change from stereophonic sound to monophonic, change interactive document-sharing semantics, drop one of the video channels, introduce compression. (2) They can change network and processing bandwidths; e.g.,reduce image size, reduce audio-sampling size, change the quality parameters of a compression algorithm. (3) They can change the frequency at which they operate; e.g., drop the frame rate from 25 to 15 fps, reduce audio sampling rate, adjust camera position once per second instead of five times per second.

QoS adaptations should be carried out to maximize QoS improvement for a given increase in resources, or minimize QoS degradation for a given reduction in resources. The quality of service that counts is often the quality of service as perceived by a human user. It is, therefore, important that the user can influence how QoS adaptations are carried out — in other words, the user must be allowed to determine which media may enjoy additional or must suffer reduced resources and which QoS parameter of such media should be affected.

Perceived Quality of Service for video depends on image size (number of pixels), image quality (effects of lossy compression and lost or late data), frame rate (images per second), jitter (irregularity of frame arrival times), and, for interactive applications, latency (time *en route* for video data). For audio, perceived QoS depends on sampling frequency, sample size, data loss (due to compression or transmission), and latency.

Achieving a certain quality of service requires the allocation of a certain amount of resources. Obviously, higher frame rates and better image resolution uses up more network bandwidth, to name just one resource. In general, a higher quality level requires a bigger allocation of resources.

But note that modern image-compression techniques can dramatically reduce the bandwidth required to transport a video image, while barely affecting quality. Such compression potentially improves latency (less data to transmit) at the cost of very minor loss in image quality. The same perceived quality can often be achieved with or without compression. With compression, a substantial CPU allocation is necessary to perform the calculations for compression and decompression, while the network bandwidth allocation can remain low. Without, the CPU allocation can be less, but more bandwidth is needed. There is, as we can see, no obvious monotonic relationship between QoS and resource allocations.

An application can apply the resources it obtains to achieve optimum QoS. Resource scheduling within an application is up to the application itself. When there are multiple, independent applications, however, both resource allocation and resource scheduling must be done by the operating system.

Allocation strategies need to be in place that allocate resources to applications in such a way that the overall QoS — the QoS of all applications combined — is optimal. How overall QoS can be determined is an interesting problem of cognitive ergonomics which, for now, we shall not attempt to solve.

Applications can, in principle, obtain more resources than they deserve by over-claiming. Users of time-sharing systems were known to apply this technique to get better service: they would start up a large number of parallel jobs to get better personal service, even though it was detrimental to other users and system throughput.

This technique of over-claiming resources in order to get a larger share has become less useful now that most systems are personal workstations. The same is

true of multimedia applications: they run, to a large extent, on personal workstations where the user is best served by having the applications work harmoniously
together. It is, therefore, entirely reasonable to assume that operating systems
do not have to operate in a *competitive* environment, but rather in a *cooperative*
one.

When two applications both need, say, 60% of the CPU to perform optimally,
and only one of them is capable of QoS adaptation and make good use of only
50% or 40% of the CPU, then it is clear that fairly dividing the CPU over the
two applications by giving them 50% each is not nearly as useful as giving the
non-adaptive one the 60% it needs and the other the remaining 40%.

A QoS architecture is a collection of interfaces and algorithms for an operating system, that allows applications to describe the Qualities of Service they
can deliver and the resources they need to deliver them, that allows the operating system to determine the best possible overall Quality of Service with its
attending resource allocation, and that allows the applications to adapt to that
allocation. Preferably, all this takes place in a dynamic setting, where, resources
allocations can change whenever the QoS settings of the applications change.

QoS architectures are a a topic of many multimedia research groups. Approaches roughly follow one of two paths: *reservation* and *adaptation.*

The reservation-oriented groups assume a full knowledge of the properties of
the running multimedia applications and try to reserve exactly the right amount
of resources for this. Capacity reserves, as used in [MST94], are a way to try to
implement an estimation of the resources.

Adapatation of a multimedia application can be achieved by algorithms that
can produce usable partial results and alternative implementations that take
less resources than the primary implementation does. This kind of processing is
known as imprecise computations [ABRW91].

The adaptation path is used when the researches find that the load of multimedia applications is not predictable. The application is allocated some resources
and may find more available at run-time [Ros95]. This approach can produce satisfactory results when resources are not really scarce or the application is highly
adaptable like an MJPEG [Wal91] decompression application [Hyd94].

The Hyugens approach tries to use the best of both apporaches. Estimates
are made for the nominal and worst case resource needs. A suitable amount is
preallocated gambling on the fact that the resources will be present when the
peak need occurs. This apporach tries to maintain statistical QoS guarantees at
run-time.

The Dynamic QoS control approach of [FN96] has a similar run-time concept.
But lacks the central entity we call a *QoS manager* to prevent oscillation of QoS
levels. Others have the central entity but not the fluent adaptation [FHS96].

4   Multimedia Scheduling

The observation was made earlier that one of the biggest problems of continuous-
media processing is that one must make do with the resources one has, even when

the combined applications would be better served with much more. Somehow, we are prepared to accept this much more easily when considering network resources, perhaps because network resource scarcity has always been a problem primarily in public networks where one has little control over the allocation in any case.

When it comes to the CPU resource, we are used to time-sharing systems in which the CPU is virtualized — the API presents the illusion that each process has the whole CPU to itself; it only becomes a slower CPU when it gets shared with other processes. In non-real-time applications, this doesn't matter, but in real-time applications such as those that process continuous media, it matters a great deal.

The time-dependency of continuous media suggests that operating system support for multimedia mights well be provided by real-time systems. This is not the case, even though there are many similarities in the techniques used in multimedia systems and real-time systems.

Real-time systems can meet their deadlines because the real-time load placed on the system is bounded *a priori* and upper bounds are known for the processing times of all real-time tasks. In multimedia systems, demanding such *a priori* bounds is not realistic: multimedia applications will be 'ordinary' user-space applications that cannot be expected to meet processing-time limitations dependably, and users will not put up with low limits on the number or mix of multimedia applications they can run together.

To compute schedules that meet the deadlines, real-time systems require *a priori* known and bounded loads and predictable and bounded run times for real-time processes. None of these conditions are met in the operating systems that we are interested in: Continuous-media processes run in user space and may or may not meet the run times promised by their developers; the system load is not bounded, users will fire up more simultaneous multimedia applications until the system stops giving reasonable service.

If a conventional real-time system would be used to schedule multimedia applications, it would work fine as long as loads are within bounds, but when those bounds are exceeded it would probably break horribly: real-time systems do not specify what to do in an overload situation because it is assumed that, by design, overload cannot happen.

In most multimedia applications, missing a deadline as a consequence of overload is not at all disastrous, as long as the system only misses an occasional one. If a single frame is missing from an incoming video stream, one can leave the previous frame displayed until the next one comes in and nobody will notice. If this happens to a number of frames in a row, however, or to every second frame, then it would be noticeable. The same is true for audio, when the unit of loss is small.

Data loss will happen in the network (e.g., as a consequence of policing or transmission errors) and retransmission is rarely an option due to lack of time to do so. Data loss is, therefore, a fact of life in multimedia systems and it can happen in transmission as well as in processing. The possibility of allowing a deadline to be missed occasionally can be exploited in operating system scheduling algorithms.

Interactive multimedia applications seek end-to-end latencies of no more than a 100 ms or so. This implies that, for processing steps, only a few milliseconds are available. Multimedia applications will, therefore, need to be scheduled with intervals and deadlines in the millisecond range.

On a host executing several multimedia applications, there will be a substantial amount of context switching, typically on the order of a thousand times per second. It pays to optimize the operating system for this.

Making scheduling decisions at this rate is likely to impose a significant load on an operating system. The scheduling algorithm will either have to be very simple or it should be run off line. In the Huygens project, we have opted for the latter. We made the observation that, after assigning resources to processes for their particular QoS settings, the system has information about the frequencies, deadlines and run times for all tasks. This allows the calculation of a schedule in advance. Since all tasks are periodic, the schedule will be periodic as well [SM95].

5   Scheduling in Huygens

In Huygens, the calculation of such a periodic schedule results in a table that the dispatcher uses to identify the next task to run. The dispatcher is activated by the system clock which generates interrupts at a rate of between one per ten milliseconds and one per 100 microseconds. At every clock tic, a number of periodic tasks can be invoked. When one returns control, the next one is invoked. When all tasks of a particular clock tic have been run, the dispatcher returns control to the process that was interrupted by the clock.

This works fine until a periodic tasks misbehaves and takes more time than allocated to it. Once a task has the CPU, it can hang on to it until the next interrupt returns control to the operating system. In Huygens, we catch such processes at the next clock interrupt. Periodic tasks that should have been run behind the offending task will miss their opportunity to run, but only once: the offending task can be removed from the schedule, or, less drastically, it can be scheduled as the last task of the group for a particular clock tic.

At this level, all periodic tasks run to completion. This ensures the best system throughput. Periodic tasks with long run times of ten milliseconds and more, however, cannot be run to completion without starving high-frequency periodic tasks of the CPU. Viewed from the low-level dispatcher, tasks with long periods are run as background processes that are preempted by the system clock.

The low-frequency long-run-time tasks are dispatched by a higher-level dispatcher. This dispatcher is invoked by a low-level periodic task at a frequency of 10 Hz or so. To the low-frequency dispatcher, the actions of the high-frequency dispatcher only manifest themselves as variations in the number of CPU cycles available between low-frequency clock tics. Otherwise, the low-frequency dispatcher operates exactly like the high-frequency one.

During the calculation of the schedule, the time available at each dispatcher level is known and taken into account. The fact that a task runs at a higher frequency and thus preempts another task at a lower frequency does not imply it has a higher priority or a right to more CPU cycles.

The hierarchy of dispatchers can be made more than two levels deep, although this is not usually necessary. The scheduler that computes the dispatch tables can be run as a non-real-time background process. The scheduler that schedules the background processes can be run as a low-frequency periodic real-time task.

Applications provide the operating system with a list of their possible QoS settings. This list typically contains between one and half a dozen settings. An applications that cannot adapt has one setting. Multimedia background applications, such as an application that shows the current five-day test match, but only appears when the resources are available, may have its lowest-quality setting have no resources associated with it.

For each QoS setting, the application provides the following information:

- The QoS rating of the setting, a number between 0 and 255 — the higher this number, the more desirable this setting is.
- Two flags, named *deliverable* and *desirable*. The former indicates that the system (the QoS scheduler) is currently prepared to schedule this QoS setting. The latter indicates that the application is currently prepared for the system to schedule the QoS setting. The use of these flags is explained below.
- A list of tasks (periodic threads). Each task has an entry with the following information:
  - Task entry point. This tells the system how to invoke the task.
  - Sources and sinks. These are (possibly empty) lists of references to other tasks or connections and tell the scheduler where the task fits in a continuous-media pipeline. This information defines a partial order that lets the scheduler determine a scheduling order for the tasks.
  - *Optional* flag. This indicates that the task need not be invoked when CPU cycles are scarce.
  - Task period in μs.
  - Task CPU consumption in cycles per second.
  - Task memory consumption in kilobytes.
- A list of connections (virtual circuits). Each connection has an entry with the following information:
  - Connection type and direction; e.g., inbound MJPEG-compressed video over AAL5.
  - Peer; the address or name of the peer entity at the other end of the connection.
  - Sources or sinks (depending on direction). These are (possibly empty) lists of references to other tasks or connections and tell the scheduler where the connection fits in a continuous-media pipeline.
  - Connection period in μs. This is the time between transmission of logical units (e.g., a video frame).

- Connection bandwidth in kilobytes per second.
- Connection buffer size in kilobytes.

6 QoS Resource Allocation

The QoS scheduler attempts to allocate the available resources to applications in such a way that the overall QoS is maximized. The overall QoS is simply defined as the weighted sum of the QoS ratings of all running applications. We refer to the *weight* of an application as its *importance*. It is an integer between 1 and 255. If the importance of application i is I_i and its QoS rating is at setting Q_i, then the QoS scheduler attempts to maximize $\sum_i I_i \times Q_i$.

The number of multimedia applications on a typical host will be a small number, as well as the number of QoS settings for each of these applications. Finding an optimum or near-optimum setting, therefore, is not overly compute intensive.

The dispatching tables produced by the QoS scheduler will contain for each application the threads of the selected QoS setting. The order in which the threads are invoked by the dispatcher matches the partial order given by the *sources/sinks* specification. As a result, a group of threads forming a pipeline will see the data pass through the complete pipeline in period of the group.

This arrangement of the dispatching table not only reduces the latency of continuous-media data through the pipeline, it also helps in dynamically switching from one QoS setting to another. This works as follows.

When a new QoS setting for an application is chosen, a new schedule is computed in the form of a new dispatching table that contains the invocations of threads as specified by the newly chosen QoS setting. This dispatching table is than activated by having the dispatcher run itself off the end of the old dispatching table into the beginning of the new one. When the dispatcher has finished dispatching the last thread of the old table, all pipelines formed by multiple threads are empty and a fresh start can be made by starting the first thread in the first pipeline in the new table.

If the QoS setting changes not too drastically, it is unlikely that the user will notice such QoS changes much. Audio and video streams continue uninterruptedly.

This type of dynamic QoS resource management works fine in a centralized setting where the changeover from one dispatching table to another can be made atomically. In a distributed setting such atomic changeovers are not possible. They must be initiated in one host and trigger the changeover in the other hosts involved. Before this can happen, however, it must be ascertained that each host is prepared to support the new QoS setting.

To this end, a QoS setting contains two flags, named *deliverable* and *desirable*. The former is set by the operating system and read by the application, the latter set by the application and read by the operating system. The *desirable* flag indicates that the application is prepared to have the system schedule the QoS setting. The application may need to set this flag to `false` when peer applications on other hosts currently cannot deal with the QoS setting — usually as a consequence of lack of resources.

As a concrete example, consider a distributed application that can send compressed or uncompressed video. A single process cannot unilaterally decide to switch from one to the other because the other processes may not have the resources to deal with that. As long as it is not clear whether the peer processes can deal with a particular QoS setting, the *desirable* flag is kept set to `false` and the system will not schedule the QoS setting.

The *deliverable* flag indicates that the system has the resources to run the QoS setting (but it will not do so unless the *desirable* is also set). Distributed applications will communicate this fact to their relevant peer processes which can then set their *desirable* flags to `true`.

When a QoS setting is both *deliverable* and *desirable*, we call the setting *possible*. The scheduler and the application together choose one of the *possible* settings to run. The details are given in the following section.

7 Huygens QoS Application Programmers Interface

The *QoS manager* is the application programmer's interface for an application's resource allocation and QoS management. The interface is implemented by the operating system, either as a system process in user space, or as part of the operating-system kernel.

For maximum flexibility, it is conceived as a message-passing interface allowing RPC from the application into the QoS manager and *callbacks* from the QoS manager to the application.

Application processes are assumed to be multithreaded with *management* threads in the non-real-time domain and *continuous-media* threads or *tasks* in the real-time domain. Although all communication *about* QoS settings takes place in the non-real-time domain, there are time-outs on all operations. If a process fails to respond to, for instance, an upcall within the timeout period, that is viewed as a programming error and may lead to the removal of the process.

The tasks (real-time threads) are essentially subroutines that are invoked by an upcall from the dispatcher. These subroutines are expected to return control to the dispatcher within the time specified in the relevant entry of the application's QoS table. Failure to return in time can lead to the removal of all tasks in the current QoS setting from the dispatching table. When this happens, the application is informed through an upcall to a management thread.

Processes belonging to distributed applications, especially, cannot simply be switched over by the operating system from one QoS setting into another. Remote peer processes may not be able to cope with such a switch.

The first stage of the QoS negotiations is an exchange between the processes in the application in which they determine the QoS settings they can support. If two processes are connected through a 64 Kbps ISDN link, for example, they have no choice but to send video in compressed form — there is no point in specifying

QoS settings without compression (unless, of course, such setting are without video as well). This determination involves querying the operating system for performance data of operating-system, CPU, device, and network.

This stage culminates in sets of possible QoS settings for each of the participating processes and knowledge within the application of the possible combinations of QoS settings in the set of processes. How this negotiation takes place is up to the application. The operating system offers a standard interface for resolving queries concerning the system's capabilities.

The second stage starts when the application, using its knowledge from the first stage and flagging the initially *desirable* settings, communicates the table of negotiated QoS settings to the QoS manager.

The QoS manager then calculates a new schedule that accommodates the new application process. When such a schedule cannot be found, the (real-time part of the) application process is not admitted. The process may notify the rest of the application of this failure and exit. When such a schedule can be found, however, it is installed and the process is informed of the QoS that was selected. The QoS manager also informs the application which other QoS settings are *deliverable*.

Before the QoS manager installs a new resource allocation, it notifies the applications of the new allocation. When the applications signal their readiness, the new allocation can be installed by replacing the dispatching table. In centralized applications that communicate with a single QoS manager, this method works fine.

Seamless switch-over from one QoS setting to another in a distributed setting, however, requires a sort of *two-phase commit* (2PC) protocol: during the first phase, the processes and operating systems prepare for the new setting and then, when all parties are ready, one of the application processes (typically a continuous-media data source) actually switches over, e.g., by starting to send compressed video instead of uncompressed. As processes notice the changeover, they tell their systems that the old QoS setting is no longer active. The details are as follows

Either the application, or one of the QoS managers takes the initiative for the change by suggesting a new QoS setting from the *possible* set. The application, acting as coordinator of the 2PC, informs all QoS managers involved of the suggested new setting. When a manager cannot accommodate the change, then the changeover fails and the QoS managers are duly informed. Note that applications can thus refuse changing their QoS setting.

When a manager *can* accommodate the changeover, it installs a *dual schedule*, a dispatch table in which both the old and the new setting are present. The condition of this installation is that the application will either use the resources of the old setting or that of the new, but not both. When all QoS managers have installed the *dual schedule* — and notified the application of this — the changeover happens as explained earlier.

When an application process has switched to the new setting, it informs the QoS manager and a schedule can be installed containing only dispatch instructions for the new QoS setting.

It is possible that, during the changeover from one QoS setting to another, resources are temporarily overcommitted and some deadlines are lost. This will be likelier when multiple applications have to change their QoS setting simultaneously, for instance, for admitting a new application. However, the changeover will happen quickly enough that the disruption of service is barely noticeable.

8 Conclusions

We have presented the Huygens Quality-of-Service architecture for general-purpose multimedia applications. Parts of the architecture have been implemented in the Nemesis operating system which has been developed in the Pegasus Esprit project of the Universities of Twente and Cambridge.

The Pegasus project is about to continue into its second phase, Pegasus II; this time Cambridge and Twente are joined by the University of Glasgow, the Swedish Institute of Computer Science and APM Ltd., the producers of ANSA-ware. The goal of Pegasus II is to bring the multimedia solutions of Pegasus to a broad audience and to incorporate it into industrial-strength operating-system platforms.

As a demonstration of the sort of applications that Nemesis will support, Twente developed a digital TV director — an application that controls several cameras in a meeting room in order to broadcast a report of the meeting taking place. The TV director detects and locates speakers (using triangulation over multiple microphones) and tracks them on camera (using a pan/tilt/zoom device and a combination of motion detection and skin-colour detection[3]). The TV director demonstrates that it is possible to write an application that carries out significant continuous-media data processing (audio triangulation and camera tracking) in real time. It adapts dynamically to the availability of resources by prioritizing its actions and the frequency with which it carries them out.

References

[ABRW91] N.C. Audsley, A. Burns, M.F. Richardson, and A.J. Wellings. Incorporating unbounded algorithms into predictable real-time systems. Technical report, University of York (UK), Sep 1991.

[DHH⁺93] Luca Delgrossi, Christian Halstrick, Dietmar Hehmann, Ralf Guido Herrtwich, Oliver Krone, Jochen Sandvoss, and Carsten Vogt. Media scaling for audiovisual communication with the Heidelberg Transport System. In *Computer Graphics (Multimedia '93 Proceedings)*, pages 99–104. ACM, Addison-Wesley, August 1993.

[EA95] Alexandros Eleftheriadis and Dimitris Anastassiou. Meeting arbitrary qos contraints using dynamic rate shaping of coded digital video. In *5th NOSSDAV ,Durham, NH, USA*, apr 1995.

---

[3] Our skin-colour detection algorithm has been checked for absence of racial bias.

[FHS96] Anne Fladenmuller, Eric Horlait, and Aruna Seneviratne. Qos management scheme for multimedia applications in best effort environments. *Journal of Electrical and Electronics Engineering,*, Mar 1996.

[FN96] S. Furuno and T. Nakajima. A toolkit for building continuous media applications using a new dynamic qos control scheme. In *Proceedings of the Multimedia Japan 96 - Yokohama March 18-20*, pages 268–277, Mar 1996.

[Hyd94] Eoin Andrew Hyden. *Operating System Support for Quality of Service*. PhD thesis, Wolfson College, University of Cambridge, February 1994.

[LMM94] Ian M. Leslie, Derek R. McAuley, and Sape J. Mullender. Operating-System Support for Distributed Multimedia. *Proceedings of the Summer Usenix Conference*, Boston, MA, pages 209–220, June 1994.

[MST94] C.W. Mercer, S. Savage, and H. Tokuda. Processor Capacity Reserves: Operating System Support for Multimedia Applications. In *Proceedings of the IEEE International Conference on Multimedia Computing and Systems*, May 1994. To appear. (This is a condensed version of tech report CMU-CS-93-157.).

[Ros95] Timothy Roscoe. *The Structure of a Multi-Service Operating System*. PhD thesis, Queens' College,University of Cambridge, April 1995.

[SM95] Paul G.A. Sijben and Sape J. Mullender. An architecture for scheduling and qos management in multimedia workstations. Technical Report Pegasus paper 95-05, University of Twente, Dec 1995.

[Wal91] Gregory K. Wallace. The jpeg still picture compression standard. *Communications of ACM*, 34(4):30–44, Apr 1991.

A CORBA Compliant Real-Time Multimedia Platform for Broadband Networks

G. Coulson and D. G. Waddington

Distributed Multimedia Research Group,
Computing Department,
Lancaster University, Lancaster LA1 4YR, UK

e-mail: [geoff,dan]@comp.lancs.ac.uk

ABSTRACT

We describe the architecture of a CORBA-based platform offering end-to-end multimedia communications and processing support in a broadband network environment. The design gives application programmers an extended CORBA computational model incorporating explicit support for continuous media including quality of service abstractions. The proposed architecture goes beyond existing multimedia-in-CORBA platforms by integrating continuous media data types as first class types in the application programmer's computational model. This is in contrast to currently proposed platforms which typically adopt an 'off line plumbing' approach where application programmers connect together 'standard' multimedia objects and then monitor and control the flow of media inside these objects. We present our extensions in detail using code examples based on Iona's Orbix CORBA 2.0 compliant platform. We also offer a scenario illustrating the use of our extensions and the implementation of a simple binding object.

1. INTRODUCTION

This paper describes the architecture of a CORBA-based platform offering end-to-end multimedia communications and processing support in a broadband network environment. The design gives application programmers an extended CORBA computational model incorporating explicit support for continuous media like digital audio and video, including quality of service (QoS) abstractions.

The proposed architecture goes beyond existing multimedia-in-CORBA platforms (e.g. the IMA's MSS [IMA,96], Columbia's Xbind [Aurrecoechea,96] or Sandia's DAVE [Mines,94]) by integrating continuous media data types as *first class types* in the application programmer's computational model. This is in contrast to currently proposed platforms which typically adopt an 'off line plumbing' approach: application programmers connect together 'standard' multimedia objects (e.g. source and sink devices, processing objects, communication objects, etc.), and then monitor and control the flow of media inside these objects. In such platforms, application programmers are not expected to require access to the *internals* of the standard objects; these are written by systems programmers and provided to the application writer in the form of libraries.

The drawback of the 'plumbing' approach is a certain lack of flexibility. If application programmers need to perform application-specific processing on a continuous media stream (this is commonly referred to as 'touching the bits'; see for example [Lindblad,94]), they must drop below the level of the generic computational model into the internals of the 'standard' multimedia objects: i.e. into a system-specific OS, protocol and network environment. This is clearly undesirable as it complicates the task of the application programmer and thus reduces his productivity. In contrast to the above, our design allows application programmers to directly source, sink and process real-time media streams in a similar way to conventional static data types in the standard CORBA programming environment. This is achieved by systematically extending the CORBA computational model in two main ways:

- *augmented interface definitions*

  In addition to standard IDL control interfaces, programmers declare interfaces containing *event*[1] interaction points (potentially with attached QoS information). Programmers provide implementations of these interaction points in a similar way to operation implementations in standard CORBA.

- *binding objects*

  Programmers use binding objects as place holders for the specification and realisation of communications with a given QoS when run-time bindings are established. QoS specifications are translated into machine specific resource allocation and QoS support mechanisms.

Importantly, our design makes it easy to define new interfaces and associated binding types to support new applications and new demands. The remainder of this paper is structured as follows. First, section 2 outlines the component technologies that have influenced our design. In section 3 we present the proposed extended CORBA object model which is followed by a description of the necessary supporting infrastructure in section 4. Section 5 then outlines an example scenario whilst section 6 draws our conclusions.

2. COMPONENT TECHNOLOGIES AND THEIR LIMITATIONS

2.1 The Component Technologies

Our computational model and its supporting infrastructure have been heavily influenced by four main component technologies which are described in this section. These are CORBA 2.0, the ISO's Reference Model for Open Distributed Processing, the SUMO project at Lancaster University and Columbia University's Binding Architecture. In the design described in this paper, the low level communications resources identified in the Columbia Binding Architecture and in the SUMO system are made accessible via CORBA interfaces, and used to support a computational model incorporating bindings and QoS, in both the end system and the network.

2.2 The OMG's CORBA

The Common Object Request Broker Architecture version 2.0 [CORBA,96] from the Object Management Group forms the basis of our platform design. CORBA provides a technology independent object-based computational model in which distributed objects with strongly typed interfaces can be invoked with full location transparency.

The limitation of CORBA with respect to our application domain is that there is no support for 'streaming' interaction styles (only request/ reply operation invocation is offered) or for QoS as required by continuous media applications.

---

1   Events in our sense are unrelated to the CORBA 2.0 COSS Event service (the latter is a high level facility for supporting event streams which is built on top of CORBA request/reply communications and has no associated notion of QoS).

2.3 The ISO's RM-ODP

Our multimedia computational model extensions are influenced by the ISO Reference Model for Open Distributed Processing [ITU-T,95a], [ITU-T,95b]. This model includes the key notions of *flows*, *signals* (*events*, in our terminology), *QoS annotations* and *explicit bindings* as introduced above and detailed in the remainder of the paper.

The limitation of the RM-ODP model is that it is highly abstract in nature and needs considerable refinement and expansion before it can be implemented in the context of any particular platform/ operating system/ network environment. Specifications for such refinement and expansion are not currently available.

2.4 Columbia University's Binding Architecture

The Columbia Binding Architecture [Aurrecoechea,96], developed by the COMET group at Columbia, exposes the low level communications resources (e.g. ATM switching tables) of broadband networks via a high level distributed programming environment (e.g. CORBA), so that network connections can be established by remotely configuring the resources from this high level environment. This architecture considerably eases the implementation of the 'signalling protocols' required to establish new services; new services need no longer be inherently a part of the network but can be viewed more as application programs.

The limitation of the Columbia Binding Architecture with respect to our application domain is that it does not comprehensively address computational model issues: a 'plumbing' based computational model is still assumed. In addition, the emphasis of the work has been on network internals; end-system issues have not been looked at in any detail.

2.5 The SUMO system

SUMO [Coulson,95b] is a joint project involving Lancaster University and CNET, France Telecom which has developed a micro-kernel based operating system to support distributed multimedia applications. SUMO provides optimised data and control pathways specifically designed for continuous media manipulation and offers efficient low level management of system resources (i.e. CPU cycles, physical memory and network access). The limitation of the SUMO system is essentially the converse of that of the Columbia Binding Architecture: it addresses low level resource management issues in the end system but not in the network. It is thus complementary to the Columbia work.

3. ENHANCING CORBA FOR REAL-TIME MULTIMEDIA

3.1 Computational Model

We now describe our extended CORBA-based computational model for distributed multimedia applications. As explained above, the programming model is based closely on the ISO/ ITU Reference Model for Open Distributed Processing [ITU-T,95a], [ITU-T,95b].

Event interfaces and events For multimedia, a communications abstraction is required which captures the concept of information flowing over time [Blair,95]. Of course, it would be possible to model continuous media flows as repeated operation invocations; with this approach however, there could be no concept of a connection governed by an overall quality of service as each invocation is a separate, isolated event. In addition, such an implementation would be extremely inefficient as a round trip communication would be incurred for each media packet communication. To facilitate this requirement we add the concept of *event interfaces*. Event interfaces contain *event* interactions rather than operation interactions. Events are *unidirectional* as opposed to the bi-directional request/reply style of operations. Events, like operations, may, but are not required to, carry typed data objects as arguments.

Event interfaces, encapsulating event interactions, are not defined with standard IDL. Rather than extend IDL, we have defined a special language called the Event Definition Language (EDL) for the specification of such interfaces. EDL, an example of which is illustrated below, is derived from CORBA IDL.

```
events VideoDecompressor : QoS_events {
    in FrameCompressed(INDEO_T frame);
    out FrameDecompressed(RAW_T frame);
    out DecompressionFailed(MESSAGE_T reason, TIME_T time);
};
```

This example shows an EDL interface for a video decompressor object (the *QoS_events* interface from which *VideoCompressor* inherits is assumed to define some generic, standard, events and types). Note that the directionality of events is indicated by the *in* or *out* keywords. Note also that, as illustrated above, events can be used as the basis of *QoS monitoring* (cf. the *DecompressionFailed* event) as well as for their primary use of carrying continuous media data units.

Binding Objects A *binding object* is used to connect together two or more event interface references so that communication may take place between them. Binding objects encapsulate the underlying communications infrastructure and may also encapsulate end-system functions (e.g. transparent conversion of media formats, pre-fetching and caching of video frames etc.). Binding objects also serve as control points at which applications may specify, monitor and adjust the ongoing QoS of the communication. Generic control functions, such as start and stop, are performed via a standard operational interface that all binding objects support (see below). New binding object types written by application programmers (see section 5) inherit their binding control interface from this interface.

```
interface binding_ctl: QoS_specification {
    enum status {ok, error};
    struct QoS { ... };
    readonly attribute QoS currentQoS;

    status change_QoS(in QoS newQoS)
    status start();
    status stop();
    closeBinding();
};
```

Third Party Binding Binding objects support a *third party* style of binding in which the application setting up the binding can be entirely remote from the interfaces being bound. This is in contrast to the standard CORBA model where binding is initiated by a client and there is no explicit client interface involved.

We shall now briefly describe the third party binding process in a TCP/IP communications implementation. The ORB daemon within a particular domain listens on a "well known" port (which is usually advertised in a particular configuration file). The binding object initially dispatches a CORBA *LocateRequest* message on the daemon's listening port. The daemon replies with a *LocateReply* message indicating both that the request has been forwarded and the object reference (IOR)[2] to which further requests to the object be made. In addition the daemon is responsible for locating and launching the server process as necessary. At this point the server-to-be-bound is awaiting requests on a known network address. In setting up the client side, the binding object must pass the IOR received from the *LocateReply* message, to the client object, which is then at liberty to accept the binding and then make invocations on the server. It is suggested that a possible implementation of this be through another CORBA invocation, hence making the client a servient.

Binding objects are created with a given end-to-end QoS specification. The specified QoS governs the ongoing flow of events (e.g. continuous media data unit arrivals/ departures) and is expressed in terms of parameters such as throughput, jitter, latency and packet loss. An attempt to create a binding using a binding object will succeed if the desired quality of service can be supported by both ends of the communication and also by the underlying communications infrastructure. Note that the interfaces must also be type-compatible for a legal binding to be established.

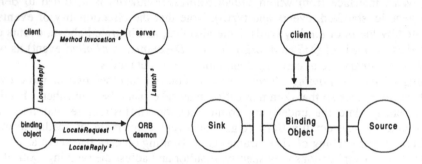

Figure 1: Third Party Binding and RM-ODP Binding Model

Binding for Operational Interfaces It is possible to use to binding objects to bind standard IDL specified operational interfaces. In this case, the primary QoS parameter would be end-to-end latency although other possibilities exist such as independently specified request and reply latencies, and reliability.

Local Binding The binding model described above appears recursive in that an object must seemingly bind to a binding object using a further binding object and so on. In fact, the recursion 'bottoms out' by the provision of a *local binding*. Communication across a local binding is assumed to be instantaneous and reliable. Any overhead is subsumed into one or both of the objects whose interfaces are being locally bound.

QoS Specification In order to temporally constrain events we adopt a suitable QoS specification notation. The general form of such specifications is a list of *<name, value>* pairs where *name* is a QoS characteristic identifier (e.g. latency) understood by a particular binding object type. Scalar *values* are adequate for many purposes but for more general QoS specification, *value* can be a complex description in its own right.

---

2   The Interoperability Object Reference (IOR) is a CORBA 2.0 defined universal identifier which includes version information, network host, network port and object key.

We have adopted a simplification of a real-time logic, called QL, for general QoS specification [Stefani,93]. The constituents of QL expressions are *signals* (i.e. arrivals or departures of data items at/ from interfaces), *time stamps* on those signals and boolean connectives between them. Signals are used in QL expressions so that QoS specifications can be made independently of any given interaction style (i.e. they underpin both events and operations). Signals relating to events are denoted in QL by the interface type plus the name of the event; e.g. *type1.e1*. Signals relating to operations are denoted by an operation name and an associated *direction*. The direction can be either a signal emission (SE) or a signal reception (SR). For example, the signal pertaining to the arrival of a signal *s1* in an interface of type *type1* would be *type1.s1.SR*. A very simple example of a QL specification based on the previous example could be:

```
T(VideoDecompressor.FrameDecompressed, n) -
     T(VideoDecompressor.FrameCompressed, n) < 7ms
```

This says that the decompression function should be bound by a delay of 7 milliseconds. The function T is a time stamp function which takes as arguments an event and an integer denoting the n'th occurrence of that event.

Using similar facilities, one can specify a range of other quality of service properties such as jitter and throughput. For example, a jitter constraint can be expressed as:

```
10   < T(VideoDecompressor.FrameDecompressed, n) -
     T(VideoDecompressor.FrameDecompressed, n-1) < 20ms
```

Similarly, throughput can be expressed as:

```
T(VideoDecompressor.FrameDecompressed, n + 1000) -
     T(VideoDecompressor.FrameDecompressed, n) < 100ms
```

A complete QL specification takes the form of a list of clauses such as the above. There is an implicit AND between each clause: all clauses must be satisfied if the QoS specification as a whole is to be supported. It is useful to apply QoS annotations to both event interfaces and to bindings. QoS specifications on interfaces typically indicate a level of QoS that an object is willing to offer to bindings in general. QoS specifications on binding objects indicate the particular QoS required for that particular binding. Further details of QL are given in [Stefani,93]. This reference also considers issues such as the expressibility and decidability of the QL language.

Multiple Interfaces per Object The standard CORBA model only permits one interface to be associated with an object[3]. In the extended computational model where both IDL and EDL interfaces are used, objects must be able to support multiple interfaces. In fact, multiple interfaces are useful for other reasons particularly for separating logically distinct sets of operations on a single object (e.g. management operations from service operations).

3.2 Object Support Environment

The object support environment for the extended model builds naturally on the standard CORBA design. Aspects of the object support environment such as writing and registering servers are essentially unchanged except that the extended model does not maintain such a clear separation between client and server roles. The major extensions required are as follows.

---

[3] Actually, some CORBA implementations such as IONA's Orbix, do provide macro-based mechanisms to achieve the effect of multiple interface definitions per object instance but these do not address the generality of our requirements.

Event Object Adaptor A new Object Adaptor called an Event Object Adaptor (EOA) is provided to allow programmers to supply implementation classes corresponding to EDL interfaces. The following illustrates a C++ implementation class corresponding to the EDL interface of section 3.1.

```
// C++ implementation of VideoDecompressor.edl
#include "VideoDecompressor.hh"

class VideoDecompressor_i: public
VideoDecompressorEOAImpl,QoS_events
{
public:
    VideoDecompressor_i();
    virtual ~VideoDecompressor_i();

    void FrameCompressed(RAW_T frame,
        CORBA::Environment&=
        CORBA::default_environment);
    void FrameDecompressed(RAW_T frame,
        CORBA::Environment&=
        CORBA::default_environment);
    void DecompressionFailed(MESSAGE_T reason,
        TIME_T time,
            CORBA::Environment&=
        CORBA::default_environment);
}
```

The *VideoDecompressorEOAImpl* class, among other functions, contains a virtual method *bind_request()* for which the application programmer provides an implementation. This method is upcalled by the EOA when a third party requests a binding to the object. The application programmer's code returns either an accept or reject result to the EOA.

In the above implementation class, all the events, whether of *in* or *out* directionality, have an implementation provided by the programmer. The interaction semantics of *in* events are clear: the binding upcalls the programmer's implementation when an event arrives. For *out* events, the programmer is upcalled whenever the binding *expects* an event to be provided by the object. This is termed an *active binding* interaction style. The advantage of active binding interactions is that they permit the delegation of as much as possible of the responsibility for QoS management to the binding itself. For example at bind time the binding, rather than the application, allocates buffers for bindings and provides the thread on which the upcalls will be made at both source and sink. At data transfer time, the binding decides to upcall the application to obtain/ deliver data at instants determined by the QoS specification provided by the application. Further benefits of the active binding style are discussed in [Coulson,95a]. It is also possible to adopt a *passive binding* interaction style (where the application is responsible for initiating events) for both *in* and *out* events. To achieve this, the EOA itself provides a C++ object implementation of class VideoDecompressor_i. Operations in this object are then called by the application either to initiate an event (assuming an *out* event) or to block and wait for an incoming event (assuming an *in* event). A pointer to the EOA's instance of VideoDecompressor_i is passed to the application at bind time. It is determined which interaction style is required for both in and out events when a binding is established.

Binding Establishment Having provided implementations of the to-be-bound interfaces as described above, the programmer binds the interfaces by means of a binding object. The process of creating and using a binding object appears as follows:

```
binding my_bdg = bind_factory.create("bind_type");
binding_ctl my_ctl = my_bdg.bind(src_obj, snk_obj, QoS);
status = my_ctl.start();
```

Here, a binding object is created by invoking an operation on a suitable *binding factory* object. Then the pair of interface references to be bound are passed to the resulting binding, together with their required levels of QoS (specified in a CORBA context object; see section 5.2) and a binding control interface is returned. Subsequently, the binding is enabled by invoking the start() operation on its control interface. For bindings of event interfaces, if the *out* events in the interfaces bound are configured to operate in an active binding interaction style, the start() operation will cause the binding to immediately upcall these event implementations to obtain data to be communicated. Otherwise the binding will wait for implementations to explicitly start providing data to be communicated.

Different binding types can define different sets of parameters to the bind operation. For example a multi-cast binding may take a source interface followed by a list of sink interface and a pipeline binding will take a list of interface references.

EDL Compiler In addition to the usual function of stub generation, the EDL compiler generates *QoS monitors* from EDL interface specifications and their associated QoS specifications. QoS monitors are procedures containing code which evaluates actual QoS by recording the occurrence of events at event interfaces. They then compare this information with the expected temporal behaviour as indicated in the QoS specification, and signal any violations to the binding object. The binding object implementation may then take appropriate action (e.g. informing the application or reconfiguring component objects making up the binding).

The EDL compiler is also responsible for providing a C++ implementation class for passive binding interactions as described above.

Multiple Interface Support To achieve multiple interfaces per object we have extended the standard CORBA IDL *module* facility which provides a name space scoping mechanism for groups of interfaces. In standard CORBA, IDL *modules* map to C++ *namespaces* in the compilation process and a flat set of implementation classes is produced. In our extension, each interface within a module is mapped onto a base C++ class which is inherited (using multiple inheritance) by a single derived class representing the module as a whole. This latter implementation class then represents the object with multiple interfaces.

4. INFRASTRUCTURE SUPPORT FOR THE EXTENDED PLATFORM

4.1 Binding Implementation

As described above, binding objects are responsible for taking source and sink interfaces, together with an end-to-end QoS specification, and transparently building a suitable configuration of components to form the required binding with the required QoS. Internally, binding object implementations deduce the necessary components (see below) in an implementation specific manner and then instantiate and bind these components to form the end-to-end binding. In doing this, the binding object will enlist the help of various services described in section 4.3 below.

'Component level' binding may involve either the recursive use of other binding object types or local binding. Local binding is used either where the to-be-bound components are co-located, or in the special case of switch objects and network objects described below.

For co-located components, the establishment of a local binding involves the exchange of information between two adjacent components. This information includes shared resource identifiers, pointers to callback procedures, implementation object specifiers and network port identifiers.

Binding object implementations may also need to perform an admission test to determine whether or not sufficient resources are available to meet the end-to-end QoS specification. To facilitate admission testing, the low level component objects support interfaces which binding objects can use to query resource availability and commit resources for new bindings.

4.2 Binding Components

A small set of 'standard' service components with IDL and EDL interfaces are provided which binding object implementations can instantiate and configure into end-to-end bindings. In the network, the component objects are abstractions over the resources contained in network elements. In our ATM based environment, the following component types are provided.

- *Switch objects.* These represent the local control elements of a switch fabric. Method invocations on the IDL interface of a switch object enable the direct configuration of the VPI/VCI blocking table and the assignment of channel identifiers to VCI/VPI pairs. In addition, the switch object facilitates the committal and removal of the reservation entries of a given input and output VPI/VCI/Port triplet, to the physical routing table of the switching fabric.

- *Link objects.* These represent the output multiplexers associated with an ATM switch port. The link object simply models the output port of the switch where there is contention for buffer space and switching time). Link objects are aimed purely at actual resource management units of the physical device.

In the end-system the following component types are provided;

- *Stub/ skeleton objects.* These encapsulate the stubs and skeletons produced by the EDL compiler. Bindings co-operate with the EOA to connect stub and skeleton objects to the C++ implementation classes which produce/ consume the data flowing into/ out of bindings. Stub/ skeleton objects support EDL interfaces containing standard events to accept and emit typed data items and packets.

- *Media objects.* These encapsulate media devices such as cameras, microphones and loudspeakers. 'Virtual' devices such as video windows are also modelled as media objects. Processing components, such as compressors and filters, are classed as media objects and all media objects support EDL interfaces to accept and emit media frames and an IDL interface for device control (cf. the interface of figure 1).

- *Protocol objects.* These encapsulate protocol machines which are used to interface component objects on an end system to the network. Protocol objects support EDL interfaces to accept and emit packets from/to stubs/ skeletons and network objects. QoS capable protocol objects (cf. the SUMO transport protocol [Coulson,95b]) also support an IDL interface for QoS re-negotiation.

- *Network objects.* These encapsulate the end-system's network interface card. They are used as an intermediary between protocol objects and the nearest switch object involved in the end-to-end binding.

Local binding of switch objects is achieved by calling operations in their IDL interfaces which allocate VCIs and configure switching tables to effectively connect a pair of switch objects or a switch object and a network object.

4.3 Per Node Services

In addition to the ORB daemon, the following runtime services are provided on each node to support the extended CORBA platform.

- *QoS mapper.* This performs a translation between end-user QoS requirements and component level QoS requirements. As our design is open with respect to QoS notations, we envisage a number of QoS mappers being made available each of which understands some particular QoS notations. The QoS mapper takes the configuration and end-to-end QoS specification and then translates this information into a set of component-level QoS specifications.
- *Event interface type checking service.* This takes two event interfaces and determines whether or not they are type compatible and thus eligible to be bound by a binding object. For two event interfaces to be type compatible, there must exist a known configuration of service components which successfully maps between the two type dependent sets of events.
- *Node QoS manager.* This service is essentially an interface to underlying OS services and manages the CPU, memory and communications resources on the end-system. It is solely responsible for the management of resources and the co-ordination of components associated with a particular stream through a particular node. In particular, the QoS manager is responsible for system resource reservation, admission control and resource control. The QoS manager is a *per-binding, per-node* service component. Within an end-system the manager interacts with the OS services for resource utilisation and within a network node, it interacts with the resident control interface. Multiple streams and hence multiple QoS managers may reside on a single node at any one time and therefore, a global 'resource registry' is needed between QoS managers. The implementation of such a registry is considered to be OS specific and therefore outside of the scope of this model.

Figure 2 illustrates the composition of the per node services within the end-system.

4.4 QoS Management

In the end-system, QoS is managed at three distinct levels in a hierarchical arrangement. The three levels are as follows.

- i.) *Component level QoS management.* Multimedia service components attempt to maintain QoS according to their agreed QoS specification. This is achieved through QoS monitor code generated from the user's QoS specification. Examples of component level QoS management strategies are frame dropping and queue management.
- ii.) *QoS manager control.* QoS indications are fed up to the QoS manager from lower level QoS monitors. The QoS manager uses a pre-defined adaptation table to determine the appropriate action to be taken. Such action may include

making invocations on the control interface of selected binding components, or alternatively passing the indication further up the stack to the client.

iii.) *Client QoS control.* Should all underlying mechanisms fail to maintain the agreed QoS specification the client is given the responsibility of QoS control. This may involve instigating QoS re-negotiation in the form of an alternative service type selection. For example, a client receiving an audio/video stream, may in the event of QoS failure or degradation, decide to reduce the frame rate of the video stream. Clients inform the infrastructure at bind time of the addresses of QoS callback functions which are to be called on QoS failure/ degradation.

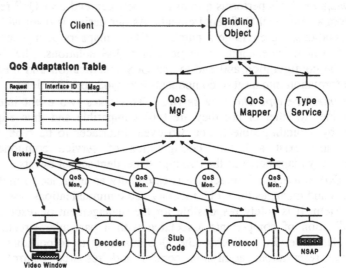

Figure 2: Per Node Services

5. AN EXAMPLE BINDING SCENARIO

5.1 The Scenario

This section clarifies the perspective of i) the application programmer and ii) the binding object implementor in our enhanced computational model. To do this, we explore a remote camera to video window connection scenario. In our scenario, we assume the application programmer has acquired an event interface reference to a remote camera object and intends to bind this to a software decompressor object and feed the output of this to a video window object. The application programmer has implemented the decompressor and video window according to interface definitions understood by an *Indeo_Video_Stream*[4] binding object. The camera object is on one machine, the binding object (which is co-located with the client program) is on another and the decompressor and video window objects are on a third machine.

---

4   Indeo Video[TM] is a Intel/Microsoft video compression technology which offers a variable rate compression scheme. Capture devices, such as the Intel Smart Recorder Pro, are capable of capturing directly to Indeo Video and hence an intermediary software compression stage is not required.

5.2 Programmer Implementation

The programmer provides the following EDL event interface and IDL control interface descriptions for the two service components to be provided, i.e. the video window and decompressor.

```
//EDL event interface definitions
events VideoWindow : QoS_events {
    in FrameDecompressed(RAW_T frame);
    };
events VideoDecompressor : QoS_events {
    in FrameReady(Indeo_T frame);
    out FrameDecompressed(RAW_T frame);
    };
// IDL control interface defintions
interface VideoWindow {
    void SetFrameDropRate(in short fdr);
    };
interface Decompressor {
    void SetFrameDropRate(in short fdr);
    };
```

These interfaces are compiled into support QoS mechanisms linked with the implementation code. A QoS specification must also be associated with the event interfaces. This is achieved by passing simple scalar name-value pairs via the CORBA *context object*[5] facility to the binding object. The context object is as follows.

```
CORBA::Context QoS_ctx = CORBA::Context::Context()
QoS_ctx -> set_one_value("FramesPerSec", 25);
QoS_ctx -> set_one_value("MsDelay", 50);
```

The following illustrates the resulting mappings to C++ headers for the VideoWindow implementation to be provided by the programmer.

```
class VideoWindow_i : public
VideoWindow_ci, ideoWindow_ei;
class VideoWindow_ci : VideoWindowBOAImpl {
    public:
    VideoWindow_ic();
    virtual ~VideoWindow_ic();

    void SetFrameDropRate(short fdps,
    CORBA::Environment&=CORBA::default_environment);
    };
class VideoWindow_ei : public
VideoWindowEOAImpl, QoS_events {
    public:
    FrameDecompressed(RAW_T frame,
CORBA::Environment&=
CORBA::default_environment);
    };
```

These classes are compiled and linked into CORBA servers which create an instance of the above classes which wait to be bound by a third party. This process is as follows for the video window (the case of the camera is similar).

---

5   CORBA context objects contain lists of properties in the form of <name, value> pairs. By convention, context properties represent information about the client, environment, or circumstances of a request that are inconvenient to pass as parameters. Once a server has been invoked it may query its context object for such properties.

```
#include "VideoWindow_i.h"

main() {
    CORBA::Object *b;
    VideoWindow_i vw(); // Create a videowindow object

    // "vwSrv" is server name as registered in

    // Implementation Repository
    b = CORBA::ORB.wait_for_bind("win1:vwSrv");

    /* Register callback with per-binding QoS
    manager; will need to find out the type of b via
    CORBA::Object::_get_interface() -- this will be
    binding object type specific. */
    b.QoS_manager_register(QoS_callback);

    cout << "Server terminating" << endl;
}
```

The *wait_for_bind()* call is used to make the server listen for incoming bind requests
(see below). Once a binding has been created, *CORBA::ORB.wait_for_bind()*
returns a pointer to the QoS manager for the new binding. This allows local
application code to carry out local operations on the binding such as registering
callbacks for QoS degradation.

Once the application programmer has described and implemented the service
objects, the binding can be created. First a call to a *binding factory* is made to
request a suitable binding object; then a binding is established via a call on the
bind() method of this binding object. References to the interface instances within the
servers mentioned above plus the QoS specification context are passed to the *bind()*
call. Note that two interfaces are used by the decompressor; one for input and the
other for output.

```
binding bo = bind_factory.create("Indeo_Video_Stream");
binding_ctrl indeo_control = bo.bind("cam1:camSrv",
    "decin:decSrv", "decout:decSrv", "win1:vwSrv", QoS_ctx, &env);
```

5.3 Binding Implementation

5.3.1 Binding Creation Phase

The first task of the binding object's *bind()* operation on being invoked is to carry
out some checks of type safety on its arguments. To do this, *bind()* retrieves,
through the *CORBA::Object:_get_interface* service, the interface signatures
corresponding to the implementation interface references it has been passed (i.e. the
cam1:camSrv, *decin1:decSrv*, *decout1:decSrv* and *win1:vwSrv* interface references
in our scenario). These are obtained from the Interface Repository on the host on
which the interfaces reside. The *bind()* implementation type checks the resulting
interface signatures by passing them to the local type checking service.

In making a request on a remote object, the ORB returns to the binding object the
network addresses of the associated servers. The binding object uses this
information to contact each server. On receiving a bind request message from the
binding object, library code in the server upcalls the object's *bind_request()* (see
section 3.2 above) method to ask if the object is willing to be bound. At the same
time, the library code passes a proxy interface to the application object which the
application object can later use for passive binding interactions (see section 3.4).

Assuming the application object accepts the binding, the server then arranges to instantiate the necessary binding components. In the case of the camera object, the camera server asks its local QoS manager to dynamically link instances of the appropriate stub, protocol and network components into the server process. The camera server then performs local bindings between these components. Similarly, on the decompressor/ video window machine, component objects are instantiated and local bindings established. The binding object must also arrange for the two machines to be connected via the network. To do this the binding object creates another, lower level, binding object[6] that understands network connections. This binding object works by obtaining a list of interface references to switch control objects running on each of the switches on the chosen route, and then making invocations on these objects to request that they make local bindings to their neighbours. The list of control object interface references is obtained from a general purpose routing server.

Having established the chain of components necessary to build the binding, a QoS mapper is invoked to translate the user's end-to-end QoS requirement into a set of component level QoS requirements (in terms of latency, jitter, throughput, loss rates). This has the following implications for the various QoS parameters:

- *Throughput.* This involves mapping a measure of 'media units per second' from the application programmer's media units to an equivalent rate involving the possibly differently sized units dealt with by individual components (e.g. media frames to network packets).

- *Latency.* Involves appropriately allocating latencies to components while ensuring that per-component latencies are less than or equal to the overall end-to-end latency requirement.

- *Jitter.* This also involves partitioning the total jitter allowance between components. It is likely that only components on the receiving end system will be involved in jitter correction.

- *Error rates.* The interpretation of this parameter will be primarily restricted to the protocol components. As with throughput, an appropriate translation from the user's media units will be required.

Having calculated an appropriate set of low level QoS targets, the binding object invokes each component object, informing it of its component level QoS target and asking whether it can meet this target. Assuming all components can meet their targets, the binding object asks the components to commit their resources. Finally, the binding object builds and returns the binding control interface to the client application.

5.3.2 Binding Operation Phase

On successful establishment of the binding, the client has a reference to a control interface on the binding. The following shows a possible control interface signature (note that this inherits from the *binding_ctl* interface described in section 3.1).

```
interface IndeoVideoStreamControl : binding_ctl {
    setCompressionRate(in short value);
    setImageQuality(in short percentQuality);
};
```

---

[6] Note the recursive use of the binding architecture.

Some invocations (e.g. *setCompressionRate()*) by the client on this interface are simply redirected by the binding object to the appropriate component object. Other operations (e.g. *setFrameRate()*) may result in more widespread changes such as global QoS re-negotiation. QoS re-negotiation involves re-mapping the user's end-to-end QoS requirements and then re-configuring the set of bound components.

When the *start()* operation on *IndeoVideoStreamControl* has been invoked, an operation in the camera is repeatedly called to obtain the next frame. Each frame is sent to the decompressor object via the binding which receives the frame on a *FrameCompressed()* upcall. The decompressor decompresses the frame and then delivers the decompressed frame on a *FrameReady()* call. This call, which is essentially provided through the *VideoDecompressorEOAImpl*, upcalls the locally bound VideoWindow *FrameDecom-pressed()*.

5.3.3 Binding Termination Phase

Having finished with the binding, the client application terminates the binding through a call to *closeBinding()*. This call results in the binding object making *release()* invocations on each of the binding components. As a result each component frees any used resources and terminates its server if a reference count of the server's interfaces has become zero.

6. CONCLUSIONS

We have described an enhanced CORBA programming model and infrastructure for real-time/ multimedia applications. Importantly, programmers in our environment are not constrained to structure their applications in the 'plumbing' style necessitated by, say, the IMA MSS model or in terms of standardised virtual classes as is necessary in, say, the Columbia binding architecture. In effect, the Columbia design offers specific object types that the system knows how to bind together. In contrast, we 'standardise' at a lower level (i.e. EDL, EOA, component types etc.) so as to support the typesafe binding of arbitrary types while remaining in the context of a simple, general programming model.

The programming model offers real-time event-based communication as a first class, language based, facility. The infrastructure adopts ideas on distributed resource allocation from the multi-service network community and applies them in an end-system/ application environment. The resulting platform offers great flexibility to the application programmer. With the aid of an initial set of binding types, generic component objects and standard services, the programmer can write real-time event/ stream based applications as easily as traditional request/ reply based applications in standard CORBA. Furthermore, programmers can easily extend the initial set of binding types by refining and building on existing types (as illustrated in section 4.3.1), and can thus support applications with arbitrary event interface types and binding semantics.

Currently we are engaged in implementing our extended CORBA model in an ATM network environment. Our approach is to use the Winsock 2.0 API to build a primitive ATM AAL5 network binding type and to add richer binding types on top of this in the end-system environment. We are using Xerox Parc's Inter Language Unification (ILU) public domain CORBA implementation as a basis for our platform and using the Windows NT operating system on PCs as our end-system environment.

ACKNOWLEDGEMENT

We would like to acknowledge the kind support of BT Labs in funding this research under the Management of Multi-service Networks project within BT's University Research Initiative (BT-URI). We would also specifically like to acknowledge the collaboration of our colleagues at Imperial College who are also funded under this BT-URI project.

REFERENCES

[Aurrecoechea,96] C. Aurrecoechea, A. Campbell and L. Hauw, "A Review of QoS Architectures", Multimedia Systems Journal , 1996 (to appear).

[Blair,95] G. S. Blair, G. Coulson, M. Papathomas, P. Robin, J. B. Stefani, F. Horn and L. Hazard, "A Programming Model and System Infrastructure for Real-Time Synchronisation in Distributed Multimedia Systems", IEEE Journal on Selected Areas in Communications, Special Issue on Multimedia Synchronisation, 1995.

[Campbell,96] A. Campbell, "A Quality of Service Architecture", PhD Thesis, Lancaster University , England, January 1996.

[CORBA,96] Corba 2.0 Specification, OMG Technical Document PTC/96-03-04

[Coulson,95a] G. Coulson and G.S. Blair, "Architectural Principles and Techniques for Distributed Multimedia Application Support in Operating Systems", ACM Operating Systems Review, Vol 29, No 4, pp 17-24, October 1995.

[Coulson,95b] Coulson, G., Campbell, A., Robin, P., Blair, G.S., Papathomas, M. and D. Shepherd, "The Design of a QoS Controlled ATM Based Communications System in Chorus", IEEE Journal on Selected Areas in Communications, 1995.

[Halteren,95] A.T. van Halteren, P. Leydekkers and H.B. Korte, "Specification and Realisation of Stream Interfaces for the TINA-DPE", Proc. TINA-95 Workshop, 1995.

[IMA,96] Interactive Multimedia Association's Multimedia System Services at http://www.ima.org/forums/imf/mss/.

[ITU-T,95a] UIT-T, ISO/IEC Recommendation X.902, International Standard 10746-2, "ODP Reference Model: Descriptive Model", January 1995.

[ITU-T,95b] UIT-T, ISO/IEC Recommendation X.903, International Standard 10746-3, "ODP Reference Model: Prescriptive Model", January 1995.

[Leydekkers,95] P. Leydekkers and V. Gay, "ODP View on Quality of Service for Open Distributed Multimedia Environments", Proc. International Workshop on QoS (IWQoS), Paris, March 1995.

[Lindblad,94] C.J. Lindblad, D.J. Wetherall and D.L. Tennenhouse, "The VuSystem: A Programming System for Visual Processing of Digital Video", Proc. Multimedia 95, San Franciso, October 1994.

[Mines,94] R.F. Mines, J.A. Friesen and C.L. Yang, "DAVE: A Plug and Play Model for Distributed Multimedia Application Development", Proc. Multimedia 95, San Franciso, October 1994.

[OMG, 95] CORBA2.0/Interoperability - "Universal Networked Objects" Document 95.3.xx[REVISED 1.8 jm], March 1995.

[Stefani,93] J.B. Stefani, "Computational Aspects of QoS in an Object Based Distributed Architecture", 3rd International Workshop on Responsive Computer Systems, Lincoln, NH, USA, September 1993.

[TINA,95] "TINA Object Definition Language Manual", Doc. No. TR_NM.002_1.3_95, TINA Consortium, June 1995.

[Xbind, 96] Code available at: http://www.ctr.columbia.edu/opensig/opensig.html.

Implementation of Hidden Concurrency
in CORBA Clients

Patrick Hellemans
Frank Steegmans
Hans Vanderstraeten
Han Zuidweg

Alcatel Telecom

Francis Wellesplein 1
2018 Antwerp
Belgium
Tel: +32/3/240.7605
Fax: +32/3/240.9932
e-mail: phe3@rc.bel.alcatel.be

Abstract

This paper reports on the introduction of concurrency at the client side, as an engineering solution to improve performance. It is shown that, by combining a wait-by-necessity principle, where the calling process only blocks when a return value of a function call is needed, with the handle concept, used to control the access to an object, hidden concurrency can be introduced into CORBA-based client components. Concurrency is achieved by splitting sequential calls to servers through the creation of dedicated threads. Hidden signifies the fact that the split is hidden for the client code by including the thread creation in the serverStub, while the synchronisation needed at some point in the client process is done through the handle mechanism combined with the wait-by-necessity principle. The introduction of this kind of concurrency can be done transparently from the client and server application code. The principle of hidden concurrency through the introduction of multiple threads at the calling side has been contrasted with the single thread scenario through an example, which takes on the TINA (Telecommunication Information Networking Architecture) Connection Management Architecture as a particular case study.

1. Introduction

The Object Management Group (OMG) is setting the standards for the definition of a distributed software platform which adheres to the object oriented programming paradigm. This standard is referred to as the Common Object Request Broker Architecture (CORBA). CORBA also adheres to the client/server paradigm for supporting distributed processing. Pre-products and products are starting to appear on the market which implement the CORBA standard. Most of these products use OS-native multithreading capabilities to support multithreading at the server side. This paper reports on the introduction of concurrency at the client side, as an engineering solution to improve performance.

Section 2 presents a short overview of the most important CORBA concepts. Section 3 clarifies the notions of sequential versus parallel execution and synchronous versus asynchronous operation invocation. In section 0 we elaborate the concept of how client multithreading can be implemented at the client side of a client/server configuration in such a way that it is transparent to the actual client application code. The Wait-by-necessity principle and the handle concept are explained and it is elaborated how these concepts can be applied to implement hidden concurrency in client components. Finally, section 4.4 presents a case study where the programming technique is applied to the TINA (Telecommunication Information Networking Architecture) connection management architecture.

2. Common Object Request Broker Architecture

CORBA was originally intended as an "open" alternative to the proprietary solutions like OLE from Microsoft. CORBA is sometimes called a "software bus", as it supports the distribution and interworking of heterogeneous software modules. It involves the following components:

- an Object Request Broker (ORB), which provides distribution and implementation transparency. The ORB hides the complexity of communications from the applications.
- the Interface Definition Language (IDL) is the common language that acts as the "glue" between the different application components. An IDL specification is automatically compiled to "stubs" and "skeletons", pieces of code that enable the ORB to take care of communication between the objects.
- a set of Common Object Services (COS) which provide generic support for object life cycles, naming, persistence, transaction processing and asynchronous multi-casting communications.
- a set of Common Facilities which are generic applications, for example object browsers.

Fig. 1 illustrates the CORBA architecture. The interface of each application is defined in IDL and specifies exactly those operations that can be remotely invoked. An application can be a client (of other applications), a server, or both. The unit of distribution and implementation is a "CORBA Object". A CORBA object is defined by an interface described in IDL, which is associated with an implementation. Note that one interface can be associated to different implementations (even in different languages). A CORBA Server corresponds to a process, which can contain one or more CORBA objects.

There are currently over 20 commercially available CORBA platforms, including products like Orbix (Iona Technologies), NEO (SUN), Object Broker (DEC), DSOM (IBM), ORB Plus (HP), and many others. The product range is still expanding, and the existing products are becoming increasingly performant, mature and stable. The market for CORBA products is continuously evolving, but for the moment Iona Technologies seems to be emerging with Orbix as one of the market leaders.

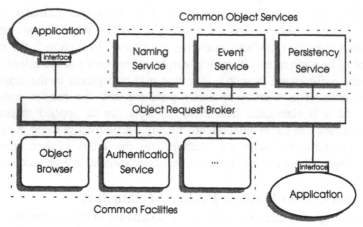

Fig. 1. Overview of CORBA

3. Concepts of Concurrency in Operating Systems and Programming Languages

A multi-tasking Operating System (OS) foresees at least one way of executing processes in parallel. In the sequel, the term 'concurrency' addresses this parallel execution of processes (a process is, in general, an executing program or part of a program). Concurrent processing is one of the most applied performance optimisations in computer systems. Concurrency increases the throughput of the system by sharing its CPU(s) between processes that are mostly waiting for external events. More detailed discussions concerning the usefulness of concurrency are beyond the scope of this work. More details concerning implementation issues on concurrent processes at OS level can be found in [6] and [7]. The aim of this paper is to introduce concurrency in the previously defined architecture without changing the core code of the components.

3.1 Sequential and Parallel Execution

A 'client/server' architecture, such as the CORBA, in most cases supports only one way of concurrency, namely *server concurrency*. This means that a server can process multiple client requests at the same time. Classically this is done by forking a new server process each time a client request is received. Special precautions have to be taken to share information between processes. Most Object Request Brokers (ORB) offer at least this kind of server concurrency. More advanced ORBs can be configured to support concurrency per server, per object or per method, but the service implementer has to manage the concurrent access of information.

Another kind of parallelism could be addressed, analogously to the previous one, as client concurrency. Fig. 2 illustrates how different statements in a scope can be executed. The first way is sequentially. Almost all programming languages are based on the sequential paradigm. A number of languages also support parallelism as demonstrated in the second diagram e.g. parallel C, ADA, Java. Here the statements between the start and the stop are logically executed in parallel. The start acts as a kind of split, while the stop forces synchronisation. The power of such a language approach is clearly the possibility to distribute the *'statements'*. If the statements are calculus routines, they can be executed on different processors. In the same way, the final result can be reached faster if the statements include calls to parallel running servers. The latter approach will be implemented in this paper.

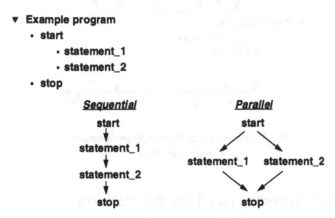

Fig. 2. Sequential Versus Parallel Execution

3.2 Synchronous and Asynchronous Operations

CORBA defines the Interface Definition Language (IDL) to formally describe the interfaces between application components. These interfaces represent a kind of remote function calls between Objects. The function call paradigm as well as most languages uses sequential execution. A function call passes parameters from the current scope to the scope of the function. At the same time, the execution is transferred to the function. Results and execution are only transferred back to the calling program when the function terminates.

The first part of Fig. 3 demonstrates the synchronous execution of a function call based program. It is obvious that it is difficult to send requests in parallel to servers in this way of working. The second part of Fig. 3 demonstrates the most widely used solution to this problem, namely asynchronous communication. The application can send and receive messages at any time. It will process them if it is ready (e.g. by reading from a message queue). Asynchronous applications are mostly implemented as state machines.

Although many theories exist, proving the correctness of an algorithm containing asynchronous communication and concurrency, is still a hard job. Proving the correctness of a sequential, synchronous algorithm is much easier. The next section provides a technique for introducing parallelism in a client program while maintaining its sequential and synchronous character. Both client and server code can even be reused by using the communication abstraction principle offered by CORBA. The next section will gradually explain the technique.

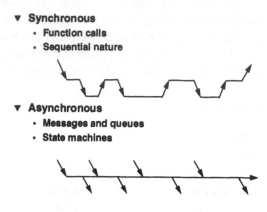

Fig. 3. Synchronous Versus Asynchronous
Communication

4. Client Multithreading on a CORBA Platform

Two things are, as pointed out before, very important in concurrent applications: splitting the current thread of execution and synchronising a number of executing threads. In Fig. 2 these points are indicated with start and stop, but they could also be addressed as respectively split and join. Parallel programming languages have special instructions for this purpose. ANSI Version 4 of C++ (which we used for the implementation) does not have such language constructions incorporated. Solaris 2.4 and higher versions include multi-threading in the OS. The application programmer can use the multi-threading facilities by means of library functions. The implementation will use these library calls, but they will be shielded from both the client's and the server's core code.

4.1 Wait-by-Necessity

Denis Caromel explains in [8] how *'Wait-by-necessity'* can be implemented for converting synchronous calls in asynchronous messages. As the words *'Wait-by-necessity'* summarise: the client of an object is only blocked if it is really necessary. In his approach, each operation invoked on an object results in a message to the object for processing. After the message is sent, the client will proceed as if the call returned. The operation returns a fake result to the client if a result is required. The real result or reply of the operation is returned by a subsequent message. If the fake result is used before the reply arrives, the client is blocked. Fig. 4 summarises the wait-by-necessity principle.

▼ server->op(parameters)
- Sends a message to the 'server'
  (request on the method)
- Execution continues

▼ res = server->op(parameters)
- Sends a message to the 'server'
  (request on the method)
- Execution continues
- Wait if 'res' is used and the reply has not come back

Fig. 4. Wait-by-Necessity Principle

Practically the communication between the client and the server is function call based. The ORB probably converts the client calls in messages, transfers them to the server and invokes the correct object in the server's address space, but this is invisible to the client and the server applications on the ORB. Instead of sending an asynchronous message, a new thread is created which will perform the synchronous ORB call. Logically this thread will also receive the return values. The creation and the termination of the threads can be implemented in the serverStub code linked with the client. This will shield the client (and of course the server) from the thread operations.

In short: the asynchronous calls to servers are implemented by launching new threads that perform concurrently synchronous calls. This split operation is covered by the serverStub. The last thing that should be taken care of is the synchronisation that is previously addressed as the 'join', between the threads. The next section will introduce the concept of handles that allows to implement a 'wait' if necessary.

4.2 Handle Concept

Bjarne Stroustrup explains in [5] how a handle class can be used for implementing access control on an object. The handle class can be applied for example to count the number of accesses to an object or for managing the memory usage of objects. Fig. 5 illustrates the handle concept.

The handle contains a reference to the object it represents. This is currently implemented as a pointer to the object. Other information can be stored in the handle object if required. The handle object can implement a number of operations. In the C++ implementation, it will almost always contain an overloading of the dereferencing operator (->). The dereferencing operator is implemented as a function. This function can do a number of operations (e.g. incrementing a counter) before returning the pointer to the real object. The returned pointer will then be used to call the operation on the real object. Syntactically the dereferencing of the handle will look *exactly* the same as the dereferencing of a pointer to an object. The only difference is the possibility to introduce extra code into a number of manipulations of the handle (dereferencing, copying, creating, deleting, ...).

▼ **Logical**

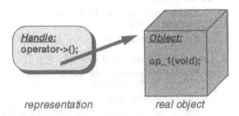

representation   real object

▼ **C++ syntax:**
- **dereferencing handle ≡ dereferencing pointer**
  - **e.g. h -> op_1();**

Fig. 5. The Handle Concept

The handle class can be implemented as a template, as depicted in Fig. 6. The objects addressed by the handle class do not need to be derived from a common superclass.

```
template <class T>
class    handle {
T*              rep;
private:
        void    set(T* pt) { rep = pt; }
public:
        handle(T& t) : rep(&t) {}
        handle(T* pt) : rep(pt) {}
        virtual T*        operator->() { return rep; }
};
```

Fig. 6. Handle Class Definition

4.3 Hidden Concurrency

A combination of all the elements that are explained so far, allows the implementation of concurrency in a client process hidden for the clients core code. First of all the client and the server are implemented on the ORB. This means that clients use a local serverStub that forwards remote calls to the server on the ORB. Results (both out and inout parameters) are passed back in the C++ model as handles. Even if there is no concurrency, a pointer to a handle pointing to the result is returned in the C++ operations on the serverStub (This means that the developed C++ model takes into account that certain parameters are out or inout parameters. Return values are returned as a pointer to a handle.). The reason why a pointer to a handle is returned will be clarified later. To introduce concurrency, the stub implementation of the server operations will create a new thread that will take care of the synchronous call to the real server. The stub operation will return a dedicated derived handle class, as depicted in Fig. 7.

```
template <class T>
class     handle_c : public handle<T> {
          semaphore      s;
public:
          handle_c(void) : s(semaphore::LOCKED) {}
          handle_c(T& t) : handle<T>(t), s(semaphore::UNLOCKED) {}
          handle_c(T* pt) : handle<T>(pt), s(semaphore::UNLOCKED) {}
          void    initialize(T* pt) { set(pt); s.unlock(); }
          void    initialize(T& t) { set(&t); s.unlock(); }
          virtual T*      operator->() {
                              if(s.unlocked()) // blocks until unlock
                              return handle<T>::operator->(); }
};
```

Fig. 7. Handle Class For Hidden Concurrency

Each object in the concurrent specialisation of the handle class contains a kind of synchronisation mechanism (e.g. semaphore or condition variable). For the handles returned by the serverStub operations, this blocking mechanism is locked and there is no referenced object. As soon as the remote call returns, the formerly created thread will create return objects with the information of the returned remote call. It will make the previously returned handles reference these newly created return objects and will unlock the blocking mechanism of the handles. The blocking mechanism is checked whenever the handle is dereferenced for accessing the information of the object it represents. In this way the main client thread will create a number of threads to handle the server calls. It will dereference the returned handles if it needs the information the handles represent. The main thread will be blocked whenever it dereferences a handle that is not yet been cleared by the thread responsible for the server call. This explains why a pointer to a handle is returned in the C++ operations on the serverStub.

Fig. 8 gives an overview of the introduction of hidden concurrency in the model as it is applied to the issue identified in section 5.2.

▼ **Concurrency**   ▼ **Hidden == invisible for client code**
  • Split: creation new thread   • Split: in serverStub
  • Join: synchronisation   • Join: in handle

▼ **Synchronous call returns handle**
    • h1 = server1->op_1();   // synchronous operations
    • h2 = server2->op_2();   // launch parallel requests

▼ **Wait-by-necessity == if returned handle is dereferenced**
    • if(h1->success() && h2->success())   // synchronization
      else
      ...
    • Only the access to a returned object forces a wait(-by-necessity)
    ==> synchronization point

Fig. 8. Hidden Concurrency Overview

38

4.4 An Alternative Approach

Alternatively, the deferred synchronous invocation paradigm could be used to implement the server stub. However, this approach relies on the CORBA dynamic invocation interface (DII) and has the following disadvantages:

- use of the DII significantly increases the code at the client side
- use of the DII impacts the performance, because it requires more parameter analysis

5. Application of Hidden Concurrency In TINA Connection Management

5.1 TINA DPE

TINA is designed to be an open architecture for telecom software applications. Performance is a crucial parameter for the validation of TINA. TINA incorporates a Distributed Processing Environment (DPE) which is heavily based on CORBA. The TINA DPE, illustrated in Fig. 9., is a software platform which allows TINA software components to communicate with each other as though they were located on the same processor. In the engineering viewpoint, the DPE is actually supported by a software layer - referred to as the DPE Kernel - which runs on top of the

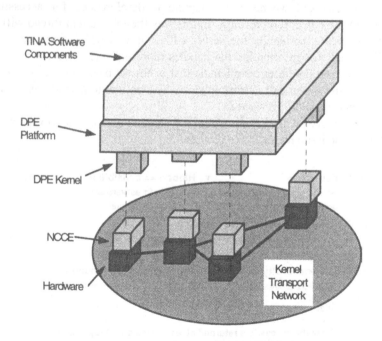

Fig. 9. TINA DPE

Native Computing and Communication Environment (NCCE) of the hardware platform. The NCCE typically includes the Operating System (OS) and additional networking facilities. The different DPE Kernels are interconnected by a network which is referred to as the Kernel Transport Network (KTN).

5.2 Problem Statement

This section presents a simple example in the context of TINA connection management, to illustrate where the introduction of concurrency in a client application is recommended. Fig. 10 shows both the example network and the

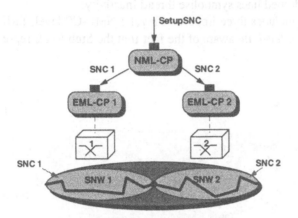

Fig. 10. Connection Setup Example

software configuration. The configuration in this example is a subnetwork (SNW) containing two switches. The master SNW is represented by the Network Management Layer Connection Performer (NML-CP) while the two switches are represented by two Element Management Layer Connection Performers (EML-CP). Setting up a subnetwork connection (SNC) on the NML-CP will result in the set-up of two SNCs in the corresponding EML-CPs. The NML-CP is a sequential application and the calls on the DPE are completely synchronous. Therefore, the set-up of the second SNC on the EML-CP level can only be performed as soon as the set-up of the first one is completely finished. As a consequence, the connection set-up time at the NML-CP level will be at the least the addition of all the connection set-up times at the EML-CP level. This is a pure waste of time because mostly the set-up of the different SNCs happens on independent machines that can work concurrently. In telecommunications, this problem is classically avoided by implementing processes as concurrent state-machines that communicate via asynchronous messages. Here, the proposed solution maintains the synchronicity. As such, the sequential code in the NML-CP can be maintained, avoiding the need to introduce complex state machines to follow the state of the asynchronous calls, while on the other hand the time required for the sequential code to execute is minimised.

5.3 Multithread Scenario

This section illustrates how the performance of the TINA connection management can be improved by introducing client multithreading in the NML-CP. The symbols in Fig. 11 must be interpreted as follows:

- Straight arrows down symbolise function calls;
- Straight arrows upward symbolise function call returns;
- Arc arrows symbolise a special event (e.g. fork, server call, server returns or unlocking of handles);
- Horizontal full lines symbolise computations or calculations at that level;
- Horizontal dashed lines symbolise thread inactivity;
- The picture includes three important levels: NML-CP level, EML-CPStub *level* and ORBStub *level*. Be aware of the fact that the Stub *levels* represent more than one object.

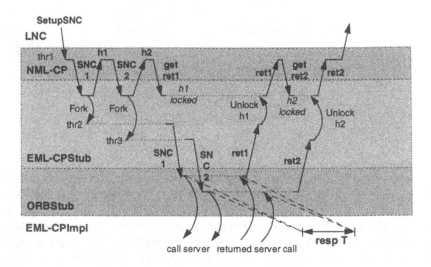

Fig. 11. Multithreaded Connection Setup

We distinguish the following steps:
1. The LNC calls the SetupSNC on the NML-CP.
2. After some computations are done, the NML-CP calls a SNC setup on the first EML-CPStub (SNC1).
3. After some computations are done, the first EML-CPStub creates a new thread. It creates a locked handle h1 and returns it.
4. After some calculations are done, the NML-CP calls the set-up on the second EML-CPStub.
6. The NML-CP tries to retrieve the result of the call to the server via dereferencing h1. The current thread is blocked in the dereferencing action because the handle is locked.

7. Thread thr1 is put in the waiting queue and thr2 gets active. 'thr2' forwards the SNC1 to the remote server. Then it is also put in the waiting queue of the scheduler.
8. Only thr3 is left in the ready queue. After scheduling in, thr3 performs the SNC2 call on the remote server object whereupon it also gets inactive.
9. After some time, the first result of the remote server call is received by the ORBStub. In the example, this will be the first ORBStub. 'thr2' gets active again and the call is returned to the first EML-CPStub. This processes the result and creates a return object, initialises the formally returned handle h1 with a reference to this object and unlocks the handle. Finally thread thr1 terminates.
10. Thread thr1 gets active again because the handle h1 is unlocked. The dereferencing continues and the result ret1 is returned to the NML-CP.
11. The result of the second remote server call is received by the ORB, but will not be processed because another thread is still active.
12. The NML-CP continues and tries to retrieve the result of the SNC2 call by dereferencing h2.
13. The result is already received from the remote server, but has not been processed yet. Therefore h2 is still locked. As a consequence, thr1 is blocked.
14. Thread thr3 is scheduled in again. The reply on the remote server call is processed and returned to the second EML-CPStub. The second EML-CPStub creates a return object with ret2 and updates h2 with a reference to it. At last, h2 is unlocked and the thread terminates.
15. Thread thr1 gets active because h2 is unlocked. The dereferencing action continues and ret2 is returned to the NML-CP.
16. The NML-CP still does some post processing and returns the set-up call to the LNC.

6. Conclusions

The introduction of concurrency at the *client* side of client/server applications has been proposed as an engineering solution to improve performance. It is shown that, by combining a wait-by-necessity principle, where the calling process only blocks when a return value of a function call is needed, with the handle concept, used to control the access to an object, hidden concurrency can be introduced into the engineering model of TINA-based application components. *Concurrency* is achieved by splitting sequential calls to servers through the creation of dedicated threads. *Hidden* signifies the fact that the split is hidden for the client code by including the thread creation in the serverStub, while the synchronisation needed at some point in the client process is done through the handle mechanism combined with the wait-by-necessity principle. It should be emphasised that the ~introduction of this kind of concurrency can be done transparently from the client and server code. The principle of hidden concurrency through the introduction of multiple threads at the calling side has been contrasted with the single thread scenario through an example, in which the NML-CP sets up connection points in two switches in sequence.

Acknowledgements

Part of this work has been performed in the ACTS European Research Project VITAL (AC003).

References

[1]   M. Kawanishi, H. Oshigiri, J. Pavón, M. Schenk: *"Connection Management Architecture"*, March 1995 (TB_JJB.005_1.5_94).

[2]   M. Lengdell, H. Oshigiri, J. Pavón, M. Kawanishi, L. Richter: *"Network Resource Information Model Specification"*, December 1994, (TB_LR.010_2.0_94).

[3]   C. Aurecoechea, A. Hopson, H. Oshigiri, J. Pavón, F. Ruano: *"Connection Management Specification"*, 6 March 1995 (TP_NAD.001_1.2_95).

[4]   N. Natarajan, F. Dupuy, N. Singer, H. Christensen, M. Chapman: *"Computational Modelling Concepts"*, November 1994 (TP_A2.HC.012_1.1_94).

[5]   B. Stroustrup: *"The C++ Programming Language"* Second Edition, AT&T Bell Laboratories, Inc., Murray Hill, New Jersey 1991 (printed by Addison-Wesley), ISBN 0-201-53992-6.

[6]   A S. Tanenbaum, *"Modern Operating Systems"*, Prentice Hall, Englewood Cliffs, New Jersey 1992, ISBN 0-13-595752-4.

[7]   J. L. Peterson, A. Silberschatz, *"Operating System Concepts"* 2nd Ed., Addison-Wesley Publishing Company, 1995.

[8]   D. Caromel, *"Service, Asynchrony, and Wait-By-Necessity"*, Journal of Object Oriented Programming, November/December 1989.

[9]   D. Caromel, *"Concurrency And Reusability: From Sequential To Parallel"*, Journal of Object Oriented Programming, September/October 1990.

Passing Objects by Value in CORBA

Ennio Grasso

CSELT

via Reiss Romoli 274   10148 Torino (Italy)

e-mail: ennio.grasso@cselt.stet.it

fax: +39-11-2286862

Introduction

The CORBA specifications [OMGa] define an Interface Definition Language (IDL) to describe object interfaces. This approach allows the separation between the interface description and the actual implementation of object operations, which may be realized in any programming language.

An IDL interface specification declares the object attributes and the signature of the operations supported by the object indicating the types of the arguments and whether they are **in**, **out**, or **inout** parameters. The IDL language defines a concrete syntax for a non-pure object-oriented model, meaning that it distinguishes between object types on the one hand and non-object types on the other. While object types identify IDL interfaces, non-object types correspond to the traditional types that can be found in many programming languages, such as *int*, *boolean*, *char*, etc. (basic types), *struct*, *union*, *sequence*, etc. (constructed types).

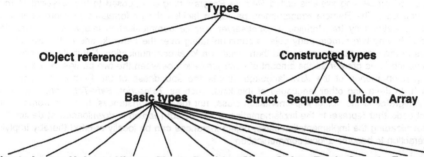

The IDL language is object-oriented in that it allows object interfaces to be organized into an inheritance hierarchy[1]. There is one root interface called *Object* from which all other IDL interfaces inherit giving rise to an inheritance graph[2]. Both object types and non-object types may be specified as **in**, **out**, or **inout** arguments of IDL operations.

As for non-object types, the invocation has pass-by-value semantics, meaning that the actual values of the parameters are copied in the call. In particular, the values of the **in** parameters are copied from the client to the target object at operation invocation, while the values of the **out** parameters are copied from the target object to the client at operation reply[3].

---

[1] *It should be noted that CORBA terminology of "interface inheritance" is a bit misleading since inheritance usually applies to code reuse whereas at the interface level the proper term should be "interface subtyping".*

[2] *Since IDL allows multiple inheritance for interfaces, it gives rise to a graph rather than simply a tree.*

[3] **inout** *parameters are copied both at operation invocation and reply.*

As for object types, the invocation has pass-by-reference semantics, meaning that the actual values of the parameters are references to object interfaces and are not the objects themselves. When the reference to an object interface is passed in a remote operation invocation, the receiving object will be able to use that reference to invoke operations provided by the referred interface.

In the IDL to C++ mapping specified by OMG [OMGa], the reference to a remote object interface corresponds to a C++ smart pointer, i.e. a C++ class that overloads the dereferencing operator "->" and encapsulates the logic to access the remote object. In general, a C++ smart pointer is an object that acts as a pointer and performs some action when is used to access an object. In the IDL to C++ mapping, a remote interface reference is viewed as if it were a local C++ object pointer and any interaction with the local C++ object pointer causes a remote invocation to the remote object.

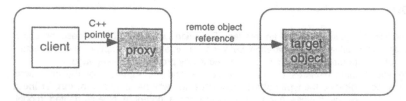

Although the above behaviour is reasonable in the majority of the circumstances, there are scenarios where a different approach might be required. In fact, high-latency and low-bandwidth transport networks, such as the Internet, require a reduction in network traffic to improve the overall performance of the system. These limitations of the transport network have led to a different paradigm in distributed processing systems called *Remote Programming* as opposed to the classical *Remote Procedural Call*. The Remote Programming paradigm tackles the performance problem caused by remote invocations by transforming a client/server remote communication into a local interaction. Instead of having two remote party objects communicating over the network, one of the two objects migrates to the other object's place and then initiates a local communication. Naturally, the benefit of this approach is as greater as the amount of communication between the two parties increases. The booming phenomenon of the *Java* language attests the soundness of the Remote Programming approach. In Java and other languages of this kind, such as *Telescript, Safe-Tcl, Obliq*, etc., what actually migrates is the object implementation class, not the object instances. In other words, some piece of code that represents the implementation of the object (*applet*) is downloaded at destination. After downloading the implementation class, object instances can be locally created thereby implying any interaction to become a local communication.

The crucial point of languages such as Java, which enable the Remote Programming paradigm, is that they are interpreted languages as opposed to compiled languages such as C++. Interpreted languages tend to defer almost any decision at run-time thereby increasing the flexibility of the code but at the cost of increasing the run-time overhead. On the other hand, compiled languages are subjected to a compilation phase in which some decisions are statically made that reduce the amount of flexibility but avoid having to insert run-time checks thereby improving performance. There is no doubt that C++ code is faster then Java code, though Java is more flexible than C++.

Performance issues

In distributed and real-time environments where performance is a crucial issue, interpreted languages fall short in meeting the expectations of the applications. In these environments a compiled language (usually C++) is a mandatory choice.
Does this mean that C++ (and possibly other compiled languages) will not reconcile with the Remote Programming paradigm? After all, Remote Programming is used to improve network performance, which is a prime demand in real-time systems. In fact, the Remote Programming approach is useful

not only for low-bandwidth networks, even in high-bandwidth networks the time spent in remote communications often exceeds by several magnitudes the time for the actual computation.

To deal with compiled languages, such as C++, we propose a model based on *object copying* rather than class migration. In the proposed model, the code is not downloaded at run-time because we are in a compiled environment. Nonetheless, a looser form of Remote Programming can be achieved by copying an object instance from one place to another. This mechanism implies that the receiving place already has the implementation class of the object to be copied, or else it may be dynamically linked if the system supports DLLs. What is copied is not the implementation class but the internal state of a particular object instance. What are the advantages of this mechanism? Plainly, by copying the object instance, an interaction with that object will be locally resolved instead of causing a remote communication.

Recall that in the IDL to C++ mapping, when a reference to an IDL interface is passed as an argument in a remote invocation, a smart C++ pointer object is created that encapsulates to logic to interact with the remote interface. The straightforward idea is to make this C++ object pointer even smarter: instead of merely encapsulating the logic for the remote invocation, the smart object pointer is itself a precise copy of the remote object so that it can locally execute any operation without making a remote invocation. Note that the client is not aware that the object has been copied. The only thing it deals with is a C++ object pointer regardless of whether this pointer refers to an object that merely represents a proxy to a remote object or is a real server object in its own right.

To summarize, when an object reference is passed as an argument in a remote invocation, the state of the object to which this reference refers is copied in the invocation and a new instance is created at destination and initialized with the state received so as to recreate a precise copy of the object. This mechanism realizes a pass-by-value semantics of objects as opposed to the classical pass-by-reference which may be useful in circumstances where performance is a crucial issue.
In our model the pass-by-value semantics does not supersede the pass-by-reference semantics. Rather, both options are available and the client cannot tell which has been applied since the mechanism is completely transparent: all the client deals with is a C++ pointer that may either correspond to a proxy object or be a precise copy of the remote object. This transparent behaviour permits greater flexibility because the client is not affected by either choices. Only the copied object is indeed aware of the mechanism and must cooperate to achieve the bass-by-value semantics. In fact, being objects units of encapsulation, they must be willing to externalize their internal state and then internalize that state.

OMG LifeCycle and Externalization Services

The proposed mechanism bears a close resemblance with both the Externalization Service and the LifeCycle Service defined by OMG in the CORBAservices specifications [OMGb]. Is our approach yet reinventing the wheel? Why not simply use the Externalization or the LifeCycle services? The answer is simple: both the LifeCycle Service and the Externalization Service have several drawbacks to being effectively exploited in realizing a pass-by-value semantics for objects.

The *copy* operation of the LifeCycle Service delegates the responsibility for copying an object to the object itself. Given a factory finder, the object must create a new object instance within the scope of that factory finder and then initialize that instance so as to be a copy of itself. How the object manages the initialization of its copy is outside the scope of the specifications, though we feel that this is a prickly issue that cannot be neglected.

On the other hand, the Externalization Service provides a thorough support for streaming objects but is more geared toward object streaming on stable storage rather than a light-weight mechanism for object copying. Indeed, the great number of IDL interfaces and the contrived interaction model needed to use the service makes it a heavy-weight service that can hardly be exploited for realizing a pass-by-value semantics. However, some principles of Externalization Service are very close to a pass-by-value mechanism and can be profiled so as to obtain a light-weight version of the Externalization Service that can be exploited in our context. Moreover, the usage of the LifeCycle Service and the Externalization Service implies a remote invocation to create a copy of the object. This is exactly what we would like to avoid in order to lower the amount of remote invocation and improve performance.

However, there is even a more remarkable difference between the LifeCycle and Externalization services on the one hand and a pass-by-value mechanism for objects on the other. Both the LifeCycle and the Externalization services create new CORBA objects, meaning that the original object and its copy will be identified by two different object references.

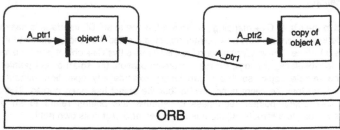

A_ptr1 and A_ptr2 are two distinct object references

On the other hand, in the pass-by-value mechanism the very same object reference is altered at the receiving domain space so that it identifies the new instance rather than its remote counterpart. Unbeknown to the client that uses the receiving object reference is that the object reference has been altered and now identifies a local copy.

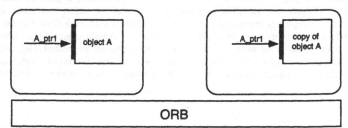

The very same A_ptr1 refers to two different objects depending on the domain space

Pass by value Service

The interoperability model of CORBA 2.0 specifications [OMGa] points out the difference between *ORB Services* and *CORBAServices*. CORBAServices are general purpose services defined in IDL as normal CORBA objects and made available by the ORB throughout the network. Conversely, ORB Services are invoked transparently by the application code and reside within the ORB, either as part of the ORB core or layered over it. ORB Services range from fundamental mechanisms, such as reference resolution and message marshalling/unmarshalling, to the support of advanced features such as transactions and security. Indeed, there are emerging specifications for CORBAServices that require specific context information to be implicitly transmitted along with remote invocations and replies. These sophisticated CORBAServices need to be supported by ORB Services to add the implicit context in the course of requests and replies. The interoperability specifications define mechanisms for identifying and passing this implicit context and assume that:

- the implicit context is specified as an IDL data type;
- ORB callbacks are provided that allow services to supply and consume the implicit context at operation invocations and replies;

A CORBAService requiring implicit context information to be transmitted during operation invocations and replies is allocated a unique service ID value by OMG. Currently, the only CORBAService that exploits implicit context is the Transaction Service [OMGb], though the Security Service is expected to use this feature as well. In the CORBA Transaction Service specifications, a pseudo IDL interface has been defined to permit the cooperation between the ORB and the Transaction Service thereby enabling implicit propagation of the transactional context as part of a remote invocation. According to this mechanism, the ORB behaves as a client and calls the Transaction Service to piggyback the transactional context in the invocation. The specifications define the *CosTSPortability* module with two interfaces. The *Sender* interface provides the *sending_request* and *received_reply* operations invoked by the ORB in the client domain space respectively before sending an invocation and after receiving the reply. The *Receiver* interface provides the *received_request* and *sending_reply* operations invoked by the ORB in the server domain space respectively after receiving an invocation and before sending the reply. The only argument of these operations is the transactional propagation context.

The mechanism for adding implicit context information is a fundamental building-block for the realization of the pass-by-value semantics for objects. The following pseudo IDL type defines the implicit context structure used to transmit objects' state as part of operation invocation and reply:

```
module CosPBVInteroperation { // PIDL

        typedef sequence<any> ObjectState;

        struct ObjectInfo {
                Object objRef;
                ObjectState state;
        };
        typedef sequence<ObjectInfo> ObjectsInfo;
};
```

ObjectState is defined as a sequence of *anys*, while the implicit context *ObjectsInfo* is defined as a sequence of *ObjectInfo*. Each element of the sequence is enough to completely characterize the object: the object state and the object reference so as to create a precise copy at destination. The pass-by-value semantics for objects is defined as a simplified version of the Externalization Service. The *CosPassByValue* module defines the *Copiable*, *CopiableFactory* and *Identify* interfaces:

```
module CosPassByValue {

        exception DoNotCopy {};
        exception AlreadyRegistered {};
        exception NotRegistered {};

        interface Copiable;
        typedef sequence<Copiable> Copiables;

        interface Copiable {
                void get_object_state(out CosPBVInteroperation::ObjectState state,
                                      out Copiables related_objects);
                                      raises (DoNotCopy);
                void set_object_state(in CosPBVInteroperation::ObjectState state);
        };

        interface CopiableFactory {
                Copiable create_uninitialized();
        };

        interface Identify { // PIDL
                void register_copiable(in Copiable object);
```

```
                              raises (AlreadyRegistered);
            void unregister_copiable(in Copiable object);
                              raises (NotRegistered);
            void register_factory(in CopiableFactory factory,
                              CORBA::InterfaceDef object_type
                              CORBA::ImplementationDef object_impl);
                              raises (AlreadyRegistered);
        };
};
```

An object that wants to support the pass-by-value semantics must inherit form the *Copiable* interface that provides two operations: *get_object_state* and *set_object_state* which will be called by the pass-by-value service respectively to externalize and internalize the object's internal state. The get_object_state may raise the *DoNotCopy* exception meaning that the object refuses to be copied. This provides Copiable objects the opportunity for deciding whether to apply a pass-by-value or a pass-by-reference semantics on a per invocation basis. Also note that the get_object_state operation returns a sequence of references to some other Copiable objects that should be copied along with this object. The pass-by-value can use the *hash* and *is_equivalent* operations provided by any object references[4] to compare objects when detecting cycles or overlapping references in objects being copied in the same invocation.

When copying objects, the pass-by-value service must be able to create instances of the objects being copied at destination before calling the set_object_state operation of those objects. Therefore, for each Copiable object there must exist a *CopiableFactory* object that supports creation of that Copiable object through the *create_uninitialized* operation.

The *Identify* interface is designed to be supported by the pass-by-value service as a pseudo object and used by Copiable objects and CopiableFactory objects to register their involvement in the pass-by-value mechanism. A Copiable object calls the *register_copiable* operation of the Identify interface to express its interest in being copied in remote invocations. After having registered, the Copiable object should expect the pass-by-value service to call its get_object_state operation whenever a reference to it is to be passed in a remote invocation. As said above, the object maintains the control on deciding whether applying a pass-by-value or a pass-by-reference semantics on a per invocation basis. At any time a Copiable object that registered with the pass-by-value service can waive its interest in the pass-by-value semantics by calling the *unregister_copiable* operation. The *register_factory* operation must be called by a factory object to inform the pass-by-value service that this factory is capable of creating instances of Copiable objects supporting a certain interface type as indicated by the *InterfaceDef* parameter[5] and providing a certain implementation as indicated by the *ImplementationDef* parameter. The pass-by-value service will use the InterfaceDef parameter as a match-maker to select a factory that creates objects supporting a certain interface type and may use the ImplementationDef parameter to select objects with implementation in a certain equivalence class.

ORB callbacks

To enable a uniform model for describing the pass-by-value mechanism that works with multiple ORBs, we need to define a standard interface between the ORB and the pass-by-value service:

```
module CosPBVPortability { // PIDL
```

---

[4] *The Object interface is defined in pseudo IDL meaning that the operations are implemented directly by the ORB, not passed on the object implementation class.*

[5] *The InterfaceDef describes the most derived interface which must be a descendant in the inheritance hierarchy of the Copiable interface.*

```
     typedef sequence<Object> Objects;
     exception AlreadyRegistered {};
     exception NotRegistered {};

     interface SenderCallbacks {
       void sending_request(in Objects outgoing_objects,
                            out CosPBVInteroperation::ObjectsInfo copied_objects);
       void received_reply(in CosPBVInteroperation::ObjectsInfo copied_objects);
     };

     interface ReceiverCallbacks {
       void received_request(in CosPBVInteroperation::ObjectsInfo copied_objects);
       void sending_reply(in Objects outgoing_objects,
                          out CosPBVInteroperation::ObjectsInfo copied_objects);
     };
};
```

The *SenderCallbacks* and *ReceiverCallbacks* interfaces must be supported by the pass-by-value service and will be called by the ORB before and after operation invocation and reply. The pass-by-value service will register its interest in being notified by the ORB by calling the *identify_sender* and *identify_receiver* operations of the *PBVIdentification* interface, which must to be supported by the ORB as an ORB Service. Both the *CopierCallback* and the *Identification* interfaces are defined in pseudo IDL so that the invocation of the operations is performed in the same domain space as the ORB with the only overhead of local procedure calls.

```
interface PBVIdentification {
        exception NotAvailable {};
        exception AlreadyIdentified {};

        void identify_sender(in CosPBVPortability::SenderCallbacks sender);
                             raises (NotAvailable, AlreadyIdentified);
        void identify_receiver(in CosPBVPortability::ReceiverCallbacks receiver);
                             raises (NotAvailable, AlreadyIdentified);
};
```

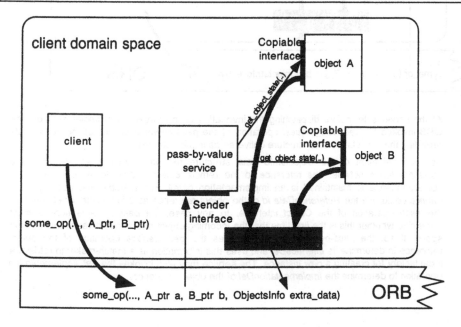

The behaviour of the callback mechanism is as follows:

- At the client side, before sending a remote invocation the ORB calls the *sending_request* operation of the pass-by-value service providing the list of object references that are being passed as **in** or **inout** parameters in the current invocation (*outgoing_objects*).

- The pass-by-value service determines which of these object references refer to Copiable objects that have registered their interest in the pass-by-value semantics and then invokes the *get_object_state* operation of such objects.

- The Copiable objects are responsible for returning their internal state and possibly a list of references to other Copiable objects that should be copied in the same invocation.

- As said above, the pass-by-value service can use the *hash* and *is_equivalent* operations of the *Object* interface to determine cycles. In the end, the pass-by-value service builds the *ObjectsInfo* data structure to be delivered in the invocation as implicit context. Then the ORB delivers the call to the server.

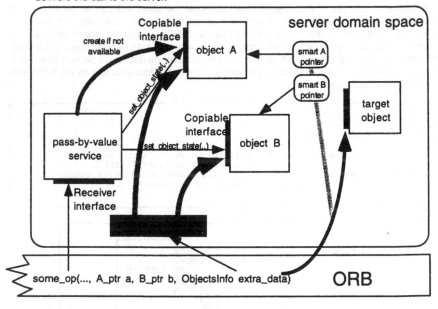

- At the server side, before dispatching the invocation to the target object implementation, the ORB invokes the *received_request* operation of the pass-by-value service at the server side providing the ObjectsInfo data structure delivered as implicit context.

- For each element of the ObjectsInfo data structure the pass-by-value service makes a correspondence between the reference to the remote object and its local copy. How this correspondence is maintained is an implementation detail. For example, the pass-by-value service could use the *ReferenceData id* of the object reference as a key value, or else exploit the *hash* operation of the *Object* interface. In any case, the pass-by-value service must determine whether this is the first time that the incoming object reference arrives in this domain space. If so, the pass-by-value service invokes the *get_interface* operation of the object reference to determine its *InterfaceDef* and uses this information as a match-maker to retrieve a local factory for creating a new instance. The service may also invokes the *get_implementation* operation to determine the *ImplementationDef* of the object reference.

- After having created a local copy, the pass-by-value service must alter the incoming object reference so as it refers to the local copy. This is important because the target object will receive this very object reference among its parameters and we want this reference to refer to the local copy rather than the remote object. Again, how the object reference is altered is an implementation detail. For example, the pass-by-value service may call the *change_implementation* operation of the BOA interface providing the implementation of the local copy:

```
// get the object's incoming information
Object incoming_object = ObjectInfo->objectRef;
// if 1st time for incoming_object, then...
{
        // get the interface definition of the incoming object
        InterfaceDef intf = incoming_object->get_interface();

        // retrieve a foctory for this object using "intf" as a match-maker
        CopiableFactory fact =....

        // create a local copy of the object
        Copiable local_copy = fact->create_uninitialized;

        // get the implementation of the local copy
        ImplementationDef impl = local_copy->get_implementation();

        // change the implementation of the original object reference to be
        // the same of the local copy
        boa->change_implementation(incoming_object, impl);

        // release the local object reference
        local_copy->release();
}
// set the object's state
ObjectState state = ObjectInfo->state;
incoming_object->set_object_state(state);
```

- Note that if this is not the first time that the incoming object reference arrives in this domain space, there already exists a local copy corresponding to this object reference and there is no need to create a new one.
- Finally, the pass-by-value service invokes the *set_object_state* operation of the local object to initialize the object's internal state and then the control returns to the ORB that can dispatch the invocation to the target object.

The same procedure applies when the target object operation completes and the reply is returned. This time the ORB calls the *sending_reply* at the server side and the pass-by-value service determines which Copiable objects are to be transmitted in the way back as **out** or **inout** parameters. Likewise, when the reply arrives at the client side, the ORB invokes the *received_reply* operation of the local Sender object whose behaviour is the same as the received_request operation.

Implementation issues

In the previous sections the pass-by-value semantics for objects has been defined in all its parts. The support for pass-by-value semantics cannot proficiently rely on a simple plug-in service but a tight collaboration between may parties is necessary. First, the objects being copied must provide operations to externalize and internalize their internal state. This has been achieved by defining the *Copiable* interface. Secondly, the pass-by-value service must offer an *Identify* interface so that *Copiable* objects and *CopiableFactory* objects can express their interest in the pass-by-value semantics. Thirdly, for portability across different ORBs, the *SenderCallbacks* and *ReceiverCallbacks* interfaces define standard callback interfaces supported by the pass-by-value and invoked by the

ORB. Finally, the pass-by-value service registers the callback interfaces through the *PBVIdentification* interface of the ORB.

The callback model described here has been inspired by the solution adopted for OMG Transaction Service which may well be exploited in future standard CORBAServices. The pass-by-value service and the ORB have a peer-to-peer relationship: the ORB acts as a client of the pass-by-value service when it needs to invoke a remote operation by asking the pass-by-value service to provide the implicit context to transmit during the call (piggybacking of extra data). On the other hand, the pass-by-value service acts as a client of the ORB when it needs some basic functionalities from the ORB or the BOA.

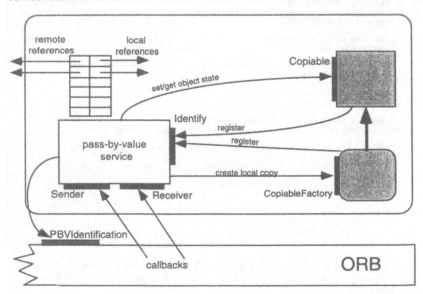

Because of the tight integration between the pass-by-value mechanism and the ORB it is clear that any reasonable implementation of the pass-by-value semantics should exploit any relevant features of the target ORB provided the interfaces described above are supported. An implementation may even avoid supporting the *PBVPortability* interfaces and use proprietary protocols between the pass-by-value service and the ORB but at the cost of a non-interoperable approach between different ORBs. In the remainder we will describe a possible implementation of the pass-by-value service for Orbix by IONA [IONA].

Pass by value on Orbix

Two Orbix features are particularly relevant for the pass-by-value service: Process filters and Smart Proxies.

Process filters[6] are objects invoked by the ORB before and after each remote invocation is delivered and the reply returned. A process filter provides four methods[7]: *inRequestPreMarshal*, *outRequestPreMarshal*, *inReplyPreMarshal* and *outReplyPreMarshal*. The implementation of these methods is left to the programmer who is given the hooks to customize the behaviour of the ORB.

---

[6] Besides process filters, Orbix provides object filters, but they will not be mentioned in this context.
[7] Actually, Orbix's filters provide eight operations distinguishing between Pre- and Post-marshal.

Process filters realize the callback mechanism between the ORB and the pass-by-value service that allow the latter to provide extra data to be implicitly transmitted in the invocation.

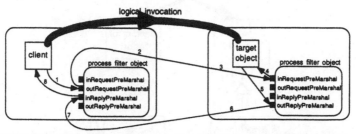

1. the client issues the invocation and the ORB calls the outRequestPreMarshal method of the process filter;
2. the outRequestPreMarshal piggies back the transactional context and the ORB delivers the remote invocation;
3. the invocation arrives at the server and the ORB calls inRequestPreMarshal method of the process filter;
4. the inRequestPreMarshal obtains the transactional context and the ORB dispatches the invocation to the target object;
5. the target objects completes the operation and the ORB calls the outReplyPreMarshal method of the filter;
6. the filter may or not add extra data and then the ORB returns the reply to the client;
7. the ORB calls the outReplyPreMarshal of the filter which checks if extra data has been added to the message;
8. finally, the ORB returns the reply to the client.

Besides process filters, another useful feature provided by Orbix is the concept of "smart proxy". An Orbix proxy is simply what CORBA calls a *client stub*, namely the representation at the client domain of a remote object interface. In an IDL to C++ mapping, a proxy is a C++ object that locally represents the remote object and encapsulates the logic that allows the invocation of the remote object. In this way the client sees the remote object as if it were a normal C++ object. Orbix allows the programmer to define smart proxies by adding new semantics. As a rule, a smart proxy adds some logic that tries to resolve the invocation locally and issues the remote invocation only as a last resort.

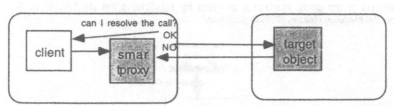

For each IDL interface, the IDL compiler creates a C++ class named after the interface. This is the proxy class from which proxy objects will be created at run-time by the ORB. Smart proxies are created by subclassing the proxy class and informing the ORB of this new specialized behaviour. Therefore, whenever the ORB needs to create a new proxy object, it will instance the specialized class.

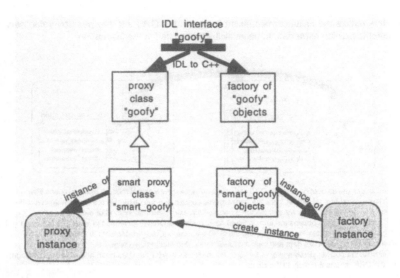

In the picture above, the compilation of the IDL interface *goofy* will create a C++ class named *goofy* and a factory class named *goofyProxyFactoryClass* which is used by the ORB to create instances of the goofy class. To create a smart proxy, the programmer must subclass the goofy class, e.g. *smart_goofy*, adding the desired behaviour. The programmer must also subclass the factory class so that the ORB will create instances of the smart_goofy class rather than goofy.

For the pass-by-value service smart proxies can fruitfully be exploited. In the server side, the implementation of the goofy interface is provided by subclassing the *goofyBOAImpl* class, which represents the skeleton class in CORBA parlance.

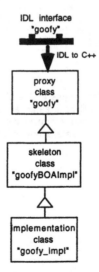

The strategy is to define a smart proxy class which inherits both from the proxy class *goofy* and the real object implementation class *goofy_impl*. By inheriting from the goofy class the ORB is informed of the presence of a smart proxy, while by inheriting from the real implementation class we recreate locally the precise behaviour of the transmitted object. Plainly, it will suffice to create a smart proxy that inherits from the actual implementation class.

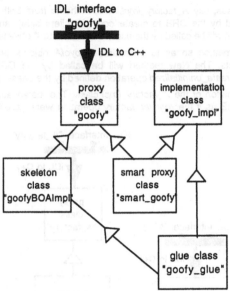

The inheritance graph depicted above shows how the pass-by-value mechanism could be implemented on Orbix. The *goofy_impl* class represents the actual implementation of the *goofy* interface. In the server, the *goofy_glue* class inherits from both goofy (through the skeleton class) and goofy_impl thereby tying the interface and the implementation. Instances of the goofy_glue class are CORBA objects at the server side. Also the *smart_goofy* class inherits from both goofy and goofy_impl, so that when the ORB creates a proxy in the client domain space it will actually instantiate a real implementation of the object. In other words, the smart_goofy class is the client counterpart of the goofy_glue class of the server.

How does this model map onto the specifications of the pass-by-value service described here? The mechanism used by Orbix to customize the behaviour of the proxy class (i.e. definition of smart proxies) exploits C++ inheritance and therefore is a static mechanism. On the other hand, the pass-by-value service expects a dynamic registration of factory objects through the *register_factory* operation of the *Identify* interface. Yet, the full conformance with the interfaces of the pass-by-value service would require the access to low-level functionalities of the ORB, which unfortunately are not available. Nonetheless, Orbix provides some mechanisms that permit the implementation of the pass-by-value semantics through static inheritance. For a certain IDL interface *A* that inherits from *Copiable* and given a factory interface *A_factory* that inherits from *CopiableFactory*:

```
interface A : CosPassByValue::Copiable {
     .....
};
interface A_factory : CosPassByValue::CopiableFactory {
     A create();
};
```

The programmer should:

-   create a smart proxy class, say *copyofA*, which inherits from the A class (generated by the IDL compiler) and the implementation class, say *A_impl* (note that the implementation class must

56

exist in any case for objects to be copied). Each method of copyofA will delegate its behaviour to the A_impl superclass;

- create a factory class, say *A_factory_impl*, which inherits from both the *AProxyFactoryClass*, which will be called by the ORB to create *copyofA* (client side), and the *A_factoryBOAImpl*, skeleton class which will be called by the user code to create *A* objects (server side);

- redefine its *New* method so as to instantiate *copyofA* objects and the *create* method to instantiate *A* objects. The New method will be called by the ORB to create proxies and correspond to the *create_uninitialized* operation defined by the pass-by-value service.

- instantiate one singleton of the *A_factory_impl* class. The instantiation implicitly registers this factory with the ORB as if the *register_factory* operation were called in the constructor of the class.

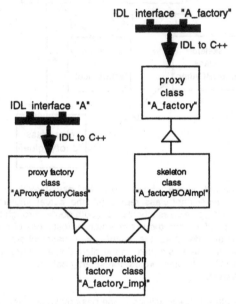

Note that the implementation of the factory provides two different methods to create *A* objects, namely *New* and *create*. This is because in Orbix a smart proxy class cannot coincide with the real implementation of the object so that we need to define a *copyofA* class and a *glueofA* class (see above).

References

[IONA] IONA Technologies, "Orbix 2 Programming Guide", Dublin, November 1995.
[OMGa] Object Management Group, "The Common Object Request Broker Architecture and Specification", Revision 2.0, OMG doc. n. 95-07-01, Framingham, MA, July 1995.
[OMGb] Object Management Group, "CORBAservices: Common Object Services Specification", OMG doc. n. 95-03-31, Framingham, MA, March 1995.

Communication Middleware for Reliable Workflow Management Systems

Hans Schuster

University of Erlangen-Nürnberg, Department of Computer Science VI
Martensstr. 3, D-91058 Erlangen, Germany

Abstract. In distributed workflow management systems (WfMSs) many workflow servers and clients should work together cooperatively using client/server communication. Depending on the communication partners, different characteristics are required for a client/server interaction. In this paper we introduce a middleware service for WfMSs which supports client/server interaction qualities. These qualities characterize the behavior of client and server in case of failure and recovery independently of underlying base services like TP monitors. Our middleware service separates a WfMS from communication base services and provides interoperability among them.

1 Motivation

Workflow management systems (WfMSs) are a middleware framework (according to [3]) to implement business processes of an enterprise. An enterprise depends on its business processes. Therefore, the execution of workflows implementing business processes does not only have to be performant but also reliable. It is not acceptable at all that data are lost during workflow execution or that inconsistent states are entered because of system failures [15].

The components of a distributed WfMS work together using a client/server protocol to execute workflow instances [14]. Since execution must be fast and reliable, client/server communication must also fulfill these requirements. However, it turns out that different components of a WfMS have their own communication requirements. For example, if the WfMS wants some log component to write information into the history, this job may be done asynchronously and without returning any result or acknowledgment as long as it is done exactly once. If a user requests the execution of a workflow, his request is again to be performed exactly once but a synchronous execution with result message is necessary. In summary, the examples show that requests and responses within a distributed WfMS are of different nature depending on the kind of involved clients and servers. Therefore, a middleware service which can offer different communication qualities is the most appropriate one.

This paper develops a communication middleware service supporting different communication qualities for client/server interactions. The middleware layer executes a request for a server according to parameters which specify the required quality, like exactly-once, with/without result or acknowledgment, synchronous/asynchronous. Then a suitable implementation technology is selected. Our middleware layer integrates different standard technologies by the introduction of client/server qualities and allows interoperability among them. Figure 1 shows the overall architecture of a WfMS using our middleware layer: at the top level the functionality of a WfMS is implemented by independent modules, i.e modules for control and data flow, application integration (WFA), agent assignment (Policy), logging (History), and a coordinator module (Kernel) [14]. These modules communicate using client/server protocols and execution qualities of our middleware service called Executable Objects; Executable Objects offer execution qualities based on different recovery mechanisms. The Executable Objects middleware layer is implemented on top of heterogeneous (operating system) technologies and communication base services.

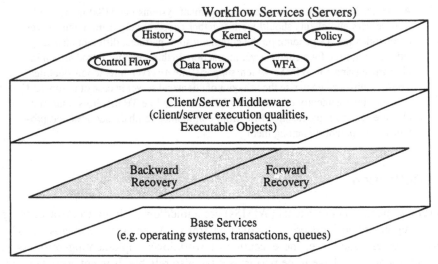

Fig. 1. Layered architecture of a workflow management system

Current approaches to WfMSs do not cover different communication properties: The FlowMark WfMS [13] consists of a monolithic workflow engine (server) together with build-time and run-time clients. The FlowMark server is built on top of a database system. Different communication characteristics are not exploited. The Exotica project deals with several extensions of FlowMark. [1] introduces an architecture for FlowMark based on server clusters but communication issues are left open. In [2] an implementation of FlowMark based on persistent queues is proposed. From the perspective of our work, this corresponds to one type of client/server execution quality. Other communication mechanisms are not supported but [2] states that using non-persistent queues for some communication steps may improve performance. The Mentor project [25] covers the distributed execution of workflows. To preserve reliability, the WfMS is implemented on top of the distributed transaction and persistent queue facilities of the Tuxedo TP monitor [24]. There is no flexibility with respect to communication mechanisms; especially heterogeneity of base services is not covered.

The rest of this paper is structured as follows: Client/server execution qualities are defined in Section 2 and recovery mechanisms to enforce these qualities if failures occur are analyzed. Upon this, Executable Objects are introduced as middleware service which supports client/server qualities (Section 3). Other communication middleware services which can be used to implement Executable Objects are discussed in Section 4. Section 5 concludes the paper an gives a short outlook.

2 Execution Qualities for Client/Server Communication

According to the terminology of Bernstein [3] a WfMS can be regarded as a framework, i.e. some kind of middleware for the execution of business processes. Frameworks are implemented on top of lower level middleware services. In this section we show requirements of WfMSs with respect to middleware communication services (Section 2.1). Then we deduce client/server qualities which have to be guaranteed by middleware services suitable to implement WfMSs (Section 2.2). Client/server call semantics, the most important type of client/server qualities, are detailed in Section 2.3. To enforce given call semantics, recovery mechanisms have to be introduced (Section 2.4).

2.1 Examples for Communication Within Workflow Management Systems

In general, WfMSs consist of multiple distributed components. Dividing a WfMS into several component systems is a consequence of modular design and scalability requirements. Though many different WfMS architectures have been proposed [1], [2], [13], [14], [25], all of them consist of (distributed) components. Also the reference model of the Workflow Management Coalition [12] defines a WfMS as a collection of different components (but without taking distribution issues into account). During workflow execution, these components work together cooperatively using some kind of client/server interaction.

A client/server interaction in a WfMS is influenced by the semantics of the request. Focusing on the client/server interactions within a WfMS, it turns out that the communication behavior which is mandatory for a correct workflow execution depends on the communication partners:

- If a user wants to execute a workflow by selecting the start operation at his worklist, the worklist has to contact the workflow engine to initiate the operation and to synchronize with other concurrent users. Since the user is waiting for his operation to complete, the interaction has to be synchronous and the outcome has to be returned as fast as possible.
- If a workflow has finished, the workflow engine has to determine the subsequent step(s). In a distributed workflow engine, like the engine of the MOBILE WfMS [14], several server processes are involved. These client/server interactions can and should be done in parallel. Thus, they have to be executed asynchronously. Additionally, some workflow services, e.g. logging, do not produce any results. Since throughput of the workflow engine should be as high as possible [11], asynchronity and elimination of unnecessary result transmissions have to be exploited.

These examples of client/server interactions within WfMSs show that a suitable client/server middleware service has to support a variety of client/server interaction qualities. In the following, we present a classification of client/server qualities in order to define a basis to develop a suitable middleware service.

2.2 Classification of Client/Server Qualities

Requirements regarding client/server interaction are very heterogeneous. Nevertheless, these requirements cannot be regarded to be equally important. For example, if a 'start workflow' operation is not performed exactly-once, the client/server interaction is not correct. However, if response time is too high, working with the system may be boring but the execution is still correct. In order to fulfill different requirements, we introduce a classification for client/server qualities (Figure 2).

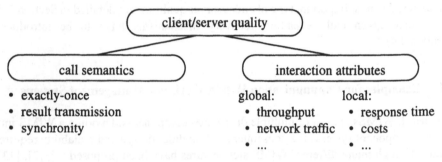

Fig. 2. Classification of client/server qualities

We divide client/server qualities into *call semantics* and *interaction attributes*. Call semantics define the mandatory behavior of a client/server interaction. A violation of the call semantics of a client/server interaction is regarded to cause inconsistency. Thus, call semantics define the correctness criterion for a client/server interaction in our model. In Section 2.3 call semantics are elaborated in more detail.

Interaction attributes define additional requirements for client/server communication. Violating them will not hurt system integrity but taking interaction attributes into account will lead to smart system behavior. Interaction attributes can be further separated into global and local ones. *Global interaction attributes* consider overall system behavior. For example, throughput is a relevant factor for the overall performance of a WfMS. However, throughput is irrelevant for a single call. Thus, it is regarded to be a global attribute. Absolute response time is regarded to be a *local interaction attribute* because it is relevant for one call (recall that mean response time is a global attribute). Besides, costs for resource allocation are covered by a local attribute of a client/server interaction.

Client/server qualities according to the scheme shown in Figure 2 are not independent. For example, optimizing some calls with respect to response time may lead to worse throughput. Therefore, it is impossible to support all combinations of call semantics and interaction attributes. If there are multiple solutions to accomplish the required call semantics, that one should be chosen which matches best with the requested call attributes. In the following, we will concentrate on call semantics and do not discuss interaction attributes at all. Thus, we will use the terms call semantics and client/server qualities synonymously.

2.3 Client/Server Call Semantics

According to Section 2.2 call semantics define the mandatory behavior of a client/ server interaction. Call semantics for client/server interaction in WfMSs are constituted by the following issues:
(1) Execution semantics: exactly-once
(2) Result transmission: result/acknowledgment/no-result
(3) Synchronity: synchronous/asynchronous

From an abstract point of view it does neither matter how the above criteria are implemented nor what kind of errors might occur as long as the call semantics hold. We have chosen these kinds of client/server call semantics introduced above because of their relevance for WfMSs (Section 2.1). However, depending on the application environment the introduction of further kinds of call semantics may be valuable.

The only *execution semantics* supported by client/server call semantics is *exactly-once*. This reflects the fact that without having knowledge about the functional semantics of a requested call, only exactly-once can be regarded as correct execution. Besides, client/server call semantics shall build an abstraction from errors during client/server communication. Consequently, common execution semantics for RPCs like at-least-once or at-most-once [23] are not appropriate at this level of abstraction. However, if client/server call semantics are implemented for a concrete client/server interaction, at-least-once can be used, for example, to implement an idempotent request because this implementation is equivalent to exactly-once execution semantics in this scenario.

Result transmission determines the feedback which is awaited after requesting a call. If *result* is specified, the server must return the result of the call. *Acknowledgment* enables the server to inform the client only about the end of the call execution but no results are sent back. 'Acknowledgment' is a special kind of result; the effort of sending back the computed result can be saved. For this reason, 'result' and 'acknowledgment' can be treated equally during recovery and implementation (Section 2.4). *No-result* means that the server will produce neither results nor will inform the client about termination of its processing.

Synchronity allows to determine whether a client/server interaction will be *synchronous* or *asynchronous*.

In our model client/server call semantics are tuples (res, sync) with res ∈ {result, acknowledgment, no-result} and sync ∈ {synchronous, asynchronous}. Note, execution semantics are always exactly-once and therefore not contained in the tuple. The combination (no-result, synchronous) is invalid because *no-result* and *synchronous* are somehow contrary. If the server will send neither a result nor an acknowledgment, it is impossible for the client to wait until the server has finished processing. All other combinations are valid.

2.4 Recovery Strategies to Enforce Client/Server Qualities

Errors during client/server interaction hurt exactly-once execution semantics and/or transmission of result or acknowledgment. Synchronity is not affected directly by failures. As a prerequisite of enforcing client/server qualities, errors during client/server interaction must be detectable. This assumption is not trivial; especially communication errors, for example loss or delay of messages, are difficult to detect. However, there are techniques and communication protocols to solve these problems [23]. If failures occur during client and/or server processing, there are in general two possibilities for reaction:

(1) *Forward recovery*, i.e. after eventually restarting the failed process the last state of the client/server interaction is reestablished and the interaction is continued. Using this strategy a client/server call will always terminate correctly, i.e. the given client/server qualities hold, if it terminates at all. However, if the client or the server fails because of an unrecoverable error, e.g. division by zero, this strategy will result in an infinite retry loop.

(2) *Backward recovery*, i.e. after a client or server failure the whole client/server interaction is undone. As a consequence, consistency is preserved because an undone client/server interaction can be regarded as never have happened.

Besides using the same kind of recovery at client and server, a combination of forward and backward recovery can be used. Figure 3 shows possible combinations for recovery at client and server with respect to result transmission semantics. 'Result' and 'acknowledgment' can be treated equally. For these two types of result transmission semantics only the combination backward recovery at the client and forward recovery at the server is invalid. In this case the call will be always executed because of forward recovery at the server but the result cannot be delivered if the client fails and aborts its processing. Thus, the result guarantee would be violated. However, the combination forward recovery at the client and backward recovery at the server is valid: forward recovery at the client ensures that the client will never forget a request. If the implementation of backward recovery at the server assures that the client is notified about a server abort, the client is always able to retry its request.

Result transmission	Client recovery	Server recovery
result/acknowledgment	backward	backward
	forward	backward
	forward	forward
no-result	forward	forward

Fig. 3. Possible recovery methods to achieve result transmission semantics

If a client/server interaction has the quality 'no-result' only for ward recovery is possible. 'No-result' always implies asynchronous client/server interaction (Section 2.3). To ensure the exactly-once execution semantics the client relies on, the server must not abort the call because there is no possibility to inform the client. Also, the client must not loose a call during client/server interaction.

3 Supporting Client/Server Qualities by Executable Objects

Executable Objects (ExOs) [22] are a middleware service to support client/server inter-action which was developed in the *MOBILE* workflow management project [14]. Section 3.1 describes the goals of ExOs. Their user interface is introduced in Section 3.2. Section 3.3 points out the implementation of client/server interaction qual-ities with ExOs. Recovery is introduced in Section 3.4 and 3.5.

3.1 Objectives

ExOs have been introduced to support the implementation of the *MOBILE* WfMS. According to [22] ExOs offer an asynchronous call interface (Section 3.2) that hides implementation details. Therefore, ExOs provide full transparency with respect to dis-tribution and heterogeneity. ExOs mainly support the distribution of large grained objects like components of the *MOBILE* WfMS.

In this paper we will concentrate on support of reliability by client/server qualities. Thus, ExOs must provide high level methods for the implementor of a WfMS to pre-serve consistency if parts of the system or even the whole system fails. To achieve this goal, ExOs support client/server interaction qualities that introduce a well defined behavior also in the case of failure.

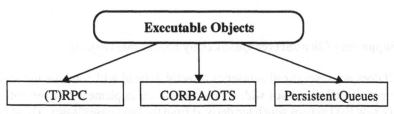

Fig. 4. Executable Objects and other middware services

Since current communication middleware services (see Section 4) already provide valuable services but fail to offer a solution for all of the above mentioned objectives, ExOs are implemented on top of current services (Figure 4). Thus, ExOs integrate them providing interoperability and additional functionality. In contrast to class libraries (e.g. the ACE toolkit [20]) which encapsulate communication services into objects but which do not hide characteristics of these services, ExOs provide full transparency with respect to base services. Therefore, using ExOs a WfMS can run in heterogeneous envi-ronments because the WfMS code is fully decoupled from other communication mid-dleware. By this means ExO provide interoperability among different lower level mid-dleware services.

3.2 Functionality and Use of Executable Objects

ExOs use the proxy mechanism [21] to cope with distributed objects. There are two cases of object calling: if the implementation of an object (*implementation object*) to be called resides within the same process as the calling program, the object can be accessed directly. If it resides on a remote node, a *proxy object* is called instead. The calling program always assumes the called object to be available locally (either as implementation object or as proxy object). The calling program plays the client role, the called object plays the server role.

ExOs offer an asynchronous calling interface with usual semantics (*Executable Call Interface* (ECI) of the abstract base class Executable, Figure 5). Additionally, two call-back methods (OnResult() and OnFailure()) are available. These methods allow for a more convenient use of asynchronous calls than pure polling. ExOs are specialized to a proxy class ExO_Proxy and an implementation class ExO_Impl which offers an additional set_result() method (not shown in Figure 5).

```
class Executable
{
        call(method_nr,param);
        is_ready();
        wait();
        get_result();
        get_failure();
        OnResult();
        OnFailure();
};
```

Fig. 5. ExO classes and Executable Call Interface

3.3 Supporting Client/Server Qualities by Executable Objects

The ECI does not support call semantics directly. Instead will combine the ability to provide certain call semantics with an ExO class. To implement call semantics, we introduce new ExO classes which are derived from the ExO base classes. These classes offer get_call_semantics() and set_call_semantics() methods to retrieve and request qualities.

Both at proxy and implementation side forward and backward recovery is possible (Section 2.4). Therefore, ExO_Proxy_FW/ExO_Impl_FW are derived from ExO_Proxy/ExO_Impl. They inherit the ECI from ExO classes and have knowledge about client/server qualities. ExO_Proxy_FW/ExO_Impl_FW are the abstract base classes for all ExOs supporting client/server qualities and forward recovery. Analogously, ExO_Proxy_BW/ExO_Impl_BW are defined as abstract base classes for ExOs supporting backward recovery. The hierarchy of ExO classes is shown in Figure 6.

Client/Server call semantics are made up by synchronity and result transmission. Synchronity, i.e. both synchronous and asynchronous execution, is covered by ExOs: call() is always asynchronous and wait() can be used to wait for the completion of a call synchronously. The result transmission quality determines the behavior of the

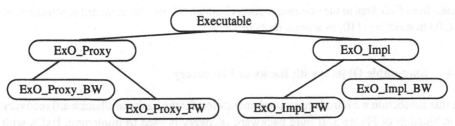

Fig. 6. Class hierarchy for Executable Objects

get_result() and wait() methods: if 'result' is set, get_result() returns the result of a call if the call has already terminated; wait() blocks until the termination of the call. In case of 'acknowledgment', get_result() will return only information about the termination status of a call but no result. 'No-result' causes get_result() and wait() to become obsolete, i.e. they always return successful termination.

The kinds of client/server qualities which are supported by a server depend on two issues:

(1) A concrete ExO class (both proxy and implementation) supports both kinds of synchrony and at least one kind of result transmission.

(2) The user-defined server code knows whether it will produce results.

Therefore, when a server (i.e. user-defined server code and ExO_Impl) is created, the set of client/server qualities is determined which can be guaranteed by this server in general. For example, a server which knows that its service may fail in some situations will only offer 'result' and 'acknowledgment' result transmission quality. It will not support 'no-result' in order to avoid infinite loops (see Section 2.4). If a user client wants to invoke a client/server call, it sets the desired calls semantics at the ExO by set_call_semantics(). If the requested call semantics are supported, the call can proceed otherwise an error code is returned.

```
class ExO_Runtime
{
        ExO *bind (server_name, quality, recovery_type);
        ExO *rebind (ObjectId);
        ...
};
```

Fig. 7. Bind methods of the Executable Object runtime class

In order to connect implementation and proxy objects some bind methods are available in the ExO runtime component (Figure 7). The bind methods are used both for making a connection to a server (bind()) and for starting forward recovery in the case of failure (rebind(), see Section 3.5). The required server is specified by a logical name and also a client/server quality (quality) which should be supported is given. Because a user client may be able to deal with several kinds of recovery the recovery type can be also specified in the bind() call (recovery_type). Valid recovery types are BW, BW_call (both Section 3.4), and FW (Section 3.5).

In the following we will show how ExOs support client/server interaction qualities and how recovery can be used. As a prerequisite atomic units of work have to be defined. For example, results may be lost if failures occur when results are communicated from ExO_Impl to the communication channel. We use the standard mechanism of ACID transactions [10] as atomic units of work.

3.4 Executable Objects with Backward Recovery

In this subsection we introduce an implementation for the backward/backward recovery combination of Figure 3. If pure backward recovery is used to implement ExOs with call semantics, the so-called *call cycle* (Figure 8) has to be atomic independently of the concrete client/server quality of the call, i.e. the call cycle has to be executed transactionally. This applies to both proxy and implementation objects. It is possible to execute multiple call cycles within the same transaction.

```
BOT();
exo.call(my_method, p);
... /* do something: for example exo.wait()
                     or exo.is_ready() */
exo.get_result();
COMMIT();
```

Fig. 8. Using ExOs with backward recovery

When a client/server interaction is initiated at a ExO_Proxy_BW object within a client transaction, the call is forwarded to a corresponding ExO_Impl_BW object. The resulting call cycle at the ExO_Impl_BW object has also to be executed in a server transaction. To preserve consistency, these transactions have to be coupled by abort dependencies. Otherwise, it would be possible that a client will receive neither a result nor an acknowledgment, which would hurt the result transmission guarantee. As a consequence, client and server transactions can be implemented by the following possibilities:

(1) Client and server transaction form a distributed transaction, i.e. ExO_Proxy_BW communicates with ExO_Impl_BW by normal TRPC using a TP monitor like Encina [8] or Tuxedo [23] (note, at the ECI it is transparent which TP monitor actually has been used). In this case, there is a bidirectional abort dependency between the client and the server: if the client aborts, the server must also abort and vice versa. This recovery type is indicated by BW in the bind() method.

(2) The server transaction is implemented as a subtransaction of the client transaction. This variant may be implemented using nested transactions of the Encina TP monitor [8]. Here, the abort dependency is unidirectional: if the client aborts, the server has to abort, too. However, if the server aborts, the client will receive only a notification and will not be forced to abort. Recovery type BW_call selects this behavior.

3.5 Executable Objects with Forward Recovery

This subsection deals with the implementation of the forward/forward recovery combination (Figure 3). Using forward recovery, neither the client nor the server can completely abort; processing is always restarted. However, infinite retry loops may occur

(Section 2.4). To implement client/server interaction with forward recovery by ExOs, the call cycle has to be broken into two parts (Figure 8), which are both executed within a separate transaction (note, the second part is obsolete for 'no-result' calls):

(1) The first part is made up by the invocation of the call() method of the ExO and by storing the object identifier of the ExO by the caller. The object identifier is necessary for recovery. Besides these steps the caller may do some other actions. This procedure ensures that failures will not result in lost requests. Depending on the communication channel used, the proxy object will have to repeat request messages, eventually using call sequence numbers to avoid multiple executions.

(2) The second part consists of reading the result from the ExO and doing some user defined actions. By doing this within a transaction, loss of results is avoided. Communication errors during result transmission are handled analogously to request transmission.

```
BOT();
exo.call(my_method, p);
/* save Id of exo */
... /* do something: eventually other calls */
COMMIT();

... /* do something: for example exo.wait()
                     or exo.is_ready() */

BOT();
exo.get_result();
... /* do something with the result */
COMMIT();
```

Fig. 9. Using ExOs with forward recovery

If an error occurs during the call cycle the ExO can be recreated after restart using the rebind() method of the ExO runtime component and the object identifier of the ExO. A recreated ExO will restart processing according to the last call() invocation.

If ExOs with forward recovery are used, special effort has to be made at the implementation object. Since an error may also occur during the execution of the user defined server code, an invocation and recovery scheme has to be defined:

(1) When the call() method initiates the execution of a server function, the server function is executed within a transaction.

(2) The server function has to call the set_result() method also within a transaction.

(3) If the server function uses multiple transactions internally, the server function has either to be idempotent or to be able to detect the restart or a special restart function may be provided.

During recovery an ExO_Impl will restart server processing. A server function that uses a single transaction is automatically idempotent. If multiple transactions are used, the server code has to detect the restart and we assume that it will be able to recover to its last state. ExOs cannot provide further support for forward recovery of server code because no assumptions can be made about its structure.

The forward/backward recovery combination (Section 2.4) is not further detailed in this paper: it is realized just by a pair of ExO_Proxy_FW and ExO_Impl_BW classes.

4 Investigation of Conventional Communication Mechanisms

To implement client/server interaction qualities we are going to discuss the error behavior of popular middleware services that are used to implement client/server models. The following mechanisms are investigated:
- Message passing, Remote Procedure Call (RPC), remote operation calls (CORBA)
- Persistent queues
- Distributed transactions
- Advanced communication services (e.g. Isis [4])

If a client/server model is implemented by pure message passing, standard RPC mechanisms [23] or an object request broker without further functionality [18], all kind of failures may arise. A discussion of selected failure situations and protocols can be found in [23]. These services provide no support of higher level failure semantics.

Implementing client/server interaction qualities using persistent queues is easier than using remote operations or messages. Persistent queues guarantee that enqueued data will not be lost due to system breakdowns. A data item can only be removed from a persistent queue by the dequeue operation [10]. For this reason, persistent queues support safe request and result transmission.

Distributed transactions [10] and the Object Transaction Service [19] are a special case of a client/server model implementing backward recovery both at server and client side. All activities of a client run within a transaction. Service requests are performed transactional. Thus, the server processing the request participates in the client's transaction. If any error occurs, the distributed transaction will be aborted and partial work will be undone (backward recovery). Some research prototypes for distributed systems like Camelot [7], Argus [16], Arjuna [6], or Clouds [5] offer object models with atomic actions or facilities similar to distributed transactions.

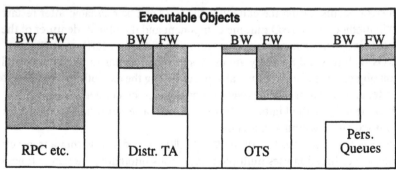

Fig. 10. Implementation of ExO on top of base services

Figure 10 summarizes the discussion and gives an overview on the effort of implementing ExOs with backward/forward recovery using common base services. The grey rectangles indicate effort for the programmer of ExOs. RPC mechanisms will result in high additional programming effort for both kinds of recovery. TRPC (i.e. distributed transactions) and especially OTS reduce effort for implementing ExOs with backward recovery significantly (OTS is more appropriate because of CORBA's dynamic invocation interface which facilitates the implementation of the ECI). Persistent (transactional) queues support the implementation of ExOs with forward recovery very well. However, ExOs with backward recovery cannot be implemented on top of persistent queues.

Advanced communication services like Isis [4] and Electra [17] provide virtual synchrony and support reliable communication and synchronous object replication using dedicated multicast techniques. They are a good basis especially for implementing ExOs with replicated servers. However, server replication is not in the scope of this paper.

5 Conclusion

We have shown how to provide ExOs as a middleware service which supports reliable communication within WfMSs. Besides transparency and scalability, reliability is considered as one of the key requirements for an implementation framework of WfMSs. Currently, ExOs are used to implement the *MOBILE* WfMS. The experience gained from this implementation effort is promising. ExOs prove themselves to alleviate the implementation of large WfMSs in heterogeneous, distributed environments since many system details are made transparent.

In the future we will implement also invocation attributes by ExOs, i.e. we will support the full range of client/server qualities. An interesting approach to solve this problem is to enhance the functionality of the bind() method in the ExO runtime class. Since different implementations of ExOs using different base services can be transparently used, the bind() method can select the ExO implementation which matches best the required invocation attributes.

Acknowledgments

Parts of this research were conducted with support of the special research project SFB 182 "multiprocessor and network configurations" sponsored by the German Research Society.

References

1. Alonso, G.; Kamath, M.; Agrawal, D.; El Abbadi, A.; Günthör, R.; Mohan, C.: Failure Handling in Large Scale Workflow Management Systems. *Technical Report, IBM Almaden Research Center*, 1994
2. Alonso, G.; Mohan, C.; Günthör, R; Agrawal, D.; El Abbadi, A.; Kamath, M.: Exotica/FMQM: A Persistent Message-Based Architecture for Distributed Workflow Management. In: *Proc. IFIP Working Conf. on Information Systems for Decentralized Organizations*, Trondheim, August, 1995
3. Bernstein, P.A.: Middleware: A Model for Distributed System Services. *Communications of the ACM*, 39(2), February, 1996, pp. 86-98
4. Birman, K.P.; van Renesse, R. (Eds.): *Reliable distributed Computing with the Isis Toolkit*. IEEE Computer Society Press, Los Alamitos, 1994

5. Chen, R.C. ; Dasgupta, P.: Linking Consistency with Object/Thread Semantics An Approach to Robust Computation. In: *Proceedings of the 9th International Conference on Distributed Computing Systems* (Newport Beach, California), 1989, pp. 121-128

6. Dixon, G.N. ; Parrington, G.D. ; Shrivastava, S.K. ; Wheater, S.M.: The Treatment of Persistent Objects in Arjuna. In: *Proceedings of Third European Conference on Object-Oriented Programming ECOOP89*, 1989, pp. 169-189

7. Eppinger, J.L. ; Mummert, L.B. ; Spector, A.Z.: *Camelot and Avalon: A Distributed Transaction Facility.* Morgan Kaufmann Publishers, 1991

8. *Encina++ Programmer's Guide and Reference.* Transarc Corporation, 1995

9. *Encina RQS Programmer's Guide and Reference.* Transarc Corporation, 1995

10. Gray, J. ; Reuter, A.: *Transaktion Processing: Concepts and Techniques,* Morgan Kaufmann Publishers, San Mateo, 1993

11. Design and Architecture of High Performance Workflow Management Systems. In: Jablonski, S. (Ed.): *Database Support for Open Workflow Management Systems.* Work Report of the IMMD 29(5), University of Erlangen-Nuremberg, May 1996, pp. 60-79

12. Hollingsworth, D.: *Workflow Management Coalition: The Workflow Reference Model.* Document TC00-1003, Workflow Management Coalition, Dec. 1994

13. *FlowMark - Managing Your Workflow, Version 2.1.* IBM, 1995

14. Jablonski, S. ; Bußler, C.: *Workflow Management - Modeling Concepts, Architecture and Implementation.* International Thomson Computer Press, to appear: September 1996

15. Krishnakumar, N. ; Sheth, A.: Managing Heterogeneous Multi-System Tasks to Support Enterprise-Wide Operations. In: *Distributed and Parallel Databases,* 3, 1995, pp. 155-186

16. Liskov, B. ; Scheifler, R.: Guardians and Actions: Linguistic Support for Robust, Distributed Programs. In: *ACM Transactions on Programming Languages and Systems,* 5(3), 1983, pp. 381-404

17. Maffeis, S.: *Run-Time Support for Object-Oriented Distributed Programming.* PhD Thesis, University of Zürich, 1995

18. Object Management Group: *The Common Object Request Broker: Architecture and Specification.* Revision 2.0, 1995

19. Object Management Group: *CORBAservices: Common Object Services Specification.* OMG Document Number 95-3-31, 1995

20. Schmidt, D.C.: The ADAPTIVE Communication Environment: Object-Oriented Network Programming Components for Developing Client/Server Applications. In: *Proc. of the 12th Sun Users Group Conference,* June 1994

21. Shapiro, M.: Structure and Encapsulation in Distributed Systems: The Proxy Principle. In: *Proc. of the 6th International Conference on Distributed Computing Systems (Cambridge, Massachusetts, May 19-23, 1986).* 1986, pp. 198-204

22. Schuster, H. ; Jablonski, S. ; Kirsche, T. ; Bussler, C.: A Client/Server Architecture for Distributed Workflow Management Systems. In: *Proc. of the 3rd Int. Conf. Parallel and Distributed Information Systems PDIS'94* (Austin, TX, Sept. 28-30), 1994, pp. 253-256

23. Tanenbaum, A.S.: *Modern Operating Systems.* Prentice Hall, Englewood Cliffs, 1992

24. Unix System Laboratories: *Tuxedo ETP System Release 4.2 - Application Development and Administration.* Decision Support Inc., 1992

25. Wodtke, D. ; Weissenfels, J. ; Weikum, G. ; Kotz Dittrich, A.: The Mentor Project: Steps Towards Enterprise-Wide Workflow Management. In: *Proc. 12th International Conference on Data Engineering,* New Orleans, February 1996

Metadata Modelling for Healthcare Applications in a Federated Database System[*]

M. Roantree[1], P. Hickey[1], A. Crilly[1], J. Cardiff[2], J. Murphy[1]

[1] School of Computer Applications, Dublin City University, Dublin, Ireland.
{mark.roantree@compapp.dcu.ie}
[2] Regional Technical College, Tallaght, Dublin, Ireland.

Abstract. *One of the problems facing federated database management systems is how to handle change among entities in the federation. Change can occur when a new site is added to the federation, a new set of security privileges is introduced, or one of the schemas has been modified. One powerful mechanism for constructing an adaptive federated architecture is metadata. Mowbray [MZ95] describes metadata as self-descriptive definition of services and information. In this article we present our ideas for modelling federation metadata in the LIOM project.*

1 Introduction

A federated database system (FDBS) is a collection of autonomous database systems which cooperate to provide a combined view of individual data stores. We have based our work on the 5-level schema architecture described in [SL90] and will use the terminology adopted in [HM85] and [SL90] when describing the architecture. One of the major issues facing designers of federated database management systems is how to handle change. By change, we mean the addition and removal of participating sites, the generation of new export and federated schemas, and schema modifications to any of the schema layers in the federated architecture. In this paper, we describe our research on modelling federation metadata and our plans to implement this research in a healthcare environment. The paper is structured as follows: the remainder of this section provides an introduction to the LIOM project and federated databases in general; §2 describes the system architecture and our metadata model; §3 provides a description of the target healthcare environment and issues concerned with participation in a LIOM federation; and finally §4 offers some conclusions.

1.1 The LIOM Project

The goal of the LIOM project [Mur95] is to provide interoperability services to a federation of loosely-coupled autonomous and heterogeneous database systems. The software method of the LIOM project is the Minerva method, which is the

---

[*] Supported by Forbairt Strategic Research Programme ST/94/720

focus of the Object Model Sub-group in LIOM. Early results on the Minerva method and model can be found in [Mur96].

Interoperability is the means of connecting software systems in a manner which facilitates transparent access to enterprise data resources which may be distributed among applications across multiple and heterogeneous software and hardware platforms. Our target environment for the implementation of a prototype is the HIV section of the Genito Urinary Medicine (GUM) clinic at St. James' Hospital in Dublin. A full description of each participating application is provided in §3. A healthcare computing environment consists of a heterogeneous collection of usually independent information systems. They often range from centralised Hospital Information Systems and Laboratory Information Systems, to departmentally-based systems such as Pharmacy, Accident and Emergency, Intensive Care Unit and Radiology systems. Patient data can also exist on GP packages and community based systems. In many cases, information such as patient demographics are replicated across these systems. In most cases, the facility to pass information among these systems does not exist. An architecture such as that offered by federated database systems offers one possible solution for information interchange between these systems.

Our prototype uses Orbix [Ion95], an implementration of the OMG's Common Object Request Broker Architecture (CORBA) [OMG95] to provide a framework for interoperability betwen databases. Each local database is encapsulated by a standard IDL interface [OHE96] [MZ95] to enable it to participate in a LIOM federation. In §3 we discuss a number of approaches to interoperating with different healthcare data models.

1.2   Federated Databases

A federated database management system (FDBMS) allows local databases (LDB) to interoperate with other LDBs even though they may use a different data model. This is achieved by converting each LDB data model into a canonical data model (CDM) representation. We have chosen an object-oriented data model as our CDM as we concur with the conclusions reached in [SCG91] which describe the expressive qualities required of a CDM. The conversion process involves the creation of a new schema called the *component schema* [SL90] which is modelled using the CDM and contains mappings to the local schema. A separate conversion process for each type of data model is required which involves many issues discussed elsewhere [PBE95], [LM91], [FHM91]. Once the component schema has been generated, various *export schemas* are derived on top of each component schema in the same way as we derive views on traditional data models. This helps to provide a layer of security for the architecture. *Federated schemas* are then constructed using export schemas.

2   System Architecture and Metadata Models

Although our CDM is not fully specified, we have made the decision to define some metadata constructs required for a federated database system and to explore possible architectures for a data dictionary. It is possible that some modifications will be required after the specification of the CDM. We then describe our usage of metadata and how it is managed in the object dictionary. Our architecture contains two types of metadata: CORBA metadata and LIOM metadata. CORBA metadata describes the interfaces offered by the components of the LIOM federated architecture. LIOM metadata describes the information sources in the architecture.

2.1 System Architecture

We will compare the 5-level schema architecture [SL90] with the LIOM architecture to demonstrate how we manage LIOM schemas[3]. In *figure 4(a)* the local schemas [SL90] are at the bottom of the layer. Each of the four datastores will have their own local schema and possibly different data models. For a local database to participate in the federation, it is necessary to construct a component schema which is a direct representation of some portion or all of the local schema in CDM format. In the LIOM architecture the component schema is modelled as a CORBA object. There is one CORBA object[4] for each component schema. The *ComponentSchema* class (a subclass of the *LIOMSchema* class in §2.2) is used for this purpose. The function of this object is twofold: to interoperate with local data models, and to supply a standard interface to the LIOM services. Thus, the component schema is a CORBA object[5] although schema attributes are not modelled as IDL attributes. In §2.2 we describe a template for modelling LIOM schemas. Component schemas do not contain data but mappings to attributes in local schemas. They contain a description and location of data i.e. metadata.

To complete the integration process, it is necessary to define a layer of export schemas on top of the component schema. One of the services provided by the middleware layer is a facility for creating an export schema. Our model treats export schemas in a similar manner to component schemas. They contain metadata only: a series of mappings to attributes in component schemas, and are modelled as CORBA objects. A further service provided by the LIOM framework is a facility for generating federated schemas. Since federated schemas are simply mappings to attributes in export schemas [PBE95] [SL90] and contain only metadata, they can be modelled in the same manner as component and export schemas. In essence, all three schemas above the local schema contain only metadata and are modelled as CORBA objects. By representing schemas as CORBA objects, we use the inherent capabilities of CORBA to distribute, provide names for, and provide access to LIOM schemas.

---

[3] By LIOM schemas we mean schemas created for usage by the federation. These include component schemas, export schemas and federated schemas.
[4] The LIS appears to have 2 CORBA objects in *figure 4(b)*. This is explained in §3.
[5] Later we will see that all CDM schemas are CORBA objects.

a) Schema Inheritance

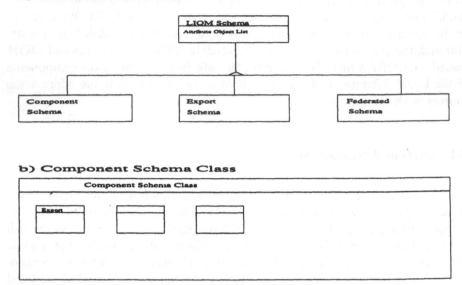

b) Component Schema Class

Fig. 1. *Metadata Objects*

2.2 Modelling Metadata

We concentrate our discussion on LIOM metadata as CORBA metadata has been discussed extensively elsewhere [OHE96] [MZ95]. The LIOM object dictionary contains federation metadata. This may cover a broad range of information from usernames, user privileges, a collection of standard terms for a healthcare[6] environment or location information for each participating database. However, we limit our discussion to the fundamental metadata objects, which are the LIOM schemas. Our research has been focused on modelling component, export and federated schemas. *Figure 1(a)* demonstrates how each schema inherits from the *LIOMSchema* class. In *figure 1(b)* we can see how the component schema class is an aggregate class containing *n* other classes [Col94]. One of these is the export schema class. (This may not represent the final implementation. For example, *ComponentSchema* objects may be referenced through *ExportSchema* objects or the relationships between objects may be stored in the object dictionary.)

A LIOM schema contains only metadata. Since LIOM schemas are dynamic,

---

[6] In the LIOM project these would be healthcare terms. However, another project may contain banking, flight control, or engineering terminology depending on the environment.

the physical data attributes cannot be directly expressed in the interface definition. Instead a schema contains a collection of attributes[7] which can change
during the lifetime of the federation. A standard interface exists for manipulation
of the attribute collection.

```
interface LiomSchema
{
    string SchemaName;
    attribute sequence<SchemaAttribute> AttributeList;

    SchemaAttribute GetAttribute(in short index);
}
```

```
interface SchemaAttribute                  interface AttributeMap
{                                          {
    string identifer;                          TYPE Type;
    int MapCount;                              string SchemaId;
    attribute sequence<AttributeMap> MapList;  string AttributeId;

    AttributeMap GetAttribute(in short);       GetAttribute();
                                           }
}
```

The attribute list (or schema) can be modified without having to reconstruct
the IDL interface of the *LiomSchema* class. Since a *SchemaAttribute* object is a
mapping which may or may not contain conversion information, it must have the
expressive capabilites to represent this. A section of the *SchemaAttribute* class
is also illustrated to demonstrate the structure and behaviour of an attribute
in a LIOM schema. It contains an identifier, and type and location information
of the target attribute. The attribute itself is actually modelled as a method
(*GetAttribute()*)rather than a value. This allows us to perform manipulations on
the mapped data before returning it to the next layer in the architecture. For
example, the conceptual schema of the participating database (local schema)
contains the raw data, which may represent an entity called *salary* in dollars.
The component schema which maps to this data may return it to the export
schema layer in pounds or Dmarks. Some export schemas may return this value
to the federated schema rounded to the nearest whole number. This conversion
information can be encapsulated in the *SchemaAttribute* class.

Our metadata model contains three schema classes: the *FederatedSchema*
class, the *ExportSchema* class and the *ComponentSchema* class. The *ComponentSchema* class has an *'is referenced by'* relationship with the *FederatedSchema*
class through instances of one of its attributes (the *ExportSchema* class).

Federated Schemas. A federated schema in the LIOM framework contains an
identifier attribute and a collection of mappings. Our model requires a direct

---

[7] A schema attribute can be an object attribute or method

mapping from a federated schema attribute to a single attribute in n export schemas, with type and possibly conversion information for each of them. Each export schema attribute must map to a component schema attribute which in turn maps to the raw data in the local schema. In *figure 2* we see that an attribute in the federated schema called *city* is mapped to an attribute called *city* in export schema E_1, which has a subsequent mapping to *city* in a component schema C_1. The *city* attribute in C_1 maps to the raw data in DB_1, identifed by *address3*. The federated attribute *city* also maps to attributes in export schemas E_3, E_5 and E_6.

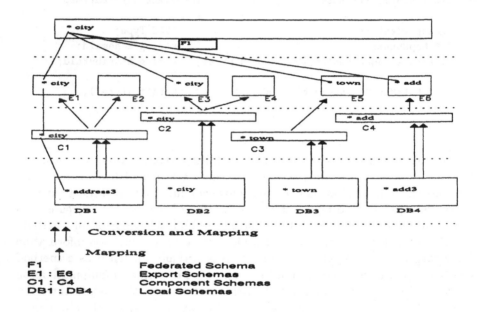

Fig. 2. *Federation Mappings*

Thus, the structure of a *SchemaAttribute* object in a federated schema is comprised of an identifier and several attribute objects containing mapping and type information.

- Attribute identifier in this Federation
- Attribute Identifier in Export Schema n
- Type and semantic information for attribute n[8]

---

[8] A 1-to-many mapping between attributes may exist.

In *figure 2* the attribute *city* in the federated schema is mapped to a number of attributes with the same semantic information in four separate export schemas. Our metadata model captures this information through each of the *SchemaAttribute* objects in the federation. A *SchemaAttribute* object contains any number of links to export *SchemaAttribute* objects. The *type* and *conversion* information can differ across export schemas. For example, a patient's height could be required as *cm* at the federated schema level and could be represented as *cm* and *inches* in various export schemas.

Export Schemas. An export schema contains an identifier attribute and a collection of mappings. Unlike the mappings in a federated schema, these attributes map to a single attribute in a single component schema. Otherwise, their behaviour is modelled in identical fashion. An export schema attribute contains:

- Attribute identifier in this Export Schema
- Attribute Identifier in Component Schema
- Semantic and Type information

One of the main reasons for deriving export schemas is to restrict access to the component schema. Thus, security details can be encapsulated in the *ExportSchema* class or the *SchemaAttribute* class. For example, we may restrict access to an entire *ExportSchema* object or to a selection of *SchemaAttribute* objects inside the schema.

Component Schemas. The generation of component schemas involves data model conversion. This process differs for each local data model and involves issues such as legacy system interoperability [Ber96], semantic and structural heterogeneity of data types [SL90] and issues concerned with proprietary software applications[HRCM96]. As a result the process for integrating applications into the federation requires manual interaction. The structure of the *ComponentSchema* class is identical to that of the *ExportSchema* class:

- Attribute identifier in this Component Schema
- Attribute Identifier in Local Schema
- Semantic and Type information

Local Schemas. Local Schemas are the conceptual schemas of databases participating in the federation. Local database information is not represented in our metadata model as the component schema is the entry point for participating databases.

2.3 Metadata Management

In this section we describe our design of the metadata dictionary. Where CORBA is used, the CORBA Information Repository stores CORBA metadata and where

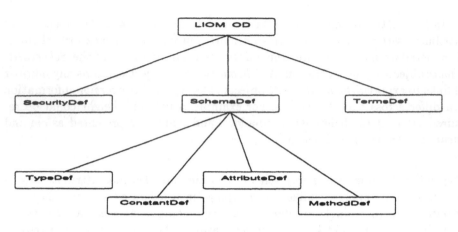

Fig. 3. *LIOM OD Hierarchy*

instances of LIOM objects are used, the LIOM Object Dictionary is used to store metadata objects.

At the implementation stage, we model federated, export and component schemas as CORBA objects and thus require an entry for each of them in the Interface Repository (IR), which is a database of IDL interfaces for LIOM schemas. This structure, explained in detail in [OMG95] demonstrates how metadata is structured in the CORBA architecture. The benefit of using the CORBA IR is that it supports runtime discovery and invocation of its services.

The LIOM Object Dictionary (LiomOD) is used to store federation metadata specified by the LIOM framework. We have based our design on the CORBA IR (*figure 3*). The OD manages LIOM objects which reside in the federation. It permits runtime discovery of LIOM federation information such as schema descriptions although it has a more rigid structure when compared with the CORBA IR. This is due to the fact that the LIOM OD is designed specifically for federated databases whereas the CORBA IR is designed for more generic distributed applications. *Figure 3* demonstrates the LIOM OD hierarchy which is closely related to the CORBA IR hierarchy [OHE96] (pp. 101-103). The main difference is that we have specific modules rather than a generic set of modules. We have specified only the schema definition so far, but other definitions could include user definitions and terminology definitions. We are currently specifying a LIOM Dictionary Service for managing the metadata stored in the LIOM OD.

3 A Description of the Healthcare Environment

In this section we deal with the integration stage where local schemas are converted to component schemas. After a brief description of the healthcare application, we discuss how the integration process is accomplished for each system. Some common issues involved in interoperability are mentioned together with issues specific to each application and the solutions we have adopted in each case to overcome some of these issues.

a) Federation Architecture

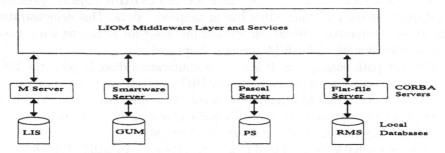

b) Interoperability Path for LIS

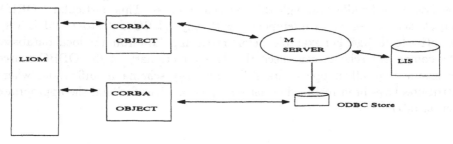

Fig. 4. *System Architecture*

The target environment for our federated architecture and metadata model is the Genito Urinary Medicine (GUM) clinic at St. James' Hospital in Dublin. There are four autonomous systems which are used to store and retrieve patient data. These four systems will be integrated to form a federated database environment based on the research we have carried out in the LIOM project. In earlier work [Roa96] they are described in more detail together with details of how CORBA objects are used to interoperate with the individual applications.

3.1 Laboratory Information System

The Laboratory Information System (LIS) is MUMPS legacy system with a hierarchical data model. It runs on a DEC ALPHA machine and can be accessed using the M [Shu96] [MTA94] programming language. There are six different databases in the LIS which model the same type of data: patient demographics and laboratory results. They each use an attribute called Medical Record Number (MRN) as a primary key.

Integration Issues. To retrieve live data from the LIS, an M-language interface is used to communicate with the LIS. There are two interoperability paths for the LIS which can be seen in *figure 4(b)*. Note that only one component schema exists for each local schema. In *4(b)* there are two CORBA objects operating at different speeds, retrieving either live or snapshot[9] data. This demonstrates that we have employed different background processes for retrieving data. User profiles determine which CORBA object is employed.

The first path employs an M server communicating directly with the LIS. The M server is passed a query by the CORBA object, which in turn passes a modified query to the LIS. Having retrieved the results from the LIS, the M server passes the output back to the CORBA object. Due to the performance constraints, LIS queries retrieve most recent data only.

A second CORBA object is used to interoperate with an ODBC [SCS95] data store. Data is retrieved from the LIS through an M server on a periodic basis and stored in an ODBC compatible database. All data processing functionality and persistence is handled through this external process. This particular CORBA object can be reused to interoperate with any ODBC datastore and is very adaptive to change. For example, before retrieving data from the local database, the component schema can check the data directionary of the ODBC source to ensure that all mappings are still valid. Any schema modifications where attributes have been modified or deleted must be identified and the appropriate action taken.[10]

3.2 Genito Urinary Medicine System

The Genito-Urinary Management (GUM) system is a proprietary application developed in a language called Smartware using a relational data model. The MRN attribute is again used as primary key.

Integration Issues. A CORBA object (see SmartWare server in *figure 4(a)*) is used to provide interoperability with the native GUM data files. This is constructed with the standard IDL interface for the *ComponentSchema* class but the functionality to interface between the SmartWare data files and LIOM is

---

[9] A snapshot is refreshed every 15 minutes.
[10] For example, return NULL where an attribute no longer exists.

specific to this application. This is contrary to the adaptive nature of the LIOM model but is employed where necessary. It is used where schema changes to the local application are unlikely to occur. For this application, dynamic querying is only achieved by building a static link to raw data in the SmartWare data files.

3.3 Pharmacy System

The Pharmacy System (PS) is a Pascal application with a proprietary data model. The primary key used is a drug dispensing code. This will provide issues for correlating query results with results from other local databases. The type of information stored in the PS is a description of the drug which was dispensed, date it was dispensed, cost and quantity of drugs, and and a script number, which is the primary key. The central object in this system is not a patient object, but a drug prescription object.

Integration Issues. The CORBA object contains functionality to read the PASCAL data files through a process which exists to query the data dictionary of the native pharmacy database. This provides access to the local schema attributes to populate the *SchemaAttribute* objects inside the *ComponentSchema* object. We assume ODBC style functionality for all datastores as it allows us to query a data dictionary for the purpose of constructing a component schema.[11] Where the ODBC style of functionality does not exist, we must provide it by building an interface between the native data files and the *ComponentSchema* class.

In the following section we describe how we construct this functionality for a flat-file format. We believe that the process of constructing component schemas will require human interaction but our goal is to automate some of this process where possible. By reading the data dictionary of the participating application, LIOM can generate a first 'pass' of the component schema.

3.4 Radiology Management System

The Radiology Management System (RMS) was developed in COBOL on an ICL UNIX box. Data is not required on a 'live' basis. Instead a daily snapshot is requested for data retrieval. Data is exported to a flat-file format which is used by the federation for querying purposes.

Integration Issues. The *ComponentSchema* object is used to query a flat-file data model. A template file exists which acts as a data dictionary for flat-file formats. The template file describes the data in the flat-file. When the format of the flat-file changes, the template file must be changed accordingly. Although

---

[11] This functionality which exists in the *ComponentSchema* class was mentioned earlier in §3.1.

the template file is itself a flat-file, it has been designed to handle object-oriented data. It permits inheritance, user-defined data types and encapsulation.

An entry in the template file contains a class name, the number of attributes the class contains, and a description of each attribute. The template handles inheritance by including the class name of the superclass beside the class name. If the entity *Patient* was modelled as an object which inherited from another object *Person* then the entry in the template file reflects this inheritance:

[Patient[Person]], 5, PatientNumber, TXT, 8, LastName, TXT, 30, FirstNames, TXT, 30, Address, TXT, 80, DOB, DATE:

We can also support complex types by using the descriptor CPLX. If *PatientNumber* were of the type CPLX rather than TXT, then a description of the *PatientNumber* complex type must also appear in the template file. This provides us with a mechanism for encapsulating information. We accept that a trained user is required to modify the template file but argue that the task of schema modification is equally complex, and the same user should perform both tasks.

4   Conclusion

One of the goals of the LIOM project is to construct a federated system architecture that is adaptive to change. To specify this architecture it is necessary for it to contain as many layers of metadata as possible. We have concentrated on modelling three types of metadata for federated database management systems: component schema metadata, export schema metadata and federated schema metadata. We have described how we model these metadata objects and the relationships between them. We accept that without a full specification of the canonical data model this process is not complete. However, we argue that this work will provide valuable input into the specification of the CDM.

We are now focused on expanding our metadata objects to handle constructs such as object relationships and primary keys in LIOM schemas. We are also concentrating on the design and implementation of a LIOM Dictionary Service to manage metadata in a persistent fashion. The Dictionary Service can also provide information on keys that can be used to combine the results of sub-queries against component schemas. For example, the pharmacy system is concerned with prescriptions and the LIS deals with patient laboratory tests. What common attribute(s) can a LIOM service use to join the results of sub-queries? These issues will become clearer as we finalise our specification for an object dictionary service.

Acknowledgements

The authors wish to acknowledge the comments of the anonymous referees whose comments helped with the final draft of this paper.

83

References

[Ber96] P. Bernstein. Middleware: A Model for Distributed System Services. *Communications of the ACM*, Vol. 39, No. 2, Feb 1996.

[Col94] D. Coleman et al. *Object-Oriented Development: The Fusion Method.* Prentice Hall, 1994.

[FHM91] D. Fang, J. Hammer and D. McLeod. The Identification and Resolution of Semantic Heterogeneity in Multidatabase Systems. *1st International Workshop on Interoperability in Multidatabase Systems*, IEEE Press, 1991.

[HRCM96] P. Hickey, M. Roantree, A. Crilly, J. Murphy. Architectural Issues for Integrating Legacy Systems using CORBA2 in the LIOM Project. To be published in *1996 International Conference on Object Oriented Information Systems*, Springer, 1996.

[HM85] D. Heimbigner and D. McLeod. A Federated Architecture for Information Management. *ACM Transactions on Office Information Systems*, Vol. 3, No. 3, 1985.

[Ion95] IONA Technologies Ltd. *Orbix 2 Programming Guide.* Iona Technologies, 1995.

[LM91] Q. Li and D. McLeod. An Object-Oriented Approach to Federated Databases. *1st International Conference on Interoperability in Multidatabase Systems*, IEEE Press, 1991.

[MTA94] M Technology Association. *M: The Open Production System* (White Paper), 1994.

[Mur95] J. Murphy et al. LIOM Language Definition. *LIOM Report no. LIOM-DCU-95-01*, Dublin City University, 1995.

[Mur96] J. Murphy at al. Minerva: The Method and Model of the JUPITER/LIOM Interoperator. *LIOM Report No. LIOM-DCU-96-04*, Dublin City University, 1996.

[MZ95] T. Mowbray and R. Zahavi. *The Essential CORBA: System Integration Using Distributed Objects.* Wiley, 1996.

[OHE96] R. Orfali, D. Harkey and J. Edwards. *The Essential Distributed Objects Survival Guide.* Wiley, 1996.

[OMG95] The Object Management Group. *The Common Object Request Broker Architecture: Architecture and Specification*, Object Management Group, Framington, 1995.

[PBE95] E. Pitoura, O. Bukhres and A. Elmagarmid. Object Orientation in Multidatabase Systems. *ACM Computing Surveys*, Vol. 27, No. 2, June 1995.

[Roa96] M. Roantree. Interoperability Issues for Healthcare Data Models. *LIOM Report No. LIOM-DCU-96-03*, Dublin City University, 1996.

[SCG91] F. Saltor, M. Castellanos and M. Garcia-Solaco. Suitability of Data Models as Canonical Models for Federated Databases. *SIGMOD Record* vol. 20, no. 4, 1991.

[SCS95] R. Signore, J. Creamer and M. Stegman. *The ODBC Solution.* McGraw-Hill, 1995.

[Shu96] D. Shusman. Programming with M. *Database Development,* Dr. Dobbs Sourcebook, Jan/Feb 1996.

[SL90] A. Sheth and J. Larson. Federated Database Systems for Managing Distributed, Heterogeneous, and Autonomous Databases. *ACM Computing Surveys*, vol. 22, no. 3, September 1990.

ReGTime — Rent Gigaflops someTimes

Bernd Dreier[1], Annja Huber[1], Holger Karl[2], Theo Ungerer[2], Markus Zahn[1]

[1] University of Augsburg, Institute of Informatics, D-86135 Augsburg, Germany
[2] University of Karlsruhe, Institute of Computer Design and Fault Tolerance,
D-76128 Karlsruhe, Germany

Abstract. ReGTime[3] (*Rent Gigaflops some Times*) is a software package that helps to rent unused computing power. Sites offer unused resources on a "computing power market". Customers specify their requirements using World Wide Web. ReGTime creates an offer based on available capacities. If the offer is accepted, ReGTime helps to establish a contract, organizes the access, observes the compliance with the contract, and collects data for invoicing. This way e.g. smaller companies may purchase additional computing power without investing in hardware.

1 Introduction

Today computer networking continues to grow in both size and importance. As a result of increasing bandwidth and capacity of computer networks, information can be transferred in reasonable time even across wide area networks. Using high–speed networks, heterogeneous and distributed computer systems offer the possibility to combine a team of computers over large distances to *one virtual machine*. By "distributed computing", tasks can be solved which are too complex for a single computer.

Selling computing power is already widely used in the area of mainframes and today's parallel computers. There are only a few providers well–known to their customers. The access is done via ftp/telnet or similar means. The (parallel) program is transferred to the remote computer. It is executed on the provider's machines and after termination all results are sent back to the customer. No distributed computing occurs.

Recently, research in this area are research aims at "metacomputing" [1] and "virtual computing centers" [2], i.e. the cooperative use of several parallel computers by collaborating computer centers. One example is the "Virtuelle Rechenzentrum Südwest" [3], another one the connection of an Intel Paragon XP/S10 of KFA Jülich and an IBM SP2 owned by the GMD using an ATM–connection [4]. A parallel program can be distributed over both parallel machines, however, the remote connection is much slower than internal connections. Here, too, only a few participants exist which are well known to each other.

Workstation clusters — sometimes even several collaborating clusters — are also used as a virtual machine. Spreading work over several workstation clusters

---

[3] ReGTime is available at http://www.informatik.uni-augsburg.de/info1/regtime/

requires accounts on each computer of every cluster. Several software packages (e.g. MPI [5], PVM [6] and Linda [7]) or distributed systems (e.g. DCE [8] and CORBA [9]) allow networked computers to appear as a single concurrent computational resource. Up to now, this way of using networked computer systems is mostly found at universities and research institutions. However, both technical and theoretical know–how for parallel and distributed computing will be available in middle and small sized companies soon.

It is the idea of ReGTime that managers of networked computers offer their free capacity on a "computing power market", and customers are able to rent resources on a short–term basis. ReGTime negotiates the offers between providers and customers. Small and middle–sized organizations are able to use high computing capacities temporarily without high investments for powerful computer systems. The managers themselves increase the profitability of their machines through this additional income.

ReGTime primarily aims at small and middle–sized companies as customers. As providers, institutions with one or several workstation–clusters are our main focus. Another target group are corporations with computers linked via corporate networks — thereby improving the utilization of their own resources.

Considering the fast progress of networking via internet and intranet, the prerequisites to offer and sell unused computing power on a market are fulfilled. This lays the foundations of the envisioned "computing power market". In such a market, many potential participants (providers and customers of computing power) exist. There is substantial demand for brokering, since the potential users of distributed systems still miss a system that provides easy access to rentable computing power. These are our reasons for creating ReGTime, a software package to offer, broker and rent computing power.

The idea of an internet–based brokering service showed up in several contexts recently: FAST [10] is a project intended to manage the procurement of electronic parts. The BargainFinder [11] searches at several internet–CD–shops for cheap CDs. The MeDoc–project [12] deals with searching for (mostly computer science related) publications in the internet. The "Information Broker" of MeDoc takes requests for some kind of information and answers with references where the information can be found. Except for ReGTime, none of today's brokering services is concerned with renting computing power.

2 Functionality of ReGTime

2.1 The Basic Building Blocks

There are two main groups in ReGTime: providers and customers. A customer needs high computing power and is looking for providers that allow the rental of their underutilized computers. Providers will grant the necessary rights based upon a contract.

A provider offers his computers (grouped into one or several clusters) for rental. A computer is characterized by its hard- and software features and by the times at which the machine is available for rental. The provider specifies the computing nodes and the accounts available to the customers. To easily administer these informations, ReGTime provides an easy–to–use configuration tool to set parameters like offered nodes, prices, and rental times.

To simplify the negotiations between customer and (several) providers, a *broker* can be used (in resemblance to existing market mechanisms). It mediates requests of customers and contracts between customer and one or several providers. The broker itself does not contract with either party. After publishing his offer (e.g. via World Wide Web) or registering with some brokers, a provider is part of the "computing power market". This registration can be done automatically, no further human interaction is necessary.

ReGTime is independent of any distributed programming environment (e.g. PVM or MPI) a customer wants to use. Providers specify their available software packages, customers request any particular system explicitly. ReGTime could even broker non–distributed software like hardware synthesis tools or numerical packages.

2.2 A Session with ReGTime

To give an impression of the dynamic appearance of ReGTime, we present a short guided tour of a session with ReGTime from request to invoice (see Fig. 1).

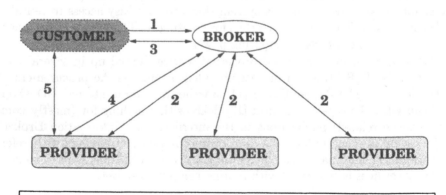

1 Customer initiates request	4 Broker establishes the contract
2 Broker generates an offer	5 Customer uses the rented cluster,
3 Broker makes offers and customer accepts	provider sends invoice directly

Fig. 1. Flow chart of ReGTime

A customer requests computational power by entering parameters like number and types of acceptable computers, operating system and software prerequisites, and the contract's time frame in a WWW form (see Fig. 2). The time

frame can be specified flexibly by an earliest and latest starting point and a
duration. Additionally, price limits can be set for fixed costs, time–dependent
costs, cpu–, memory–, and I/O–related costs individually.

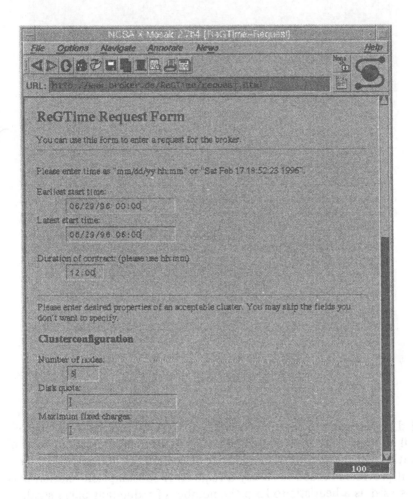

Fig. 2. ReGTime's request WWW interface

Upon receipt of a customer's request, the broker queries all it's registered
providers. If a provider is able to satisfy the request even if only partially, the
provider answers the request with an exact description of all available computers,
the available times and costs. The broker assembles the replies of the providers
to one or several offers for the customer (see Fig. 3). Usually, the customer
receives several offers one of which he may choose. Some of these offers may
combine several providers. Combined offers are necessary if a request cannot be

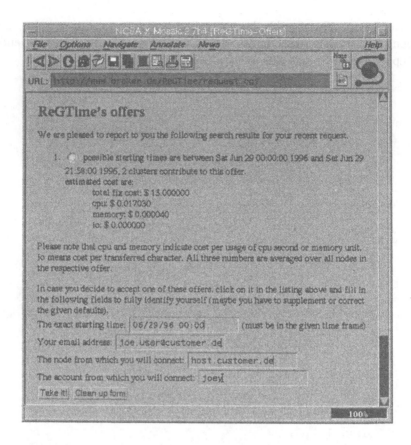

Fig. 3. A sample offer of a contract

satisfied by a single provider. Wether the customer accepts a combined offer or not will strongly depend on the granularity i.e. the communication needs of the application which is to be distributed. The broker tries to minimize the number of different providers needed to satisfy a request. A subsumption relation between offers is used as a heuristic to keep the number of redundant offers small.

The customer can choose from the offers which are presented in a WWW form. After accepting a specific offer the customer has to provide his email address, account name, and the internet name of the computer from which he will use the rented systems. The final steps to make a contract with the providers are initiated by the broker. The participating providers receive the contract. A provider may require the customer to sign the contract (see Sect. 2.3 for a discussion of the security issues involved). Finally, each provider sends a confirmation to the broker, which generates a message for the customer, containing the machine and account names the customer rented.

At the starting time — set in the contract — access to the rented systems is provided by regular accounts. Access authorization is granted to the customer by means of the *.rhosts*-mechanism. This allows e.g. PVM or MPI users to add the rented hosts to their parallel vitual machine for further distributed processing. Shortly before termination of the contract the customer is advised to finish working soon and to transfer back results. All customer processes on the rented machines are notified by sending them a SIGPWR. Upon termination of a contract, all these processes of a customer are terminated (SIGTERM), and after a short grace period, all potentially remaining processes on the rented machines are killed (SIGKILL), the account is locked and the home directory is deleted.

During a contract, all customer activities are logged. These accounting informations are used to compute the invoice. CPU–times, average memory consumptions and I/O–activities of the customers' processes may be charged for. The prices for each category are part of the contract. Additionally, fixed costs for a contract and costs based solely upon the duration of a contract are possible.

The invoice is still a bill sent by email. This will change as soon as electronic cash is widely available.

2.3   Security issues

Considering the bad security properties of today's UNIX–systems granting access to an unknown customer is risky. At least, a provider should be certain about the identity of his customers. ReGTime approaches this problem by using authentification procedures based upon the public–key mechanism PGP [13].

In the procedure detailed in Sect. 2.2, authentification of the customer is solely based upon node and account names. This information can be manipulated easily and is therefore not acceptable for authentification.

Both provider and customer may demand that contracts must be signed. In this case, a provider sends the complete contract back to a tool executed on the customer host. It passes the contract to PGP for signature and sends the signed contract back to the provider. The provider asks PGP to check the signature against a copy of the customer's public key. If PGP validates this signature, and both the original version of the contract and the signed one are identical, the provider considers the customer to be correctly authenticated and the contract is accepted.

Due to the PGP method it is essential under which prerequisites a provider is willing to add someone's public key to his key ring. If a provider accepts a key received in an email message, the whole authentification is not securer than the email system itself, which is not very secure. The highest security level would be achieved, if keys are only accepted after a personal introduction with a valid identity card. A provider can choose any level of security somewhere along these lines. This additional effort is necessary only once to guarantee the identity of public keys.

The question of how to make legally binding contracts over the internet still remains open.

3 Implementation

ReGTime implements the tasks listed above by a set of three Unix dæmons (see Fig. 4): *brokerd* acts as the broker i.e. it communicates with the customer by World Wide Web. The *providerd* is working as a provider's manager, it negotiates on behalf of a provider and establishes contracts. To observe compliance with the contract, a third dæmon acts on the provider's side, running on every rentable machine: *guardiand* mainly controls access, terminates processes at the end of a contract and computes invoices. For portability reasons most of the guardian's functionalities are implemented as Perl scripts (cp. [14]).

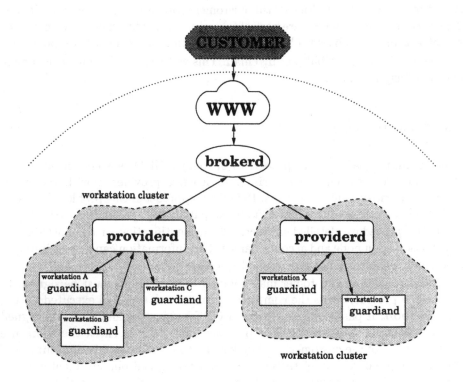

Fig. 4. Implementation of ReGTime

ReGTime's customer interface is designed as a WWW form. Customers' input is forwarded (via sockets) to the associated broker (*brokerd*) by CGI scripts. Thus, the broker may run on a different host as the http–dæmon does. Every request is handled by a separate process forked by the broker. To provide a secure signature, a program called *sign–it* establishes an interface between ReGTime and PGP and the customer's site.

Accounting information is gathered by the operating system of each rented machine. Today, almost all wide–spread UNIX-systems offer a *pacct*-like accounting system. Using this system, the kernel generates information for every terminating process, containing its run–time and resource consumption (like cpu time, memory and I/O). As already mentioned, access to rented workstations is based on regular accounts, therefore the required informations about the customer's resource consumption can be derived from the standard accounting system. At the end of a contract, accounting information is gathered from the enlisted hosts and is used by a distinguished *guardiand* to assemble the invoice. The invoice is sent to the customer via email.

4 Installation

Prerequisites for a successful installation are:

- UNIX operating system
- ANSI–C compiler (e.g. gcc)
- Perl (Version 4.036)
- *pacct*–accounting system (optional)
- PGP (Version 2.6.3 or higher) for electronic signatures (optional)
- Tcl/Tk (Version 7.3/3.6 or higher) to use graphical configuration tools (optional)

At first the file *config.data* in the *sources* directory has to be modified. *config.data* includes a number of variables that have to be set according to the local system configuration. Then, *make config*, *make* and *make install* builds the complete system, i.e. the *providerd*, *guardiand* and *brokerd*. The accounts used for renting must be set up separately. The *brokerd* can also be installed independently from the provider's software. Finally, the graphical configuration tools of ReGTime allow the provider to specify the node and cluster information (like prices and availability) in a user–friendly manner.

If a customer doesn't want to use signatures, no special software for ReGTime is needed by a customer. Otherwise, a customer only needs an ANSI–C compiler and PGP and has to install *sign–it*.

5 Results and Experiences

ReGTime was tested on SUN SparcStations running Solaris 2.4 and on IBM RS/6000 workstations with operating system AIX 4.1. The demonstration system consisted of two independent workstation clusters at the universities of Augsburg (up to 20 IBM workstations) and Karlsruhe (four SparcStation5). ReGTime turned out to be easy to use, access to computing power is provided fast and comfortably. We have successfully tried several existing distributed applications (based upon PVM) in conjunction with ReGTime.

A first prototype was presented at CeBIT'96 in Hannover. The described clusters were accessed from the exhibition, an additional IBM RS/6000 on the fair ground acted as a third cluster. The audience widely accepted ReGTime and its idea of a "computing power market", although doubts concerning provider's security risks were raised. Therefore, ReGTime puts a strong emphasis on authentification of customers. If a provider is able to restrict the range of customers to trustworthy persons (like members of the same corporate network, or the same company or university), the security problems are cut down. From the customer's point of view, its software is unlikely to be abused as it is (as a rule) only a small part of a distributed application. With distributed systems like DCE, data transfer between different components of a distributed application can also be encrypted.

Further experiments were done to test the potential loss of communication speed when parallel programs — distributed over several, remotely coupled workstation clusters — are executed. The latencies incurred by small messages between two workstations clusters, one in Karlsruhe and one in Augsburg, were surprisingly small, sometimes even within one order of magnitude to the latencies in a local ethernet–based cluster. A master–worker–paradigm turned out to be nearly as efficient when running on two remote clusters as when running only locally.

6 Conclusions and Future Work

ReGTime is a software package for an envisioned "computing power market". It consists of three main parts. Firstly, ReGTime helps customers to search for providers who allow rental of their workstation clusters. Secondly, it manages the rental of disposable machines on provider's side and establishes the contract with the customer. Thirdly, it is responsible for granting access to rented systems and compliance with established contracts. Furthermore, it supports secure authentification between business partners by PGP signatures.

Testing of ReGTime is successfully finished. During our presentation of ReG-Time at CeBIT'96 in Hannover, visitors showed great interest in renting remote workstations and providing resources to the "computing power market".

Our next aim is to test ReGTime in industrial projects. Therefore, we have to explore the integration of ReGTime into the existing electronic market and the way to originate the mentioned "computing power market". We will examine which economical principles have to be considered, such that both customers and providers are willing to accept this new market.

References

1. Larry Smarr and Charles E. Catlett. Metacomputing. *Communications of the ACM*, 35:45–52, June 1992.
2. Friedhelm Ramme. Building a virtual machine-room — a focal point in metacomputing. *Future Generation Computer Systems*, 11:477–489, 1995.
3. Rechenzentrum Karlsruhe. Virtuelles Rechenzentrum Karlsruhe. http://www.uni-karlsruhe.de/Uni/RZ/VRZ/, 1996.

4. M. Weber and E. Nagel. Metacomputing zwischen KFA und GMD: Ein verteilter massiv-paralleler Rechner. *PARS-Mitteilungen*, 14:9–18, December 1995.
5. Message Passing Interface Forum. *MPI: A Message Passing Interface Standard*, June 1995.
6. V.S. Sunderam, A. Geist, J. Dongarra, and R. Mancheck. The PVM concurrent computing system: Evolution, experiences, and trends. *Parallel Computing*, 20:531–546, April 1994.
7. N. Carriero, D. Gelernter, T.G. Mattson, and A.H. Sherman. The Linda alternative to message-passing systems. *Parallel Computing*, 20:633–655, April 1994.
8. Jr. Harold and W. Lockhart. *OSF DCE Guide to Developing Distributed Applications*. McGraw-Hill, Inc., 1994.
9. Object Management Group. *The Common Object Request Broker: Architecture and Specification*, July 1995.
10. Craig Milo Rogers, Anna-Lena Neches, and Paul Postel. Transitioning to the web. In *Online Procurement at ISI*. World Wide Web Fall Conference, 1994.
11. Andersen Consulting. BargainFinder Agent. http://bf.cstar.ac.com/bf/, 1996.
12. A. Brüggemann-Klein, G. Cyranek, and A. Endres. Die fachlichen Informations- und Publikationsdienste der Zukunft — eine Initiative der Gesellschaft für Informatik. pages 2–12. GISI, 1995.
13. Simson Garfinkel. *PGP: Pretty Good Privacy*. O'Reilly & Associates, Sebastopol, CA, March 1995.
14. Larry Wall and Randal L. Schwartz. *Programming Perl*. O'Reilly & Associates, Inc., Sebastopol, CA, 1991.

Structuring Call Control Software Using Distributed Objects

H. Blair[†], S. J. Caughey[‡], H. Green[†] and S. K. Shrivastava[‡]

[†]GPT Ltd.,
New Century Park, Coventry, CV3 1HJ, England.

[‡]Department of Computing Science,
University of Newcastle,
Newcastle upon Tyne, NE1 7RU, England.

Abstract

Present day telecommunications systems make use of computing technology that places excessive reliance on specialist equipment and techniques for delivering core services of switching and call management. It is becoming increasingly difficult to maintain and enhance these systems to incorporate new services and functionalities. Continuing advances in distributed computing technology hold the promise of a way out of this difficulty. The paper analyses the problems facing telecommunications software and describes how it can be restructured using object-oriented techniques. The approach presented opens up a way of structuring telecommunications applications using CORBA technology.

1. Introduction

Telephony systems have two very onerous, and potentially conflicting requirements. Firstly, as such systems are largely concerned with protecting the ability to communicate, they have very strict requirements for availability (downtime in current systems: < 10 minutes / year, typical next generation system requirements: < 3 minutes / year). Secondly, they require high performance.

These are "traditional" telecommunications system concerns, which have been the daily fare of switch designers for many years. Our work is motivated by the observation that in present day systems, the requirements stated above have been met by making use of computing technology that places reliance on specialist equipment and techniques for delivering core services of switching and call management. It is becoming increasingly difficult to maintain and enhance these systems to incorporate new services and functionalities, and customers increasingly wish to take advantage of the rapid improvement in price/performance offered by industry standard hardware. Continuing advances in distributed computing technology hold the promise of a way out of this difficulty. However, the ideas developed in the arena of distributed computing (objects interacting via invocations, with dependability achieved by utilising techniques such as atomic transactions and object replication) will need considerable refinement before they can be adapted to deliver the availability as well as the timeliness requirements demanded by next generation telecommunications services. In particular, the asynchronous nature of telecommunications signalling protocols and the resulting state machine specifications needs to be taken into account.

This paper analyses the problems facing telecommunications software and describes how it can be restructured using object-oriented techniques. The approach presented opens up a way of structuring telecommunications applications using CORBA technology by making use of a suitably enhanced ORB [1] and CORBA services [2].

2. Structure of Telecommunications Applications

The idea of a client-server interaction, in which a user "asks the system a question" and the system responds, is deeply embedded in the way the data processing industry thinks about what it does. Telecommunications, by contrast, has always required at least two users and a system, or a network of systems, for a meaningful interaction. The system becomes an intermediary between the users, forming connections (or more abstractly bindings) on their behalf.

Current telecommunications applications are still essentially bound by the "step-by-step" setup of circuits. In this context, we are creating a bearer model and then establishing what the users want. In the terms above, the binding to a service is *implicit* (since basic telephony is the only service on offer). When we move to a network providing variable bandwidth, one-to-many communications and many qualities of service, this model is clearly inadequate.

TINA has promoted the notion of a "separated" service layer, in which services are provided by a network-wide distributed processing infrastructure, which makes requests of a lower bearer layer to create connections [3]. The service layer is responsible for coordinating the creation, modification and destruction of service agreements amongst users. For a given call, this leads to the identification of the required stream model, which identifies for each participant the information streams sent and received, with the appropriate information characteristics. The bearer layer receives requests from the service layer and is responsible for setting up the stream model connecting a set of endpoints.

Within the service layer, the original "step-by-step" principle for call control is still maintained, but in the more abstract context of piecewise binding creation. At each step, starting from the originating user agent, we can create a new binding segment by binding to an entity (e.g. a network interconnection point or node) "in the direction of" the terminating user agent. Each of these binding segments may possess state. In this context, the invocation of a telecommunications feature (e.g. call waiting), or the traversing of a transparency constraint (e.g. network boundary) may be modelled by the creation of a new binding segment (i.e. adding an independent state machine representing the feature to the total relationship state). Below we discuss this aspect in detail.

2.1. State Machines

Within telephony services, call functionality is traditionally modelled as a state machine in which external events are received from the users active in a particular call (or the system administering the call) and each event drives the machine into some new state. This model is particularly suited to the world of call processing where, due to the limited user interface (traditionally a small number of buttons), complex call features may only be initiated by sequences of user actions, each driving the state of the call forward. In any real-world telephony system the total state diagram, which specifies the system's responses to all possible combination of events is hugely complex, describing a myriad of interactions between users and the system. In order to reduce this complexity, the state machine is structured as a number of smaller state machines, each dedicated to handling some particular portion of the state diagram (often relating to a particular call feature). These state machines consume external events but additionally may produce internal signals which can be communicated between state machines to drive them forward. The total state of a call is therefore described by the total state of all its individual state machines.

Structuring in this manner has two advantages. Firstly, as the number of states which can be represented by two state machines is the product of their individual number of states, by creating smaller state machines the total number of states to be represented can be greatly reduced. Secondly, improved modularity means that changes in functionality can be limited to some (hopefully small) subset of state machines and the introduction of new functionality can be expressed, largely, by creating a new state machine. These changes could be introduced without effecting other state machines. As telephony functionality tends to grow by the steady introduction of new and increasingly complex features, reached by extending sequences of user actions, this design approach has proved popular.

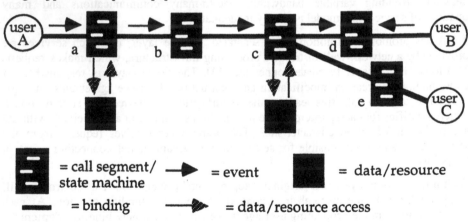

Fig. 1.

As the specification is structured in terms of state machines, reflecting each of these as a software entity (a *call segment* in our terminology) is the natural, and traditional, mechanism for implementing call processing software. Calls progress through a series of state transitions towards a specific goal, generally communication with some party, and so call segments tend to be bound together in *chains* connecting the parties (these chains may bifurcate i.e. split, in the case of multi-party calls) with messages passing along the chain in all directions. We have used this chaining as an organising principle for our current call control software implementation [4,5]. Call segments all support a common vocabulary of telephony events (essentially, a "superset" of network signalling protocol). For the reasons above, telephony features are represented by separate call segments, which may dynamically break in and drop out of the chain. The order in which these segments appear in the chain allows for precedence in the handing of events, and may be used as a basis for the management of "feature interaction". Fig. 1 shows three users connected together by a chain of call segments. We discuss problems with the above way of structuring call control software.

In most implementations, call segments are contained within 'heavyweight' communicating processes, where each process manages large numbers of calls, and keeps track of the progress of each call through the segment by maintaining call records. Events are implemented as asynchronous messages. Each process waits for messages and on receiving one directs it to the appropriate call record. A key feature of this model is that a process handles only one message at a time. This avoids any concurrency control problems. As these processes are single threaded, it becomes necessary to make all inter-process communication asynchronous (synchronous, request-response, communication will block a process, thereby making it unresponsive to incoming messages). Unfortunately, this makes the programming of a given state machine more complex than need be. Call segments may have to access persistent data services (or interact with hardware devices) which are structured as separate entities. Such accesses are 'request-response' interactions, that are best structured as (synchronous) remote procedure calls. However, call segments have no provision for making synchronous calls, so need to explicitly program using messages. This introduces complexity, since code and states must be written to deal with incoming events happening before the response. Moreover, it leads to a conflict of objectives between efficiency and modularity. Efficiency considerations demand that the call processing software be broken into only a small number of processes, so as to minimise the number of inter-process messages (because sending/receiving of a message requires expensive kernel calls), but software engineering concerns of modularity and extensibility demand that the software be broken into larger number of processes.

The present way of restructuring a single state machine (say X) into a number of smaller state machines (say a,b,c,d) has another problem. A state machine selects a message from its queue of input messages, performs some action and, optionally, outputs one or more messages. This entire process is atomic (free from interference), in the sense that the processing of the action is not interrupted to service other input messages. A single state transition of X could represent a sequence of transitions of $a,..,d$. Although each individual state transition of this sequence is atomic, no attempt is made to make the entire sequence atomic. This can lead to situations where different state machines have conflicting views of the state of the call or of resources attached to it. Some of these situations are inherent to the telecomms problem, and must be catered for in any case. For example:

1. User A calls User B. At some point during the setup, User B picks up his phone. (In Fig 1 above, suppose the state machine d represents the agent of User B.) If the event 'call seize' reaches d before the event 'off-hook' from User B, then d must deal with the problem. If d has got so far as to ring B's telephone, then d assumes B is answering A's call. If the 'off-hook' from B precedes the 'seize' from A at d, then B is treated as busy.

2. It is possible for network circuits connecting exchanges A and B to be selected from both ends. This creates the possibility that A may select a particular circuit x for a new call using the route A->B, since x is free in its busy-free tables. At the same time, B may already have selected x for a call using B->A. This will be discovered when A

signals to B. The network protocol resolves this problem by getting one end or the other to "back off".

However, where state machine decomposition is being used to simplify the behaviour of one particular actor in a call, extra complexity can arise from differences in the ordering of events. This is true, for example, of the user agent and user features (i.e. features modifying the behaviour of the user agent). Where the features are represented as separate state machines from the user agent, new possibilities for interleaving appear (particularly as the feature state machines may be dynamically inserted and removed from the call chains). The approach developed in the next section explores transactional solutions to this problem.

2.2. *Fault-tolerance*

Switches have traditionally been designed with extensive hardware level redundancy to provide a highly available hardware platform. All major telecommunications manufacturers have spent much time and money in developing and improving their own processor technology, because until now there has been no commercial platform available that could deliver the availability required of a switching system. Typical architectures involve microprocessors with proprietary instruction sets targeted at efficient bit operations and indexing, with all elements (processor, memory I/O, power supply etc.) replicated with no single points of failure.

Despite the fact that call control software executes on highly reliable hardware platforms, application software is known to get into inconsistent state. A major cause of unreliability of software must therefore be due to faults (bugs) in software itself. There is much evidence to suggest that many of these faults are of a transient nature (e.g., [6]). For example, interference during call processing, as discussed previously, may cause seemingly random faults which are difficult to diagnose or prevent. Additionally, programming errors which have remained undetected through the development phase may be present, manifesting themselves only within certain, rare, states.

For this reason, call processing relies upon the use of backward recovery, i.e. the ability to reset the system to some predefined or earlier state, following error detection. Code is inserted by programmers to check the validity of messages received and consistency of internal data. Errors detected are reported to a distributed rollback service which analyses reports and decides upon appropriate recovery action based upon the severity and frequency of the reports. Recovery actions range from reinitialising particular pages of data belonging to a suspected process, through process and processor reset, with the ultimate level being a complete restart of the system.

Switching systems need to maintain persistent data, e.g., subscriber data, configuration information statistics etc. (data/resource entities shown in fig. 1). This data is shared between many calls and call segments and frequently held within a number of databases which offer simple transactional support to control concurrent access. In general this data consists of a working copy (often held in main memory for efficiency considerations) and one or more backup copies. The higher levels of recovery recover portions, or all, of these backup copies.

The fault-tolerance approach discussed above suffers from drawbacks both at the hardware as well as at the software level.

At the hardware level, reliance on the use of specialist fault-tolerant hardware is becoming increasingly unattractive. There is intense pressure to reduce costs and at the same time, meet increased performance requirements. It would be cheaper to use processor types that are widely available commercially - but one of the most difficult technologies to master is that of hardware-based replication, especially as processor busses become wider, and clock rates become faster. Further, every new microprocessor architecture requires considerable re-design effort. Software-based replication (whereby replica synchronism is maintained at the process level by making use of appropriate software implemented protocols) is therefore an attractive technology [7, 8]. The telecomms applications are, however, particularly demanding for such a strategy, since they have very high rates of interaction with the environment, and each such interaction must be agreed between the processors. In terms of performance, a hardware-implemented platform will always out perform its software equivalent. In the medium term therefore, switching systems are expected to make use of commercially available microprocessors and use hardware-based replication techniques for fault-tolerance. In the long run, the situation is likely to change in favour of software-implemented approaches.

At the software level, structuring call processing as communicating state machines concentrates upon the encapsulation of functionality but fails to encapsulate data. This is unfortunate as it is data which is of primary interest within software error recovery and so using this approach makes it difficult to contain errors and prevent their effects spreading into the system. Recovery action is taken upon the units of encapsulation familiar to the rollback service i.e. pages, processes and processors, rather than the units of concern to the application programmer e.g. call processing activities. In such an approach the rollback service must often take a conservative approach and recover parts of the system which may be unaffected by a fault, in order to ensure recovery. Indeed as an individual call's data can span pages, processes, processors and even exchanges, backward recovery of these units can place calls into inconsistent states which then need to initiate further recovery.

3. Structuring Using Objects

In this section we discuss how structuring of call control software using distributed objects can help reduce software level problems mentioned above. The main problems with the call segment based software structuring is that it lacks a conceptually simple way of dealing with consistency problems caused by processing of multiple events (discussed in section 2.1) and further, recovery action is taken upon the units of encapsulation familiar to the rollback service rather than the units of concern to the application programmer. We remedy this by introducing the notion of an activity. Activities are units of recovery and deadlock resolution. An attractive feature of the model that we present here is that it can be implemented by making use of a suitably enhanced ORB and CORBA services.

3.1. Distributed Objects

We now develop an object oriented approach for restructuring call processing software in a way that masters complexity without compromising efficiency. Segments are objects (instances of appropriate classes) and inter-segment communication is via method invocation. Multi-threaded processes are used, where each process is capable of managing several objects. This means that breaking the call control software into a number of segments need not lead to corresponding increase in inter-process communication, as objects within a process communicate using procedure calls. Objects may request the creation and deletion of other objects. (Note that our model does not assume dynamic creation/deletion but allows for objects to be obtained/returned from some free pool).

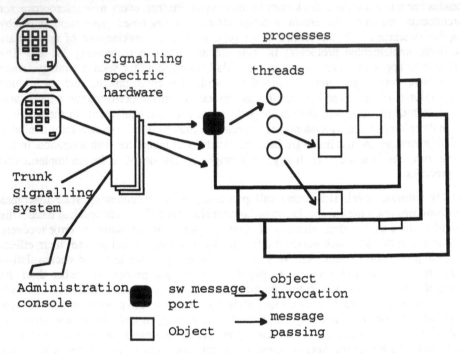

Fig. 2

Fig. 2 illustrates the basic architecture. External events e.g. events generated by subscriber telephones, are transformed into software messages by signalling specific hardware e.g. a Line Handler Unit, and delivered at a software message port. A thread, dedicated to listening at the port, allocates each incoming message to a thread which is then responsible for processing that particular event. This thread performs an invocation on some relevant object, passing it the message contents as parameters to the invocation. Objects process events by carrying out invocations on other objects. If an invocation is upon a remote object then a message is passed to the relevant process (which may be on a different processor) via its message port and the invocation is performed there. Invocation is distribution transparent from the perspective of the invoking and invoked objects

An object directly represents a state machine: input messages represent requests for object method invocations, a state transition represents a method execution and output messages represent asynchronous method invocations on other objects (an asynchronous method invocation is non-blocking; the caller invokes the method but does not wait for results). In addition, we also permit an object to make synchronous (blocking) invocations. When an object invokes another object and expects results from that invocation, then such invocations are made using blocking calls. Generalising, a method of an object may contain both asynchronous (non-blocking) as well as synchronous (blocking) calls. To ensure interference free execution of object methods, each object enforces concurrency control permitting multiple (simultaneous) execution of its read-only methods but exclusive execution of its methods involving state changes. Concurrency control raises the possibility of deadlocks. In the next subsections we discuss how we deal with deadlocks, consistency problems caused by processing of multiple events and call recovery.

Examples of simple 2-party and 3-party calls using our object infrastructure are illustrated below. We omit the mechanism by which telephony events are delivered to objects by modelling the process as a direct invocation performed by the subscriber's telephone upon its Line object, where a Line object is the software representation of the telephone, holding line specific information such as whether incoming or outgoing calls are barred.

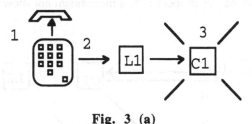

Fig. 3 (a)

With reference to Fig. 3(a), when a phone goes offhook (1) an 'offhook' operation is invoked on the telephone's Line object, L1, (2) and, if outgoing calls are allowed, L1 creates a Call object, C1, to handle the resulting call (3).

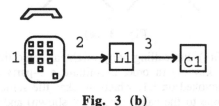

Fig. 3 (b)

With reference to Fig. 3(b), digits which are entered (1) cause a digit operation to be invoked on L1 (2), which propagates the digit by invoking the digit operation on C1 (3).

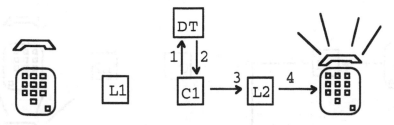

Fig. 3 (c)

With reference to Fig. 3(c), digits continue to be accepted until C1 ascertains that sufficient have been received and invokes the 'translate' operation on the Digit Translation object (1), the response (2) indicating the Line object, L2, associated with the called party. (Note that this call/response can be implemented as a synchronous call). An 'incoming call' operation is invoked on L2 (3) and L2 causes the phone to ring (4).

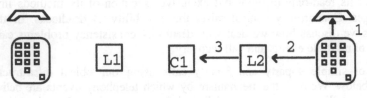

Fig. 3 (d)

With reference to Fig. 3(d), whenever the called party answers (1) the 'answer' operation is invoked on L2 (2) which then invokes the same operation on C1 (3). C1 then connects the two parties in speech (by a mechanism not shown here).

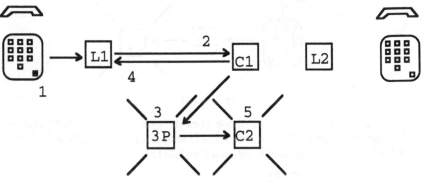

Fig. 3 (e)

With reference to Fig. 3(e), the calling party might at some time within the speech phase press the 'recall' key (1) in order to initiate a 3-party call. This causes the operation 'recall' to be invoked on L1, which invokes the same operation on C1 (2). C1 connects the 'held' tone to the called party (not shown) and then creates a 3-Party object (3) and informs L1 that it has done so (4). The 3-Party object meanwhile creates another Call object, C2, (5) which will be responsible for the call set-up to the third party. As a result of this process the 3-Party object has been inserted into the call chain.

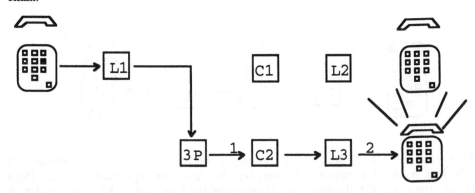

Fig. 3 (f)

With reference to Fig. 3(f), digits may now be entered (1) as in the 2-party case, except that in this situation they go via the 3-Party object, until sufficient digits are received by C2. The Digit Translation Table is then accessed (not shown) and the called phone is rung (2) as in the 2-party case. When the third party answers, they and the controlling party are connected in speech. Finally, when the controlling party presses recall, all 3 parties are connected in 3-party speech.

3.2. Activities and References

Objects involved within call processing activities require *firewalls* which prevent errors spreading, through interaction, to other objects. We describe later how object references can be used for this purpose. Some form of recovery is also required behind such firewalls to ensure that, having detected erroneous behaviour, some (hopefully small) set of objects may be identified as being responsible and recovery action taken upon those objects to return them a consistent state. We accomplish this by introducing the notion of an *activity*. An activity represents the computation carried out as a result of processing an external event. Processing of an external event starts a new activity and all the processing related to that event is executed as apart of this activity. Activities are units of recovery and deadlock resolution.

An ideal way of making activities recoverable would be to make them transactional. Then, all activities will follow some protocol for concurrency control, such as the well-known two-phase locking protocol, to ensure interference free (serializable) execution: locks on objects are acquired as invocations are made and released only when the activity ends. Any erroneous situation would cause the relevant activity to be aborted. However, despite the desirability of making all activities transactional, in real-world telephony applications this may prove impractical. First, an activity can (and does) perform unrecoverable actions. Second, supporting serializable activities requires additional synchronisation between objects involved within the activity and this imposes communication overheads that may prove unacceptable for activities spanning multiple switching domains.

We propose a *lightweight* solution for constructing recoverable activities by permitting an activity's computation to be a mixture of both transactional and non-transactional. In other words, objects may be *transaction aware* or *transaction unaware*.

As we mentioned earlier, telecommunications applications have to support a traditional data processing function in that large amount of shared persistent data (representing user data, hardware configurations, billing tariffs etc.) needs to be maintained; updates to this data must be carried out atomically. Hence, persistent objects would normally be transaction aware, whilst volatile objects would be transaction unaware. Naturally, only transaction aware objects will follow a concurrency control protocol to ensure serializability (e.g., two-phase locking), whereas other (volatile) objects will use only local concurrency control to ensure interference free execution of local object methods.

The recovery action undertaken for volatile objects involved in call processing e.g. C1, C2 and 3P in the previous diagrams, consists of simply deleting them. This is made possible through the novel use of *object references* to be described below. The action of deleting the objects of a call may be less drastic than it first appears as the state of a call in the speech phase (a high percentage of the calls in progress) may often be recovered by interrogation of the various hardware devices responsible for maintaining the speech path, and the user need not be aware that the recovery has occurred.

References provide the capability to communicate with a designated object, and in our model they may be freely held, copied and exchanged. References are created when an object is instantiated, being returned to the instantiator as a part of that process. Objects also obtain references by being passed them in messages from other objects, and this includes references returned as the results of invocations on objects acting as name services (e.g. traders). Communication by a particular object is therefore limited to those objects for which it holds references. Synchronous communication is a special case, in which the reference to the calling object is automatically passed in the request message (so that the results may be returned) but the called object may not retain the reference.

The underlying object support infrastructure is required to guarantee *referential integrity*, meaning that an object will continue to exist (will not be terminated) whilst any object retains a reference to it. This provides security against a faulty object wrongly attempting to terminate an object (the firewall referred to earlier); the object will continue to exist whilst any correctly functioning object retains a reference to it. The infrastructure must also provide distributed garbage collection of objects that is both *safe* and *lively*: objects with references are not garbage collected (safety) and objects without any reference are eventually garbage collected (liveness).

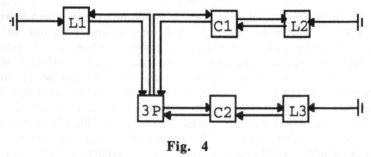

Fig. 4

Fig. 4 shows the objects involved in 3 party speech and the references held by those objects. The references from each of the telephones to the Line objects are permanent (as illustrated by the earth symbols) and those objects will never be deleted. All persistent objects e.g. the Digit Translation object presented earlier, are permanently referenced and therefore cannot be incorrectly deleted by an erroneous object. Our model specifies that for every call the objects representing the communicating parties e.g. the Line objects in the example above, act as the roots of a directed, fully connected graph, i.e. every object in the call may be reached by following a path of references from any root. Note that the referencing graph shown above represents one example of the call segment chains mentioned previously.

As references provide the capability to access other objects then the controlled exchange of references prevents one call from interfering with another. Calls cannot erroneously delete objects which are correctly referenced, and although they do require access to certain persistent objects e.g. the Line and Digit Translation objects in the diagrams, updates to persistent objects may only occur transactionally and rigorous checks can be introduced as necessary in order to minimise the possibility of incorrect updates. Calls may therefore be implemented with an efficient firewall which prevents errors being propagated to other parts of the system.

Objects detecting inconsistencies within a transaction cause the transaction to abort (either by informing the transaction manager, by refusing to commit, or by raising exceptions which indirectly cause the abortion). A transaction manager might itself suspect an inconsistency and abort the transaction. Errors detected within some activity but outside of a transaction, for which no specific exception handler is available, cause the entire call to be terminated (this will also cause termination of any ongoing transactions within the activity). This is possible, as root objects have the ability to terminate a call by sending messages informing all root objects of the fact and then deleting all their references. Objects which hold a path to a root object may inform the root object and have them terminate the call. Unreferenced objects will automatically be garbage collected.

The treatment of deadlocks is straightforward given that activities are recoverable. One simple way of preventing deadlocks is to assign unique timestamps to activities and resolve lock conflicts uniformly in favour of say 'older' activities. All object invocations carry the identity of the activity. So if a lock conflict is detected, and the holder of the lock is 'younger' than the requester, then the holding activity is aborted.

Currently available ORBs do not provide the necessary guarantees of referential integrity and garbage collection of unreferenced objects. A research object support system built by us [9] does provide these facilities. The techniques used there can be adapted easily for incorporation in an ORB.

3.3. Supporting Transaction Aware Objects

The Object Transaction Service (OTS) specification [2] describes the protocols and services necessary to enable distributed objects to become transaction aware. The transaction class library and related services of the distributed object system Arjuna, built by us [10], is in the process of being adapted to be OTS compliant and can be used to provide the necessary transactional support for persistent objects.

As stated before, all object invocations carry the identity of the activity. On receipt of an activity identity only a transaction aware object will register its participation in a transaction with some transaction manager. We illustrate our basic approach to transactional support with an imaginary call feature invoked from within 3-party speech. In the previous 3-party call illustration we described how Line objects hold state regarding some particular telephone e.g. whether incoming calls are barred or not. Let us imagine a call feature which, through the pressing of some sequence of keys, allows a party within a 3-party call to set a time at which all 3 phones will simultaneously ring and on answer the 3-party conference is re-instated. One implementation of such a feature has the 3-party object recognise the appropriate key sequence and then invoke operations (directly or indirectly) on the 3 Line objects informing them of the required time. Each Line object then holds the time (as persistent state which outlives the present call). This feature requires that the update of all the Line objects with the required time should occur atomically. Fig. 5 illustrates an implementation of the feature which makes use of transactions on persistent objects.

With reference to Fig. 5(a), in which all parties are in 3-party speech, the 3-Party object on receiving the appropriate key sequence (1) begins a transaction by creating a Transaction object (2).

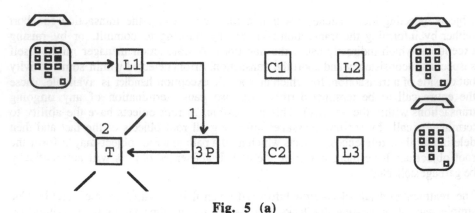

Fig. 5 (a)

With reference to Fig. 5(b), the 3-Party object now invokes synchronous 'update time' operations on all 3 Line objects, the identity of the Transaction object being passed with the message. In response each Line Object registers itself as belonging to the transaction (2) (via a synchronous 'register resource' invocation on the Transaction object) before returning a confirmation to the 3-Party object (3). (Only L1's response is shown in the diagram).

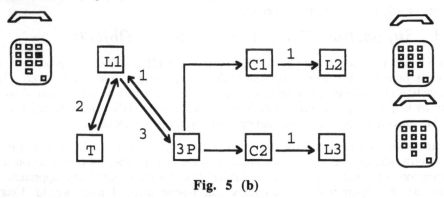

Fig. 5 (b)

Whenever all the Line objects have responded correctly the 3-Party object invokes 'commit transaction' on the Transaction object which then executes the commit protocol with the Line objects. Only when they receive the commit instruction will the Line objects commit the updated time to persistent store. A failure of any Line object to respond correctly to the 'update time' operation e.g. due to a communication failure or to a party having cleared down, causes the 3-Party object to invoke the 'rollback' on the Transaction object. The 3-Party object is informed whenever the commit or abort is completed and may then delete the Transaction object.

4. Concluding Remarks

We have presented a way of structuring telecommunications applications using CORBA technology. Our approach of structuring the software system as communicating objects allows better fault containment and provides localised recovery at the level of individual calls. For fault containment we require that objects involved within call processing activities be protected by firewalls which prevent errors spreading through interaction to other objects. We achieve this by insisting that the underlying object support infrastructure provide referential integrity for objects. This provides security against a faulty object wrongly attempting to terminate an object. Although currently available ORBs do not provide the necessary guarantees of referential integrity, the techniques developed by us and described elsewhere [9] can be adapted in an ORB. To provide localised recovery at the level of individual calls, we have introduced the notion of an activity which represents the computation carried out as a result of processing an external event. A lightweight solution for constructing recoverable activities has been proposed by permitting an activity's computation to be a mixture of both transactional and non-transactional. We have described how Object Transaction Service can be used to provide the services necessary to enable distributed objects to become transaction aware. We are implementing key aspects of the model described here by developing a telecomms ORB. At the same time we are also adapting the transaction class library and related services of Arjuna [10] to be OTS compliant so that it can be used by this ORB in the manner desribed here.

Acknowledgements

The work of the University authors has been supported in part by a research grant from GPI Ltd. Discussions with G.D. Parrington clarified our ideas on Object Transaction Service (OTS) specification

References

[1] CORBA: Common Object Request Broker Architecture and Specification, OMG Document Revision 2.0, July 1995.

[2] CORBA services: Common Object Services Specification, OMG Document No. 95-3-31, March 1995.

[3] H. Berndt et al., "TINA service architecture", TB_MDC.012_2.0_94, TINA Consortium, Redbank, NJ, March 1995. (http://www.tinac.com/).

[4] H.M. Blair, "Attacking Product Complexity: Broadband Call Control for Vision O.N.E", Proc. of XIV Intl. Switching Symposium, Yokohama, October 1992.

[5] H. Green, "Distributed Systems Issues for Telecommunications", Proc. of 1995 European Research Seminar on Advances in Distributed Computing, ERSADS'95, April 1995.

[6] Y. Huang and C. Kintala, "Software fault tolerance in the application layer", in Software Fault Tolerance, M.R. Lyu (ed), Trends in Software, Vol. 3, John Wiley and Sons, 1995.

[7] S. K. Shrivastavaet al., "Principal features of the VOLTAN family of node architectures for distributed systems", IEEE Trans. on Computers, 41, 5, May 1992, pp. 542-549.

[8] F. Brasileiro et al., "Implementing fail-silent nodes for distributed systems", IEEE Trans. on Computers (to appear).

[9] S.J. Caughey and S.K. Shrivastava, "Architectural support for mobile objects in large scale distributed systems", Proc. of IEEE Intl. Workshop on Object-Orientation in Operating Systems, Lund, August 1995, pp. 38-47.

[10] G.D. Parrington et al., "The design and implementation of Arjuna", USENIX Computing Systems Journal, vol. 8 (3), 1995, pp. 255-308.

Design and Implementation of a Multimedia Communication Service in a Distributed Environment Based on the TINA-C Architecture

M. Khayrat Durmosch, Christian Egelhaaf, Klaus-Dietric Engel, Peter Schoo
Research Institute for Open Communication Systems, GMD-Fokus
Hardenbergplatz 2, D - 10623 Berlin
Tel.: +49 30 25499 200, Fax: +49 30 25499 202, http://www.fokus.gmd.de/
[durmosch\egelhaaf\engel\schoo]@fokus.gmd.de

Abstract

This paper discusses our experiences with the development of a distributed telecommunication application. The application performs a multimedia communication service which has been designed based on the Telecommunications Information Networking Architecture Consortium (TINA-C) Service and Management Architectures. The implementation has been installed and tested across a set of different CORBA2 platform products. The report focuses on the impact of using such platforms for the design of distributed applications. In addition some observations on testing and operating of distributed telecommunication applications in the project specific test bed are reflected.

1   Introduction

The project TANGRAM started in spring 1995 supported by DeTeBerkom[1] at GMD–FOKUS in Berlin. Its main objectives are to design and develop a distributed processing environment (DPE) consisting of existing platform products supporting distributed object technology[2], and, secondly, to provide support for the development of distributed telecommunication applications.

The primary interest of the first objective is to evaluate the extend to which interoperability is achieved between different CORBA2 platforms, and how such software products actually support the distributed applications which are being installed across this environment and which are used to provide telecommunication services to end users. It encompasses a variety of hardware and operating systems. The products actually used are the CORBA implementations Orbix of IONA [1], and HP-Distributed Smalltalk of Hewlett-Packard [2].

The second objective concentrates on increasing the efficiency and effectiveness of application development and engineering. The application's key points are to enable services which support user and service mobility, personalisation and customization of services. Another important issue is, that these applications are prepared for service management, i.e. they must be able to handle subscription and accounting information for telecommunication services.

---

1. A subsidiary of the Deutsche Telekom AG.
2. Through out his paper the term platform will be used to indicate this type of software.

Due to the influence of the emerging distributed computing technology the telecommunication industry takes a new approach for the development, construction and operation of software for telecommunication systems. A consortium of about forty international companies (service providers, network operators and telecommunication vendors) founded in 1993 the Telecommunication Information Networking Architecture Consortium (TINA-C). TINA-C's goal is the development of on an environment comprising open distributed processing platforms positioned in telecommunication systems which include a variety of existing and forthcoming network technologies. Much of this work is based upon the Reference Model of Open Distributed Processing (RM-ODP) [13]. On the other hand the OMG CORBA activities [5][6] have also greatly influenced the TINA-C distributed processing environment and its services.

The paper is organised as follows: Section 2 describes briefly the functionality of the implemented application which is primarily driven by the enterprise perspective for which this service is viable. The next section introduces the Distributed Processing Environment. The computational design is discussed in Section 4, while experiences with our implementation can be found in Section 5. The paper is concluded by an outline of further issues and future work.

2 TINA-Multimedia Communication System - Requirements and Design

The TANGRAM project has developed a distributed application which essentially enables the exchange of audio and video data between a group of participants. Although service functionality is important, the main focus of the project is on design and realisation of this service example. However, the application is designed to fit commercial situations in which a customer books for her users the ability to use a service by signing a *contract* with a service provider. For example, a company may subscribe with a service provider to provide a service for its employees, or a single user may book a service for her own use. This contract determines customization and also the accounting, tariffing and charging which is to be performed when the service is used. On the other hand, when a contract is signed, the service provider is expected to guarantee the contractually fixed functionality and qualities. A stakeholder model is used to describe this commercial situation which consists of particular roles and their relationships.

To this end TANGRAM's multimedia communication service (T-MMCS) typifies the category of commercial telecommunication service which enables a group of users during a session to isochronously exchange data through a network. Additional capabilities to control a session, or the ability to commonly share other resources, such as, for example, sharing applications, would specialise this application to a conference service.

The role of this application within the project is not to gain a far reaching functional richness, but to serve as a test of the project specific DPE, and to specify a starting point for the development of abstract object-oriented frameworks which support the rapid creation of service variations. This is due to the projects interest in the evaluation of the TINA-C results and the CORBA products maturity and applicability for the telecommunication industries.

2.1 Basic Design Considerations

The design considerations regard primarily two areas: first the environment for the target of the T-MMCS application, and second the software structure to be implemented.

In order to decouple technology domains which have different innovation cycles and thus protect immense investments, and to appropriately position the domain of distributed software technology, the architectural principles of TINA-C [3] have been followed.

Three parts can be distinguished (Figure 1): a *network technology* based part, comprising the infrastructure resources which enable data transport (WANs, LANs, switches, bridges, etc.), a part comprising *computing capabilities* to access and control the infrastructure. These computing capabilities comprise distributed software technology platforms (e.g. CORBA2 products) forming a DPE. They support the administration and execution of *application software* which resides in the third part.

On the other hand, the T-MMCS design is a discrete software structure made of units, called *components* or *computational objects*[3] which have clearly distinguishable processing tasks. The aims were to apply the suggestions made in the TINA-C Service

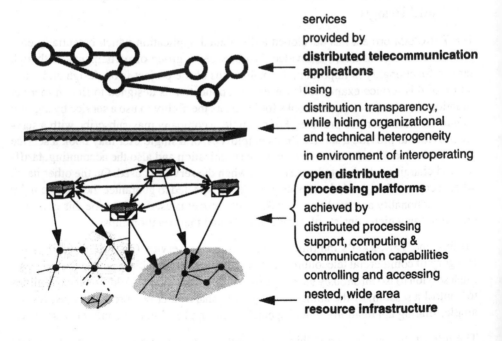

services
provided by
distributed telecommunication applications
using
distribution transparency, while hiding organizational and technical heterogeneity
in environment of interoperating
open distributed processing platforms
achieved by
distributed processing support, computing & communication capabilities
controlling and accessing
nested, wide area **resource infrastructure**

Figure 1: Telecommunication Information Networking Environment

Architecture [4] to structure software for telecommunication services, and to identify components which are service independent and thus (re-)usable for other application contexts. The motivation for the general separation principles [7] which guide the structure and a detailed discussion of their application in the design of the T-MMCS [9] has been presented.

3 The TANGRAM DPE

The Tangram DPE is used to support the T-MMCS on a variety of hardware platforms including SUNs, Windows PCs, Apple Macintosh. The platform products actually used are the CORBA implementations Orbix of IONA [1] and the HP-Distributed Smalltalk of Hewlett-Packard [2]. The Tangram DPE forms a distributed processing platform that offers only distribution transparency to the components and thus masks the heterogeneity of the underlying systems (Figure 1). The complete set of transparencies that *should* be supported by DPE functions consists of: *access transparency, location transparency, migration transparency, relocation transparency, replication transparency, concurrency transparency, persistence transparency* and *transaction transparency.*The complete Specification of the CORBA communication facilities and the CORBA services can be found in [5] and [6].

3.1 CORBA 2 Interoperability

The CORBA 2 interoperability part adds multivendor interoperability to the ORBs. This includes initialization services, and enhancements to the Interface Repository. With CORBA 2, an ORB can broker interactions between objects that reside within a single process as well as between objects that globally interact across multivendor ORBs and operating systems.

An ORB is considered to be interoperability-compliant when it supports

- the Dynamic Invocation Interface, the Dynamic Skeleton Interface, the specification around the Object References converting and manipulating operations, and the ORB and OA Initialization and Initial References specification [CORBA2: p9-5]
- and a native or half-bridge support of the Internet Inter-ORB Protocol (IIOP) which specifies how General Inter ORB Protocol (GIOP) messages are exchanged over a TCP/IP network.

The Interface Repository (IR) is a logical part of the ORB and provides persistent storage of interface definitions. It manages and provides access to a collection of interface (object) definitions specified in IDL. These object definitions are available to an ORB as "interface objects" accessed through IDL-specified interfaces. In particular the object definitions in the IR assist the ORB in providing interoperability between different organizational domains (e.g. different types of systems), and between different technological domains (e.g. different ORB implementations).

---

3. These terms are used as synonyms through out the paper.

3.2   ORB Interoperability Extension

Interoperability between several heterogeneous ORBs means a transparent crossing of domain boundaries. Conceptually this is done by translating the necessary information when an object request traverses domain boundaries. This translation is provided by a mapping or *bridging* mechanism which resides at the boundary between the domains, and which transforms requests expressed in terms of one domain's model into the model of the destination domain. The object models of the two domains need to be compatible to achieve full interoperability. This should be the case if both domains comply with the CORBA Object Model.

Interoperable Object References

Clients should be able to use object references to invoke operations on objects in other ORBs. The client does not need to distinguish between references in local or remote ORBs. An *Interoperable Object Reference - IOR* has been defined to provide this transparency. This new data structure should only be used when crossing object reference domain boundaries within bridges, and should not be visible to application level ORB programmers. IORs are created from conventional object references when required to cross a referencing domain boundary.

General Inter-ORB Protocol

The GIOP is used for information exchange between different ORBs. Its specification consists of the Common Data Representation (CDR), GIOP Message Formats, and GIOP Transport Assumptions. The CDR is the transfer syntax into which the OMG-IDL data types are mapped for transfer between Inter-ORB Bridges. The mapping of GIOP message transfer to a specific TCP/IP connection is the Internet Inter-ORB Protocol (IIOP). The GIOP and IIOP support protocol-level ORB interoperability. The exchanged messages are encoded in the Common Data Representation (CDR) format. The TCP/IP address of the servers are published in IORs. The clients initiate a connection with the address specified in the IOR. The listening server may accept or reject the connection.

4   T-MMCS Computational Design

Computationally, the components and their relations (Figure 2) are identified distinguishing responsibilities with respect to the entire T-MMCS. The figure discussed is a simplification, since some details are omitted here for reasons of brevity. The figure presents a two-party session, although the components have been designed to handle an arbitrary number of parties.

The system implemented and running at GMD FOKUS consists of computational objects (CO) of 17 different types. A two party session is built from 25 instances of these types, for every further party 10 more COs are created. In addition, 17 instances of infrastructure components used for life cycle management are needed for a two party session.

113

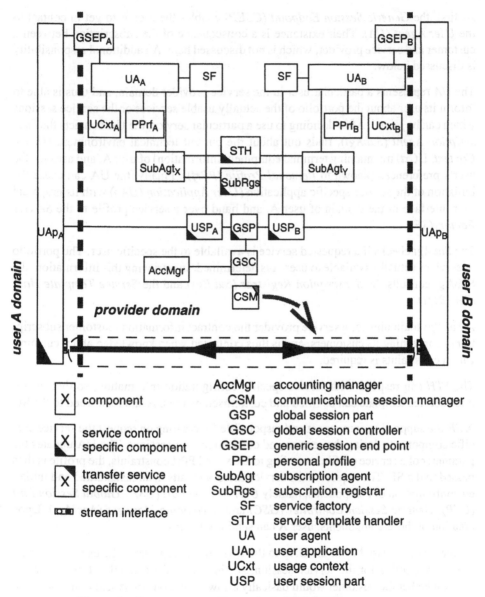

Figure 2 : Component configuration of T-MMCS

The components are implemented in SmallTalk, C++ or C, are installed across instances of HP-DST and ORBIX such that their interactions pass IDL specified interfaces and cooperatively achieve the T-MMC service provided to the users.

The following section is intended to give an idea of the complexity of the T-MMCS rather than a comprehensive discussion of the system. It is a rough description in a timely order. The components are briefly explained when they are involved the first time.

At first, the *Generic Session Endpoint (GSEP)* enables the user A to get in contact to the *User Agent (UA)*. Their existence is a consequence of the subscription between a customer and service provider, which is not discussed here. An additional responsibility is discussed below.

The *UA* represents a particular user in the service provider domain, and thus is able to inform its user about the portfolio of the actually usable services or the service sessions which can be joined. After deciding to use a particular service, the UA contacts the *Subscription Agent (SubAgt)*, finds out about the current technical environment *(Usage Context, UCxt)* maintaining terminal equipment information) of user A, and asks for the user's preferences (known to *Personal Profile (PPrf)*). Finally, the UA can cause the initiation of the service specific application *(User Application (UAp)* with its graphical user interface in the domain of user A, and hand over a service profile to the *Service Factory(SF)*.

The *SubAgt* checks if a requested service is available to the specific user. The portfolio of services actually available to user A is determined. In retrieving this information, the SubAgt consults the *Subscription Registrar (SubRgs)* and the *Service Template Handler (STH)*.

A *SubRgs* maintains for a service provider the contract information (customer subscriptions) concerning its customers, and is thus contacted when knowledge about customization constraints is required.

The *STH* can respond with service specific configuration information, so that the replied service template can be filled and customised by the UA and forwarded to the SF.

A *SF* is a supporting component and responsible for creating on request the service specific components during the service and communication sessions. The UA updates the parameter of a service profile according to UCxt and PPrf constraints, the profile is then passed to the SF. The request to the service factory results in an instantiated and initiated configuration of components, namely *User Session Part (USP), Global Session Part (GSP), Generic Session Controller (GSC)* and *Accounting Manager (AccMgr)*. Upon creation of these components, user A can send invitations.

Invitations are passed from the UAp to the *USP*, which represents the user and its customer perspective for the service session. At this stage, for example, it is possible to check whether the customer would basically allow invitations to be sent to the other users. An invitation request is forwarded to the GSP.

The *GSP* has a global view on the service session and disregards aspects which are local to the user A. Received invitation requests are forwarded to the associated UAs, which will check again customer restrictions, user preferences and environmental constraints, before invitations are passed via GSEPs to the invited parties. When an invited user accepts the offer to join a session, its UA will accordingly create an USP.

Once all USPs have been created, they negotiate via the GSP the remaining open service characteristics and their requirements or constraints for the communication session. The latter are formulated by the GSP in terms of modification rights (for example, based on the applied charging policy split charging), port capabilities, and the connectivity between these ports. This information is handed over to the GSC.

The *GSC* is responsible for creating an appropriate *Communication Session Manager (CSM)*, and acts as a moderator between the GSP and the set of controlled CSMs. This component is accountable and thus related to the AccMgr.

The *AccMgr* triggers the logs of usage metering data produced by the GSC, and evaluates and forwards this information for charging purposes.

The *CSM* finally reformulates the connectivity requirements of the service for a particular communication session into creation and control of network based connections (indicated by the thick arrows in the figure). Thus, this component is responsible for enabling the control and exchange of streams that can mediate through the network infrastructure.[4] Now the user applications are connected by streams and the session set-up including A/V communication is complete.

5   Experiences

In the following the technical approach taken is briefly presented and the support of methods or techniques is illustrated which was considered useful or necessary from the design phase up to final integration tests[5].

5.1   Using ODP and TINA-C Methods

The background for the activities was the TINA-C Service and Management Architectures [4], [10] and the Reference Model on Open Distributed Processing (ODP) [11]. While the former supplied telecommunication domain specific design support, the latter was used to organise the various aspects of the intended T-MMCS, and its realisation with CORBA products.

Among other things, ODP suggests five viewpoints to be taken in the development of a system to manage the complexity of distributed applications.

The *enterprise viewpoint* considers the environmental constraints which the product has to fit for the benefit of its users. In aiming to identify service-independent constituents, use cases (inspired by Jacobson [12]) were developed, which are organized according to a session model suggested in the TINA-C Service Architecture. This session model distinguishes: *access sessions*, when accessing and using services which a customer has subscribed; *service sessions*, when a particular service is under user control, e.g. during invitation phases; and, finally, *communication sessions*, when the transfer of data through the resource infrastructure between the devices takes place.

---

4. For the T-MMCS the emphasis has not been on details of the TINA-C communication session, which involves connections management aspects and details to a much higher extend.

5. At time when this paper was delivered, performance evaluation or comparison were not yet been performed. Thus, any remark on this topic must be deferred to a later stage.

The use cases developed have been used for two purposes. First, to identify and describe the the second ODP viewpoint, the *information viewpoint*. Its purpose is to define the information which has to be processed. This definition is independent of its data representation. The information models have been described in OMT defining the information classes and their relationships.

Information processing is described by the third ODP viewpoint, the *computational viewpoint*. Problem domain specific solutions have been strongly influenced by the TINA-C Service Architecture. In particular, it was helpful regarding the different information classes and how to structure the software into discrete components. The computational model finally derived is illustrated in Section 4.

Up to this stage in the development process, the resulting computational model of the T-MMCS is basically independent of the distributed software technology which was used for the implementation. Basically, the components of this model have been specified by a superset of the OMG IDL, namely ODL, this enables the initial assignment of the supported and required interfaces to objects[6].

The RM-ODP suggests two further perspectives: the *engineering* and *technology viewpoint*. While the latter is concerned about real products and systems and their properties, the engineering viewpoint concentrates on the capabilities of and support for distributed systems in secondary applications like the T-MMCS.

The complexity of the T-MMCS, compared to other communication applications, is introduced by the stakeholder model, which is essential for telecommunication services. More complicated stakeholder models are currently under discussion to reflect the vision of the "service supermarket", where services as commercial products are bundled for retailing purposes. Regarding this discussion, the chosen stakeholder model is rather traditional. An example how the TINA service architecture has been applied to a project which realises an information supermarket, can be found in [8].

Regarding the T-MMCS design, three aspects are discussed here: The usage of information models to derive the component configuration, the means used in that computational model and the contents of its constituents, plus, finally, its properties regarding the subsequent engineering process.

Information model

A particular point in the design process is the common understanding of terminology, concepts and where they apply in the context of information processing in a larger system. An information model can assist here, since it enables the expression of classes of information and their relationships.

---

6. A conceptual difference becomes visible here: Whereas the OMG considers objects, these are considered as interfaces in ODP and TINA-C, and respectively in the TINA-C Object Definition Language (ODL).

However, the problem has been observed, that the transformation of information to the computational view is complex task. When the information model is mapped one-to-one as a pragmatic approach, inflexible solutions are established. For example, when an identified information object is taken directly as a computational object. Changes or extensions to the information model during the design process often are accompanied by changes in the computational objects which should not have been affected. The reason is that the computational object represents the information object explicitly, instead of being just responsible for maintaining data structures representing that information.

Computational model

This section discusses some issues on the means used to express the computational model of the T-MMCS. In addition, the constituents appearing in the T-MMCS design are described.

Operational and stream interfaces

Whereas in CORBA there is little difference between the concepts *object* and *interface*, they are clearly distinguished in ODP and TINA. Here an object may have more than one interface. The interfaces can be of different types. An object can have operational interfaces, which provide a set of operations to be used by other objects. This functionality is described in interface types. Secondly, an object can have stream interfaces across which it is able to produce or consume flows, representing continuous flows of data of which the actual data structures are of no interest, e.g. audio or video types of information. Moreover, for both categories of interfaces, an object may have more than one interface instance for each interface type.

Problem domain specific grouping of computational objects

The components that were discussed in Section 4 have been identified and structured according to the outlined environment for information processing. As discussed earlier, the DPE provides a distribution transparent environment which hides the heterogeneity of the involved technology and organisations.

This environment spans across the domains of end users, service provides and potential network operators. Their spheres of influence have to be appropriately reflected within this environment. This is the reason for the appearance of agents, such as for example, the UA or the SubAgt. The basic trade-off between autonomy and controls in the different domains is handled by capturing and maintaining the required and necessary information in constituents, like the user, in a domain which is not under his authority. Vice versa, the service providers, maintain for the purpose of control, the overall behaviour of the T-MMCS by means of the SSM. That allows each participant to have its local, heterogeneous capabilities involved in the services. The reason for the existence of the USM is to handle this.

5.2 Specification Work - using OMT and ODL

ODP viewpoint specific models have been outlined which were used during the development of the T-MMCS. This section discusses how these models was specified and reports some experiences using them.

The information model was specified in OMT. The reason for choosing this technique was, that a considerable amount of work on this has been done already in TINA-C. This enabled the work to be based upon available results for which refinements and extension were made. The OMT technique has not been used to its full extent, for example, operational models were not developed. Instead the computational model of the T-MMCS has been selected. This is the reason, why in the development of computational objects it has been quite difficult to follow the information flow through the involved components.

This activity resulted in an ODL specification of the T-MMCS. It describes for each component a set of interfaces plus a (non formal) description of the expected behaviour. The interfaces are organized in "initial", i.e. available upon instantiation, "supported" as functionality provided to other objects, and "required" expressing the assistance of other objects. These interfaces have been made according in CORBA IDL including exceptions. Included data type declarations have been organised in modules to handle naming and scoping problems. The modules have been structured accordingly to groups of computational objects – reflecting the TINA-C session concept – in access, subscription, end user system, service, and accounting parts. The entire specification is object based and does – at a computational level – not take advantage of inheritance or polymorphism. Quite naturally, one of the major problems has been to find and meaningful balance between the available TINA-C specifications and the required extensions.

5.3 Engineering Aspects

Tackling the transformation from computational to the engineering level requires one to resolve some issues regarding the interpretation of object having multiple interfaces. A second issue is the inclusion of software which already exists, avoiding re-developments.

Modelling objects with multiple interfaces

Objects in the T-MMCS design at the computational level have multiple interfaces. This is useful for distinguishing different kinds of access rights to the operations which objects can provide at their interfaces. On the other hand, it is necessary because the objects may be aggregated and the sets of operations are maintained at interfaces of configured object instances. To map this property of objects to CORBA it was decided to associate to each interface of an computational object to an engineering object plus a core object, which implements the semantics defined by the computational object. The purpose of the resulting interface engineering objects is to hand over invocations of operations to the core object. The core object, in turn, has to react to such invocations and any result is passed back again via the appropriate interface engineering object. The

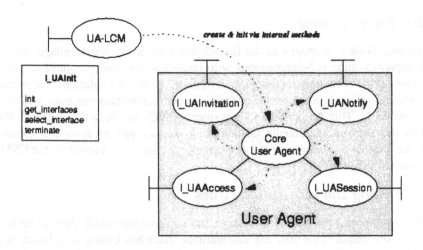

Figure 3: Life-cycle Manager of User Agent (UA-LCM), and created

structures defined at the computational level are thus maintained, while the implementation freedom for the programmer is not restricted, i.e. the implementation of the internal structure of the core object is not prescribed.

A consequence of this approach is that it is necessary to handle configurations of engineering objects (a set of interface objects plus a core object). Primarily, this is a life cycle issue, and computational object type specific life-cycle managers have been developed (Figure 3). Instances of these life cycle managers are specific to types of computational objects, and react on appropriate parameterization. Their purpose is to instantiate and initiate a set of interface objects plus their core object. The IDL specifications were helpful for the generation of appropriate code, which programmer used as skeletons for the extension of type specific requirements.

Configurations of computational objects

As described in the T-MMCS design, there are configurations of computational objects which have to be instantiated and configured during the operation of the applications, for example, USP, GSP and GSC. Configuration managers have been developed to handling these dynamic situations at the engineering level. Their purpose is to obtain a configuration of computational objects, which is appropriately instantiated and initiated. This is achieved by means of the life-cycle managers. In addition, the configuration manager registers itself at the CORBA naming service. As a result, when the need arises to find a particular CORBA interface reference, the naming service is accessed to derive the interface reference of the configuration manger, which knows about its life-cycle managers. In turn, life-cycle managers can resolve the request for the CORBA interface references of the interface objects that have been instantiated. This is how the TAN-GRAM project implemented a mechanism to achieve the ODP location transparency.

Including legacy systems

Although SmallTalk was chosen as the first choice implementation language, the T-MMCS implementation is heterogeneous with respect to the used programming languages. One reason is the required integration of existing software solutions. For example, an existing implementation for the audio/video communication was used, which is implemented in C. This Audio Video Component (AVC) has been developed in the context of the Berkom Multimedia Collaboration Service project activities. Consequently, the T-MMCS control over the AV communication, as achieved by the CSM, is implemented in SmallTalk/HP-DST [2].

5.4 Testing and Integration Issues

When the development reached its final stage, the implementors made their white box tests, which were required for their implementations. Black box testing was also carried out, based on the individual operations an computational object had to provide. It showed that the dependencies between the timing of operation invocation on object interfaces (what is the next "allowed" operation invocation that is expected to come now?) caused some problems. The reason was that behaviour descriptions in the IDL and ODL specifications were not sufficient, and thus the integration of the different parts was a quite difficult task. As an solution for this, Message Sequence Charts were used, indicating the flow of operation invocations between the various involved components. This aided the integration of components into the entire application of the T-MMCS. It was noticed, that this could be an useful approach, which should have been taken alos during the design phase of the T-MMCS.

6 Conclusion

Some experiences gained during the development of a distributed telecommunication application have been reported. The development and the resulting implementation cope with heterogeneity to a high degree in a number of areas including applied modelling techniques, programming languages and the actually implemented CORBA2 products.

Despite the fact that the participating developers had to adopt two technologies (SmallTalk and CORBA) which were entirely new to them, an implementation of the T-MMC service was achieved in a considerable short time. Some of the reasons for this were the availability of the TINA-C architecture which was used as a design aid, and the use of the ODP viewpoints to drive the T-MMCS development process, which is considered helpful for managing the complexity of the development task.

Improvements are possible in the components descriptions for this work. An object-oriented construction of objects supported by a description technique would be beneficial, plus specification of the behaviour visible at the interfaces as well as for entire computational objects. This could extend the reusability of designed computational objects, if mechanisms are available to specialise and extend components. On the other hand, behaviour descriptions could improve the understanding of IDL specifications and might even be used to devise component specific test cases. These test cases could then be applied to implementations. Meanwhile, a newer version of ODL provides some support for inheritance; however, the capability is not given to express objects or interface related behaviour.

Further work for the project will concentrate on issues related to the development of abstract object oriented frameworks. This will enable more rapid development of property variations for sets of computational objects. For this, a code generator using IDL specifications as input will provide assistance. So far, a generator was developed which produces code skeletons, and injects code into engineering objects, so that the support of the interpretation used for the ODP location transparency is enabled. Additionally, this generator prepares engineering objects of distributed applications for monitoring across heterogeneous platforms.

7 References

[1]   IONA Technologies, *The Orbix Architecture*, August 1993.

[2]   Hewlett-Packard, *HP Distributed Smalltalk 4.0, White Paper*, January 1995

[3]   TINA-C, *Overall Concepts and Principles of TINA*, TINA Baseline, TB_MDC.018_1.0_94, February 1995.

[4]   TINA-C, *Service Architecture*, TINA Baseline, TB_MDC.012_2.0_94, 31 Mar. 1995

[5]   OMG, The Common Object Request Broker 2.0: Architecture and Specification, July 1995

[6]   OMG, CORBA Services: Common Object Services Specification, March 31, 1995

[7]   H. Berndt, M. Chapman, P. Schoo, I. Tönnby, A Comparison of Architectures for Future Telecommunication Services, *3rd Int. Conf. on Intelligence in Broadband Services and Networks*, Heraklion, Crete, Greece, October 1995

[8]   M.J. Ellis, P.B. Farely, M.D. Chapman., Information Services Supermarket, Proceedings of *IFIP/IEEE Int. Conference on Distributed Platforms (ICDP)*, Dresden, Germany Feb. 1996

[9]   J.Dittrich, K.-P.Eckert, P.Schoo, Design of a Multimedia Collaboration Service for an Environment of Distributed Processing Platforms, Proc. of *International Workshop on Distributed Object Oriented Computing (DOOP'95)*, Oct. 95; see also http://www.fokus.gmd.de/ovma/Tangram/pub/entry.html

[10]   TINA-C, Management Architecture, TB_GN.010_2.0_94, Dec. 1994

[11]   ITU-T|ISO/IEC Recommendation X.901 | International Standard 10746-1, *Open Distributed Processing Reference Model: Overview*, January 1995.

[12]   Jacobson, I., *Object-Oriented Software Engineering – A Use Case Driven Approach*, Addison Wesley, 1993

[13]   ISO/IEC 9596-1 : 1991. *Information technology - Open Systems Interconnection - Common management information protocol specification*. International standard, 1991.

Exercise of TINA Concepts for a Video Broadcast Service over ATM Networks

Tania R. Tronco Fudoli[*]

CPqD - Telebrás/ UNICAMP

Km 118 Rodovia Campinas-Mogi-Mirim (SP-340)

CEP 13088-110 Campinas- SP - Brazil

E_Mail: tania@cpqd.br

Elie Najm

ENST - Telecom Paris

46, Rue Barrault

75013 - Paris- France

E_Mail: najm@res.enst.fr

Abstract

The Telecommunications Information Networking Architecture (TINA) is a software architecture that is currently under development by the TINA Consortium (TINA-C). This architecture will provide an environment for the construction, operation and management of a broad range of services, ranging from standard to new sophisticated types, like multimedia. TINA adopts the Open Distributed Processing (ODP) approach that is an emerging ISO/ITU-T standard. ODP provides a framework of abstractions based on multiple viewpoints to specify open distributed applications and systems. A viewpoint is a part of the specification of a complete system determined by a particular interest. TINA principles and concepts are specified using enterprise, information, computational and engineering ODP viewpoints. This paper considers the TINA computational and engineering viewpoints to specify a video broadcast service. In the TINA Computational Model, a Communication Session is specified and represented as a communication path (called binding object) between video server and the clients. In the TINA Engineering Model, the infrastructure that provides this communication is revelead. Finaly, TINA computational and the engineering specifications are mapped onto an ATM based technology. ATM offers important characteristics required by multimedia applications such as variable bit rate, QoS guarantees, effectiveness of the transport and adaptation functions for the transport of all types of services in a single network. In this technology mapping, ATM call and connection control operations are considered and related to TINA architecture.

1 Introduction

The new emerging distributed multimedia applications based on broadband communications have influenced the development of a plethora of system architecture that provide similar solutions. Distributed object-based architectures are now emerging as the most pertinent basis for supporting distributing, heterogeneous computing and telecommunications systems. The Telecommunication Information Networking Architecture Consortium (TINA-C) is defining a distributed object-based framework that will provide an unified architecture for the specification of a broad range of services. TINA-C is using the ISO/ITU-T Reference Model of Open Distributed Processing (ODP) [11, 12, 13] to specify this environment. ODP

---

[*] This research is supported by CNPq and CPqD - Telebrás

provides a framework for distributed systems and applications development in a heterogeneous environment. An ODP specification consists of multiple descriptions, with different abstractions levels, where by each abstraction focuses on a different aspect of the global system. Five viewpoints have been defined within ODP: enterprise, information, computational, engineering and technology. The enterprise viewpoint defines the purpose, scope, and policies for the system while the information viewpoint focuses on the semantics of information and information processing activities in the system. The computational viewpoint focuses on the functional decomposition of the system into objects which are candidates for distribution. The infrastructure (collection of computer systems and networks) that provides the distributed processing environment is revelead in the engineering viewpoint; and finally, the technology viewpoint focuses on the technology solutions applied to implement the system. TINA conceptual framework is specified at four of five ODP viewpoints: enterprise, information, computational and engineering viewpoints and is independent of underlying technologies [4]. ATM is only used as model for defining generic capabilities of the transmission network.

The present paper focuses on TINA Connection Management Architecture (CMA) computational and engineering viewpoints to specify a video broadcast service. TINA CMA realizes functions like setting up, maintaining and releasing connections and includes a Communication Session Manager (CSM) function [4, 14]. In the computational viewpoint, the CSM is specified by means of a binding object which provides the communication path between the video server and the clients. It also offers guarantees of Quality of Service (QoS). In the engineering viewpoint, the basic structure to support the CSM computational model is showed and in the technology viewpoint an ATM network infrastructure is defined to support these specifications.

The paper is structured as follows: section 2 is devoted to explain the video application together with the concepts and principles of TINA Connection Management Architecture; section 3 and section 4 consider, respectively, the CSM computational and engineering models; section 5 is devoted to the use of the ATM technology to implement the system and section 6 concludes the paper with some remarks about the TINA and ATM architecture and future work.

2 The Video Application in the TINA Environment

The video application that we consider consists of a source that emits two synchronised flows, an audio and a video flow. The source broadcasts the two flows to a dynamically changing set of clients across the ATM network. The transfer of audio/video flow requires high bit rate point-to-multipoint connections between the server and the clients. This configuration should optimize the network resources and permits clients to join a video session in progress.

The number of clients can change during the session. This is due to the fact that the application provides control operations and makes possible, at any time, a client request to join or to leave the audio, the video or both streams. Supplementary low bit rate connections between each client and the server are necessary to implement this function.

The video stream is displayed at 25 frames per second (PAL) and the sound is sampled at 8000 samples/s (telephone quality).

The video broadcast should be as natural as possible for the clients. This implies that the QoS requirements, like intra and inter synchronisation of flows need to be taken into account in the specification. The inter synchronization of flows is known as lip synchronisation. The lip synchronisation is considered acceptable if the sound is not too far (back or ahead) from the corresponding lip movement. The actual figures are +/-80ms [16]. A jitter of +/-100 samples and a delay of +/- 500 samples is considerate whithin the acceptable range for the sound while the video allows a jitter of +/-1 frame and a delay of +/-3 frames [1].

To fulfil these requirements, the video broadcast specification will be given, consistently, in the ODP computational, engineering and technology viewpoints of the TINA Connection Management Architecture. According to the concepts and principles of the TINA [3,4], the service specification environment consists of a *Service Architecture (SA)* and a *Connection Management Architecture* (CMA) as depicted in Figure 1. In this Figure, different flows (that we called F1, ... , F6) between the participating objects have been identified.

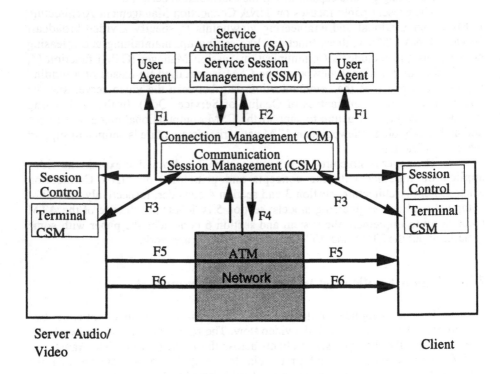

Fig. 1. Video Broadcast in the TINA Architecture

The Service Architecture defines object types and interfaces that are used to build services. The SA includes a Service Session Manager (SSM) that supports the initiation, interaction and termination of services [3]. It relates service users together by providing a group-oriented view, so that they can interact with each other and share entities. A service session is active only during the service activation phase and deleted when the user leaves the session. A user can be simultaneously involved in multiple service sessions, and a service session has one or more users associated with it such that for each associated user there will be a related user session. A service session manager offers operational interfaces and service specific operations that allows users to join and leave a service.

The Connection Management Architecture is responsible for setting up, maintaining and releasing connections and includes a Communication Session Manager (CSM). A Communication Session is a service-oriented abstraction of connections in the transport network. It maintains the connections state of a particular service session, such as the communication paths, end-points and quality of service characteristics [3, 4]. Moreover, it provides a connection graph interface for the service session to manipulate. The Communication Session Manager calls upon connection management objects to establish physical connections between the network access points.

Considering this architecture, the sequence of the procedures for the video service establishment are briefly described as follows:

1. the client sends a service request to the user agent to establish a video broadcast service session. After authentication and authorization from the service provider, the client can specify the Quality of Service (QoS) parameters and an audio and/or a video signals (F1 flow). The user agent creates a video service session manager and joins the user to the session, causing a user session to be created. Afterwards, the user must identify the called user's agent, and a request is passed over to this user agent. The destination user accepts the call and the acceptance is fed back to the service session. The SSM supports the negotiation capabilities among the users and serves as a control center of consensus basis. A QoS negotiation process between end-users can take place before the video connection establishment. After the QoS negotiation, the SSM asks for the CM (via F2 flow) to establish a communication session that connects the parties (two in the example).

2. the SSM sends to the CM the QoS parameters and the traffic characteristics required for this communication. These parameters will define the type of the connection that should be set by the CM.

3. the CM, via the Communication Session Management (CSM), will originate the instantiation of a computational binding between the server and the client and will split the request, via F4 flow, to an ATM network connection establishment (F5 and F6 flows). The F3 flow provides an interface between CSM and the Terminal CSM (TCSM) that are responsible for the connection set up inside the nodes. The establishment of an ATM network connection can be controlled by an external function placed in the CM. This function is called "third party model" in opposite to "first party model" where a user directly demands a connection to the network. The network connection setup is thus independent, controlled by TINA CM. Other users can join at later stages, and additional network connections are set up [4]. In short, there are six types of information flows for the video service establishment:

- the F1 session control flow that transports the messages related to access, authentication, authorization, service selection and service invitation; it uses a user-to-network protocol over a low bit rate bi-directional channel.

- the F2 flow for the messages exchanging between the SSM and the CSM; this procedure will result in a communication session set up.

- the F3 flow that provides the interface between TCSM and CSM; it uses a user-to- network protocol over a low bi-directional channel.

- the F4 flow for the network connections establishment via an external function placed in the CM (third party model);

- the F5 Audio flow and the F6 Video flow that transport the audio and the video streams to the clients.

In the sections that follow, this model will be detailed in the computational, the engineering and the technology viewpoints.

3 Video Broadcast in the Computational Viewpoint

The computational viewpoint treats the specification and the execution of the distributed application on the distributed computing platform [5]. At this level, the specification of a distributed application minimizes the details of underlying distributed execution platform. In the computational model, an application is composed of a dynamic configuration of objects (distributed object model) that interact with each other at well-defined interfaces. *Operations* realized at these interfaces can modify the state of the object. A computational interface is characterised by a signature, a behaviour and a specific environment contract [5]. Interfaces may be dynamically created or deleted. There are three types of interfaces: signal, operational and stream interface. A signal interface has a signature that defines an unambiguous name, a set of signals and, for each signal, whether the interface have the role of source or sink [11]. Signals are the most primitive description of interactions between computational objects. Operational and stream interfaces can be described as a compound or special types of signal interfaces. An operational interface consists of a set of operations (operation name, type of arguments and results that may be exchanged in each operation), a behaviour specification (ordering of invocations at or from this interface) and a role indication (client or server). A stream interface is a set of flows supported at this interface where each flow determines whether the interface has the role of producer (sender) or consumer (receiver) [11]. Stream interfaces are described as continuous sequence of symbols. Examples include the flow of audio or video information.   Interactions between given computational interfaces are only possible if a binding (i.e. some communication path) has been established between them [11]. In the computational model, binding actions are described either explicitly or implicitly. Explicit binding actions can be issued at operational and stream interfaces while implicit binding actions are only issued for operational interfaces. This is because these interfaces contain information about the ordering of invocations and responses. Explicit bindings have a reference for an environment contract where QoS requirements can be described and defined in terms of *primitive binding actions* or *compound binding actions*. Primitive binding actions permit the binding of only two interfaces of the same or of different objects (of the same type). On the other hand, compound binding actions permit the binding of two or more interfaces (of the same or of different types) by means of a *binding object*. The binding object (i) allocates a set of interfaces that will be bound, (ii) allocates a set of control interfaces, through which its operations can be controlled and (iii) returns the interface identifiers to the initiating object [11]. Hence, in the computational model there are two kinds of objects: basic objects and binding objects.

To deal with the complexity of a video broadcast, a binding object will be used as a basis for the computational specification. The binding object is an important concept to model continuous data flows in distributed systems. When binding objects are specified, it is possible to define QoS (Quality of Service) requirements (such as order, timeliness, throughput, etc.) on the transport of interactions supported by the binding object. This object manages both, the stream interfaces which are used for the audio/video interactions and control operations that can be performed on the binding object. In the TINA Architecture, the CSM has been identified as the object that provides all these capabilities; so, the CSM will be used as the control part of the binding object for the video broadcast computational specification. Figure 2 represents the CSM and its environment from the computational viewpoint.

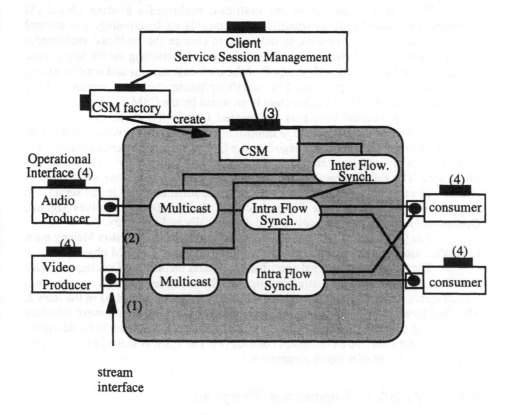

Fig. 2. CSM Computational Model

In this Figure, the stream interfaces (1and 2) are used by the producers and consumers to exchange audio and/or video. Stream interfaces represent an abstraction of audio/video devices. The binding of stream interfaces is an abstraction of a connection. The topology selected for the group communication consists of one sender (audio or video producer) and several receivers, named 1 -> N, where N is the number of clients. Such (1->N) simplex connections are called multicast streams.

Then, there are two multicast stream interfaces that only emit signals (audio or video) and 2N stream interfaces that can only receive signals (audio and/or video). This videobroadcast communication is made up of two media each of which will be transferred on a multicast stream with adequate performance. Unambiguous identifiers for each multicast stream interface, named interface references, must be available in order to allow potential receivers to recognize a multicast stream that has already been established. A client can specify the references of the required interfaces to be interconnected and the characteristics of the connections. At this level, the communication resources required by the clients are represented in terms of the Logical Connection Graph (LCG) because the physical connection is invisible for the client. The CSM provides the mapping from the Logical Connection Graph to the Physical Connection Graph. The mapping of logical addresses to physical addresses is done with collaboration between the CSM and the TCSM (Figure 2).

The control interface of the multicast multimedia binding object (3) provides operations to the environment that controls its functioning. The control interfaces will be used to create, to delete or to change the multicast multimedia binding, Moreover, this control interface notifies errors disrupting the binding in case of engineering failures, controls the QoS of the multicast streams and notifies events of relevance to the application like start/stop/pause multicast stream. These functionalities in the TINA Architecture is provided by the CSM.

The operational interfaces (4) created for the the client to manage the connection, will be used to exchange information between the server and the client. Via this interface, the clients can negotiate the QoS in the binding establishment and join or leave a multicast stream in an established binding by specifying its identifiers. The establishment of the multimedia binding with one server and N clients will result in the establishment of one operational interface in the server and N operational interfaces, one for each client, that emits and receives signals. Operational interfaces are normally bound dynamically and implicitly.

The CSM factory will serve requests from the Service Session Management to create a multicast stream binding, impliying the creation of a CSM object.

The CSM computational specification should include the QoS requirements between the two multicast streams (lip synchronisation) as well as the QoS requirements for each flow (throughput, jitter and delay) as described in the item 2. The QoS parameters of lip synchronization should be described at control interface environment contract while the QoS requirements for each flow should be described at each stream interface environment contract [8]. The CSM is able to map this QoS description in terms of network parameters.

4 Video Broadcast Engineering Viewpoint

The engineering model is still an abstraction of the distributed system, but focuses on the infrastructure required to support distribution [6]. Th e set of basic services and mechanisms, identified in the engineering model, are modelled as a collection of interacting objects which together provide support for the realization of the computational model. The infrastructure which enable, regulate and hide distribution in the ODP distributed platform, are modelled as objects, called *engineering objects*, which may support multiple interfaces. There are different types of engineering objects, some of them correspond to the application functionality and are called *basic engineering objects (BEOs)* while those which provide distribution functions are classified as protocol objects, or support objects, etc. Several basic engineering objects may be grouped into *clusters* and a host may support multiple clusters in its addressing domain, know as *capsule*. A capsule is the unit of allocation and encapsulation of clusters and includes basic engineering objects, transparency objects, protocol objects and other local operating system facilities [6].

The ODP infrastructure consists of interconnected autonomous computer systems (hosts), which are called *nodes*. Each node supports a nucleus object and multiple capsules. The nucleus co-ordinates processing, storage, and communications resources of the corresponding node. The communication within this infrastructure are realized through the *channel* in the engineering model. The channel is a configuration of *stub, binder, protocol and interceptor* objects which provide distribution support. The *stub* provides adaptations functions to support interactions between basic engineering object interfaces in different nodes; the *binder* object maintains binding between interacting basic engineering objects and the *protocol* object assures that engineering objects can interact remotely with each other in different clusters. When protocol objects are in different domains they interact via an interceptor object, which performs transformation functions such as protocol conversion or enabling interactions.

The video broadcast computational specification of Figure 2 will be represented as a collection of basic engineering objects and channels, i.e., stub, binder and protocols objects in the engineering viewpoint, as showed in Figure 3.

This Figure depicts the channels used by the transport of audio and video flows. This type of channel is named *stream channel* in opposite to *operational channels* that are used to transport control operations such as clients requests, QoS negotiation, etc. For the stream channel, the stub provides the mechanisms to encode and decode video/audio information, controlling operations to local resources (e.g. increase buffer-size) and notification of events concerning the stream (e.g. QoS changes, no buffer space available, etc.). A stub has a control interface for QoS management. The binder objects maintain the integrity of the binding and are also responsible for validating the interface reference and for interacting with the relocates object to recover information about the interface location after a binding error. For streams, information is maintained with respect to the required QoS. A binder has a control interface which enables changes in the configuration of the channel and destruction of all, or part, of the channel [7]. There is only one binder in each channel end which then is capable of controlling several pairs of stub/protocol. For the multicast multimedia binding object, a specialized protocol, called stream protocol is necessary. Continuous flows require relationships between calls and a stream protocol is applied which creates a virtual channel between two protocol objects for the duration of audio/video flow exchange. The CSM engineering object implements the control interface of the binding object and the TCSM manages the connections insides a node. For the video broadcast service, a point-to-multipoint stream channel will be established.

A new client can request to participate in an already established binding. The client issues an add request specifying the interfaces references of the binding. If the request is successful, the server will add the receiver to the streams channel. If the request fails, the reason for the failure will be transmitted to interface of the client.

At any time a client can request to join or to leave the video and/or audio streams by providing the reference of one (or two) receiving interface(s).

In the TINA architecture, operational channel will also be created for the controlling operations exchange; these channels will be maintained during the lifetime of the binding. For the operational channel, the stub provides marshalling/unmarshalling of operation parameters to enable access transparent interactions [7]; the operational protocol is necessary to the operations exchange and QoS negotiation, the service requirements have to be distributed to all involved and intermediate nodes. At engineering specification the QoS parameters are expressed in terms of Mbit/s for the throughput and ms for jitter and delay. The CSM contains a QoS adapter to perform the QoS mapping between the QoS computational specification and QoS engineering specification.

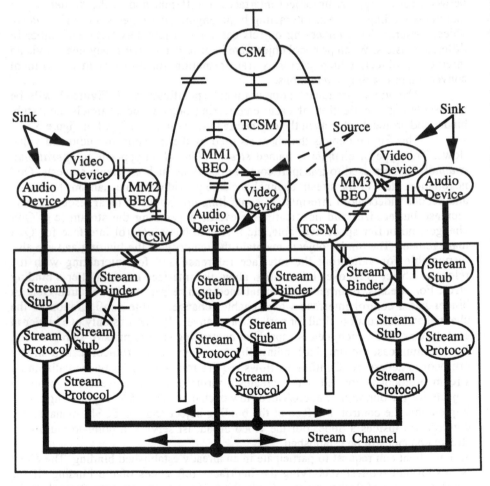

MM: MultiMedia

Fig. 3. Video broadcast Engineering Viewpoint

5 Video Broadcast Technology Viewpoint

The technology specification focuses on the choice of technology to support the abstract models described in the previous sections. ATM (Asynchronous Transfer Mode) technology was selected to support the multicast stream and operational channels of ODP standard. In the following, many steps of the binding establishment phase are related to the ATM call control and management. We will first provide a quick description of those parts of ATM that are of interest to our example. We then give the mapping of ATM concepts to the technology viewpoint.

ATM call and connection control operations makes possible to set up connections on demand between users and the ATM network. This procedure is also know as a switched virtual call (SVC) in older terminology [2]. The ATM User-Network Interface (UNI) signalling [1] supports SVCs. It specifies the procedures for dynamically establishing, maintaining and clearing ATM connections at the User-Network Interface of the Control Plane of the B-ISDN Reference Model [2]. ATM UNI contains the Q.2931 signalling protocol, which is used to set up connections in the ATM network, and supports both point-to-point single connection and point-to-multipoint connections. A point-to-point connection establishment procedure begins by a user issuing the SETUP message as showed in Figure 4. This message is sent by the calling user to the network and is relayed by the network to the called user. This message contains several information fields to identify the message, specify various AAL (ATM Adaptation Layer) parameters, calling and called party addresses, requirements for QoS, etc. After reception of the SETUP message, the network returns a CALL PROCEEDING message to the initiating user, forwards the SETUP message to the called user, and waits for the called user to return a CALL PROCEEDING message. The called user, if its accepts a call, will then send to the network a CONNECT message. This connect message will then be forwarded to the calling user. As soon as the CONNECT messages arrives, the calling user and the networks return the CONNECT ACKNOWLEDGE to their respective parties [2].

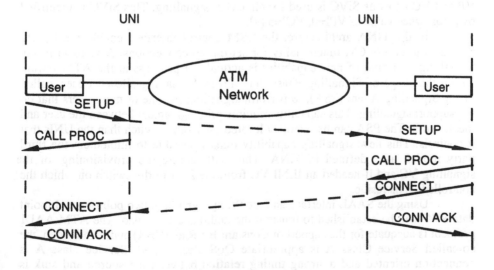

Fig. 4. Connection Set-up

The calling and called party addresses specified in the signalling messages are obtained by an address registration procedure. The ATM UNI Interim Local Management Interface (ILMI) [1] provides a procedure for the user and the network to register the ATM addresses. For the ILMI function, the access method is an open management protocol called SNMP (Simple Network Management Protocol)/AAL over a preallocated VPI(Virtual Path Identifier)/VCI(Virtual Channel Identifier) values (VPI=0, VCI=16). The ATM AAL5 protocol is appropriate to support this interface.

A point-to-multipoint connection is defined as a collection of associated VC (Virtual Channel) and VP (Virtual Path) links that are associated with endpoint nodes. One ATM link is designated as the root link, which serves as the root in a tree topology. When the root receives information, it sends copies of this information to all leaf nodes on the tree. Communications must occur between the leaf nodes through the root node. A multipoint connection is set up by first establishing a point-to-point connection between the root node and one leaf node. After this set-up is complete, additional leaf nodes can be added to the connection by "add party" requests from the root node. The "add party" message can only be used on an active connection [9].

Signalling messages that the user and other network elements generate must be reliably transported between end users. The signalling ATM Adaptation Layer (SAAL) protocol and procedures define how to transfer the signalling information for call and connection control within the cells of the ATM layer on VCs used for signalling. The SAAL resides in the ATM control plane and it is composed of a Common part, which represents the functionality common to all users and a Service specific Part, which identifies the protocol and procedures associated with the signalling needs at the UNI. The SAAL provides reliable delivery of signalling messages. The Service-Specific Part is further subdivided into the SSCF and the SSCOP; SSCOP provides the recovery of lost or corrupted SDUs(Service Data Units); SSCF maps the service of SSCOP to the needs of the SSCF user; it provides the interface to the next layer, in this case, the Q.2931 signalling protocol. Figure 5 depicts the SAAL protocol stack. At ATM layer, a default bi-directional associated VP and VC know as SiVC is used for all access signalling. This SiVC is identified by preassigned value of VPI=0, VCI=5 [9].

In the TINA architecture, the CSM control interface enable third party providers to access CM functionality for setting up connections. A work in Proxy Signalling as a kind of new capability is actually in progress at the ATM Forum within the scope of Signalling Phase 2[1]. Proxy Signalling allows a user, called Proxy Signalling Agent (PSA), to perform signalling for one or more users that do not support signalling. This capability requires prior agreement between the user and the network. The PSA can be remotely located on another switch than the UNIs that it controls. This new signalling capability makes possible to implement the third party model, as a defined in TINA. This will require the provisioning of the signalling VC and if needed an ILMI VC from the PSA to the switch on which the controlled UNIs reside.

Using the SAAL interface and the Proxy signalling, two point-to-multipoint data SVC will be established to transmit the audio and the video. The ATM AAL1 protocol is adequate for the support of Constant Bit-Rate (CBR) audio and video, the so-called Service Class A is appropriate QoS class [6, 8]. Service class A is connection oriented and a strong timing relation between the source and sink is required but where the bit rate is constant. QoS parameters in this class consist of cell transfer delay, cell delay variation and cell loss ratio. A QoS adapter is required for the QoS mapping from the engineering to the technology viewpoint. The disavantages of CBR transmission for burst traffic such as video is that it is either inefficient or introduces considerable delay. Studies about renegotiation of the bandwidth are actually under development [15] for the video transmission over ATM.

As a part of these new signalling capabilities in study at ATM Forum, an extending call model and a protocol architecture to support more sophisticated services is actually at development. It will be based on a separation of the call and connection concepts, which, in Phase I signalling have an one-to-one relationship [9]. In these new concepts, a call is defined as an association of one or more parties using one or more telecommunications services to communicate through the network [9]. This new concept of the call is near to the already defined concept of the TINA Communication Session. Moreover, the notion of service session in TINA is an extension of the call concept [4]; the TINA service provider controls all the calls related to a given service.

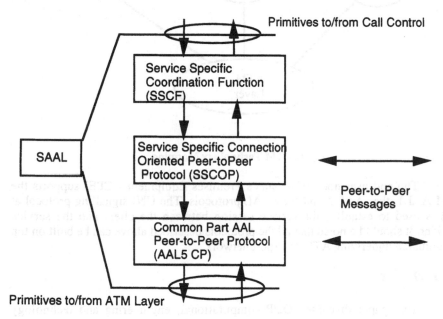

Fig. 5. SAAL Protocol Stack

The establishment of the service session management between the client and the service provider as described in the section 2 can be effected by the Remote Procedure Calls (RPC) over TCP/IP. RPC is a logical client-to-server communications system that specifically support applications that are distributed. The user-to-network signalling protocol DSM-CC (Digital Storage Media - Call Control) can be used on top of the RPC. The management protocol may be implemented, for example, using SNMP/UDP/IP over AAL5 [1]. Figure 6 depicts the resulting mapping of ATM technology in the engineering viewpoint showing the operational, the signalling, the management and the stream interfaces.

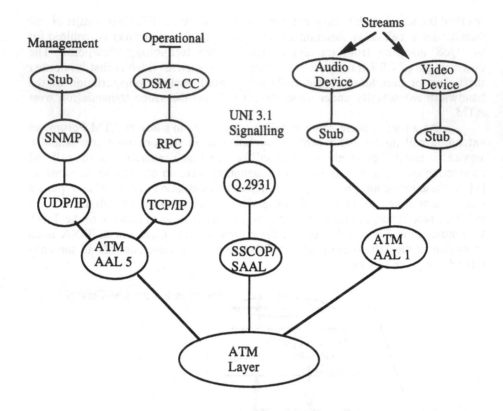

Fig. 6. ATM Technology Mapping

The end user node (Customer's Premises Equipment - CPE) supports the ATM AAL1, the AAL 5 and the SAAL protocols. The UNI signalling protocol at CPE is used to establish the service session between the client and the service provider. It should be noted that all the protocols described above can be built on top of a common underlying ATM transport network.

6 Conclusion

This paper discussed ODP computational, engineering and technology issues to specify a video application in a distributed environment. The TINA architecture was used as a basis for the specification. The technology viewpoint was used to evaluate the adaptability of the ATM protocols to implement the TINA concepts. TINA framework is independent of the underlying transport network. The ATM network showed to be adequate and advantageous to support this model; all the protocols defined in the TINA architecture to support the videobroadcast service can be built using the ATM network as transport. Further research is needed to complete this initial attempt and to include other types of applications. The advantages of the TINA approach is that it presents a single complete and consistent platform to provide a broad range of the services, which is enormous simplification for customers and telecommunications operators.

7 References

[1] ATM Forum: User-Network Interface (UNI) Specification, Version 4.0, February 1996.

[2] Blach, U. - "ATM Foundation for Broad band Networks" - Prentice Hall series in Advanced Communications Technologies, 1995.

[3] Chapman, M., Berndt, H. and Gatti, N. - "Software architecture for the future information market" - Computer Communication, vol. 18, November 1995.

[4] Demounem, L. - "Intelligent Networks and TINA Service Models - Present and Future" - Proceedings of the Sixth IFIP/ICC Conference on Information Network and Data Communication, 1996. Throndheim, Norway.

[5] Farooqui, K., Logrippo, L. - "Introduction to ODP Computational Model" - TR-94-17, August 1994, Department of Computer Science, University of Ottawa, Canada.

[6] Farrooqui, K., Logrippo, L. - "Introduction to ODP Engineering Model". Department of Computer Science, University of Ottawa, Canada.

[7] Gay, V. Leydekkers, P. and Huis, R.V. - "Specification of multiparty audio and video interaction based on the Reference Model of Open Distributed Processing", Computer Networks and ISDN Systems - Special issue on ODP, Volume 27 - Number 8, pp. 1247-1262, July 1995.

[8] Leydekkers, P., Gay, V. - "ODP View on Quality of Service for OpenDistributed Multimedia Environments" - Proceedings of the 4.International IFIP Workshop on Quality of Service - IWQoS96 - Paris, March 6-8, 1996.

[9] Minoli, D., Dobrowski, G. "Principles of Signalling for Cell Relay and Frame Relay" - Artech House, 1995.

[10] Najm, Elie, Février, A., Leduc, G. - "Compositional Specification of ODP Binding Objects" - Proceedings of the Sixth IFIP/ICCC Conference on Information Network and Data Communication, 1996. Throndheim, Norway.

[11] Reference Model of Open Distributed Processing, Overview, ITU-T X.901, 1995.

[12] Reference Model of Open Distributed Processing, Foundations, ITU-T X.902, 1995.

[13] Reference Model of Open Distributed Processing, Architecture, ITU-T X.903, 1995.

[14] Stefani, J. - "Open Distributed Processing: an architectural basis for information networks" - Computer Communications, volume 18, number 11, November 1995.

[15] S. El-Henaoui, R. Coelho, S. Tohme - "A Bandwidth Allocation Protocol for MPEG Works" - IEEE Infocom'96.

[16] Steinmetz, R., Engler, C. - "Human Perception of Media Synchronization" - IBM Technical Reporter 43.9310.

CORBA-Based Data Transfer for Financial Risk Management

M. Leclerc[1], C. Linnhoff-Popien[2], S. Lipperts[2], T. Müssener[1], H. Wegmann[2]

Abstract

Financial instruments are becoming more and more complex in order to meet the needs of end-users. This development has led to a corresponding maturation of computer systems. Distributed object products provide solutions that satisfy requirements such as data integration and interoperability. However, Distributed Platforms do not provide container objects or other means of data transfer.

This paper discusses the options of transferring data in a distributed system based on the Common Object Request Broker Architecture (CORBA). The CORBA implementation Orbix has been chosen for the financial environment of Dresdner Bank Middle Office. In order to transfer data within a financial risk management system, three aspects are considered: synchronous and asynchronous transfer; sequential transfer and multiplexing; polling and caching. A monitor for evaluating the performance of data transfer is presented. Moreover, first studies concerning data transfer using the synchronous polling and caching mechanisms are given. Finally, criteria are derived, which combinations are preferable depending on given conditions.

Keywords

CORBA, Orbix, synchronous/asynchronous communication, multiplexing, monitoring

1   Introduction

The financial industry today is characterised by rapid innovation and increasing globalization. It is common practice that whenever a task has to be dealt with, an appropriate instrument is developed or purchased and added to the computing environment. Often, however, little or no attention is paid to the interoperability of these products. As a result, functionality already provided by one component cannot be accessed by other components, thus forcing system developers to reinvent the wheel or purchase multiple applications with identical functionality [SUN96].

Several problems have to be solved when trying to avoid this development by establishing communication in such a heterogeneous environment. The Object Management Architecture (OMA), a concept published by the Object Management Group (OMG), specifies an architecture for a distributed object system, with the architecture of the Object Request Broker (ORB) being the central part. It has been further detailed with the Common Object Request Broker Architecture (CORBA) [OMG95]. Its goal is to specify a software architecture which offers interoperability of applications, independent of programming languages, operating systems and hardware

---

[1] Dresdner Bank Frankfurt, Department Treasury/Eigenhandel
[2] Aachen University of Technology, Department of Computer Science

components. Moreover, the integration of legacy applications into distributed systems with little or no modification is intended.

Having realised the nature of the problem in their own domain, Dresdner Bank has decided to evaluate the advantages of a CORBA based distributed system.

In this paper, special emphasis will be laid on the transfer of data in a distributed system. In the second chapter, the requirements of the distributed system in the financial environment are considered. In the third chapter, the main CORBA implementations are examined with regard to these requirements. The fourth chapter discusses strategies for transferring data. In the fifth chapter, tools for monitoring performance are presented as well as first results of tests concerning synchronous polling and caching. The final chapter summarises the results and gives an outlook on future activities.

2 Dresdner Bank Requirements

The problem of transferring data is relevant for most non-trivial distributed systems. For a distributed system within a financial environment in particular, data transfer is paramount. Data always has to be accurate and up to date to ensure reliable and precise calculations. In financial risk management, where numerous unpredictable or unknown factors influence the estimations, data needs to be replicated and updated, thus leading to a quest for efficient data transfer [Mul96]. A simple scenario where data needs to be transferred is described in Fig. 1.

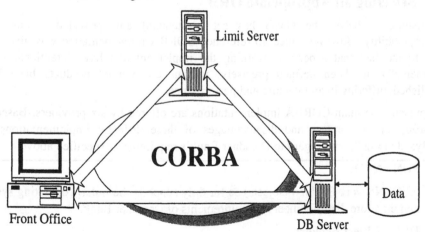

Fig. 1. Scenario of data transfer in a financial system

For a limit server to be able to calculate a limit which is requested by a front office, it has to access all relevant data managed by a database server. A front office might request the remaining limit of a particular counterparty as well as the limits of all counterparties currently known to the distributed system. Moreover, a front office might request data from the database server immediately. Therefore large amounts of differing data need to be transferred even in this excerpt of the system, neglecting requests form other system components.

As the project is embedded in a financial environment, there are specific characteristics that influence the nature of the system components. With regard to the distributed platform to be provided, the following requirements should be met:

- The various platforms and corresponding software components given within Dresdner Bank's environment should all be supported (KONDOR+ and OPTAS on Sun, STARS++ on HP, EXCEL and REPO on PC). This includes the integration of Microsoft OLE.
- The ORB (Object Request Broker) should provide a C++ language mapping, because this is the language predominantly used in the projects concerned.
- There should be indications for stable and reliable functionality of the CORBA implementation to avoid tedious and time consuming search for previously undetected errors.
- The number of clients used should be scalable.
- The distributed platform should enable high performance.
- The CORBA 2.0 Internet Inter-ORB Protocol (IIOP) should be supported. This is mandatory for CORBA 2.0 implementations [HoTo96], in order to provide interoperability between ORBs and ensure flexibility by enabling future employment of the most adequate ORBs.

However, the results are not proprietary to the specific domain and can be transferred to a far more general scale.

3   Selecting an Appropriate ORB

Publishing CORBA, the OMG has set a standard and provided a basis for interoperability. However, since no reference CORBA implementation was given and due to the fact that aspects concerning the implementation have intentionally and accidentally not been defined precisely, various commercial products have been published, differing in architecture and performance.

At present, the main CORBA implementations are offered by six providers. Based on [Hor96], the advantages and disadvantages of these different implementations are analysed in Fig 2, with regard to Dresdner Bank's requirements specified above.

- **SUN - NEO:**

  NEO (Network Enabled Objects) so far only supports the Solaris operating system and therefore does not meet the requirements of Dresdner Bank.

- **DEC - Object Broker:**

  Rather than being entirely based on the CORBA concept, the Object Broker is an extension of former DEC services. Therefore important aspects of CORBA, e.g. the object-orientation, have hardly been taken into consideration.

- **IBM - DSOM:**

  Similar to the DEC Object Broker, the Distributed System Object Model (DSOM) originally has not been conceptualised as a CORBA implementation. As a consequence, the aspects of distribution are not central. Moreover, the development using DSOM is more inconvenient than development with other products.

- **PMC - ORBeline:**

  ORBeline is a complete implementation of the CORBA 1.2 specification. So far, it does not support the CORBA 2.0 interoperability protocol. In addition, it does neither provide control of right to access nor security mechanisms.

- **HP - DST and ORB+:**

  At present, there are no real alternatives for DST (Distributed Smalltalk), if distributed Smalltalk applications are involved. DST supports all platforms that provide VisualWorks, follows the IIOP and provides the naming, events, lifecycle, relationship, concurrency and transaction service. However, the corresponding product HP ORB+ which provides a C++ language mapping has been released only recently and has not been used and tested in complex systems yet.

- **IONA - Orbix:**

  Orbix has first been developed in 1993 as a pure CORBA implementation. With most UNIX derivatives, Windows 3.1, Windows NT, OS/2 and other operating systems, all major platforms are supported. So far, none of the CORBAservices implementations have reached more than β-stadium. However, Orbix has been used in industrial applications, running more than 2000 clients stable. Especially in projects of Swiss banks, multi-threads have enabled high performance by providing quasi-parallel programming. Microsoft OLE has been integrated and the CORBA 2.0 IIOP is supported by Orbix 2.0.

Fig. 2. Discussion of existing CORBA implementations

As a conclusion it can be stated, that at the CORBA-implementations' current state of development, IONA-Orbix suits the requirements of Dresdner Bank best. It has therefore been chosen as basis for the financial risk management environment. It is emphasised though that in different systems other CORBA implementations might be more appropriate. Nonetheless, the general results drawn from the experiences with Orbix will also apply for other products.

4 Data Transfer with Orbix

We have derived three main aspects to classify the process of transferring data. These three aspects are orthogonal, i.e. they can be combined independently, thus giving $2^3 = 8$ possible combinations, see Fig. 3.

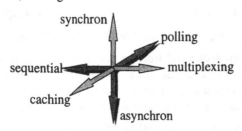

Fig. 3. Three aspects of transferring data

In Fig. 4, synchronous and asynchronous transfer are compared. After sending a data package by synchronous transfer, the sending party has to wait for the data to be processed and the result to be returned. This causes an idle time that depends on the duration of the transfer and the processing of the data.

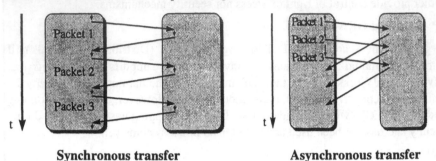

Synchronous transfer   **Asynchronous transfer**

Fig. 4. Synchronous vs. asynchronous data transfer

In order to avoid this idle time, one might consider using requests that do not wait for an answer to be returned. One way of implementing this is provided by OMG's Interface Definition Language (IDL) oneway operations. However, such an approach can only be used to implement an asynchronous transfer in one direction, i.e. if no result is returned. Otherwise, the result has to be requested and a deferred synchronous transfer is established. In that case the client might still have to wait for a response when requesting the result.

Asynchronous requests are not defined in CORBA 2.0. Yet an asynchronous transfer as shown in Fig. 4 can be simulated with the Event Service, one of the CORBAservices. In this approach, clients are notified if the response to a request is given. Thus the idle time is avoided by asynchronously sending all data packages first and receiving the processed data when being notified.

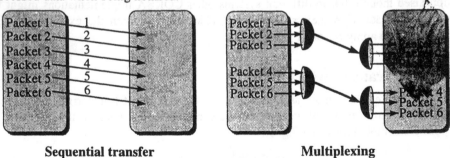

Sequential transfer   **Multiplexing**

Fig. 5. Sequential transfer vs. multiplexing

The difference between sequential transfer and multiplexing is considered in Fig. 5. Data packages are sent in sequential order. The efficiency of transferring data depends on the duration of moving a single package, since the time of an entire data transfer is the sum of the times for transferring the individual data packages.

Multiplexing requires parallel execution of requests. Several data packages are transferred at the same time. Therefore a shorter sequence of transfers is necessary to move an amount of data.

Alternatively, large data packages can be divided into a number of packages which are then transferred in parallel.

In either case, the data packages have to be brought into original ordering on the receiving end.

If frequently updated data has to be transferred, caching and polling can be applied as shown in Fig. 6. If caching is used, all changes to data are immediately committed (1,2,3). Therefore data can be transferred if needed without further action (4,5). On the contrary, data is not constantly updated if polling is employed. In case of data transfer (A,D), changes first have to be adopted (B,C).

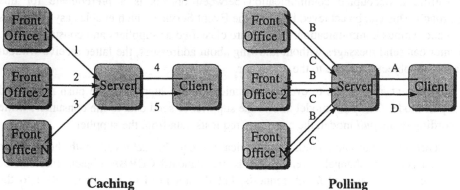

Caching   **Polling**

Fig. 6. Caching vs. polling

Orbix provides mechanisms that enable the strategies described above. Asynchronous transfer can be realised with the Event Service, one of the OMG CORBAservices [OMG96], which is provided by OrbixTalk. A β-version of this product has recently been released [Iona96]. Research on the asynchronous transfer based on the Event Service still has to be extended. Multiplexing can be achieved using the multi-threading mechanism of Orbix, which is available with the 2.0 version.

Depending on the amount of data to be transferred and the frequency of transfer, suitable combinations of the given strategies will result in best performance. It is assumed, for instance, that if large data packages have to be transferred to a server that processes time consuming operations on that data before it is returned, it is likely that an asynchronous transfer using multiplexing will give the best result. If frequently updated data is requested irregularly, synchronous polling will be most appropriate. For simply transferring data, a synchronous sequential transfer might be ideal, or an asynchronous multiplexed transfer.

An examination of synchronous polling and caching will be done in the following chapter and first conclusions will be drawn.

5   Performance Measurements

5.1   Monitoring

In this chapter, first results obtained by measuring parameters of data transfer in the financial environment of Dresdner Bank are presented along with two general concepts for monitoring performance. One is based on the Event Service, the other on the Orbix specific filtering mechanism.

A standard CORBA request is directed to a particular object and results in the synchronous execution of the corresponding operation. If this operation raises an exception, appropriate exception handling has to be taken by the calling object. In the context of monitoring performance, it would be useful to have an object that is simply notified by other objects whenever significant action is taken. However, synchronous notification would result in a distortion of the elapsed time, because the notifying objects would have to wait for the monitoring object to respond to the notification. Therefore a decoupled communication between objects is a prerequisite for this approach. This can be achieved by using the Event Service which enables asynchronous and anonymous communication. Objects are classified as suppliers and consumers. The former can send messages without knowing about addressees, the latter receive without having an object reference to the originator.

Two different approaches to event communication are supported: the push model and the pull model. The *push* model allows the supplier to send data to the consumer, while according to the *pull* model, the consumer requests data from the supplier.

Asynchronous and anonymous communication can be achieved with help of an intervening event channel. Event channels are standard CORBA objects that can be addressed by standard CORBA requests, but do not need to supply the data to the consumer at the same time it is received from the supplier. Moreover the persistence of events can be specified, i.e. an event channel may keep an event for a period of time, sending it to consumers who register within that period of time, or only pass it to consumers that are currently waiting. Event channels act both as consumer and supplier for multiple objects, thus providing the means for communication between multiple suppliers and multiple consumers.

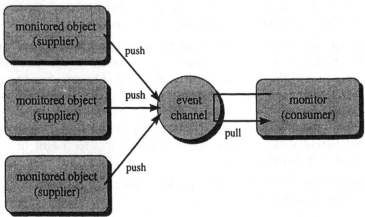

Fig. 7. Communication model for the monitoring tool

Employing a mixed style communication with an event channel, the architecture for a monitoring tool can be built as shown in Fig. 7.

All objects that are supposed to be monitored send an event to the event channel (push model), whenever a point of interest is reached. A time stamp is included for the monitoring tool to be able to timely order the events. If multiple machines are used, it is necessary to synchronise the systems clocks to obtain a correct order. Events are kept in the event channel and requested by the monitoring tools (pull model).

Since the β-release of OrbixTalk, which provides the OMG Event Service, has been available only recently, the implementation of a monitor using the Event Service had to be postponed, although this approach offers an elegant solution. So far, a monitoring tool based on an Orbix specific filter mechanism has been implemented and used in the tests discussed in this chapter.

Two forms of filtering are supported by Orbix: *per-object* filtering, which applies to individual objects, and *per-process* filtering, which applies to all objects in a client's or server's address space [Iona95]. Filters have associated monitor points that allow additional code to be executed before the continuation of normal code execution.

Per-object filters either observe a per-object-pre or a per-object-post monitor point. The former is applied to an operation invocation on a particular object before it is passed to the object, the latter after the operation has been processed by the object.

For the implementation of the monitoring tool, per-process filters have been applied. A per-process filter has eight corresponding monitor points with actions being triggered for any subset of these points. The eight monitor points are given in Fig. 8.

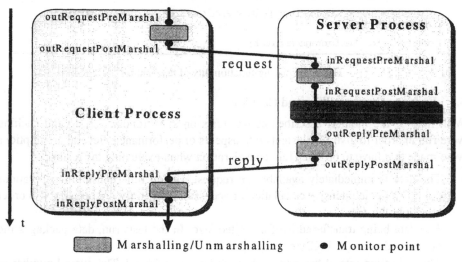

Fig. 8. Monitoring Performance using Orbix filters

Implementing a per-process filter is straight-forward, see Fig. 9. A class Filter is defined in the Orbix-C++ library containing eight virtual functions which correspond to the monitoring points. In order to observe any of these points, the corresponding virtual function needs to be redefined in a class derived from Filter. For an object to be observed, all that needs to be done is to create an instance of this class. The object will then automatically trigger the redefined functions, whenever a filter point is reached. In the extract of source code shown below, the actual measuring is done by the class EventTimer, whose member function monitorEvent is called with an appropriate parameter.

```
class ProcessFilter : public CORBA_Filter {
private:
EventTimer *monitor;

public:
    ProcessFilter() {
        monitor = new EventTimer();
    }
    ~ProcessFilter() {
        delete EventTimer;
    }
virtual unsigned char outRequestPreMarshal (CORBA_Request& r,
                                            CORBA_Environment&) {
        monitor->monitorEvent(outRequestPre);
        return 1;
}
virtual unsigned char outRequestPostMarshal (CORBA_Request& r,
                                             CORBA_Environment&) {
        monitor->monitorEvent(outRequestPost);
        return 1;
}
// tackle other six monitor points analogously
};
ProcessFilter PerformanceMonitor;
```

Fig. 9. Specifying functionality of the monitor

5.2 First Studies on Polling and Caching

With help of the monitor described above, tests on synchronous polling and caching were run in order to give first insights into aspects of performance. Several assumptions were made that have to be taken into consideration when evaluating the results:

- The data is immediately available on request, i.e. no time consuming operations due to compute intensive calculation or access of data stores are necessary in order to supply the data.
- The data being transferred is of a limited size. In the tests run, data packages did not exceed a size of 1 KByte.
- The utilisation rate of the network has not been considered. The overall number of transactions necessary to apply a certain transfer mechanism is a crucial factor for the suitability of this mechanism.
- Tests were run with Windows NT on Pentium PCs and Solaris on a SPARCstation 5, connected by a Local Area Network (LAN). A server running on Windows NT was requested by a Windows NT client and - depending on the data transfer mechanism - the required data was requested from servers or sent from clients running on Solaris, see Fig. 10.

CORBA can be used for interconnecting heterogeneous systems. However, since there are no container objects provided, objects cannot be transferred as a whole. This topic will be further explored in the near future. At present, one approach to realising object transfer is to encode entire objects in strings, which are provided as a template type in the OMG interface definition language (IDL), transfer these strings, and extract the objects at the receiving end by decoding the strings. When deciding on the type of data to be transferred, this topic has been taken as a reason to transfer unbounded sequences (IDL template type) of strings.

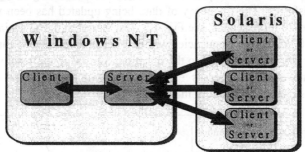

Fig. 10. The testing environment

The general idea for comparing synchronous polling and caching has been to measure the time elapsed for a given number of calls. In each test series, 50 to 500 calls have been made, thus reflecting a general tendency.

In order to examine synchronous polling, both the length of the sequences and the length of the strings contained have been varied. In order to get an impression of the quality of the transfer rates, the tests have not only been run in the environment shown in Fig. 10, but also on a stand-alone Windows-NT machine. Some significant results are shown in Fig. 11.

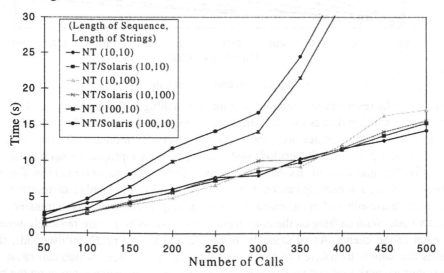

Fig. 11. Synchronous Polling

In each test series, sequences of a certain length containing strings of a certain length are involved, as shown in the legend of Fig. 11. It can be noticed that the difference in performance on a stand-alone machine and multiple machines connected by Orbix is fairly small. The number of calls is proportional to the time elapsed, with the exception of long sequences where the elapsed time increases exponentially with the number of calls. This might be caused by the internal representation of sequences as linked lists and the resulting overhead of memory allocation and deallocation.

In order to compare synchronous polling and caching, a particular polling test series has been taken as a basis, where sequences of length 100 containing strings of length 10 were being transferred. The frequency of data being updated has been varied within a range of 100 and 20 milliseconds, see Fig. 12. Test were run in the testing environment shown in Fig. 10.For update frequencies within a reasonable range it can be stated that the number of calls is proportional to the duration. Similar to the results obtained with polling, the time elapsed increases exponentially with the number of calls if the utilisation rate is close to the limit of the system.

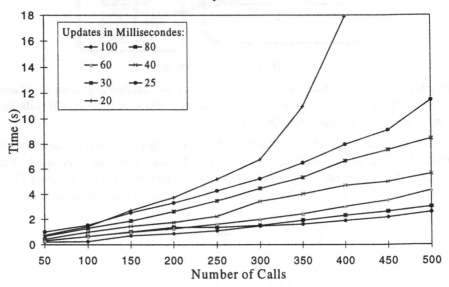

Fig. 12. Synchronous Caching

Comparing the results of synchronous polling and caching in these test series, the time required for caching data is shorter than the time required for polling the same amount of data, even if the updates are done as fast as every 25 milliseconds. However, it would be wrong to generally conclude that caching is more appropriate than polling. So far, only the time elapsed has been taken as a factor. Yet an enormous difference between polling and caching can be noticed with regard to the number of transactions necessary to use either of the mechanisms. With polling, each server has to transfer data exactly once. With caching on the other hand, data needs to be transferred continuously by each of the clients. As an example, if data is updated every 25 milliseconds, this means that data is transferred 40 times per second by each client, which can cause an enormous network load and become a bottleneck for any application running on the net. However, apart from very specific cases, minimal update frequencies such as these will not be required. Still caching can be less adequate than polling, even if data is updated less frequently. In a financial environment, for instance, it might be possible that market data of several Mbytes has to be guaranteed to be up to date, say less than a second old. The data might be requested irregularly, say once or twice per hour. If caching this amount of data does not require considerably less than a second, polling would be more appropriate, because caching would have to be done at least every second, thus leading to a continuous data transfer and causing the network to become a bottleneck.

6 Conclusions

In the tests examined, data was available to the client faster, if caching was applied, even if data was updated in very short intervals, thus causing the server to deal with large amounts of requests in addition to the request observed. An important side effect was the high network utilisation rate caused by this mechanism. Polling instead caused the client request to be dealt with less fast, but the network load was kept considerably lower. The observations lead to two general assumptions:

- If data is requested far more often than it is updated, caching can be applied efficiently while keeping the network utilisation rate fairly low.

- If data is changing rapidly and is requested irregularly, caching would cause an enormous network traffic. In this case, caching is more appropriate.

However, the topic will have to be further examined and testing will have to be extended in order to cover the entire problem domain. In addition, testing on sequential transfer vs. multiplexing and synchronous vs. asynchronous transfer will have to be realised to obtain reliable criteria to decide, which combination of these orthogonal strategies is most appropriate in a specific case. At this stage, however, it can be stated, that it will always be the individual conditions of a given system that will determine which combination is most suitable.

References

[Hor96] Peter Hornig: The children of OMA - An Overview of CORBA implementations (in German). In: OBJEKTspektrum 1/96, January 1996

[HoTo96] Chris Horn, Annrai O'Toole: Distributed Object Oriented Approaches. In: Proceedings of the IFIP/IEEE International Conference on Distributed Platforms, 1996

[Iona95] Orbix 2 Programming Guide. IONA Technologies, November 1995

[Iona96] OrbixTalk Programming Guide. IONA Technologies, 1996

[Mul96] Hans-Peter Müller: When bits are cash money (in German). In: Business Computing 2/92, February 1996

[OMG95] CORBA: The Common Object Request Broker: Architecture and Specification, Revision 2.0. OMG, July 1995

[OMG96] CORBAservices: Common Object Services Specification. OMG Document 96-3-28, March 1996

[SUN96] Sun Microsystems: Distributed Object Technology in the Financial Services Industry. White Paper, February 28, 1996

Crossing Technological Domains
Using the Inter-ORB Request Level Bridge
– Preliminary Performance Study *

K. Zieliński, A. Uszok, M. Steinder

Institute of Computer Science, University of Mining & Metallurgy
Al. Mickiewicza 30, Cracow, Poland
tel: +48 (12) 17 39 82, fax: +48 (12) 33 89 07,
e-mail: {kz, uszok, gosia}@ics.agh.edu.pl

Abstract. This paper evaluates an overhead introduced by components that build a framework for inter-ORB request level bridge. It shows that TypeCode processing complexity is the most influential factor that determines efficiency of almost each generic bridge. This has been experimentally proved by evaluation of the components of the implemented half-bridge between Orbix 1.31 and IIOP domain.

1 Introduction

Existence of many different ORB domains is justified for performance, security and management reasons. Even in a context of CORBA 2.0 emerging standard this diversity of application requirements leads to many technological domains distinguished by various data representations, communication protocols, addressing and cooperation schemes.

Providing interoperability across technological domains need a bridging mechanism which resides at boundaries between domains and transforms requests expressed in terms of one domain's model into a model of a destination domain. This activity introduces an overhead which depends on many factors. Their identification and experimental evaluation is crucial for applicability of this techniques and efficient inter-ORB bridge design. This paper concentrates on request-level generic transparent bridging defined by UNO specification as the most general approach. Implementation of this bridging technique is supported by components such as DSI, DII, and IR.

The aim of this paper is to evaluate an overhead introduced by Inter-ORB bridge components that build the framework for inter-ORB request level bridging proposed in [8]. The half-bridge components are analyzed separately to identify parts which have the greatest influence on an overall bridge performance. An advantage of this approach is that the obtained results can be also used for other applications that require DSI or DII usage.

A generic half-bridge requires dynamic interpretation of request arguments of various data types. This process is controlled by the TypeCode. Organization of the presented study is based on the thesis that TypeCode processing complexity is the most influential factor that determines efficiency of almost every generic bridge. This claim has been experimentally proved by evaluation of the components of the implemented half-bridge between Orbix 1.3.1 and IIOP domain.

---
* This work was sponsored by the European Commission under the COPERNICUS project TOCOOS no. CP940247. (http://galaxy.agh.edu.pl/research/cs/TOCOOS/COPERNICUS.html)

The rest of this paper is structured as follows: in the next section basic components of the framework for inter-ORB request level bridge have been described and their activity has been analyzed. Then, in Section 3 implementation of selected components, which are responsible for dynamic interpretation of arguments of a forwarded requests and, thus, introduce the greatest overhead, has been presented in more detail. This section focuses on TypeCode translation process, DSI and DII functionality, and organization of IR access. The implemented components of the half-bridge are very complex, thus, the extensive testing have had to be carried out. A methodology of this process is presented in the next section. In Section 5 results of preliminary performance studies of the investigated components have been presented and discussed. The paper is ended with conclusions.

2 Half-bridge functional model

Half-bridge functional model is determined by its location in a cooperation environment, on domain borders. Its task is to receive request addressed to a remote server from the local client, translate it into server's format and forward it to the server.

To perform this task a half-bridge must be able to: initialize itself, handle and understand client's request, translate objects defined in CORBA model, and construct a new request. The initialization process has been investigated in [8] and does not influence the overall half-bridge performance, so the last three activities will be elaborated here. The framework architecture of the half-bridge which carries out these activities is presented in Figure 1.

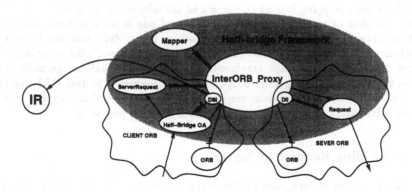

Fig. 1. Half-Bridge Framework Architecture

2.1 Incoming Request handling

A request to an object in CORBA compliant systems is taken over by an object adapter, the same which is used to activate the object. It uses Dynamic Skeleton Interface (DSI) to interpret and serve a request.

Dynamic Skeleton Interface is a CORBA 2.0 mechanism, therefore most of currently available ORB systems do not possess its implementation. This necessitates extension of these systems with DSI.

DSI provides the same functionality as the type-specific IDL generated skeletons. However, it allows an object implementation to receive any operation request on any available CORBA object without requiring compile-time knowledge of the type of the object it is implementing. The main component of this information is a set of TypeCodes, which describe operation arguments. This information is stored in IR (Interface Repository) from which it could be retrieved in run-time [5].

DSI is a server-side analogue of Dynamic Invocation Interface (DII). All requests on a particular object are performed by having the ORB invoke the same up-call routine – *invoke* method of the *DynamicImplementation* object. This function need an access to operation data including its name, parameters' types and values as well as its result, which are offered through an abstract ServerRequest object, which possesses functionality for retrieving data from a request buffer and writing return values into the request buffer. These activities are controlled by TypeCodes.

2.2   Mapping objects defined in CORBA model

CORBA 1.2 standard left some parts of the system undefined because the then state of the art did not allow standardization or some of the elements were intentionally left opaque to allow their specialization for different uses. These deficiencies in the CORBA definition allow vendors of CORBA compliant systems to specify different extensions to the same interfaces to make them usable. To allow two different ORBs to cooperate a mapping from one ORB to another and vice versa must be defined for Objects, TypeCodes, Principals, Contexts and ServiceContext. TypeCode mapping together with Object References mapping is most common and introduces the greatest overhead. The need for this kind of mapping occurs when a TypeCode is an argument of operation invocation. However, it is more common that an operation definition has to be translated when crossing domain's border. It always involves TypeCodes mapping, which describes data types of operation arguments. In the case of a half-bridge built around ORB backbone only mapping from cooperating environments to this ORB backbone and vice versa is needed. Mechanisms responsible for performing this mapping may take necessary information from bootstrapping or from external protocols.

2.3   Forwarding Request to Server

A translated request is forwarded to the server using DII. Its activity is once again navigated by TypeCodes. The new NValue list has to be created which will contain arguments of the request in a server domain. Putting these arguments into the list is controlled by their TypeCodes. This operation is symetrical to the DSI activity.

3   Sources of overhead

When considering a half-bridge implementation (in this case all presented analyses are based on a half-bridge working between Orbix 1.3.1 [9] and IIOP domain) it is easy

to recognize that the most complex computations are related to marshaling and un-marshaling messages, extracting and inserting parameters from/to ServerRequest and translating CORBA Objects. Processing all mentioned operations requires TypeCode accessibility and interpretation. This remark leads to the conclusion that a half-bridge overhead is very much depended on efficiency of the following functions:
- TypeCode format translation,
- Extraction and insertion of parameters from/to ServerRequest performed by DSI,
- Processing Interface Repository operations which are necessary to provide information for DSI and DII.

Implementation of software components that perform these processing will be described in more details. Another half-bridge activity which introduces significant overhead is Object References translation, however, it has been already evaluated in [8].

3.1 TypeCode translation

TypeCode is a value which represents type of data. The CORBA 1.2 standard defined only an abstract structure of the TypeCode, which consists of a "kind" field, and a set of parameters appropriate for that kind. It also specifies an interface enabling manipulating the TypeCode. However, it does not describe representation of this abstract structure, thus, existing CORBA 1.2 compliant environments possess their own proprietary internal representation of TypeCodes. The new CORBA 2.0 [4] standard defines TypeCode representation which should be used in IIOP messages. This led to the problem of translating TypeCode between proprietary formats when constructing the half-bridge as for instance in the case of Orbix 1.3.1 and IIOP.

The Orbix 1.3.1 TypeCode is represented as a string, containing a description of the given type. In this string the first character describes the TypeCode kind, e.g. type **long** is represented as simple "l". For complex types apart from the kind field the string stores their names, member fields and member types (following these rules if members are also complex types), etc.

On the other hand the UNO (CORBA 2) encoding of a TypeCode [4] is the TCKind enum value, followed by zero or more parameter values. For simple data types only the **kind** value is filled and the parameter list remains empty. It is significant only for complex types such as struct, union etc. Their encoding is done according to the CDR specification. Any new component of this buffer has to start from the position whose index is a multiple of four.

The two TypeCode formats between which the translation has to be carried out have completely different structures. Mapping could be done directly only for simple data types. Mapping for a TypeCode representing complex data types will involve complicated analysis of a recursive structure.

Here the description of two translation functions Orbix2UNO and UNO2Orbix with a stress on an overhead sources in their implementations is presented. They both act in a similar way: they take a TypeCode value in one encoding and construct its counterpart in the second encoding.

Translation from Orbix to UNO TypeCode encoding. The main problem encountered was evaluating the size of the created UNO TypeCode. The size of a memory area necessary to hold TypeCode is not known before the end of the whole analysis, thus it is impossible to allocate memory for the whole UNO TypeCode at the beginning of translation. Therefore it should be allocated piece by piece when required in time of translation. Memory for incoming octets is allocated by an object of a special class Buffer dynamically in small arrays stored in a list. This solution requires transformation of information stored in the object of the class Buffer into one array of octets, which is a part of the UNO TypeCode encoding, when the translation is finished.

Another problem was mapping TypeCodes being parts of another TypeCode. In case of the TypeCodes with a complex parameter list, encoded as a sequence of octets, it is important to know the length of the inner TypeCode, because this value should precede elements of the sequence. The problem was solved by recursive calls of the internal function Inner_Orbix2UNO() which returns length of the TypeCode being mapped. Each of those recursive calls works on the same _buffer defined in function Orbix2UNO(). This function interprets a contents of the Orbix TypeCode and fills _buffer with information about structure of the corresponding UNO TypeCode. The interpretation is based on the system of cases, each corresponding to one of simple or complex types. In case of complex types function Inner_Orbix2UNO() calls itself for interpretation of subtypes (for instance types of elements of array, or types of fields in structure and so on).

Translation from UNO to Orbix TypeCode encoding. Inside the function UNO2Orbix – first the UNO TypeCode is changed to the tree form, where every node contains attributes of an element of a structure (type, name, pointers to possible members when it is a complex structure). Many times jumps back have to be done in tree's structure (i.e. when "qualified" structure name has to be created – struct1::struct2, or structure declaration has to be repeated in the Orbix TypeCode twice).

The length of the Orbix TypeCode is calculated using the created tree. Then, such a number of bytes is allocated in memory. After that the tree is translated to the Orbix TypeCode encoding by recursively analyzing its structure. If a currently analyzed node represents a simple data type, it is translated directly to a corresponding Orbix value for this TypeCode. If, however, the TypeCode for a complex data types is encountered in the node, first, the beginning of this structure is produced, next, all its members (or fields i.e. for an enumerated type) are processed recursively, and finally the tail of the structure (as necessary in Orbix format) is created.

3.2   Dynamic Invocation Skeleton for Orbix

DynamicImplementation interface, whose implementation constitutes DSI, is defined in IDL as follows:

```
interface DynamicImplementation {
        void invoke(inout CORBA2_IONA::ServerRequest sreq);
};
```

The Orbix 1.3 IDL compiler constructs three C++ classes based on this interface, which were modified as follows in order to implement DSI for Orbix:
- DynamicImplementation – All methods of this class were removed.
- DynamicImplementationBOAImpl – It is a base class for all objects that wish to implement DIR. Its second constructor has been added to allow registration of the class with an arbitrary interface name. The first parameter of this constructor denotes an interface identifier of the implemented object.

- **DynamicImplementation_dispatch** – It implements dispatch method of the **DynamicImplementationBOAImpl** derived classes. When a request directed to one of the objects of a class that inherits from **DynamicImplementationBOAImpl** arrives the dispatch method of **DynamicImplementation_dispatch** class is called. The body of this method has been modified in such a way that it accepts all operation names, creates a **ServerRequest** object, invokes **invoke** method of the specified object and finally writes all inout, out and return values into the received from the client Request object. This method does not require any changes when being used in users programs.

A programmer who uses DSI has to implement the **invoke** method on his own. This method gets as a parameter a ServerRequest object. The object instance on which a request is made, can retrieve all information necessary for handling request from this object and modify the inout parameters, out parameters, and result. The object implementation also reports exceptions through this object.

ServerRequest implementation. ServerRequest object implementation in Orbix wraps up the Orbix **Request** object. Its main function – **params()** is used to unmarshal/marshal income parameters and returned values using internal functions **extract**, and **insert** respectively. Function **extract** reads parameters placed in an Orbix Request and places them in the NVList structure. On the other hand the function **insert** reads values from NVList and puts them into the Request. For thier activity it has been necessary to implement functions which determine size of data represented by a given TypeCode and read data of an arbitrary complexity from the Request. Both functions are based on TypeCode interpretation. To analyse TypeCodes function **tc_traverse()** has been implemented. Analysis of TypeCode is not complicated when simple data types are in use. In that case we have only to determine which of these types is processed. Then the proper code is executed, which deals with it. Problem gets a bit more intricate when complex data types are used (for example structures, unions, structures of unions and so on). In that case the function must be called recursively for each subtype of the examined data structure. The interior of function **tc_traverse()** consists of one multi-conditional switch, which checks the kind of type represented by TypeCode and, next, executes required sequence of operations for this type.

Function **tc_traverse()** does not operate on Orbix Request data – these actions such as writing and reading Orbix Request are all performed by functions, pointers to which are passed to the function **tc_traverse()**. On the other hand these functions do not operate on TypeCode – its analysis is made by **tc_traverse()**. For reading a value from Request function **fill_mem** was defined Operations performed by this function are very easy for simple data types – the function just extracts data from Request and writes it into the area pointed by its argument. The problem gets more complicated when operating on complex data, then it is necessary to call function **tc_traverse()** which has **fill_mem()** as its argument. In this case **tc_traverse()** is called in order to modify parameter containing TypeCode of the retrieved from the Request parameter, so that it points to a proper part of Typecode and to call function **fill_mem()** when necessary. Reading data from Request was simplified by stream operator **>>** , which was defined for all simple types of data.

For writing a value into Request function **fill_req** was defined. Writing data to Request is made with the use of stream operator **>>** defined for all simple data types. Problem of writing complex data into Request was solved in the same way as it was shown for function **fill_mem()**. In case of a complex TypeCode function **fill_req()** calls **tc_traverse()** with itself as an argument of this function.

3.3 Interface Repository access

DSI and DII require an access to the Interface Repository (IR). Orbix environment provides IR implementation that makes it possible to build client and server parts of the half-bridge in this environment. Unfortunately, when the reported research started there was no IR for the IIOP domain available. To solve this problem a service specific halfbridge called IR Access Server (IRAS) has been constructed. It is a service specific bridge because its functionality is limited to translating requests addressed to the IR objects only.

The IIOP client generates requests to IR according to its interface specification. These requests are captured by IRAS that represents IR in IIOP-domain, transformed into Orbix format, and sent by the Orbix IR client to Orbix IR server. Results of these calls are sent back following the same route.

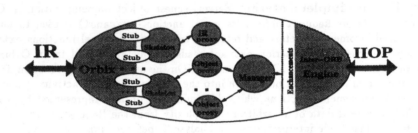

Fig. 2. Internal structure of IRAS

The IRAS internal structure is shown in Figure 2. It consists of:
1. Interface Repository Proxy Object in IIOP domain, which represents an access to Orbix Interface Repository from IIOP part of IRAS.
2. IR Objects Proxies for IIOP domain (below called OrbixEncapsulators) which encapsulate Orbix objects entries returned from Orbix Interface Repository to use them in IIOP part of IRAS.
3. IIOP Skeletons, which handle incoming requests. They are specific for individual object types (interfaces) and are pointed by appropriate Proxy Object.
4. Main Manager which manages all above components, translates requests from IIOP into Orbix format and vice versa and communicates with all requesting objects.
5. Enhancements of Inter-ORB Engine to provide management (creation and destruction) of more than one object, such as creation and destruction of objects and two level dispatching of requests — the first, choosing a target object, the second, executing appropriate skeleton function.
6. Inter-ORB Engine part responsible for utilization of IIOP standard libraries.

The IRAS activity may be described as follows. First, request generated by IIOP client is received by Inter-ORB Engine Object Adaptor (OA) and dispatched by Main Manager to the interface skeleton function pointed by the Proxy Object the request is referred to. The suitable Object is located according to Object Key in Objects Table. If this Object does not exist it is created by the OA and put into the Objects Table. The interface skeleton function retrieves a name of the requested operation from the IIOP request and on this basis passes the request to a proper implementation skeleton function. This function recovers operation parameters and performs a standard Orbix operation call on a suitable IR Object. The last step activates suitable Orbix Stub function. On return, if the objects references are passed back, the object proxies are created and registered in the object table. Next, the result is put into the IIOP request and send back to the IIOP Client.

IIOP Client Stubs for every operation of interface supported by objects in Orbix Interface Repository are implemented to provide access to IR for any process in IIOP domain. All operations provided by Orbix IR interfaces have been made accessible for IIOP clients. IRAS activity does not involve the DSI and DII mechanisms and is based on statically linked stubs. The most complex operation performed by IRAS is a TypeCode translation process whose implementation is based on the UNO2Orbix and Orbix2UNO functions described in the previous section.

4 Components testing

When the components were implemented, there was a need to check if they worked correctly as well as to evaluate their performance. Though, they were tested on some simple interfaces, which implied simple TypeCodes, it did not guarantee that they would work correctly in other more complex cases. A solution was to construct a tool that generates random IDL structures according to the IDL syntax and semantics, and uses its output as a source of a random operation definition and TypeCodes.

4.1 TypeCode mapping functions testing

The whole testing scenario is presented in Figure 3 and may be described as follows:
1. Generate a module using Random Interface Generator.
2. Compile received code with the Orbix IDL compiler.
3. Extract TypeCodes from files generated by the IDL compiler.
4. Translate Orbix TypeCode to IIOP format using Orbix2UNO function.
5. Translate the obtained UNO TypeCode back to Orbix format using the UNO2Orbix function.
6. Check if the Orbix TypeCode produced by the UNO2Orbix function is identical to this generated by the Orbix 1.3.1 IDL compiler.

4.2 DSI testing

DSI tester is an environment that enables checking on correctness and efficiency of DSI mechanisms used by server encoding operations sent by client. It consists of programs *client*, *server* and random-interface generator. Client calls chosen operations with data as arguments and server "echoes" this data back to client. In order to find out if DSI works properly client has to check if data sent by him does not differ from data echoed by server. DSI performance is estimated on both sides: in client program – by measuring lapse of time during invocation of operation, in server program – by measuring how much time server takes to extracting data from request) and inserting data to request.

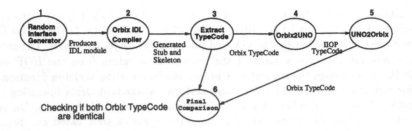

Fig. 3. Testing scenario of the TypeCode mapping functions

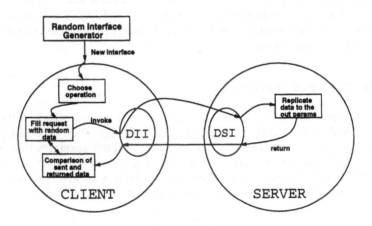

Fig. 4. Concept of DSI tester

5 Performance study

All performance results presented in this section were obtained on Sun SparcStation 10/514 and Sun SparcStation 5 machines with **SunOS 5.4** operating system. During the evaluation process, every test was repeated 5000 times in a loop for the given operation or TypeCode and the time was measured with the system **time** tool. The presented results are the average values calculated using the collected data.

5.1 TypeCode mapping functions performance

Some performance evaluation tests have been carried out to estimate time consumed by translation of TypeCode of a given complexity.

First, functions with simple "linear" structured data types (with growing number of "long" fields in a structure) were measured. In this case the time consumed also grows

157

linearly, although the `Orbix2UNO` function is considerably faster than `UNO2Orbix`. The reason is probably that `UNO2Orbix` uses more complicated tree-shaped internal structure for translating TypeCode. Next, the evaluation was done for nested structures with growing number of nests in structure, as follows:

```
struct st1 { ....
                struct stn {
                        long l;
        ....
                }field;
};
```

The obtained times of translation are shown in Figure 5 and 6.

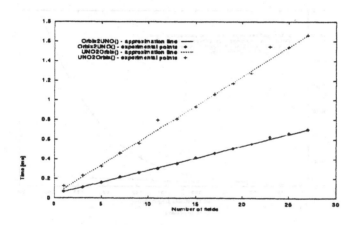

Fig. 5. Time consumed by TypeCode translation function for linear structures

Consumed time grows in the second case exponentially! This could be caused by an enormous increase of length of the Orbix TypeCode with the grow of data type complexity shown in Figure 7. It could be seen that for 200 bytes long IDL specification (what relates to 7th level of nesting) the Orbix TypeCode is nearly 7000 bytes. This forces both functions to make much work with simple reading and writing bytes and in consequence the consumed time grows faster than linearly.

5.2 DSI performance

Some performance evaluation tests have also been carried out to estimate time consumed by DSI operation versus complexity of their arguments. The tests have been performed for the invocation of operations – extract and insert, which respectively retrieve and

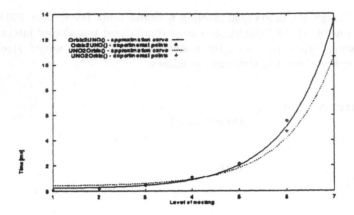

Fig. 6. Time consumed by TypeCode translation function for nested structures

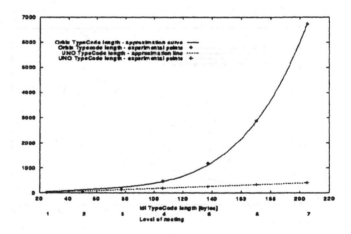

Fig. 7. Increase in TypeCode length vs. data type complexit

put data in the request. The obtained times are shown in Figure 8 and 9. In the first example only linear structure were subject to params() and insert() methods. In the second case the structure was nested as presented in the previous point.

5.3 IRAS performance

To evaluate IRAS overhead the difference in access time to IR in two situations has been measured: the first is, when the Orbix client performs the operation and the second then the same operation is called by the IIOP client via IRAS. This experiment has been

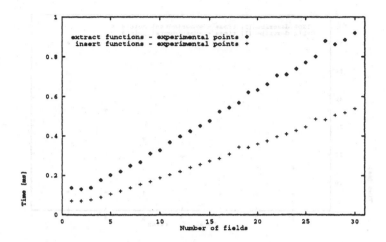

Fig. 8. Time consumed by DSI functions **extract** and **insert** for linear structures

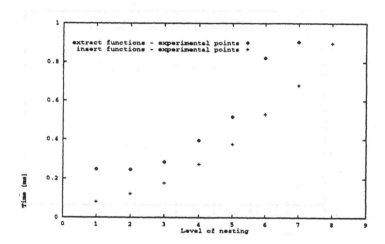

Fig. 9. Time consumed by DSI functions **extract** and **insert** for nested structures

repeated for every IR interface operation. The obtained results for describe_operation and lookup_name method are shown in Figure 10 and 11.

The presented results illustrate a general phenomenon that has been observed: IRAS introduces substantial overhead only for operations that need TypeCode translation. The process of creating proxies for Orbix IR objects in the IRAS introduces approximately only 4 [ms] delay.

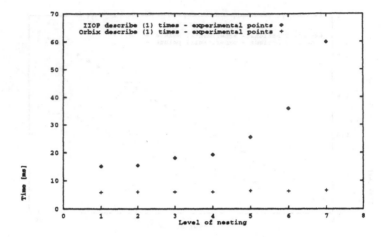

Fig. 10. Average access time to IR – `describe_operation` method

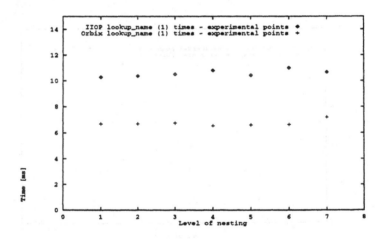

Fig. 11. Average access time to IR – `lookup_name` method

6 Conclusions

In the paper sources of overhead, when technological domains between CORBA-compilant systems are crossed, using the bridge, have been identified and evaluated. Despite of the fact that the presented results concern Orbix 1.3.1 and IIOP domain interoperability the conclusion presented below has a general meaning, as considered environments are representative for CORBA compliant systems.

The complexity of TypeCode processing has a substantial influence on DSI activity, CORBA Objects translation process and IR access time. The TypeCode encoding should not lead to substantial growth of occupied memory with comparison to a number of bytes used for textual representation of data structures in IDL. It is evident from the obtained results that growth of the TypeCode representation length results in increase of the processing time.

The TypeCode translation process is more time consuming than extracting and inserting data from ServerRequest. The DSI functions extract and insert activities are in fact controlled by the TypeCode so its length influences the processing time.

The results obtained from the study of the service specific bridge such as IRAS also prove that the TypeCode translation process introduces the most substantial overhead. The IR interface operations that do not require TypeCode translation are performed very efficiently. The process of proxy objects creation does not introduce a substantial delay.

The concept of bridge presented in this article applies not only to the interoperability between CORBA 1.2 and CORBA 2 systems. It can be very valuable as the mechanism enabling division of a CORBA-compilant system into sub-domains and serving as an administrative, security and firewall tool. It also can be used for interworking between non-CORBA compiliant systems like DCE or ANSAware.

7 REFERENCES

1. *CORBA 1.2 Revision Draft* (1993) OMG Report 93-12-43, Object Management Group (OMG) Inc.
2. W. Harrison, *The Importance of Using Object References as Identifiers of Objects – Comparison of CORBA Object References* (1994) IBM Watson, TR
3. *ORB Interoperability. Joint SunSoft / Iona Submission to the ORB 2.0 Task Force Initialization & Interoperability Request for Proposals* (1994) OMG Inc., TC Document 94-3-1
4. *CORBA V2.0* (1995) OMG Inc.
5. *Interface Repository* (1994) OMG Inc., TC Document 94-11-7
6. *ORB Initialization Specification* (1995) OMG Inc., TC Document 94-9-46
7. A. Uszok, G. Czajkowski, K. Zieliński, *Interoperability Gateway Construction for Object Oriented Distributed Systems*, (1994) Proceedings of 6th Nordic Workshop on Programming Environment Research,
8. M. Steinder, A. Uszok, K. Zieliński, *A Framework for Inter-ORB Request Level Bridge Construction*, (1996) Proceedings of IFIP/IEEE International Conference on Distributed Platforms, Chapman & Hall,
9. *Orbix Programmers Guide* (1995) IONA Technologies Ltd.,

Coordination in Evolving Systems

Matthias Radestock and Susan Eisenbach

Department of Computing
Imperial College of Science, Technology and Medicine
180 Queen's Gate, London SW7 2BZ
E-mail: {mr3,se}@doc.ic.ac.uk

Abstract. To facilitate the writing of large maintainable distributed systems we need to separate out various concerns. We view these concerns as being communication, computation, configuration and coordination. We look at the coordination requirements of long running systems, paying particular attention to enabling the dynamic addition and removal of services. We show that the key to a smooth integration of configuration and coordination into systems is a new style of communication. We show how these ideas can be incorporated into the actor model.

1 Introduction

When designing and implementing large-scale heterogeneous distributed systems the software engineer faces challenges that would not be encountered in sequential programs. The problem of *coordination* [MC94], forms a central part of the challenge – the activities of the system components need to be coordinated such that the overall system behaviour conforms to the specification. Coordination is an issue that arises *after* a range of other problems in a distributed system have been tackled. These include the distribution of components, the communication protocols, the data exchange between different platforms, fault tolerance, and migration. Typically these issues are addressed by *distributed systems platforms*, such as CORBA[MZ95]. Application design and implementation should not need to be concerned with them, apart from *using* the provided mechanisms. By contrast, coordination is often entirely embedded in the application design and implementation, and is not treated as a separate concern. This ignores the fact that coordination is a very distinct aspect of distributed systems, and that it contains application independent elements as well as elements that may be common to several applications.

To isolate the coordination elements, we can split the specification and implementation into four parts – communication, computation, configuration and coordination. Communication deals with the exchange of data, with a foundation of communication paradigms such as request-reply, synchronous and asynchronous. Computation is concerned with the data processing algorithms required by an application, with a foundation in traditional paradigms such as functional programming and object-oriented programming. Configuration determines which system components should exist, and how they are inter-connected, and is based on principles of *software architecture*[GS93, PW92, GP94]. Finally coordination is concerned with the interaction of the various system components, and is founded on recent paradigms such as *process calculi*[Mil89, MPW92, Mil91] and the notion of *interaction machines*[Weg96].

Having to perform three paradigm shifts during the design and implementation of a system is costly, since ultimately all elements have to work together to meet the overall system specification. In addition to the difference in paradigms, each element may use its own specification and implementation language. The software engineer thus potentially has to deal with four paradigms, four specification languages and four implementation languages. This makes system design complicated, analysis almost impossible, and maintenance expensive. A much preferred scenario would enable us to work within one single framework without loss of generality, ie. without losing the ability to integrate various specification and implementation languages. In this paper we argue that an enriched actor model can be the underlying paradigm for this.

We analyse the requirements of configuration and coordination and their impact on the requirements for an implementation. We introduce the notion of *implicit anonymous communication* as the key idea with which these requirements can be achieved, whilst integrating transparently into existing models. Thus from the point of view of computation, coordination does not exist. We then look at the actor model as a basis for integration and show that computation and communication concerns are already integrated into it. The model, as it stands, is not suitable for configuration and coordination, therefore we propose extensions that enable their integration. The extensions are rooted in the existing model by changing the semantics of communication. They are thus totally transparent which enables us to *add* configuration and coordination to existing designs without the need to change these.

2 Requirements of Coordination

We can view a distributed system as a collection of distributed agents[1] that interact with each other. The concerns of a distributed system can be separated into four parts (cf. Fig. 1):

- The *communication part* defines *how* agents communicate with each other.
- The *computation part* defines the implementation of the *behaviour* of individual agents. It thus determines *what* is being communicated.
- The *configuration part* defines the *interaction structure*, or *configuration*. It states which agents exist in the system and which agents can communicate with each other, as well as the method of communication. Basically it is a description of *where* information comes from and *where* it is sent to.
- The *coordination part* defines patterns of interaction, ie. it determines *when* certain communications take place.

---

[1] We use the term *agents* in a somewhat lax way as denoting an entity that 'does something'.

The communication part is the only part that is totally application independent, and thus features in the design and implementation as something that is being *used*, rather than defined or altered. The computation, configuration and coordination parts all include application dependent elements. However, each of them also has its own set of general, application independent requirements. In addition to this, inter-part dependencies yield a layered system structure. The coordination layer depends on the configuration layer because it requires information about the interaction structure in order to determine possible communications. The configuration layer depends on the computation layer since it needs to know which kinds of agents have been defined in order to be able to create new agents and to establish with which other agents an agent can communicate. The computation layer depends on the communication layer for the exchange of information. The layered structure also means that lower layers need

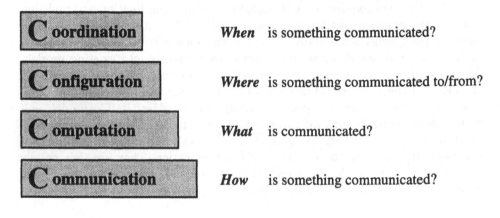

Fig. 1. The four layers of a specification of a distributed system

not, and should not know about the higher layers – as far as the lower layers are concerned the upper layers need not exist. This clear separation of concerns is extremely beneficial, enabling a high degree of reuse and easier maintenance. The aim of our research is to combine the layers in one framework without compromising their separation. This uniformity considerably reduces design and implementation time since the same methods, principles and tools can be applied to all layers. It also makes it easier to describe the inter-layer dependencies.

Before devising an integrated framework we need to investigate the requirements posed by each of the layers. The requirements of the communication and computation layer are quite well understood. By contrast, the requirements of configuration and coordination have so far received little attention. Since the coordination layer depends on the configuration layer, we first analyse the requirements of the latter and then look at the specific requirements of coordination.

2.1 From Static to Dynamic Configuration

In simple distributed systems a fixed set of interactions takes place between a fixed set of agents. The interaction structure thus only needs to be established once, at system start-up. No interaction between the computation part and configuration part is required after that, in fact, the configuration part need not even exist anymore. We shall call such a model of configuration *static configuration*. Needless to say, these systems cannot accomodate any form of dynamic change, ie. they cannot respond to a changing environment or changing requirements. In fact they cannot even cope with change if it is part of the requirements. So why bother with such a model of coordination at all? The reason is that the vast majority of distributed applications include elements of such a static nature. Typically they appear at coarse-grain levels of decomposition in the design stage. So, for instance, a video conferencing client may consist of a video camera, a microphone and a screen. These components will always exist and connections between them are fixed.

At a more fine-grain level of decomposition the interaction structure within a system changes dynamically: new agents are created, existing agents are destroyed, connections between agents are established and broken up. Such dynamic configuration activities are derived from the functional specification of the system which may state, for instance, that a new member can join a video conference after receiving an invitation. These activities thus need to be triggered by the agents in the system themselves, and so the configuration layer needs to exist during the entire life time of the system. We hence require an interaction mechanism between the computation part and the configuration part. The configuration part must have a run-time representation in order to enable dynamic access to its functionality. We shall call this model of configuration *dynamic configuration*. It subsumes the static configuration model.

2.2 From Configuration to Coordination

Coordination specifies patterns of interaction. Such a pattern may, for instance, be that the agent A can only send message X to agent B after agent C has sent message Y to agent D. Coordination requires configuration since before specifying the patterns of interaction, the parties of the interaction need to be specified – which is precisely the problem addressed by configuration.

Traditionally interaction patterns have not been specified explicitly, but were an implicit element in the design and implementation of the computation part. This makes it difficult to check and enforce adherence to the specification, limits the reuse of the thus constructed agents and complicates maintenance. To overcome these difficulties, the coordination layer should have an explicit representation, making it possible to *specify* the interaction patterns. We can also make a distinction between static and dynamic coordination. In the former case the interaction patterns are fixed throughout the life-time of a system. In the latter case interaction patterns are altered dynamically as part of the satisfaction of the application specification, ie. the changes to the structure are ultimately triggered by computational agents. So a mechanism is required that enables the interaction with both the configuration and computation part.

To enforce the adherence to the specification in a running system the coordination part needs to be able to observe and interfere with interactions. Thus, although the interaction patterns in a static configuration model are fixed throughout the life-time of the system, the coordination part must exist at run-time.

2.3 Interactive Systems

A dynamic coordination model allows us to specify systems where all possible dynamic changes to the interaction structure and patterns are known at compile time and are triggered by computational agents. However, this is insufficient in many large distributed systems, especially multimedia systems. Such systems are often long-lived, needing to be kept running for days and in some cases even years. These systems require interactive management – human agents need to be able to reconfigure the system while it is running. Furthermore they need to be able to alter the specification of the coordination, configuration and computation layers in order to make permanent changes to the overall system behaviour. An example would be a video-conferencing system where some new hardware, say a projection screen, is added to the system during a conference. The agents representing the screen need to be added to the system's computation layer. Then the configuration layer needs to be modified to forward all data of the conferencing communication to that agent. Finally we need to alter the coordination layer to ensure that the new agent interacts with the rest of the system in the desired manner. We shall refer to such systems as *interactive systems*. They are capable of accomodating changes that were not anticipated during the original system development. This is in contrast to static and dynamic systems. Both of these can contain interactive user interfaces or can interact with external components, but such interaction and the resulting changes need to be implemented as *part* of the system functionality – the system functionality itself cannot be altered.

Interactive systems require an explicit and tangible run-time representation of the computation, configuration and coordination parts, since we need the ability to modify them interactively. This is the only difference in requirements from dynamic systems.

2.4 Summary

The increasing complexity of requirements when increasing the dynamism, ie. moving from static to dynamic and finally interactive systems, can be observed for all four layers. A system can include a mixture of static, dynamic and interactive layers; however, lower layers require at least the same degree of dynamism from higher layers, as we illustrated above. Also, application requirements usually result in a varying degree of dynamism for different parts of the specification and implementation.

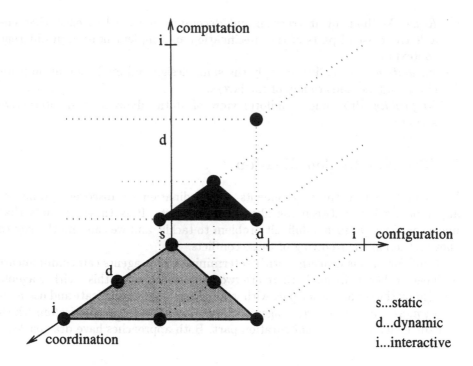

Fig. 2. Classification of Distributed Systems According to Layer Dynamism

Fig. 2 illustrates the classification of distributed systems according to the degree of dynamism in the various layers. Since the communication layer is application independent it does not contribute to the classification scheme. The lower plane contains systems with at least one static layer. The middle plane contains systems with no static, but at least one dynamic layer and the highest plane (which is in fact just a point) contains systems with only interactive layers. Additional requirements arise in a system whenever the dynamism increases in any layer. Thus systems with interactive computation, configuration and coordination are the most demanding. They require

- *Dynamic layers.* The ability to dynamically create new kinds of agents and modify their behaviour, and the ability to dynamically alter the interaction structure and interaction patterns.
- *Communication interception.* The ability to observe and interfere with communication activities in a system.
- *Layer interaction.* The ability of interaction between the coordination layer, configuration layer and computation layer.
- *Tangibility.* Explicit, tangible run-time representation of all layers.

In addition to these functional requirements there are also requirements derived from general software engineering principles:

- *Reuse.* Methods of abstraction and decomposition need to exist that enable the reuse of parts of the specification and implementation in different contexts.
- *Integration.* The ability to apply the same design and implementation principles and methods to any of the layers.
- *Uniformity.* Providing a uniform view of static, dynamic and interactive aspects.

3   The Key to Coordination

When investigating the requirements of coordination we discover a range of apparent conflicts between the above requirements. It is these conflicts that make coordination such a difficult problem to tackle, and we can find the key to coordination in the resolving of those conflicts.

Configuration is concerned with determining which agents can communicate with each other. Principally there are two ways of achieving this – either agents are told by the configuration part with whom they can communicate and use *non-anonymous communication*, or agents can use *anonymous communication* which is made concrete by the configuration part. Both approaches have drawbacks.

(a)

(b)

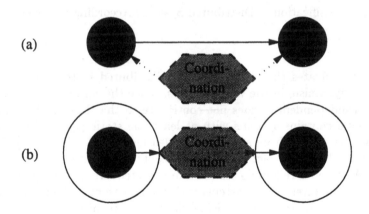

Fig. 3. Non-Anonymous and Anonymous Communication

In non-anonymous communication (Fig. 3a) messages contain a reference to a target agent. The target agents can be determined by the configuration layer, usually at instantiation time. However, this approach conflicts with the exchange of agent references in interactions, since this is a way that an agent can acquire the reference of another agent (and thus potentially communicate with it), without involvement of the configuration part. Furthermore the configuration becomes highly dependent on the implementation since it needs to know which agent references a particular agent needs to be supplied with. Specifying this, for instance in terms of roles and using some type system, is complex.

In anonymous communication (Fig. 3b) no target is specified as part of the messages. The target(s) is(are) determined by the configuration layer. This approach suffers from a lack of control on the part of the agent, since an agent cannot ensure, or even indicate that two separate interactions should take place with the same destination agent. Anonymous communication is incompatible with function call and method invocation style programming, in the sense that such types of interactions carry a substantial overhead if they are to be modelled using anonymous communication. Anonymous communication also *requires* a configuration layer, otherwise no communication is possible at all. This makes the computation layer highly dependent on the configuration layer.

3.1 Implicit Anonymous Communication

We can address the problems of anonymous and non-anonymous communication by introducing a new style of communication – *implicit anonymous communication*. The idea is to *apparently* allow agents to send messages to other agents. However, these messages will *actually* be intercepted by the coordination layer and an appropriate action will be taken, possibly sending the message to the specified agent, or even to some other agents, unknown to the sender (cf. Fig. 4). The anonymity of the communication is thus implicit – to the agent it looks like a non-anonymous communication. Explicit anonymous communication is achieved by the agent by addressing the message to itself.

Fig. 4. Implicit Anonymous Communication

As part of the implicit anonymous communication model we intercept messages and forward them to agents, thus satisfying the communication interception requirement. The intercepted messages can be sent to agents dealing with configuration or coordination, whose main task is to alter the interaction structure and interaction patterns. Thus the dynamic layer requirement is satisfied. The integration requirement is satisfied by the very fact that configuration and coordination is performed by agents. Whatever principles and methods exist for the design and implementation of the computational agents can be applied to the configuration and coordination agents. Hence we can also satisfy the reuse requirement, provided that the framework we use for the design and implementation of our agents has sufficient support for it.

Integration also means that configuration and coordination agents are subject to configuration and coordination. We can thus create meta layers of configuration and coordination. The layer interaction requirement is in turn satisfied by integration – agents in lower layers can send messages to agents in higher layers and thus achieve explicit interaction. More commonly the interaction is implicit – as the result of an intercepted communication agents in higher layers send messages to agents in lower layers. Since configuration and coordination is performed by agents we have an explicit run-time representation and thus satisfy the tangibility requirement, provided that the implementation in general has explicit run-time representations of agents. The behaviour of the agents determines how configuration and coordination takes place and this behaviour can be altered at run-time, provided the model and implementation allow the alteration of agent behaviour in general.

The most striking feature of implicit anonymous communication is that its integration into a model is transparent. As far as the rest of such a model is concerned, nothing has changed – configuration and coordination apparently does not take place. This enables the integration of configuration and coordination into existing designs by way of *adding* it without having to change any existing parts of the specification.

3.2   Structural Reflection and Interpretation

The only requirement that is not addressed by implicit anonymous communication is the uniform view of static, dynamic and interactive aspects. By that we mean that the methods and principles used for designing and implementing configuration and coordination should be independent from the dynamism of the layers. As far as the model is concerned, dynamic systems subsume static systems. Interactive systems require the availability of the layers at run-time, but otherwise seem no different from dynamic systems – the issue is *how* the layers can be accessed at run-time.

Coordination agents require access to other coordination agents since, as part of their required functionality, they must be able to inspect and subsequently modify the coordination part. The same is true of configuration agents. In the case of dynamic layers this can be achieved by providing suitable accessors, since it is known at the design stage what information about the layer needs to be gathered at run-time. However, for interactive layers a more sophisticated approach is required, as we need to have the ability to inspect and modify *any* part of the the layer, without knowing this at the design stage. Since configuration and coordination are performed by agents, this can be achieved by providing a general agent inspection mechanism.

There are two approaches to agent inspection: we could extend our model with all the necessary functionality for agent inspection, or we could employ structural reflection. The first solution has obvious drawbacks since it can make the model substantially more complex. Structural reflection[JA92, MWY91], on the other hand, has a minimal impact on the model. The idea is to make the meta-level architecture identical to the architecture described by the model. In other words, we describe the structure and functionality of agents in terms of other agents. The agent representation of the structure and functionality can then be inspected using the functionality provided by that agent. Note that this approach also simplifies the design and implementation of dynamic configuration and coordination, since no special accessors need to be defined anymore.

Structural reflection is only one part of the solution to accessing the configuration and coordination parts at run-time – it achieves uniformity as far as the model is concerned. However, this does not imply uniformity in the implementation. The latter is characterised by uniformity in the means by which the model is exploited for both dynamic and interactive configuration and coordination, ie. the inspection of an agent should 'look' the same no matter whether it is done dynamically or interactively. This can be achieved by making the implementation interpreter based. Thus, whatever constructs we use in the implementation for inspecting and modifying agents dynamically we can also use interactively. It turns out that interpretation is also required for interactive computation layers – in order to create new kinds of agents or substantially alter the behaviour of existing agents. An interpreter based implementation enables an incremental design where new kinds of agents are added to the system in precisely the same way as the agents that exist initially.

4 The Actor Model

The actor model[Agh86] is a simple yet powerful means of defining agent based systems. An actor is an entity that is represented by a *reference* and a current *behaviour*. Each actor represents an independent active entity, thus resulting in inter-actor concurrency. The basic form of interaction between actors is buffered asynchronous peer-to-peer communication. Thus, associated with every actor is a *mail queue* that serves to buffer messages that are sent to the actor until they can be accepted for processing. When an actor starts processing a message it is *locked* until a *replacement behaviour* is established that will take over the processing of the next message. Since this can take place before the processing of the message has been completed, a form of pipelined intra-actor concurrency is achieved. The behaviour of an actor determines the actions to be taken in response to a message. It typically includes a set of *acquaintances*, which are references to other actors. The content of a message may also contain references, and together with the acquaintances, they comprise the set of known actors. Fig. 5 illustrates the structure of an actor. There are two types of actions an actor can take in response to a message: the sending messages to known actors and the creation of new actors. Primitive actors are used in the model to avoid a conceptually infinite regress of message passing. An implementation will give direct treatment to passing messages to primitive actors.

4.1 Computation and Communication

All true computation ultimately takes place in primitive actors which have a built-in behaviour. Non-primitive actors use these primitive actors by sending

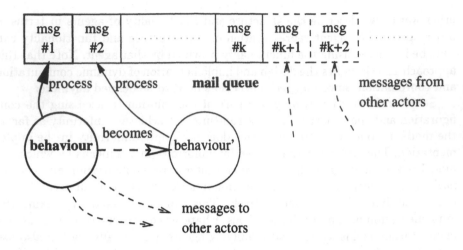

Fig. 5. The Actor Model

messages to them. In doing so they establish complex behaviours and thus perform complex computations. The buffered asynchronous peer-to-peer communication is an intrinsic feature of the model and underlies computation. Other forms of communication can be built on top of it. Causality, for instance, can be achieved using request-reply style interactions, which in turn can be implemented by embedding 'self' references in messages.

The majority of core problems of distributed systems can be addressed by implementations of the model, and thus need not be of any concern to application designers and implementors. For instance, there is nothing in the actor model that prevents distribution of actors. All implementations need to do is to give some distributions semantics to actor references. Data exchange between different platforms and actor-migration can be achieved in a similar way, by giving more concrete semantics to message passing and actor references. Note that this is precisely the way primitive actors are supported – the application developer need not have any knowledge about whether an actor is primitive.

4.2 Configuration and Coordination

The basic actor model is unsuitable for purposes of configuration and coordination because it relies on the asynchronous peer-to-peer communication. Actors can only send messages to actors they know. This knowledge is embedded in the actors, whereas it should really reside in the configuration layer. Configuration can only be achieved to some degree by having the configuration part 'tell' the agents with whom they can communicate. The same approach would have to be taken for coordination. By altering the semantics of communication in the model we can introduce implicit anonymous communication – a message sent by an actor to another actor thus not automatically ends up in the target's mail box but may instead be 'diverted' to another actor which performs configuration and coordination tasks.

Structural reflection is consistent with the actor model. An actor consists of just three entities: a mail queue, a set of acquaintances and a behaviour. By introducing method and procedure actors we can describe the behaviour in terms of actors. The behaviour can thus be unified with the set of acquaintances – an actors behaviour is determined by the procedures and methods it 'knows'. The mail queue can be viewed as a special acquaintance. The set of acquaintances can be viewed as a list of key-value pairs, so-called *slots*. Acquaintances can be identified by their key, which in turn refers to an actor. Hence an actor can be described in terms of a list containing actor references, which in turn, can be viewed as an actor. Messages can also be viewed as actors, containing a slot that refers to the target of the message and a slot that holds the content, for instance, in the form of a tuple. Thus everything in the actor model can be described in terms of actors and we can have complete structural reflection.

5 Related Research

Coordination is a relatively new research topic. Nevertheless, several coordination languages and systems have been developed. Formalisms, such as Gamma[BM90] and languages such as Linda[Gel85, Ban96] have emerged. Most of these systems are not intended to be general-purpose design and implementation frameworks. They are proof-of-concept and theoretical systems. The clear separation of layers, their transparent integration and interactive nature of the layers have not been addressed. These are important issues when coordination is viewed as a software engineering issue. For the issue of configuration this perspective has been taken by research in software architecture[GS93, PW92, GP94, RE96]. The focus has only been on layer separation though, without paying much attention to transparent integration and without recognising coordination as a separate layer. Additionally the interactive aspects have been neglected and even dynamic layers are sometimes not supported. More recently, some attempts have been made to integrate coordination into such systems – TOOLBUS[BK96] is an extension of the POLYLITH Software bus[Pur94], ConCoord[Hol96] is an extension of *Darwin*[MEK95]. ActorSpace[CA94] and Synchronizers[FA93, Fro96] are extensions of an actor language. MANIFOLD[Arb96] is based on a model where processes communicate anonymously via streams.

The TOOLBUS architecture views a system as a collection of tools that communicate with each other via a bus. While this achieves a clear separation of the configuration and coordination layers from the computation layer it does not achieve their transparent integration. The computation layer has to be modified to allow configuration and coordination, which in that case are *required* in order for anything to happen in the system. Interactive layers are not supported. Only limited means of abstraction and reuse are available.

In ConCoord a distributed system is viewed as a collection of *components* with *interfaces*. Interfaces represent services that are either provided or required. Consequently ConCoord distinguishes between provisions and requirements and it is the task of the configuration layer to establish *bindings* between the two. Communication is thus explicitly anonymous, with all the associated drawbacks. Components are either primitive or are compositions of other components, thus resulting in a hierarchical decomposition structure. Primitive components represent the computation layer. Coordination is triggered by *state notification* and results in reconfiguration. Significant changes to the coordination layer thus require alteration of the computation layer, which is not possible dynamically or interactively. Interactive layers are not supported in general. The expressiveness of the configuration language is limited and thus forces separate languages, design and implementation principles for the computation layer.

MANIFOLD is based on concepts very similar to those underlying ConCoord. The language is more powerful and in principle allows a unified design and implementation approach for the layers. However, it suffers from the drawbacks of using explicit anonymous stream-based communication as the only communication model. Events are used for layer interaction and also for interaction within the configuration and coordination layer. Configuration and coordination of the event-based communication is complicated and not explicitly supported. Interactive layers are not supported.

ActorSpaces provide an anonymous communication mechanism for actors. An actor can send a message containing a pattern which is matched against known ActorSpaces which in turn match it against the list of visible attributes of actors in their ActorSpace. The sender of the message can specify whether the message should be broadcast to all matching actors or whether it should be sent to one chosen actor. In essence, ActorSpaces determine the receiver(s) for messages and represent the configuration layer. Synchronizers constrain the invocation patterns on groups of actors by imposing temporal and causal orderings on the messages received by actors within the group. They thus represent the coordination layer. Synchronizers do not require alterations to the computation layer but ActorSpaces do. Both are not explicitly modelled as actors. Their behaviour is specified using concepts outside the actor model and thus requires new design and implementation methodologies. It also makes interactive layers impossible since no tangible explicit run-time representations of the configuration and coordination layer exist.

6 Summary

In this paper we have illustrated that there is a need for dividing the specification and implementation of distributed systems into four parts – communication, computation, configuration and coordination. We then showed that these four parts require integration into a single framework. An investigation into the dependencies between the parts reveals a layered structure where lower layers are unaware of higher layers. The coordination layer is the highest layer and as far as the other layers is concerned coordination thus does not exist. We discovered that the requirements for an integrated framework largely depend on the dynamism present in each of the layers and that there is a an interdependency between the requirements. Systems with interactive layers were shown to be the most demanding, but are the only ones that can satisfy the requirements of complex, long-running distributed applications.

We have shown that the underlying communication model plays a crucial role in meeting the requirements of configuration, coordination and their integration into an overall framework. Both non-anonymous and anonymous communication prove to be unsuitable for a general solution. We introduced implicit anonymous communication as a new model of communication. It satisfies most of the requirements, with the remaining ones being met by structural reflection and an interpreter-based approach. Most importantly it turns out to be a means by which configuration and coordination can be integrated transparently into the overall framework. Thus, for instance, the layer's conceptual unawareness of the coordination layer is preserved in the model.

We have illustrated how implicit anonymous communication can be added to the actor model by changing the semantics of communication in the model. Structural reflection can also be added easily. This again allows the transparent integration of configuration and coordination. We believe that implicit anonymous communication can be *the* means by which configuration and coordination can be integrated transparently into existing models of distributed systems design and implementation. It is the foundation upon which various higher level configuration and coordination concepts can be based.

7 Acknowledgements

We gratefully acknowledge the advice and help provided by TECC (http://www.tecc.co.uk), the Distributed Software Engineering Research Section (http://www-dse.doc.ic.ac.uk) at the Imperial College Dept. of Computing, and the financial support from the EPSRC under grant ref: GR/K73282.

References

[Agh86]   G.A. Agha. *Actors: A Model of Concurrent Computation in Distributed Systems*. MIT Press, 1986.

[Arb96]   F. Arbab. The iwim model for coordination of concurrent activities. In P. Ciancarini and C. Hankin, editors, *Coordination Languages and Models*, volume 1061 of *LNCS*. Springer Verlag, April 1996.

[Ban96]   M. Banville. Sonia: an adaption of linda for coordination of activities in organizations. In P. Ciancarini and C. Hankin, editors, *Coordination Languages and Models*, volume 1061 of *LNCS*. Springer Verlag, April 1996.

[BK96]   J.A. Bergstra and P. Klint. The toolbus coordination architecture. In P. Ciancarini and C. Hankin, editors, *Coordination Languages and Models*, volume 1061 of *LNCS*. Springer Verlag, April 1996.

[BM90]   J.-P. Banatre and D. Le Metayer. The gamma model and its discipline of programming. *Science of Computer Programming*, 15:55–77, 1990.

[CA94]   C.J. Callsen and G. Agha. Open heterogeneous computing in actorspace. *Journal of Parallel and Distributed Computing*, pages 289–300, 1994.

[FA93]   S. Frolund and G. Agha. A language framework for multi-object coordination. In *ECOOP'93 Proceedings*, volume 707 of *LNCS*, pages 346–360. Springer Verlag, 1993.

[Fro96]   S. Frolund. *Coordinating Distributed Objects: An Actor-Based Approach to Synchronization*. MIT Press, 1996.

[Gel85]   David Gelernter. Generative communication in linda. *ACM Transactions on Programing Languages and Systems*, 7(1):80–112, 1985.

[GP94]   D. Garlan and D. Perry. Software architecture: Practice, potential and pitfalls. In *Proc. of the 16th Int. Conf. on Software Engineering*, May 1994.

[GS93]   D. Garlan and M Shaw. An introduction to software architecture. In *Advances in Software Engineering and Knowledge Engineering*, volume 1. World Scientific Publishing Co., 1993.

[Hol96]   A.A. Holzbacher. A software environment for concurrent coordinated programming. In P. Ciancarini and C. Hankin, editors, *Coordination Languages and Models*, volume 1061 of *LNCS*. Springer Verlag, April 1996.

[JA92]   S. Jagannathan and G.A. Agha. A reflective model of inheritance. In *ECOOP'92 Proceedings*. Springer-Verlag, 1992.

[MC94]   T. Malone and K. Crowston. The interdisciplinary study of coordination. *ACM Computing Surveys*, 26:87–119, March 1994.

[MEK95]   J. Magee, S. Eisenbach, and J. Kramer. System structuring: A convergence of theory and practice? In K.P. Birman, F. Mattern, and A. Schiper, editors, *Theory and Practice in Distributed Systems, Proc. of the Dagstuhl Workshop*, volume 938 of *LNCS*. Springer Verlag, 1995.

[Mil89]   R. Milner. *Communication and Concurrency*. Prentice Hall, 1989.

[Mil91]   R. Milner. The polyadic π-calculus: a tutorial. Technical Report ECS-LFCS 91-180, University of Edinburgh, October 1991.

[MPW92]   Robin Milner, Joachim Parrow, and David Walker. A calculus of mobile processes, I and II. *Information and Computation*, 100:1–77, 1992. Also as Tech. Rep. ECS-LFCS 89-85/86, University of Edinburgh.

[MWY91]   S. Matsuoka, T. Wanatabe, and A. Yonezawa. Hybrid group reflective architecture for object-oriented concurrent reflective programming. In O. Nierstrasz, editor, *ECOOP'91 Proceedings*, LNCS. Springer-Verlag, 1991.

[MZ95]   T. Mowbray and R. Zahavi. *The Essential CORBA: Using Systems Integration, Using Distributed Objects*. John Wiley & Sons, 1995.

[Pur94]   J.M. Purtilo. The polylith software bus. *ACM Transactions on Programming Languages*, 16(1):151–174, January 1994.

[PW92]   D.E. Perry and A.L. Wolf. Foundations for the study of software architectures. *ACM SIGSOFT Software Engineering Notes*, 17(4):40–52, 1992.

[RE96]   M. Radestock and S. Eisenbach. Formalizing system structure. In *Proc. of the 8th Int. Workshop on Software Specification and Design*, pages 95–104. IEEE Computer Society Press, 1996.

[Weg96]   P. Wegner. Coordination as constrained interaction. In P. Ciancarini and C. Hankin, editors, *Coordination Languages and Models*, volume 1061 of *LNCS*. Springer Verlag, April 1996.

Interoperability of Distributed Transaction Processing Systems

Thomas Kunkelmann, Hartmut Vogler
Technische Hochschule Darmstadt
Informationstechnologie Transfer Office
Alexanderstr. 10
D-64283 Darmstadt
{kunkel,vogler}@ito.th-darmstadt.de

Susan Thomas
Digital Equipment GmbH
CEC Karlsruhe
Vincenz-Prießnitz-Str. 1
D-76131 Karlsruhe
sthomas@kampus.ENET.dec.com

Abstract: Distributed transactions - whose traditional domain of application is databases - have recently been brought into new areas of computer science like the management of large distributed systems and networks. There are several standards specified for distributed transaction processing in heterogeneous environments, like X/Open DTP based on DCE, and OMG OTS for CORBA environments. This paper will discuss the interoperability of these distributed transaction standards in general. A special solution for the interoperability between OTS and DTP, based on a half bridge between DCE and CORBA, is presented.

Keywords: distributed transactions, X/Open DTP, OMG OTS, interoperability, CORBA, DCE

1 Introduction

The usage of *transactions* is a very popular concept for the management of large data collections. Transactions guarantee the consistency of data records when multiple users or processes perform concurrent operations on them. Nowadays the concept of transaction processing is used, apart from the "classical" database applications, in the management of large distributed systems. An example for this is the administration of networks and network elements as well as the management of telecommunication devices [VOG96]. Here the transaction concept is applied to different layers of the network. In the context of distributed applications they cater for data consistency. In the network administration they guarantee the preservation of a consistent state of the network as well as a consistent state of network elements like routers or switches.

First we give a short overview defining transactions [GRR93]. If multiple users want to manipulate data records at the same time, data inconsistencies can occur. If the users protect their data access with transactions they can be sure that between e.g. a read operation and the resulting write operation no other user has access to this data record, preventing possible inconsistencies due to parallel update operations. In general the properties of transactions are known as the *ACID* properties (Atomicity, an indivisible set of operations; Consistency is guaranteed for the data; Isolation of parallel data acess in different transactions; Durabiliy, the events are stored permanently or completely rejected).

The access of distributed resources, e.g. databases on different computers, within a transaction is called a distributed transaction. For committing the result, the peers involved in a distributed transaction usually communicate via the *two-phase-commit* protocol (2PC): The initiator of a transaction takes the role of the coordinator, which in the first phase collects the votes about the result of the transaction from the different partners. In the second phase it transmits the result (*commit*: make the results of the transaction permanent; or *rollback*: discard all changes) to the other partners which subsequently confirm the receipt. The 2PC thus is quite robust against disturbances in the communication.

The transaction mechanism uses more general mechanisms like semaphores, deadlock detection, protocol files, logging and recovery. These are known as the *concurrency control and recovery* mechanisms (CCR).

In distributed systems transactions must be used through standardized procedures and protocols due to the heterogenity of the systems. In the last few years several service platforms (middleware) came up for communication in heterogeneous distributed systems, which have been standardized now. The most important platforms for application development are *DCE* (Distributed Computer Environment) developed by the OSF [SCH93] and *CORBA* (Common Object Request Broker Architecture) from the OMG [OMG91]. For both systems a transaction processing standard has been defined. The X/Open standard is based on services from DCE, while the OMG has defined an object-oriented standard for distributed transaction processing in the CORBA environment.

This paper illustrates problems and possible solutions of the interoperability between standardized distributed transaction systems. The next chapter presents the X/Open DTP standard. Chapter 3 explains the OTS standard of the OMG. In chapter 4 we will discuss the different forms of interoperability between these two models. The final chapter 5 presents possible developments in the area of distributed transaction processing.

2 The X/Open DTP-Model for Distributed Transactions

With the X/Open model for *distributed transaction processing* (DTP) the X/Open group [XOP93] presents a standard which allows the distribution of transactional computing on different computer nodes and applications in a standardized manner. For this the model defines several well-defined components and the affiliated interfaces.

2.1 The Components of the X/Open DTP-Model

The X/Open distributed transaction processing model describes mainly those components necessary for the distribution of a transaction on different *domains* (computer nodes). The manager of resources can, however, be designed in any fashion, they are solely responsible for the ACID properties on their data records. Merely the interface to the components of the X/Open DTP model must exist.

If a transaction should be distributed on several domains (in the model this is called a *global transaction*), in every domain there must exist the following components (see figure 2-1):

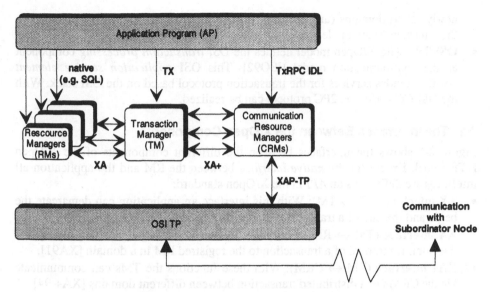

Figure 2-1 A Domain in the X/Open DTP Model

- **TM - Transaction-Manager**. The transaction manager plays the role of the co-ordinator in the respective domain. If a transaction is initiated in this domain, the TM assigns a globally unique identifier (*transaction identifier*, XID) for it. It is responsible for the correct course of the transaction and controls the commit protocol as well as the rollback and recovery. The TM monitors all actions from applications and resource managers in its domain. In every domain involved in the distributed transaction environment there exists exactly one TM.

- **RM - Resource-Manager**. This component controls the access to one or more resources like files, printers or databases. The RM is responsible for the ACID properties on its data records. The interface to the application is neither specified nor restricted in the X/Open model. In every domain there can exist several RMs which are registered at the responsible TM.

- **CRM - Communication-Resource-Manager**. This component is used by applications but also other management components for inter-domain communication. Multiple applications in the same domain also talk with each other via the CRM.

  There can be multiple CRMs in the same domain, each supporting a different communication paradigm. The X/Open model specifies the **TxRPC** as a communication model, which supports a *remote procedure call* (RPC) in the context of a transaction.

- **AP - Application-Program**. This application wants to access the resources in a transactional way and so it initializes a transaction. The boundaries of a transaction are demarcated by the function calls *tx_begin* and *tx_end* to the TM. If some RMs are called by the application, they participate in the transaction protocol, the application doesn't need to enforce further actions.

  The application can communicate to RMs and applications in other domains via the CRM. This results in a transaction tree, where the initiator is the root and the newly called domains (and probably further domains, which will be included in the transaction) are the leaves of the tree.

- **OSI TP** - The X/Open model defines the *OSI transaction processing* component as the communication model [ISO92]. This OSI *application service element* (ASE) provides services for the transaction protocol based on the OSI stack. With the OSI *CCR ASE* the 2PC protocol can be realized.

2.2 The Interfaces Between the X/Open Components

Figure 2-1 shows the interfaces between the different components of the X/Open DTP model. Except for the *native interface* between the RM and the application all interfaces are defined as an *API* in the X/Open standard:

- **TX interface** (AP ↔ TM): With this interface an application can demarcate the begin and the end of a transaction to the TM [TX95].
- **XA interface** (TM ↔ RM): The TM coordinates the begin, the suspending and the commit protocol of a transaction to the registred RM in a domain [XA91].
- **XA+ interface** (TM ↔ CRM): With these functions the TMs can communicate via the CRMs in a distributed transaction between different domains [XA+ 94].
- **TxRPC IDL** (AP ↔ CRM): The TxRPC [XOP95] is based on the *DCE RPC* [SCH93], which can use some other DCE services like the *name service* for the localization of servers. The DCE *interface definition language* (IDL) is slightly extended to support the TxRPC. The CRMs communicate with each other via the *OSI TP* protocol.

The major advantage of the X/Open DTP model is the standardization of the interfaces. Due to the modular concept all components and applications can be easily extended and replaced. So cooperation between components of different vendors is possible. In a sample environment the transaction monitors *TUXEDO* (Novell) and *Encina* (Transarc) can be involved in a single transaction and can even talk to each other via a CRM of a different vendor. The X/Open model supports changes in the configuration at runtime because the RM and CRM can also register dynamically at the TM.

Multiple transactions initiated by different applications are distinguished by the *thread of control* (ToC). It is a structure defined in the X/Open model and must be distinguished by the thread-ID or process-ID in the sense of POSIX. The TM manages the sequence of transactions by suspending them and resuming them at a later time.

2.3 Transaction Trees

A transaction is initiated by an application with *tx_begin*, so the domain of this application becomes the *root* of a new transaction tree. Involving other applications or RMs in a different domain results in a TX call from the TxRPC stub to the local TM, which informs the TM of the remote domain to join the transaction. A *branch* to the new domain is included in the transaction tree, the new domain is located at level 1 of the tree. Deeper levels of the transaction tree can be created with the same mechanism. When calling *tx_end* from the initiating application the root TM acts as the coordinator of the commit protocol for all involved domains.

181

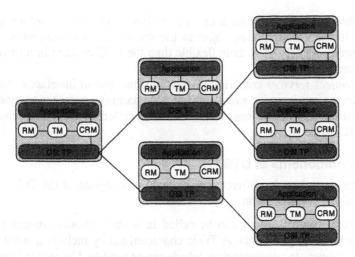

Figure 2-2 DTP Transaction Tree

Figure 2-2 shows a transaction tree as it is defined in the X/Open model.

Possible extensions to the ACID transaction model in X/Open DTP are *chained transactions*, where the end of one transaction implies the start of a new one. Furthermore there are optimizations like *vote readonly* and *commit one phase*.

The problems arising with *nested transactions* are beyond the scope of this paper.

3 The OMG Object Transaction Services Model

The *Object Transaction Service* (OTS) is part of the *Object Management Architecture* (OMA) of the *Object Management Group* (OMG), shown in figure 3-1.

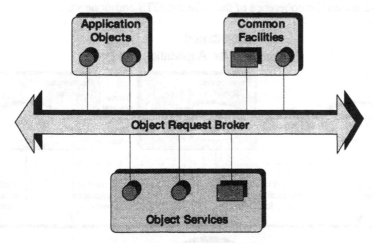

Figure 3-1 Object Management Architecture (OMA)

The kernel of this architecture is the *Object Request Broker* (ORB) defined in the CORBA specification [OMG91]. This specification describes a communication infrastructure for distributed applications in an object-oriented manner. The client/ server structure of this architecture is nearly transparent to the applications. The call of an object method is identical for local or remote objects. The calls from an application are passed to the corresponding object in the distributed environment by the ORB. The framework of CORBA is more flexible than the RPC concept in a merely client/server architecture.

The OMG *object services* comprise all fundamental system interfaces. Among others, they cover services for event notification, naming, persistence, concurrency, security, timing and transactions. The latter one is called *Object Transaction Service* (OTS) [OMG94].

3.1 The Components of OTS

This chapter describes the different components and objects of the OTS model and the interworking between them.

- An object whose methods can be called in a transactional context is called a **transactional object (TO)**. A TO is characterized by including some persistent data or pointers to persistent data, which can be modified by its methods.
  A call of a TO need not be transactional, even if the call is within the context of a transaction. It is left to the object for which calls it behaves transactional. Using TOs *transactional servers* and *recoverable servers* are implemented.
- A TO which is affected by a commit or a rollback of a transaction is called a **recoverable object (RO)**.
- A **transactional server (TS)** consists of one or more objects involved in a transaction, but doesn't have any state information about the transaction.
- A **recoverable server (RS)** includes at least one RO.
- A **transactional client (TC)** can be any program which calls methods of transactional objects in the context of a single transaction.

Figure 3-2 shows the coherence of the different OTS components.

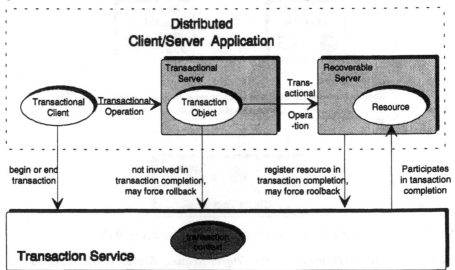

Figure 3-2 The Components and Objects of an OTS

3.2 The Architecture of OTS

The transaction service provides operations
- to control the context and the duration of a transaction
- for the participation of multiple objects in a single transaction
- to combine internal changes of object states within a transaction
- for the coordination of the 2PC protocol at the end of a transaction

Figure 3-3 shows the main components and the related interfaces of the OTS model.

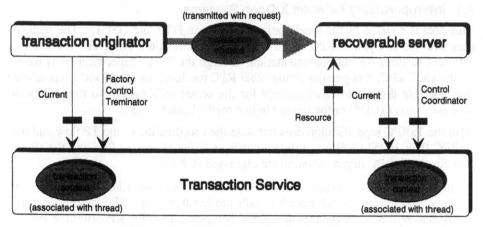

Figure 3-3 Object Transaction Service (OTS)

A typical initiator of a transaction uses the *current* object to start the transaction, which will be combined with a thread by the OTS. This current object can be used later for a commit or rollback of the transaction.

An alternative is to start a transaction by a call to a *factory*, which returns a *control* object for this new transaction. The control object provides no direct access to the transaction management, but allows access to a *terminator* object and a *coordinator* object. The terminator object provides methods for the commit or rollback of a trans-action, whilst the coordinator object allows a TO to participate in a transaction by registering a *resource* object.

3.3 Comparison of the X/Open DTP and the OMG OTS Model

	DTP Modell	OTS Modell
server localization	specific to the CRM, DCE-based systems can use CDS services	specific to the ORB, it is transparent to the application
server registration	static as well as dynamic registration	dynamic registration only
2PC-protocol	via the OSI-TP protocol	via method calls to the objects
additional functions for transaction trees	chained transactions	nested transactions
communication paradigms between the applications	currently 3 paradigms, TxRPC among others, can be extended	specific to the ORB
network protocol	OSI-TP mandatory	specific to the ORB

4 Interoperability of Transaction Processing Systems

To get from closed transaction systems to an open transaction processing environment some new and existing concepts for the interoperability must be realized. An important issue is to close the gaps in different specifications for the sake of a useful and practicable realization. We have identified three different areas for the interworking of transaction processing systems, which are explained in the following three chapters.

4.1 Interoperability between X/Open Systems

This area is covered by the specifications of X/Open DTP and OSI TP. The realization with the X/Open TxRPC and the OSI TP specification, however, leaves some different versions for the implementation. Though the TxRPC specification is based on the DCE RPC, it is possible to use other RPC mechanisms. The TxRPC specification does not define the exact concept for the server localization, so the DCE *cell directory server* (CDS) or the *string binding* method can be used.

Also the TxRPC sepecification does not state the coordination of the TP flow and the TxRPC flow. In [SLC95] two different concepts of the *separated flow* and the *single flow* for the TxRPC implementation are discussed in detail.

- In the single flow concept all communication is based on RPC. The regular TP flow and also the remote procedure calls are handled by the RPC runtime system. To realize this some changes at the IDL compiler and at the RPC runtime system can be made [SLC95]. Another possibility is to leave DCE unchanged and to use an additional pre-compiler, which generates the necessary stub routines and the corresponding DCE IDL files. This concept is realized in the *ACMSxp* implementation from Digital, for an open, distributed TP monitor [BCD95].

- The concept of the separated flow uses two different communication channels, one for the TP flow on the OSI TP stack and one for the remote procedure calls via the RPC runtime system. An advantage of this concept is that no modification of the DCE runtime system is necessary. By means of a stub routine which intercepts the TxRPC call, starts the necessary TP flow and thereafter permits the DCE RPC call, this concept can be realized. The drawback of this solution is the deficient performance. With additional listener and dispatcher routines the performance of transaction processing systems is further deteriorated.

4.2 Interoperability in OTS Systems

The interoperability of OTS systems is influenced directly by the interoperability of the ORB systems and their limits concerning naming, security and so on. Apart from these problems there are some OTS-related interoperability issues.

4.2.1 ORB Domains and OTS Domains

Different ORB domains can cooperate via an inter-ORB gateway, an inter-ORB bridge or an inter-ORB protocol. Examples for those protocols are the *Internet Inter-ORB Protocol* (IIOP), or an *Environment Specific Inter-ORB Protocol* (ESIOP), which is defined in CORBA version 2.0. By using the same OTS implementation or an inter-OTS implementation a transaction manager in one of these domains can control every resource object beyond the boundaries of its ORB domain. These ORB domains form together one transaction domain. For administrative or geographical reasons these ORB domains might form mutually independent transaction domains. In figure 4-1 the OTS domain is formed by the ORB domains #1 to #3 with a transaction manager in ORB domain #3.

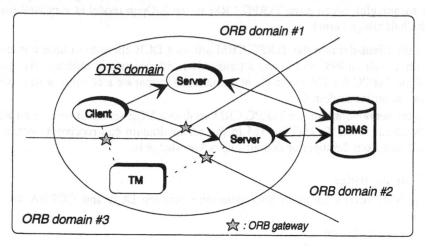

Figure 4-1 ORB and OTS Domains

4.2.2 Transaction Identifiers (XID)

In the OTS environment the identifier of a transaction (XID) is generated using the object references of the coordinator object. The problem whith this method is that object references are neither unique nor invariant beyond the ORB boundaries within an OTS domain. This leads to problems if different servers from various ORB domains access the same database.

In contrast to OTS the XID in the X/Open DTP model is globally unique. The data structure of the XID consists of two records, a global transaction identifier and an identifier for the branch, both limited to 64 characters.

For those reasons, and in view of the interoperability with an X/Open system, it is not meaningful to use an object reference as a global XID. A transactional CORBA call should therefore contain the object reference of the coordinator as well as an XID similar to the X/Open model.

4.3 Interoperability between OTS and X/Open DTP

Today´s available transaction systems, like TUXEDO, Encina or TOPEND (NCR), are based on the procedural interfaces of the X/Open standard. Due to their complexity and their widely dissemination they can only incrementally be convertet to use object-oriented systems, like OMG OTS. For this reason some systems for the interoperability between OMG OTS and X/Open DTP domains must be developed. The OTS specification contains, in fact, an XA+ interface, but does not describe the mapping of calls from one system to the other.

4.3.1 Gateway vs. Half-Bridges

Consider the fact that the interoperability of DTP and OTS implicitly contains an interoperability between DCE and CORBA. Such an interoperability between heterogeneous environments can normally be achieved by a *gateway* or a *half bridge* [SUZ96]. For the interoperability of OTS and X/Open the half bridge concept seems to be meaningful, because the TxRPC CRM in the X/Open model is very well suited for the half bridge kernel.

- In the **client-domain** the TxRPC CRM allows a DCE client to initiate a transaction, to call an RPC and to end a transaction with commit or rollback. By means of the TxRPC the TM in the client domain can propagate a commit or rollback to the subordinator domain.
- In the **server-domain** the TxRPC CRM enables a DCE server to receive an RPC. By means of the TxRPC the TM in the server domain can receive a commit or rollback from the superior domain and acknowledge it.

4.3.2 Static Bridge

In [YAV96] several forms of interoperability between DCE and CORBA are described:

- static bridge
- on-demand bridge
- dynamic bridge

For the interoperability between distributed transaction processing systems only a static bridge is planned for the present. Firstly, for the aim of an incremental transition into an object-oriented transaction system, no dynamic behaviour is expected. Secondly, for the main goal of interoperability the performance aspects must be considered in order not to impair the already worse performance of those systems. In a first version, therefore, there will be no *federating naming service* [KEL93] available. For the conversion of the different DCE IDL and CORBA IDL a translation like in [VOG95] is sufficient.

4.3.3 Structure of the Bridge

As already mentioned in chapter 4.3.1 the TxRPC CRM forms the kernel of the half bridge. Therefore no changes at the X/Open side are required. It is, however, more important to decide how to integrate a bridge object into the OTS domain. Here we have to distinguish whether the OTS domain or the X/Open domain is the initiator of the transaction.

4.3.3.1 From the OTS Domain to the X/Open Domain

If the initiator of a transaction is placed in the OTS domain, i.e. an OTS client calls an X/Open server, a new module is used in the OTS domain, which is called an *OTS-C bridge* in the following discussion. This module consists of a proxy, which acts both as a recoverable object and as a TxRPC client. Besides this the module contains a *communication manager resource object* (CM-RO), which provides a resource object interface to the superior OTS coordinator and communicates with the X/Open domain via OSI TP.

Figure 4-2 shows the structure of the OTS-C bridge and a simple example.

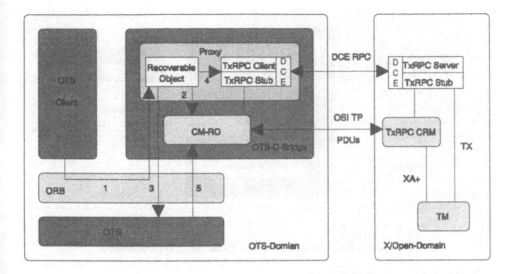

Figure 4-2 Structure and Course of Events in an OTS-C Bridge

The course of events is as follows:

1. An OTS client sends a request to include the proxy in the OTS-C bridge.
2. The proxy acts as a recoverable object, creating a CM-RO as a resource object
3. The proxy registers the CM-RO as a resource object
4. After registration the proxy can act as a regular TxRPC client and can send requests to the TxRPC server in the X/Open domain. For the corresponding data flow it uses either the TxRPC stub for the DCE flow or the CM-RO for the OSI TP flow.
5. The commit flow is handled directly via the CM-RO.

4.3.3.2 From the X/Open Domain to the OTS Domain

This is the case if the initiator of a transaction is located in the X/Open domain, i.e an X/Open client calls an OTS server (object). Here we also need a new module, called an *OTS-S bridge* in the following discussion. The OTS-S bridge consists of a proxy, acting as both a TxRPC server and an OTS transactional client, and a component called the *communication manager subordinator coordinator object* (CM-SubCO), which communicates with the client TxRPC CRM via the OSI TP protocol. Figure 4-3 shows the structure of the OTS-S bridge and a simple example.

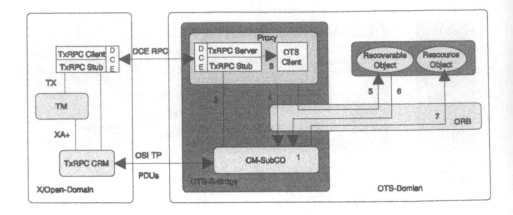

Figure 4-3 Structure and Course of Events in an OTS-S Bridge

The course of events is as follows:
1. Receiving a request from a TxRPC client, the CM-SubCO creates objects for the transaction service, like control and coordinator objects.
2. A TxRPC call is received by the proxy as if it were a TxRPC server.
3. The proxy acts as an OTS client.
4. Before sending an object call the proxy interacts with the CM-SubCO in order to execute the object call in the right context.
5. The proxy includes an OTS server.
6. After receiving an object call the recoverable server registers its resource object at the CM-SubCO, which offers a coordinator interface.
7. After receiving a commit-PDU from the superior node, the CM-SubCO transmits the corresponding semantics for the end of a transaction to the registered resource object.

5 Summary and Outlook

Distributed transactions find more and more application in new fields of operation. In the area of distributed systems the management of networks and their components with the usage of transactions must be mentioned. To distribute a transaction among different domains various standards and methods have been established. An important goal of the current research activities is to make interoperability between these standards possible.

This paper presents two currently most important transaction processing standards. For DCE-based systems this is the X/Open DTP model, for CORBA systems the OTS standard defined by the OMG. For both methods we examined the requirements for interoperability between them.

Although, interworking between X/Open DTP systems is prescribed in the standard, the realization can still be made in different ways. In this paper the single flow concept and the separated flow concept have been discussed.

A decisive role for the interoperability between different OTS systems is the interoperability of the ORB implementation it is based on. With the specification of an inter-ORB protocol in CORBA 2.0 an important step in this direction is made. But there are still many open issues, like the implementation of the transaction identifiers.

If a distributed transaction should run between an OTS system and an X/Open system, a gateway is necessary between both systems. An alternative solution is the usage of a half bridge shown in chapter 4.3. Here the components of the X/Open system remain widely unchanged, while two new modules (S- and C-bridge, for both directions of the transaction inition) are introduced into the OTS system.

A future step towards the interoperability of both systems is the development of a concept for the interworking between DCE and CORBA in general. There are some research activities in this area [YAV96]. General interoperability, however, will raise many problems, due to the fact that both concepts are too different. For the field of transaction processing the problems of the translation from a procedural to an object-oriented systems remain and require additional solutions.

The possibility of an interoperability between X/Open DTP and OTS enables the development of new fields of application for distributed transactions. In regard to the network management example from the introduction chapter this means that in future new object-oriented network elements designed for CORBA environments can be included and managed by management platforms operating in a DCE environment in a transactional manner.

Literature

[BCD95] R. Baafe, J. Carrie, W. Drury, O. Wiesler: ACMSxp Open Distributed Transaction Processing, Digital Technical Journal, Vol. 7 No. 1, 1995

[GRR93] J. Gray, A. Reuter: Transaction Processing: Concepts and Techniques, Morgan Kaufmann Publisher, 1993

[ISO92] International Organisation for Standardisation: OSI TP Model/Service, April 1992

[KEL93] L. Keller: Vom Name-Server zum Trader - Ein Überblick über Trading in verteilten Systemen; Praxis der Informationsverarbeitung und Kommunikation (PIK), Vol. 16, Nr. 3, Sep. 1993

[OMG91] Object Management Group: The Object Request Broker: Architecture and Specification, 1991

[OMG94] Object Management Group: Object Transaction Service, 1994

[SCH93] A. Schill: DCE - Das OSF Distributed Computing Environment, Springer Verlag, 1993, ISBN 3-540-55335-5

[SLC95] S. Sedillot, J. Liang, J. La Chimia: Integrating DCE RPC with OSI TP to offer a transactional RPC; First International Workshop on High Speed Networks and Open Distributed Platforms, St. Petersburg, June 1995

[SUZ96] M. Steinder, A. Uszok, K. Zielinski: A Framework for Inter-ORB Request Level Bridge Construction; Proceedings of the ICDP'96 - IFIP/IEEE International Conference on Distributed Platforms, Dresden, Feb. 1996

[VOG95] A. Vogel, B. Grey: Translating DCE IDL in OMG IDL and vice versa; TR 22, CRC for Distributed Systems Technology, Brisbane, 1995

[VOG96] F. Vogt: Werkzeuge für die Transaktionsverarbeitung heute - morgen; Proceedings of the 19th European Congress Fair of Technical Communication - ONLINE'96, Congress VI, Hamburg, Feb. 1996

[TX95] X/Open CAE Specification: Distributed Transaction Processing: The TX (Transaction Demarcation) Specification, X/Open Company Ltd., 1995

[XA91] X/Open CAE Specification: Distributed Transaction Processing: The XA Specification, X/Open Company Ltd., UK, 1991

[XA+94] X/Open Snapshot: Distributed Transaction Processing: The XA+ Specification, Version 2, X/Open Company Ltd., 1994

[XOP93] X/Open Guide: Distributed Transaction Processing: Reference Model, Version 2, X/Open Company Ltd., 1993

[XOP95] X/Open CAE Specification : Distributed Transaction Processing: The TxRPC Specification, X/Open Company Ltd., 1995

[YAV96] Z. Yang, A. Vogel: Achieving Interoperability between CORBA and DCE Applications Using Bridges; Proceedings of the ICDP'96 - IFIP/IEEE International Conference on Distributed Platforms, Dresden, Feb. 1996

Reuse and Inheritance in Distributed Object Systems

H. Gründer and K. Geihs

Department of Computer Science
University of Frankfurt
P.O. BOX 11 19 32
D-60054 Frankfurt
Germany
{gruender,geihs}@informatik.uni-frankfurt.de

Abstract. Our goal is to support reuse and extensibility in distributed object systems. This requires some form of distributed inheritance and polymorphism. Most existing distributed system architectures can only cope with the inheritance and reuse of interface specifications. We discuss reuse requirements and approaches in general and their particularities in distributed systems. An approach is proposed that enables inheritance and reuse for object implementations. Our approach is based on a decoupling of object state and behavior. The behavior is implemented by so–called object engines. Our engine design and prototype implemementation are presented and compared to other well-known reuse techniques in distributed systems.

1 Introduction

The enormous progress in computer and telecommunications technologies has led to distributed computing environments with a multitude of services, servers and clients. The terms service, server and client refer to the enterprise view of the acting entities in such an open distributed service market. From an information processing perspective these entities can be modelled as objects that represent services, clients or servers.

The object paradigm has proven to be particularly suitable to model structures and interactions of distributed systems. This is due to the fundamental properties of objects such as abstraction, encapsulation, modularity and access protection. In addition to these fundamental properties, object-orientation includes inheritance and polymorphism mechanisms. They support the reuse, substitution and extensibility of object-oriented software components. Delegation and aggregation mechanisms in object systems basically aim at the same targets. While aggregation and delegation principles can be carried over from non-distributed to distributed systems in a rather straightforward way, it is not so obvious how the benefits of inheritance can be achieved in distributed systems. This is due to the inherent heterogeneity of hardware and software, which make it generally impossible to migrate program code between heterogeneous computing systems. Aggregation and delegation avoid these difficulties by transparently transforming local invocations on proxies to remote method invocations. For the same reasons polymorhphic substitutions are not feasible generally since programs cannot be substituted across machine boundaries, unless we are dealing with interpreter based programming languages which are executable on all appropriately equipped computing platforms (e.g. [Ous94], [Sun95]).

Our work aims at conserving the widely accepted benefits of inheritance and polymorphism mechanisms in distributed systems in order to enable the reuse of program code across heterogeneous platforms. This is achieved by decoupling the object's behavior implementation from its interface and state. The polymorphism property plays an important role here when substituting an implementation by another one.

In Section 2 of this paper we review basic reuse and object specification concepts concentrating on the question of what can be reused. In Section 3 we discuss how these reuse requirements can be achieved in heterogeneous distributed systems. Section 4 presents the object engine concept which supports a form of distributed inheritance that satisfies the desired reusability and extensibility. The section also includes an overview over a CORBA-based prototype implementation. In Section 5 we summarize our results and point to further work.

2 Object model and software reuse

According to the classical definition in [Boo91], "an object has state, behavior and identity; the structure and behavior of similar objects are defined in their common class. The terms instance and object are interchangeable". The object model enables a natural structuring of the problem space and defines precise interfaces between the structural components, the objects. The object model is the basic modelling paradigm in the Object Management Architecture of the Object Management Group (OMG) [OMG92], the reference model for Open Distributed Processing (ODP) of ISO [ISO94], and the TINA–C architecture [DNI95].

In order to discuss reusability in distributed systems we have to ask first what elements can be reused during the design and maintenance process. Let us therefore recall the three principle ways of specifying objects, as shown in Figure 1 [WZ88].

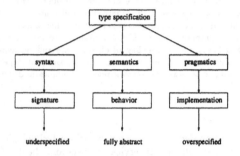

Fig. 1. Type Specification

The *syntactic specification* defines the object's user interface in form of the interface signature. Syntactic interface specifications abstract away from implementations of the operations and attributes offered by the object. The detailed behavioral semantics of objects cannot be described this way. Due to this semantic gap, interface specification is an under–specification. The *semantic specification* provides an abstract definition of the behavior of objects using natural language or formal description techniques. The complexity of objects and the limited expressiveness of specification languages mostly make exhaustive behavior descriptions impossible. A concrete object implementation written in some programming language would be called a *pragmatic specification*. There is an infinite number of possible implementations for an object. Therefore, a concrete pragmatic specification is an over–specification.

2.1 Reuse

It is quite typical for engineering approaches to take existing descriptions, properties and structures as a starting point to combine, refine and extend them in order to come up with something new. Figure 2 summarizes the different aspects of reuse in object systems for the three specification techniques mentioned above.

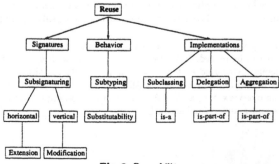

Fig. 2. Reusability

In the case of syntactic specifications one can derive sub–signatures by modifying a given signature through additive extensions or more general modifications. Reuse of a behavioral specification is reflected in a type–subtype relationship. The behavior of a subtype is compatible to the behavior of the supertype, i.e. the subtype may replace the supertype but may have additional capabilities. An object implementation as defined in the corresponding class definition is a pragmatic specification. Reuse of pragmatic specifications, i.e. implementations, can be based on three different techniques: inheritance, delegation and aggregation. Inheritance leads to a direct reuse of program code when constructing new implementations. Delegation and aggregation involve other objects to provide a service. With delegation, an object delegates parts of its service to another object. The delegation is transparent to the clients of the object. With aggregation, several objects are aggregated into a new object, i.e. the aggregate object. It offers its service at an aggregated interface. Aggregation is a special case of delegation, and both constitute a form of containment relationship. Clearly, inheritance, delegation and aggregation are related concepts. We will come back to them when we discuss their application in distributed systems.

2.2 Polymorphism

Polymorphism in object systems allows the substitution of an object of type A by an object of type B, if B is a subtype of A. The clients of the A-type would not have to know and would not notice the replacement with an A-compatible B-type. Depending on the specification technique, i.e. syntactic, semantic or pragmatic, substitution requires conformant signatures, behaviors or implementations, respectively.

Polymorphism in object systems is tightly coupled to the concept of inheritance, since polymorphism is supported along the inheritance hierarchy. An inheritance relationship can be stated explicitly in the specifications, or it may be given implicitly through the compatibility of e.g. behavior specifications. Obviously, inheritance can be exploited more easily when stated explicitly by the one who writes the specifications.

Polymorphic substitution of implementations is the key to the evolution of software systems, and in particular to the evolution of open service markets considering their variety of service types and service providers and their inherent decentralisation and autonomy. Unfortunately, inheritance and polymorphism are difficult to exploit in such heterogeneous distributed systems. The reasons for that will be discussed in the next section.

3 Objects and Reuse in Distributed Systems

The object model has been adopted by organisations such as ISO, OMG, TINA-C and Microsoft as the fundamental modelling paradigm for their distributed system software architectures. Nevertheless, the implications and realisation of inheritance and polymorphic substitutions are not completely understood yet. The cited architectures either provide a very limited form of inheritance and reuse, or none at all. We will first look at the existing approaches, before we present our solution.

3.1 State of the Art

Reuse in distributed systems may also be divided into three categories: reuse of interface specifications, behavioral specifications and implementations.

Interfaces Interfaces of computational objects in distributed systems are specified using an interface definition language (IDL). Popular examples are the OSF DCE-IDL which is also the basis for the IDL of Microsoft's Component Object Model (COM), the CORBA-IDL from OMG, and the ODL-95 of TINA-C which is an extended CORBA IDL. The DCE-IDL does not provide an explicit inheritance notation but allows for implicit inheritance-like relationships via interface versions and UUIDs. The CORBA IDL and ODL-95 support explicit interface inheritance. Typically, this mechanism is used by an application programmer to derive application-specific interfaces from built-in, system provided interface specifications. The specification of derived interfaces is supported by the CORBA Interface Repository, which contains information on the interface hierarchy and which may be accessed itself as an object. Interface inheritance and reuse are well understood in todays distributed platforms.

Behaviour The support for behavioral subtyping by far is not as well understood. Consequently, it does not play a significant role in real-life systems. Behavioural subtyping in its generality still is an open research problem, for non-distributed systems as well as for distributed ones. This is partly due to the fact that the behavior cannot completely be specified using formal notations, such as algebras or predicate logic. Furthermore, it is not possible to automatically and exhaustively check whether an implementation satisfies its specification. Often formal specifications are augmented by explanations in natural language to give a clue on the object behavior, which however hinders the automatic processing by computers. Consequently, providing reuse on the basis of a behavioral specification is not a very practical thing to do. For a thorough discussion of behavioral subtyping the reader is referred to [LW93b], [LW93a], [LW93c] and [Nie93].

Implementations Reuse of program code in distributed object systems can be based on delegation, aggregation and inheritance. While the former two are used already in distributed systems, the latter is more difficult to achieve. We will present our solution after a few words on the pecularities of delegation and aggregation in distributed systems.

Delegation Objects interact according to the client–server paradigm. One object assumes the role of a client and uses the service of a server object via a reference to that object. It is transparent to the client how and where the service methods are implemented, i.e. it is transparent whether the server object implements a method itself, or if the method execution is delegated to another object. Delegation relationships can be represented by directed graphs as shown in figure 3. Delegation is supported by almost all object based and object oriented platforms and architectures, such as ODP, CORBA, COM and TINA.

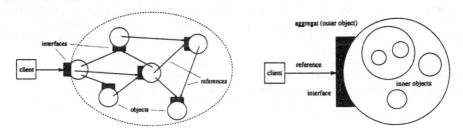

Fig. 3. Delegation   **Fig. 4.** Aggregation

Aggregation Aggregation is used in Microsoft's Component Object Model (COM). COM objects are able to have multiple interfaces. Each object by default has an interface called *IUnknown*, which is the key to aggregation. A set of objects can be grouped together to form a new object, the aggregate, which has its own IUnknown interface. The IUnknown interface contains a method named *QueryInterface()*, which allows to successively access the interfaces of all objects contained in the aggregate and to invoke methods via references to these interfaces. Objects within the aggregate potentially know all component interfaces, too. Aggregation is a special case of delegation, that additionally supports the user in building and accessing the aggregates interfaces and introduces tight bindings between the *inner* objects.

Inheritance Inheritance supports the reuse of code in a systematic, type-controlled way. We claim that in distributed systems it is not enough to support just interface inheritance (as described above). Rather we want to go further and achieve the same benefits as with inheritance in non-distributed object-oriented systems, i.e. systematic code reuse, extensibility, and polymorphic substitution.

Inheritance builds on aggregation as well as delegation. However, reuse through delegation and aggregation is not a complete substitute for inheritance, because it does not introduce any type relationships and thus does not provide the same benefits as a fully object–oriented approach. Only with inheritance an adequate and proven concept is given for the incremental construction and evolution of implementations by making use of polymorphic substitution. Furthermore, the granularity of reusable components with delegation and aggregation is the object. Such a granularity may not be appropriate for distributed systems with their potential for true parallelism in executing operations of an object.

Distributed inheritance in analogy to the non-distributed is not supported in CORBA, ODP, COM and TINA–C. Some CORBA–platforms provide inheritance in the local context but not for remote interfaces.

3.2 Polymorphic Substitution

Clients in an open service market will ask a trading service for a particular service provider and then bind to a particular service implementation [GGP+95]. The transparent substitution of the implementation is difficult for two reasons: The subsitute must provide the same type or a subtype of the one that the client has bound to, and substitution must preserve the state that has been built up in the server reflecting the context of the client–server association. Thus, the substitution of a whole service object is hindered by the fact that the object has an identity and contains individual state information.

This raises the question how the substitution of a service implementation can be achieved at all, if there is such a tight coupling between the client and the identity of a service object. We need to find a way to separate the client–server association from the implementation of the server's behavior in order to be able to exchange service implementations.

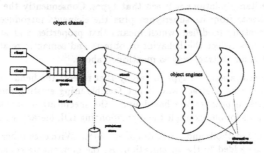

Fig. 5. Engine–Approach

4 Implementation Decoupling and Distributed Inheritance

To solve the inheritance and reuse problem in distributed systems, we propose a conceptual decoupling of an object's code from its data and interface. Note that this separation appears only from an engineering viewpoint. It is transparent to the clients' computational view of the object. The object data reflects the state of the service–association, e.g. application and client specific data, intermediate results, management information, service parameters, etc. The object's code implements the behavior of the object. In our design a so–called *engine* embodies the behavior, and a so–called *chassis* carries state and identity. An engine may attach to an object's chassis, read the state and execute operations that have arrived at the interface. Attachment requires a type–subtype compatibility. State changes computed by engines are written back to the chassis. An engine may also detach itself from a chassis. Engines may physically reside on another node of the network than the chassis, i.e. the implementation of the object becomes a distributed one. All required communication protocols and coordination mechanisms for attaching, getting invocations and detaching are supplied by the runtime environment. Fig 5 illustrates the engine concept.

Note that we still support an object–oriented modelling of the client–server interactions, because the client still sees the object as an encapsulated unit. The engineering-level separation of state and behavior enables the presence of a service offer independent from the availability of a service provider. For example, this allows temporary absence in order to perform maintenance or management activities.

The flexibility of the engine approach is underlined when looking at its support for distributed inheritance. Figure 5 shows an attached engine that as a whole implements exactly the service that is offered to the client at the object interface. In addition to such a direct type match, we support polymorphic engine substitutions when an engine implements a subtype of the object type. In this case the engine would embody more functionality as actually needed to provide the service. See [SPGG94] for details.

In this paper we want to emphasise another way of using engines. To achieve distributed inheritance of implementations, it is possible that an engine implements only parts of an object's behavior. In that case an object has several engines attached, and each one executes a defined subset of the operations. Which parts an engine is capable to implement is predefined through an inheritance hierarchy specified by the application developer. By adding operations and corresponding engines to an existing object we incrementally refine the object type, analogous to an inheritance step in an object-oriented program. In other words, we allow engines to attach to an object chassis even if it implements *only* a legal supertype of the object type. The collection of attached engines - reused and new ones - together represent the new type. Thus, service provision, substitution and evolution are supported in a very flexible way.

4.1 Service Specification

Let us demonstrate by an example how the separation into object engine and chassis helps to achieve the stated goals. Consider an arbitrary object with object type T_F (Figure 6). The type is classified according to the type hierarchy symbolized by the directed graph. The edges symbolize types and the vertices show inheritance relations between that types. Consequently the type can be specified by the elements it inherits from its supertypes plus the elements introduced by the type itself. Supertypes are incrementally modified, which means that properties and attributes are changed or added. Type hierarchies reflect the behavior of objects and semantic relations between objects (behavior inheritance) in an abstract way as mentioned above.

Since a complete specification of a type hierarchy that reflects the behavior of objects and their semantical relationships in an abstract way, is not feasible using existing formal description techniques, most approaches in practice are based upon the specification of interfaces and interface hierarchies. Figure 7 shows for our example the corresponding IDL hierarchy specifying the type T_F.

Interfaces describe the methods and attributes of an object. With each inheritance step new methods or attributes may be added to the specification. At the moment we consider only monotonous inheritance. Overloading and reduction of methods and attributes is not possible so far. This conforms to the CORBA standard. We use monotonous inheritance to identify blocks of methods and attributes that are closely related enough to be implemented by one engine. The inheritance steps determines the granularity of the engines. This can be controlled by the designer of the hierarchy. Several engines collectively implement the service of the object according to the type hierarchy (Figure 9).

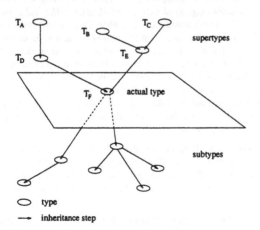

Fig. 6. Inheritance

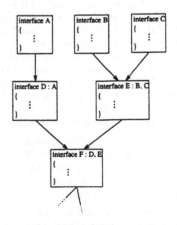

Fig. 7. IDL Description

197

Since engines need the object state to perform their functionality, a specification of the object's state structure must be integrated into the interface specification (see Figure 8). For each refinement step the state information available for engines is determined. The individual step by step state specifications together represent the object state.

4.2 Generation of Client, Service and Service Provider

An application developer, who wants to make use of the distributed inheritance mechanism, specifies his service offer of type F through an IDL description (see Figure 8). He reuses the IDL specification of D and E to build his own service. From the existence of interfaces D and E within the distributed interface repository it is assumed, that somewhere in the distributed system engines are available that implement D and E. In addition, the developer adds his new methods and attributes M to the inherited ones and specifies the additional state description S_F, which is needed to implement the offered additional funtionality. Obviously, only the additional methods have to be implemented. Implementations of the inherited ones are assumed to exist already. The interface compiler reads the description and generates the following three parts (see Figure 8):

Client Proxy A proxy is generated for clients to gain access to an instantiated object. Objects can also be accessed via the dynamic invocation interface. The client view on the object does not differ from that known from CORBA, and the full CORBA functionality is given.

Object Chassis The object chassis is the representation of the offered service. It contains the operational interface and the state representation as well as additional information needed by the engines. The object chassis is instantiated when an object is created and carries out a mediation function between service user and service provider.

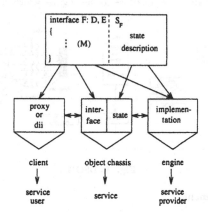

Fig. 8. Service User, Service and Service Provider

Object Engine The engine carries the implementation of the object behavior, together with runtime support functions for attaching and detaching to an object chassis, reading and writing the object state, and carrying out methods invoked on the object. It is generated as a template that contains the generic engine features. The template is completed by specific application methods, which must be coded by the service application programmer.

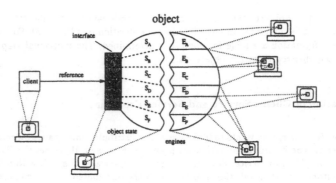

Fig. 9. Possible Runtime Constellation

4.3 Runtime Interaction

Figure 9 shows how client, object chassis and engines interact at runtime. The object, having the derived type F, offers the service to the client. The client invokes methods on the object via an obtained object reference. Client, object chassis and object engines are located in different address spaces on different host machines. This configuration behind the interface is transparent to the client. On the *back side* of the interface the engines, which were generated according to the inheritance hierarchy, cooperate to provide the service. Each engine E_i operates directly on the assigned state information S_i. In a heterogeneous, decentralised, evolving environment it is conceivable that the state expectation of an engine may be different from a given state representation in a chassis. Thus, questions on the structural compatibility of state descriptions arise. For a discussion of this subject the reader is referred to [GG95].

As with inheritance in local systems it is often necessary to access methods or state information that are defined in supertypes or superclasses, respectively. It is not possible to access them directly, since other engines in other address spaces may be responsible for implementing or holding these elements. In order to access these parts of the object, calls upwards the inheritance hierarchy are delegated via a private object interface to the engines which are actually implementing the supertypes.

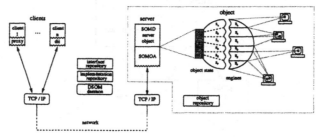

Fig. 10. DSOM

4.4 Runtime Environment

Our prototypical implementation of the engine concept and the distributed inheritance mechanism is based on the CORBA compliant implementation DSOM (Distributed System Object Model, IBM, Figure 10). The client side, the implementation repository and the interface repository are not modified. Our implementation approach concentrates on the server side. A DSOM server consists of the SOMOA, which has extended CORBA Basic Object Adapter(BOA) functionality, and the so called SOMDServerObject. The SOMDServerObject is DSOM specific and may be used by the application developer to integrate his own customized handling of objects and method invocation.

SOMOA and SOMDServerObject together administer the application objects in the address space of a server. These objects are configured according to Figure 9. This includes the sepration into chassis and engines, as well as the attachment of remote engines. In addition to the given CORBA repositories, an object repository (see Figure 10) contains information on which objects are available, what type they have, and on which server they are located. The object repository is consulted by engines when attaching to a chassis in order to ensure the type compatibility. The type information is stored in a distributed interface repository.

5 Summary and Outlook

The object model is a widely accepted basis for the modelling of distributed systems. Inheritance and polymorphism are key features for supporting software evolution and reuse. In order to exploit the inherent benefits of object–orientation in distributed systems, on the one hand one cannot do without these key features, while on the other hand their realisation is rather difficult in heterogeneous distributed environments. Consequently, most existing systems provide interface inheritance only.

We have proposed an approach to cope with distributed inheritance. It is based on the decoupling of the object behavior from the object state and interface. The object methods are implemented by so–called object engines which can execute invocations remotely. Our prototype demonstrates the viability of the approach. It is built on top of a CORBA platform.

Our current work aims at two directions: One goal is to extend the object specification by control information that governs the permissible sequence of method invocations on an object. We use Petri-nets to define the control flow. The control information processing can nicely be integrated with our engine concept which uses already a customized invocation dispatcher. That dispatcher is being extended to handle and check the control sequence. A workflow application will be the test case for this extension. The second activity investigates the use of multiple engines that execute in parallel on an object. Technically, it is no problem to integrate such a feature in our current system. However, it is quite obvious that complex concurrency, performance and reliability issues have to be examined with such a set-up.

References

[Boo91] G. Booch. *Object Oriented Design with Applications*. Benjamin Cummings Publishing Company, Inc, Redwood City, California, 1991.

[DNI95] F. Dupuy, G. Nilsson, and Y. Inoue. The TINA Consortium: Toward Networking Telecommunications Information Services. *IEEE Communications Magazine*, pages 78–83, November 1995.

[GG95]   H. Gründer and K. Geihs. An Object–Oriented Framework for Open Service Markets. In *First International Workshop on High Speed Networks and Open Distributed Platforms*, St. Petersburg, Russia, June 1995.

[GGP+95] K. Geihs, H. Gründer, A. Puder, W. Lamersdorf, M. Merz, and K. Müller. Systemunterstützung für offene verteilte Dienstemärkte. In *KiVS'95 - Kommunikation in Verteilten Systemen*, Chemnitz, 1995. Springer Verlag.

[ISO94] International Standardisation Organisation (ISO): Information Technology: Basic Reference Model of Open Distributed Processing, Parts 1-4, IS 10746 and working papers of ISO/IEC JTC1/SC21/WG7., July 1994.

[LW93a] B. Liskov and J. Wing. A New Definition of the Subtype Relation. In *ECOOP'93: Object-Oriented Programming*. Springer, 1993.

[LW93b] B. Liskov and J. Wing. Family Values: A Behavioral Notion of Subtyping. Technical Report CMU–CS–93–187, Computer Science Department, Carnegie Mellon University, Pittsburgh, July 1993.

[LW93c] B. Liskov and J. Wing. Specifications and Their Use in Defining Subtypes. *OOPSLA'93*, 28(10):16–28, October 1993.

[Nie93] O. Nierstrasz. Regular Types for Active Objects. In *Proceedings ACM Conference on Object Oriented Programming: Systems, Languages and Applications*, OOPSLA, September 1993.

[OMG92] Object Management Group (OMG), Object Management Architecture Guide, Revision 2.0, OMG Document Number 92.11.1, Richard Soley (OMG), ed., September 1992.

[Ous94] John K. Ousterhout. *Tcl and the Tk Toolkit*. Addison-Wesley, Reading, MA, 2 edition, 1994.

[SPGG94] T. Seidel, A. Puder, K. Geihs, and H. Gründer. Global Object Space: Modell und Implementation. Technischer Bericht (in German), Fachbereich Informatik, Goethe Universität Frankfurt, December 1994.

[Sun95] Sun. The java language: A white paper. WWW http://java.sun.com/, March 1995.

[WZ88]   P. Wegner and S. B. Zdonik. Inheritance as an Incremental Modification Mechanism or What Like Is and Isn't Like. In *ECOOP'88*. Springer, August 1988.

Finding Optimal Services Within a CORBA Trader

Dirk Thißen and Claudia Linnhoff-Popien
Aachen University of Technology, Department of Computer Science IV
Ahornstr. 55, D-52056 Aachen, Germany.
E-mail: thissen@zeus.informatik.rwth-aachen.de

Abstract

The growing of computer networks and transmission capacity causes the possibility of a rising amount of service offers in distributed systems. One of the CORBAservices is the trading service, which supports clients in searching for suitable services.

This paper introduces an evaluation process for selecting an optimal service offer from a trader's service directory. This mechanism uses a service distance function for computing the distance between a service request and a service offer. Minimizing this distance yields an optimal service. Therefore, existing methods for distance computation between vectors are used, and a new rulework for computing the distance between single service properties is developed. The resulting evaluation procedure is used for an implementation in a CORBA trader.

Keywords: CORBA; Trading service; Quality of service; Service distance.

1. Introduction

In a large distributed system many services are offered. To support a client in searching a special service a trader can be used. This trader has a service directory, which contains available services specified by a service type and service property values. If a client requests a service, the trader procures a convenient one. The problem in this mechanism is that the process of selecting a service only matches the client's request against the service property values. There is no possibility to take into consideration quality of service aspects as defined in the quality of service basic framework [QoS 95].

This paper treats a modification of a trader's selection procedure. The modification allows the client to include quality aspects into its request. The trader now uses a set of service distance functions to calculate the distance between the service request and each service offer. Therefore a service is viewed as a vector of properties. Analytic methods are used to calculate distances between such vectors. With respect to service quality a property can consist of several values with certain roles. Thus, to calculate a distance between these components, it was necessary to develop a new rulework. The service with minimal distance to the requested service is regarded as optimal service. In CORBA 2.0, beside interoperability between different platforms, the CORBAservices are standardized [CORBA]. In Request for Proposal 5, one of the requested services is the trading service. So, the purpose is to implement the presented selection procedure into a CORBA trader.

The paper is structured as follows. In the second chapter an overview about service trading and quality effects is given. The trading process and service notations are introduced. Furthermore the consideration of service quality leads to the concept of the service distance functions. The third chapter explains the process of finding an optimal service in a trader's service directory. Several known methods for computation and optimization concerning vector distances are discussed and compared. The new rulework for computing the distance between single properties is introduced. A concept for implementing the presented selection approach into a CORBA trader as well as some measure results using the new approach are given in the fourth chapter. Finally, the fifth chapter presents conclusions and tasks for further studies.

2. Service Request vs Service Offer

To explain the purpose of service distance functions, at first a short introduction into service notations and service trading is given.

2.1 Service Trading in CORBA

A *service* is a function provided by an object at a *computational interface* [PSW 96]. This function expresses a set of capabilities available at the interface. Such a service is an instance of a *service type*. For each service type there exists an affiliated *interface type* and several noncomputational aspects called *service properties*. Different services of the same service type may differ in their service properties. A service property is described as a (name, value) pair and is an instance of a *service property type*. The context between these types and instances is shown in figure 1.

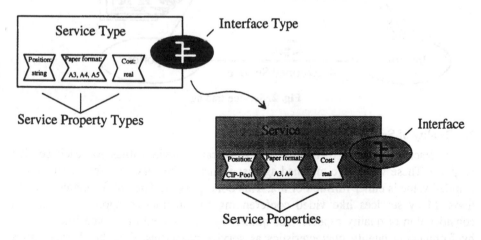

Fig. 1. Service description

A *trader* is a service procuring other services. For this purpose, a trader needs a *service directory*, which contains descriptions about all services available at the trader. A service included in such a directory is called a *service offer*. In addition to its service type and service properties a service offer can also have *service offer properties*. To structure the service offers the complete offer domain, i.e. the service directory, is divided by a context. A context hierarchy arises. Each trading context contains a set of service offers with equal administrative characteristics. An *exporter*, i.e. a server which wants to provide a service, can register this service within the service directory. The service is registrated with exporter identifier, service interface identifier, service type description and service offer properties.

A client using a trader to search a service is called *importer* [SPM 94]. It requests a service at the trader in specifying the service type, i.e. an interface type and service properties. Therefore the importer chooses the operations SEARCH or SELECT. SEARCH brings about all suitable services, whereas SELECT brings about only one of them. Such specifications for example could be made by the service description language SRDL [PM 94]. The choice of suitable services at the trader is made by matching interface type and service properties with every service offer. The result of a service import is an interface identifier. Now, the importer can directly contact the server which has exported the service. This trading process is shown in figure 2.

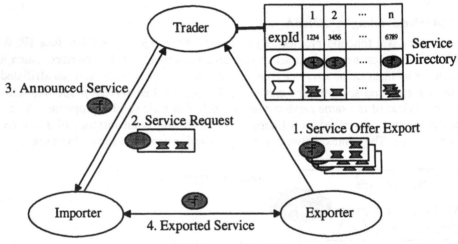

Fig. 2. Service trading

2.2 Quality of Service and Service Properties

The described trading mechanism only tolerates single values for each service property. These values are matched against values in the service offer. A single demanded value is either fulfilled or not. This concept is insufficient for many applications. Many services like video conferencing and interactive applications need a consideration of quality aspects. The *quality of service* could be taken into account by formulating quality characteristics as service properties. Quality characteristics are e.g. throughput, transmission delay or availability [Th 95]. Now, an importer needs to specify more than one value, namely a *target*, a *lower bound* and an *upper bound* on such a characteristic to formulate its wishes and limits. All these values are components of a quality of service parameter, so they all are needed to express quality [QoS 95]. Furthermore the importer must be allowed to specify the *preference* of every characteristic, so that the trader knows what characteristics are to be dealt with priority. Because of the arising complex structures of service properties, normal matching no longer can be used.

To evaluate the new specification of a service request, the trader needs a suitable evaluation component. That component only needs evaluating service properties. Therefore in the following approach only service properties are considered. The service type can be matched as before. The new component can be realized using service distance functions. A service request is represented by a vector $\mathbf{r} = (r_1, ..., r_n)$ of its service request properties. In this case service request property r_i means a record of target $r_i.t$, upper bound $r_i.u$, lower bound $r_i.l$ and preference $r_i.p$, as shown in figure 3. Likewise a service offer can be represented by a vector $\mathbf{o} = (o_1, ..., o_m)$ with records of a lower bound $o_i.l$ and an upper bound $o_i.u$. So, the trader needs no longer to match the service properties, but could compute the distance between the service request vector and the service offer vector.

Service Properties

Service request $\mathbf{r} = (r_1, ..., r_n)$ with   Service offer $\mathbf{o} = (o_1, ..., o_m)$ with

Service request property r_i: Service offer property o_i:

$$r_i = \{ \quad \text{Target t} \qquad\qquad\qquad o_i = \{ \quad \text{Upper bound u}$$

Upper bound u   Lower bound l

Lower bound l   }

Preference p

}

Fig. 3. Service property structure

A number of distance functions on vectors are well known in analysis, especially maximum metric, Euclidean metric and Manhattan metric. Furthermore methods in fuzzy set theory and the analytic hierarchy process provide approaches suitable for the distance computing on vectors. But there is no method to compute the distance between single components, because they are records of values with different roles. So, it was necessary to develop a distance function on service property records. This distance function is presented in the next chapter, just as a discussion of known distance functions on vectors.

3. Service Distance Function

To compute the distance between service vectors, two steps are necessary. The first step is to compute the distance between the components of both vectors, the service property records. This step is described in section 3.1. The result is a vector of differences. In the second step, these differences must be combined to the distance between vectors. In section 3.2 some methods are presented to achieve this. Section 3.3 presents a short comparison of the introduced service distance functions.

3.1 Service Property Record Distance

As described in chapter two, a service request property with quality consideration in our example consists of four values with the roles target, upper bound, lower bound and preference. A service offer property consists of a lower bound and an upper bound. So, it is impossible to compute a simple difference between both structures. Thus, it was necessary to draw up rules for every combination of values.

The importer is allowed to specify each combination of target and bounds. To simplify the evaluation, in the specifying process either both or no bounds are occupied. If the importer only specifies one bound, the other will be set on its extreme value. In the case of lower bound this value is zero, in the case of upper bound it is infinity. Not occupied components have the value undefined ($\perp$). Likewise the exporter can specify only one or both bounds. Service offer vector and service request vector need not to have equal size and contain equal properties, so o_i only means the property with the same name as r_i. In the following the possible cases for a component distance function d_c are distinguished.

° If the importer specifies a property not included in the provider's property vector, the distance must be set to infinity:

if $name(r_i) \neq name(o_j)$ $\forall j = 1, ..., m$
    then $d_c(r_i, o_i) = \infty$

° If the service request property r_i only defines a target, the difference is zero if the target value is within the bounds of the affiliated service offer property o_i. Outside the bounds the difference to the corresponding bound must be computed:

if $r_i.t \neq \perp$ and $r_i.u = \perp$ and $o_i.u \neq \perp$ then
    if $o_i.l \leq r_i.t \leq o_i.u$
        then $d_c(r_i, o_i) = 0$
    if $o_i.u < r_i.t$
        then $d_c(r_i, o_i) = r_i.t - o_i.u$
  else $d_c(r_i, o_i) = o_i.l - r_i.t$

° If the client only specifies bounds to a property, the distance is zero, if they lie inside the provider's bounds. If there is no intersection, the difference is set to infinity. Otherwise the distance corresponds to that size of the importer's interval, which is not contained in the provider's interval.

if $r_i.u \neq \perp$ and $r_i.t = \perp$ and $o_i.u \neq \perp$ then
    if $[r_i.l, r_i.u] \cap [o_i.l, o_i.u] = \emptyset$
        then $d_c(r_i, o_i) = \infty$
    if $o_i.l \leq r_i.l$ and $r_i.u \leq o_i.u$
        then $d_c(r_i, o_i) = 0$
    if $r_i.l < o_i.l$
        then if $r_i.u < o_i.u$
            then $d_c(r_i, o_i) = o_i.l - r_i.l$
            else $d_c(r_i, o_i) = r_i.u - o_i.u + o_i.l - r_i.l$
    else $d_c(r_i, o_i) = r_i.u - o_i.u$

° If as well target as bounds are given by the importer, the distance is zero, if the target is inside the provider's bounds. If there is no intersection between the importer's and the provider's interval, the distance is infinite. Otherwise the distance is the difference between importer's target and the provider's bound that is inside the importer's interval:

if $r_i.t \neq \perp$ and $r_i.u \neq \perp$ and $o_i.u \neq \perp$ then
  if $o_i.l \leq r_i.t \leq o_i.u$
        then $d_c(r_i, o_i) = 0$
  if $[r_i.l, r_i.u] \cap [o_i.l, o_i.u] = \emptyset$
        then $d_c(r_i, o_i) = \infty$
  if $r_i.t < o_i.l \leq r_i.u$
        then $d_c(r_i, o_i) = o_i.l - r_i.t$
  else $d_c(r_i, o_i) = r_i.t - o_i.u$

° A problem in computing the distance by calculating a difference is the variability of service property values. Properties do not require to be expressed in a numerical format. The value of a property also can be a string. E.g. reliability possibly would be expressed in terms like 'high' or 'low'. Therefore, a function must transform the non-numerical statements into a numerical format. For that purpose, a non-numerical format could be transformed in a fixed interval, e.g. [0, ..., 100], or in an interval which contains all values the service providers offer. It is to be examined in practice which interval is more suitable for distance computation. The statement which characterizes highest quality becomes the highest value of the interval, the value which represents lowest quality is to be transformed into the lower bound of the interval. Other values can be transformed into suitable values among the bounds. It must be considered that for different properties the same non-numerical value can have different meanings. E.g. 'high' expresses a high quality in throughput but a low quality in error rate.

° The computed distances must be normalized. Otherwise typically differences in one component could be high enough for all other differences to be neglected. So, for every characteristic the average distance must be used as normalization factor to bring all property distances on the same dimension.

° At last, the resulted difference must be weighted with importer specified weights. The result is a weighted component distance d_{wc}:

$$d_{wc}(r_i, o_i) = r_i.p * d_c(r_i, o_i).$$

In this way the priority of each property is considered.

Now, these rules allow to compute the distances in all components of the service request vector. The resulting differences could be put together in a difference vector $\mathbf{d} = (d_1, ..., d_n)$ with $d_i = d_{wc}(r_i, o_i)$ for i = 1, ..., n. In the next step all these values d_i are to be combined to the difference between the service vectors.

3.2 Service Property Vector Distance

The idea of a vector distance function d_v is to compute a distance between vectors by combining the individual component differences. In analysis there are a few metrics which can be employed on such vectors. In general, an analytic metric for n > 0 is defined as follows:

$$d_v((x_1, ..., x_m), (y_1, ..., y_m)) := \left(\sum_{i=1}^{m} d_{wc}(x_i, y_i)^n \right)^{\frac{1}{n}}.$$

In practice, the relevant cases are n = 1, 2 and infinity. In these cases, the metrics are called Manhattan metric, Euclidean metric and maximum metric.

° Maximum metric

For n = infinity, the meaning of the formula is committed to investigate the maximal value of d_c. So the formula becomes

$$d_v((x_1, ..., x_m), (y_1, ..., y_m)) = \max_{1 \le i \le m} \{d_{wc}(x_i, y_i)\}.$$

In this case, the optimal service is a service offer close to the service request in all properties.

° Manhattan metric

In the case n = 1, all component differences are considered equally:

$$d_v((x_1, ..., x_m), (y_1, ..., y_m)) = \sum_{i=1}^{m} d_{wc}(x_i, y_i).$$

This leads to an optimal service with minimal deviation, at which single components with great deviations can be compensated by other components with small deviations.

° Euclidean metric

For n = 2, the formula equals the standard deviation, because great differences in single components are considered stronger than components with small difference:

$$d_v((x_1, ..., x_m), (y_1, ..., y_m)) = \sqrt{\sum_{i=1}^{m} d_{wc}(x_i, y_i)^2}.$$

At last, the optimal service offer can be found by minimizing the distance d_v. Service offer vectors A and B with the same distance to a service request vector C for two properties a and b are shown for all metrics in figure 4.

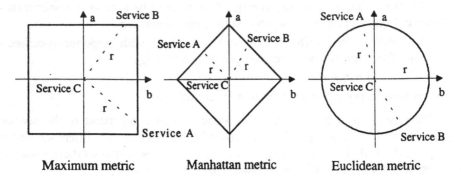

| Maximum metric | Manhattan metric | Euclidean metric |

Fig. 4. Vectors with the same distance r to a vector

Beside the mathematical functions to compute the distance between vectors, in practice there are other methods to find out an optimal service.

° Fuzzy set theory

The fuzzy set theory can be used to allow decisions in optimization problems [Zi 91]. A fuzzy set M is a set $\{(x, \mu(x)) \mid x \in X\}$, where X is a set of decision alternatives. μ is called membership function. It is a weight to express the membership of an element of X to M. In the case of service trading, X is the set of service offers. For every service request property a membership function μ exists to evaluate a service offer by this property.

An optimal decision for a set $X = \{x_i \mid i = 1, ..., n\}$ of decision alternatives and a set of goals $G = \{g_j \mid j = 1, ..., m\}$ is given by

$$\max_i\{(x_i, \min_j(\mu_{g_j}(x_i))^{w_j}) \mid i = 1, ..., n; j = 1, ..., m\},$$

where w_j is a user defined weight on goal g_j. In the case of service trading, G is the set of properties specified by the importer. For each decision alternative x_i the membership to all goals g_j must be computed. The minimal membership value is selected for x_i as membership estimation to the set G. Then the optimal decision alternative is the x_i with maximal membership estimation.

In computing distances between service offer and service request, this method can be used by exchanging the maximum and minimum forming. The only problem is finding a suitable membership function, but to this aid the distance function d_c can be used. Then w_j becomes r_j .p. So, that method corresponds to the maximum metric.

○ Analytic Hierarchy Process

The Analytic Hierarchy Process (AHP) is a complex method to achieve an optimal solution in selecting a decision alternative for a set of goals [Sa 80], [DP 94]. A user specifies a set of goals and a vector of weights to his goals. For each goal a matrix is constructed, in which rows and columns all decision alternatives are listed. The entries of the matrix are pairwise comparisons between the decision alternatives to express the fulfilment of the goal by a decision alternative in comparison to another alternative. Summing up the rows yields a vector of estimations to the goal for each decision alternative. All these vectors to the users goals are composed to a matrix. Multiplying this matrix with the users vector of weights yields a vector with estimations for the usefulness of each decision alternative. The multiplication of vector and matrix corresponds to the Manhattan metric.

In the case of service trading, the vector of user weights is given. But the pairwise comparison between service offers is very complex. At first, d_c must be used to compute the distance vector for every service offer. Then for each service property a matrix must be generated. The pairwise comparison could be achieved by comparing every vector component of every service offer with all the other corresponding values.

○ Additive and multiplicative model [Be 90]

The additive model is a simple method to consider weights in distance computing. It is a weighted sum of component distances:

$$d(\mathbf{r}, \mathbf{o}) = \sum_{i=1}^{n} w_i * d_c(r_i, o_i).$$

So it is equal to Manhattan metric. An enhanced method is the multiplicative model. In this case, distance computing ensues by

$$d(\mathbf{r}, \mathbf{o}) = \frac{\prod [1 + w * w_i * d_c(r_i, o_i)] - 1}{w}, \text{ where } w > -1, w \neq 0.$$

This method is different to all metrics, but it enhances the additive model, because great deviations are considered stronger than small deviations. The parameter w controls, how strong a great deviation should be considered in comparison to a small deviation. In the additive and multiplicative model, w_i can be substituted by $r_i.p$.

3.3 Comparison

In the previous sections service distance functions d_{wc} and d_v were presented. There is no other function to compare with d_{wc}, because the property records have a new structure. So the service ability of d_{wc} is to be examined in practice. For d_v, several methods are presented. The additive model need not be considered, because it is equal to Manhattan metric. Table 1 gives a short overview about computation complexity, result precision and implementation issues for all vector difference computing methods.

	Metrics	Fuzzy set theory	AHP	Multiplicative model
Complexity	+	+	-	o
Precision	+	+	++	+
Implementation easiness	+	+	-	+

Tab. 1. Overview about the presented methods

The computation of a distance between vectors by a metric ensues by a simple formula. So the computation complexity is low. Likewise the implementation is easy. The precision of the result in all three cases is equal. Indeed all metrics could yield different results, but each metric represents another meaning of 'optimal'. At maximum metric, a service offer is optimal, if the greatest deviation in all properties is as low as possible. At Manhattan metric, single properties with a great deviation are possible, if there are enough properties with a very low deviation to compensate the great deviations. At Euclidean metric, great deviations are weighted stronger than low deviations. So all metrics yield a precise result regarded to different meanings of 'optimal'.

The computation of the membership estimation in fuzzy set theory is similar to maximum metric. The only difference is the consideration of the importer's weights. Therefore the explanations regarding complexity, precision and implementation easiness are the same like for the metrics.

The computation with the multiplicative model possibly is more complex than the computation with metrics, because the user must know the meaning of the control parameter w. The implementation of the given formula is as easy as the implementation of the metrics. The precision of the result can differ with w, but this means different meanings of 'optimal' like at metrics.

The Analytic Hierarchy Process yields a result more precise than the result of each other method. The property differences are not only combined to a distance, but before they are weighted with each other by pairwise comparison. But this advantage in precision causes a high computation complexity. For each property a matrix must be generated and evaluated. This means a complex implementation, too. Hence, this method can be used at small service directories.

Because of the easy implementation possibilities of all methods except the Analytic Hierarchy Process, the best solution is an integrated distance computation mechanism with choice of the distance function by the importer.

4. Implementation of Service Distance Functions into a CORBA Trader

In this chapter, concepts are presented for implementing a trader evaluation component in C++ using service distance functions. This evaluation component can be integrated in an existing CORBA trader [Zl 96] of the distributed platform Orbix [ORBIX].

Because Orbix and its trader are object oriented, the quality of a service request, i.e. the service properties, are seen as object qosConstraints, see figure 5.

```
/* The class qosConstraints describes the service request properties
*/
class qosConstraints
{ private: struct_qos_specification *qosSpecification
  public : void set_qosSpecification(const iwt_types::ConstraintSpecType&
                                                          matchingConstraints,
                                     const iwt_types::PreferenceSpecType&
                                                          selectionPreference);
                         ...

          distance_type return_distanceFunction();
          preference_type return_preferenceFunction();
          struct_qos_searchVector *return_vector();
};

/* The internal state of the upper class contains the desired distance function,
   preference function and service request properties.
*/
struct struct_qos_specification
{ distance_type distance_function;
  preference_type preference_function;
  struct_qos_searchVector *qos_searchVector;
};

enum distance_type {maximum, manhattan, euclid, analytic, multiplicative};
enum preference_type {multiplicate, exponentiate};

/* struct_qos_searchVector is a list of struct_qos_searchParameter, which
   contains all in chapter two mentioned values
*/
struct struct_qos_searchParameter
{ iwt_types::NameType propertyName;
  CORBA::Double target;
  CORBA::Double upperBound;
  CORBA::Double lowerBound;
  CORBA::Double preference;
};
```

Fig. 5. Class qosConstraints for a service request

The internal state qosSpecification is a structure containing the desired distance and preference function as well as a list of struct_qos_search-Parameter. The importer must specify the service request as before, only additionally it can specify more values on a service property. Furthermore, the importer has to choose a service distance function and a weighting mechanism. The specification of the service properties and the distance function are contained in the variable `matchingConstraints`. `selectionPreference` contains the preferences on the properties specified in `matchingConstraints` and the weighting mechanism. The public function `set_qosSpecification` serves for covering the `qosSpecification` with these specifications. Furthermore, functions must be implemented to get the registered `qosSpecification`. More work is not needed on an object for a service request vector.

```
/* The class service_qos describes the service properties in a service offer
*/
class service_qos
{ private: struct_qos_offerVector *qos_offerVector;
  public : void set_qosOfferVector(const iwt_types::PropertyValueListType& spv,
                         const iwt_types::PropertyValueListType& sopv);
                  ...

          double compute_distance(struct_qos_searchVector *searchVector,
                         distance_type distance_function,
                         preference_type preference_function);
};

/* struct_qos_offerVector is a list of struct_qos_characteristik, which contains
   the property values in a service offer, as described in chapter two
*/
struct struct_qos_characteristic
{ iwt_types::NameType propertyName;
  CORBA::Double upperBound;
  CORBA::Double lowerBound;
};
```

Fig. 6. Class `service_qos` for a service offer

Likewise the property specification of each service offer is seen as an object. For service request and service offer different objects are necessary, because a service provider can specify less values on a property. So, the internal state `qos_offer-Vector` of an object for service offer properties is a list of `struct_qos_cha-racteristic`. A function `set_qos_offerVector` is needed to cover the list with the exporter's service property and service offer property values. Then, the distance to a service request specification is to be computed using the function `com-pute_distance`. This function realizes the service distance functions. The class `service_qos` for such service offer properties is shown in figure 6.

The object oriented implementation guarantees high portability. The described objects are implemented and integrated into the CORBA trader. In the trader, each service offer is an object `ServiceTableItem`. Instead of a property value list, at the service export now an object `service_qos` for each service is generated. At a service import, the matching constraints are transformed into an object `qosCon-straints`. This object is passed to the object `ContextTable`, i.e. the service directory, and then to the `service_qos` of each `ServiceTableItem`. Within this object, the service distance is computed. All suitable service offers are collected in a sequence that is sorted by the computed distance. Thus, the first entry of this sequence is the optimal service. The context between the trader and the new component is shown in figure 7.

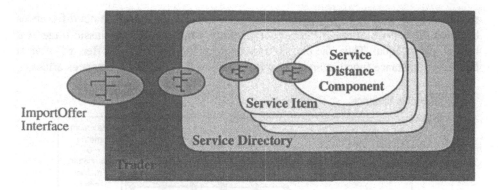

Fig. 7. The trader structure and the service distance component

To show the usefulness of the service distance component, a comparison with the classic trader is necessary. For this purpose, two comparisons are made. First, the evaluation time of the service distance component and the classic evaluation procedure are checked. Thereupon, a comparison of the import results is given.

Figure 8 shows the trader's evaluation time depending on the number of service offers in the service directory. All service offers have the same number of service properties. All service distance functions expected the AHP require the same time to search the service directory. The AHP needs slightly longer than the other service distance functions, because it has a more complex evaluation mechanism. In consequence of the scale of figure 8, it is not to see that for a small number of service offers the evaluation time for the classic trader is higher than for the service distance component. The reason is the efficient implementation of the distance functions. This advantage gets lost for a higher number of service offers.

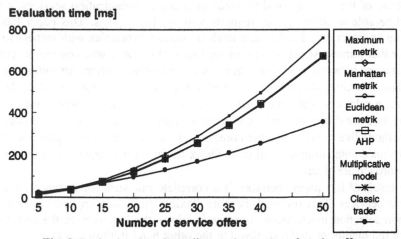

Fig. 8. Evaluation time depending on the number of service offers

To compare the import results of the service distance component and the classic trader, ten suitable services are exported. Figure 9 shows the relative distance of the service request to each service offer. It is easy to see that there are distinct differences between the service offers at the service distance component. The classic trader values all offers equal. Thus, the classic trader selects the first service offer, whereas at the service distance function an order with regard to the computed distances arises.

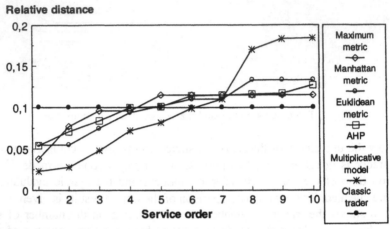

Fig. 9. Relative distance to all imported services

These measure results show, that the service distance component yields a better result than the classic trader. The price is a longer evaluation time for a great amount on service offers. For a small number of service offers there is no disadvantage by using the service distance functions.

5. Conclusions

Because of the growing quality needs of many communication services, a trader should be able to allow service requests with quality aspects. This paper has presented an approach to formulate and evaluate service properties with respect to quality. For that purpose services were viewed as vectors, so it was possible to compute the distances between a service request and each service offer. An optimal service offer has a minimal distance to the service request. To compute distances between services, a rulework was developed to compute the distance between single service properties. Such distances can be combined to a service vector distance by mathematical methods like metrics. Furthermore, aspects are presented to implement the service distance computing method in an Orbix trader. Some measure results using the new approach are given.

The result of this paper therefore is a complete rulework for distance computing between services. This rulework is more flexible and more importer oriented than common selection mechanisms, because it allows the importer on the one hand to specify the quality of its properties. On the other hand it allows to express its interpretation of an optimal service. The usefulness of service distance functions is shown by some measure results. So far, the rulework is implemented for a CORBA trader. Interworking between autonomous distributed platforms enables the use of the

CORBA trader in other platforms [MZP 95]. So it is not necessary to implement the service distance component in other traders.

Future tasks are to write a suitable importer routine to support an importer by specifying its requests. This could be realized by enhancing SRDL. Further work has to be done to enhance the presented rulework by considering thresholds on service properties and enabling the description of all property values as probabilistic or statistic.

References

[Be 90]   Bernard, R.: *Decision-Aid and Decision-Making*. In: Bana e Costa, C.: Readings in Multiple Criteria Decision Aid; Springer-Verlag, 1990.

[CORBA]   *The Common Object Request Broker: Architecture and Specification*. OMG Document Number 95.03.xx, Framingham, Massachusetts, 1995.

[DP 94]   Douligeris, C.; Pereira, I.: *A Telecommunications Quality Study Using the Analytic Hierarchy Process*. IEEE Journal on Selected Areas in Communications, Vol. 12, No. 2, pp. 241-50, Feb. 1994.

[MZP 95]   Meyer, B.; Zlatintsis, S.; Popien, C.: *Enabling Interworking between Heterogeneous Distributed Platforms*. In: Schill, A.; Mittasch, C.; Spaniol, O.; Popien, C.: Distributed Platforms; Chapman & Hall, 1995.

[ORBIX]   *Orbix - programmers guide & reference guide*. IONA Technologies Ltd., Release 2.0, 1996.

[PM 94]   Popien, C.; Meyer, B.: *A Service Request Description Language*. In: Hogrefe, D; Leue, S.: Formal Description Techniques VII; Chapman & Hall, 1994.

[PSW 96]   Popien, C.; Schürmann, G.; Weiß, K.-H.: *Distributed Processing in Open Systems* (in German). Teubner, 1996.

[QoS 95]   ISO/IEC JTC1/SC21/N9309: *Open System Interconnection, data management and Open Distributed Processing - Quality of Service, Basic Framework - Working Draft*, January, 1995.

[Sa 80]   Saaty, T.L.: *The Analytic Hierarchy Process*. McGraw-Hill, 1980.

[SPM 94]   Spaniol, O.; Popien, C.; Meyer, B.: *Services and Service Trading in Client/Server Systems* (in German). Thomson Publishing GmBH, 1994.

[Th 95]   Thißen, D.: *New Concepts of QoS* (in German). Thesis at the Department of Computer Science IV at Aachen University of Technology, April 1995.

[Zi 91]   Zimmermann, H.-J.: *Fuzzy Set Theory and its Applications*, 2nd edition. Kluwer Academic Publishers, 1991.

[Zl 96]   Zlatintsis, S.: *Design and Valuation of a Trader Gateway between ANSAware and ORB Systems* (in German). Diploma thesis at the Department of Computer Science IV at Aachen University of Technology, February 1996.

Global Trader Cooperation
in
Open Service Markets

S. Müller, K. Müller–Jones, W. Lamersdorf, T. Tu

Hamburg University, Computer Science Dept.
Vogt–Kölln–Str. 30, D–22527 Hamburg
[smueller|kmueller|lamersd|tu]@dbis1.informatik.uni-hamburg.de

Abstract

Client support for service access in open distributed systems plays an increasingly important role in the context of *Open Distributed Processing* (ODP). Examples for that include ODP's early standardisation efforts in the field of an ODP *trading* function and recent efforts of the *Object Management Group's* (OMG) to standardise a trading facility as one of its CORBA "Common Object Services". In addition to that, *integrating* different local trader functions in order to extend service access support beyond local network boundaries recently became an increasingly important new trading function.

Based upon respective standardisation activities for trader *cooperation* in open service environments, this paper first elaborates on various ways to integrate cooperating local trading facilities into a *global, distributed trading function*. It then reports on specific prototyping experiences made in the international research project on *Interworking Of Traders* (IWT). Within this context, the paper focuses specifically on various aspects of designing and implementing a trader *link management* component that forms the basis for set up, maintenance, and coordination of global trader cooperations.

1 Introduction

Driven by recent improvements in communications technology, the development of open distributed service markets [GGL+95, MML94a] has led to a situation where the dynamics is comparable to that of "real world" markets. It is this dynamic character that makes the task of finding a suitable service rather difficult for potential service users.

Flexible mechanisms have to be provided to support service *mediation* and *selection* in large open distributed service markets and *standardisation* emerges to be one of the key aspects in this field.

A possible way to solve this problem is to first generically characterise service offers by means of standardised *service types* and then to manage the exported service offers by means of *trading functions*. In this context, traders are specific service providers that enable clients to locate (i.e. *import*) suitable service offers by specifying the required service type and additional service properties. First, such offers have to be "advertised" (i.e. *exported*) to the trader by the service providers themselves. Then a potential service user merely has to specify the characteristics (i.e. the type) of service required and has to have access to at least one (local or remote) trader to send the service request to (see fig. 1 for basic principle).

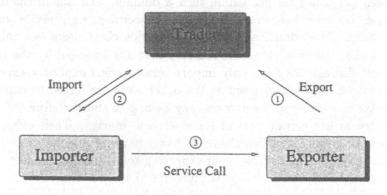

Figure 1: Trader based service mediation

Several projects have dealt with ODP–Trading recently and some respective prototypes have been developed already (e.g. [KW94, BB94, PMGG95, MML94b]). However, most of these prototypes still lack the ability to cooperate with other instances of the same trader and none of them is able to communicate with instances of different trader prototypes. In order to realize global trader cooperation in open distributed systems, additional efforts have to be made to enhance existing trading concepts to enable local trading functions to interact with one another.

One of the first projects dealing with trader cooperation is the international *Interworking Of Traders* project (IWT) [VBB95]. Initiated in 1994, its first stage has just been completed.

The remainder of this paper will introduce some of the major aspects of the IWT project and its achievements so far. Particular emphasis will be placed on the description of a *Link Management* mechanism [ODP95] proposed and implemented for global trader cooperation in a joint project of Hamburg University and the Australian *Distributed Systems Technology Centre* (DSTC) in the context of Hamburg University's *Service Trading and Coordination Environment* (TRADE) [MML95b, MML95a, LMM95].

2 Trading as a Service Mediation Mechanism

2.1 Domain Restricted Service Mediation

Due to organisational, historical or technological circumstances, traders traditionally cover one single domain (technological, administrative, security etc.), called a *trading domain*, only and efficient mechanisms for service mediation have been developed for use *within* such a domain. Domain–oriented service mediation, however, has several drawbacks concerning, e.g., service *autonomy* and *usability*. Most drastically, in such scenarios client users can only participate in those parts of electronic markets that are managed by the trader of their local domain; they can only import service offers explicitly exported to the one trader they ask. Servers on the other hand are forced to export their offer to the one trader in the domain they belong to and therefore will only be propagated in one certain part of the electronic market. Their offers remain unknown for potential service clients in other parts of a global network environment. Even importing from — or exporting to — multiple traders seems to be an unsatisfying solution for these problems as this reintroduces the problem of service location at a different level since both provider and client then would have to know explicitly how to contact all the possible traders in consideration.

Another problem lies in the *scalability* of local trading functions: for larger trading domains with large numbers of service providers and clients performance of a centralised trading architecture can become crucial. This is specifically important within domains where the number of offers and requests changes frequently; also mere optimisation in the area of hardware will not lead to satisfactory results either.

2.2 Cooperation as a Key Mechanism to Enhance Local Traders

To overcome the problems of domain–oriented trading as described in the previous section, mechanisms have to be introduced to weaken the domain boundaries for both traders and their clients while directing special attention to keeping maximum autonomy of all participants.

Basis for overcoming the domain orientation is a corresponding system support. Existing platforms — perfectly fitting into their context — have to be combined in a manner that enables transparent interaction of clients and servers developed on them. One possible solution for this supporting framework lies in the introduction of *interceptors* [GMJL96] that instantiate so called *proxies* to offer services on behalf of service providers in foreign domains. It is through proxies, that clients are then able to access service providers in spite of their potential location in different (technological) domains.

In addition to dealing with technical heterogeneity, a domain boundary crossing trading mechanism is necessary to realize large open service markets. Basic requirement for this is an opening of existing trading domains and a mutual exchange of information on services and service offers in these domains.

3 Types of Trader Cooperations

In general, there are several ways to overcome network boundaries and heterogeneity problems for cooperating trading functions. Therefore, this section introduces alternate types of domain boundary crossing for global trader cooperation: Beginning with the simplest form of sharing common service offer repositories it leads to more complex forms with maximum autonomy for participating traders by loosening diverse imposed restrictions.

3.1 Indirect Interaction

Indirect interaction represents the most simple class of trader cooperation. Here, participating traders use common service offer repositories and can access all offers all other traders have deposited there. Indirect interaction requires the least effort for cooperating traders. On the other hand, however, it has several drawbacks:

- All service types have to be well known to all participants.

- Indirect interaction is only practical in distributed systems without administrative, topological or technological boundaries.

- It is only applicable in cases where no security restrictions forbid storing offers in common repositories.

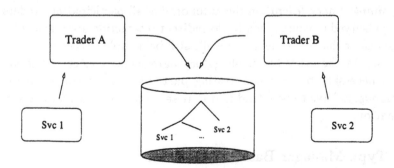

Figure 2: Indirect Interaction

Using standardised, global name services (e.g. X.500), the second and third drawback can be handled to a certain extent and some work exists already that exploits the principle of *indirect interaction* to realize trader cooperation (see, e.g., [WB95]).

3.2   Simple Trader Federation

With *simple trader federation*, obligatory agreements must exist between co-operating traders concerning, at least, call interfaces, call semantics and data structures to be used. As with indirect interaction, service types are standardised and have to be well known to all participants in advance. Service requests and their results can be freely exchanged between cooperating partners in this reader cooperation alternative.

Additionally, traders can interact in this scenario using a well known *cooperation protocol* to obtain information on one another which is stored in so called *links*. A link consists of information necessary to bind to the referenced trader and to forward service requests and also keeps information qualifying the link itself, for example the referenced trader's average answering time.

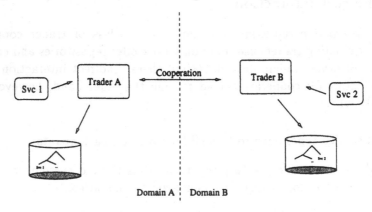

Figure 3: Simple Trader Federation

Using *simple trader federation* the autonomy of all participating traders can be better preserved in comparison to the indirect interaction approach. Clients can use the trader that suits them best while still being able to access foreign trading domains. On the other hand, obligatory agreements concerning service types are still necessary between cooperating partners. To overcome this drawback, *type managers* have to be introduced that serve to compare and transform type information.

3.3   Type Manager Based Federation

Introducing type managers and a corresponding protocol for them to interact, leads to a *type manager based federation*. With this kind of trader federation, explicit type manager functions are required and used to compare service types and to transform service type representations, if necessary.

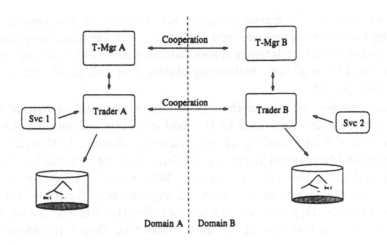

Figure 4: Type Manager Based Cooperation

This model of trader cooperation leads to an increased level of autonomy for single service and trading functions, since the necessary comparison of service types is done by type managers and service types no longer have to be agreed upon.

3.4 Free federation

Finally, giving up the requirement of a homogeneous middleware platform for all participants in cooperative open service markets leads to the most extensive form of trader cooperation, called *free federation*. Free federation relies on a mechanism of *interception* that enables services to interact with one another over heterogeneous platforms. This can be achieved by instantiating *proxies* to offer the service interface of services on one platform on another platform and is supervised by an *interceptor* [GMJL96]. In this way, both client and server have the illusion of using the same platform while all calls are transparently routed through proxies to any other platform anywhere whenever necessary.

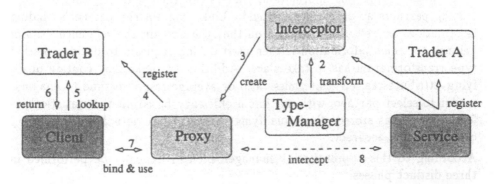

Figure 5: Free Federation using Interception

As, in an open service market scenario, also traders are just specific servers following the client/server paradigm themselves, the use of interception mechanisms enables them to interact across domain boundaries and thereby leaves them a free choice of their underlying platform as well as of their potential cooperation partners.

The main problem with the mechanism of interception and its concept of maximum transparency when used in the field of trader cooperation lies in the introduction of foreign binding information into a domain. In this case, service offers returned to clients may contain bindings that are only valid in the initial domain and not usable for the recipient. Where proxies normally just transform calls, route data in an uninterpreted way and stay "invisible" for traders and their clients, they now have to interact directly with the trader in order to enable an interpretation of the data routed and thus a transformation of bindings.

4   Establishing Trader Cooperations

Some proposals already exist for supporting global trader cooperations. Early works favoured the use of *federation contracts* [BR92, LM95]. These consist of an *import contract* and an *export contract* where the former is managed by the importer and consists of the service types available in the remote trader and mappings between local and remote or canonic service types. According to these proposals, the export contract is held by the exporter and contains path names of exported subsets of its offer space and service types offered. Due to their complexity, however, federation contracts were not considered suitable for ODP standardisation and are not used within the *Interworking of Traders* project, either.

A different approach, as e.g. described in [VBB95], has been adopted for ODP standardisation which requires less administrative overhead. With this kind of trader federation called trader *interworking*, federating traders pass necessary information on one another via an administration interface and store it in so called *links*. Using this information, traders can then send requests to cooperating partners as other clients would. Links contain the partner's binding information, as well as information on the type domain the referenced trader belongs to. This information is then used during requests to decide whether type transformation has to take place. Additionally, links may contain qualifying attributes as, e.g., hit-/miss ratio or average response time to enable a trader to select partners with maximum efficiency based on the statistical information it has stored. Such qualifying attributes are actualised after every call for utmost accuracy.

According to this approach, link management can basically be performed in three distinct phases:

1. Strategic Phase:

   During the strategic phase, links are created between all cooperating traders. The creation takes place via standardised interfaces of the traders, the so called *link management interfaces*. The links instantiated are unidirectional references that are stored in private *link spaces* of the originating traders. Bidirectional references can be "simulated" by creating additional references with opposite direction.

2. Tactical Phase:

   During the tactical phase, traders select the trader references from their link space they find most promising for the request to be made. This selection can be influenced via *policies* by both the trader and the requesting client. Policies can, for example, be used to decide whether the request shall be routed across domain boundaries, or whether the request may be handed to cooperating traders synchronously or asynchronously.

3. Operational Phase:

   During the final, operational phase the trader sends the request to selected cooperating partners via their import interface. Eventual results from remote requests are then merged with local results and handed back to the originating client, while the origin of the results stays transparent to him. At last, the qualifying attributes of the links used are actualised and their quality is reestablished.

5 Prototype Implementation

The following section describes a prototype link management component that has been developed as part of the "Interworking of Traders" project, jointly by the DSTC and Hamburg University.

The main goal of this project stage was to enable and demonstrate a trader interworking scenario between traders developed by each project partner independently (see [MML95b] and [BB94]). As part of this effort, the ODP standard draft was also tested for completeness and usability and first experiences could be gained on using *policies* as a formal mechanism to describe dynamic trader behaviour.

5.1 The Project Environment

This section introduces the prototype system environment that served as a testbed for the development of the link management prototypes.

The middleware platform used within the IWT project was OSF's *Distributed Computing Environment* (DCE) [Fou92]. In both Brisbane, Australia, and Hamburg, Germany, separate trading domains were established by respective

DCE cells and connected via DCE *Global Directory Service* (GDS), a DCE Directory Service component. In each of the two trading scenarios, each separate domain contains at least one local trader component. In case of Hamburg University's TRADEr prototype, this trading component basically consists of the following parts: an *access control* module, a *service selection management* module, a *link management* module (as described in this paper), and a *service mediation* module. The TRADEr additionally interacts with a *type manager* and an external *service offer repository*. It offers various call interfaces which belong to either service mediation or general service offer management facilities. The link management module, for example, is part of the latter group.

Both DCE cells offer local services that use their local trader facilities. A specific GUI–based trader administration tool, the *Link Configuration Manager*, enables creation of cooperation links between trading domains. The next section gives a more detailed overview of some aspects of the TRADEr "link Configuration manager" module.

5.2 Link Configuration Manager

The *Link Configuration Manager* (LCM) (see fig. 7) can be regarded as a central controlling unit of the trader's link management facility. Via a graphical administration tool it offers access to all functions of the link management

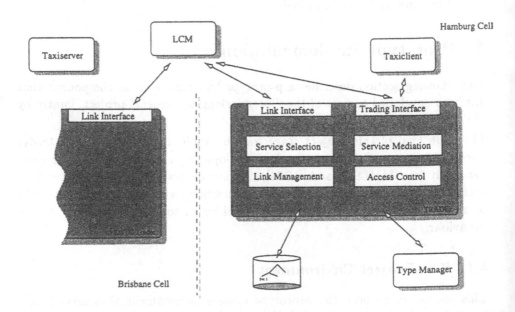

Figure 6: The Project Environment

interface. Using this tool, trading link management administrator can browse all trader service offers known to a specific trader and integrate them into global cooperation links. Additionally, the LCM can be used to supervise links held by a specific trader. By observing link attributes one can, for example, identify link problems already at an early stage (for example if response times are exceptionally high). The procedure to establish connections between traders by means of the LCM is as follows: First, the trading service offered by the foreign trader, which is to be registered as a link with the local one, has to be inquired by making a service offer request to the former one. This step is enabled in the *service offer mode* of the LCM. If successful, the next step is binding to the the Link Management Interface of the local trader and registering the binding information contained in the foreign trading service offer as part of a link. This is enabled in the *link mode* of the LCM. The Link Management Interface also allows a later control of the stored links and their attributes by means of the Link Configuration Manager.

5.3 Trader extensions

Besides the implementation of the additional Link Management Interface, the realization of interoperable trader cooperations in heterogeneous network environments also requires some modification of the Trading Service Interface of the participating traders, especially with respect to the import operation. Additional features the import operation needs to implement are the following:

- Instead of processing requests in an anonymous way, a unique identifier must be kept during the whole life cycle of a request, also when this

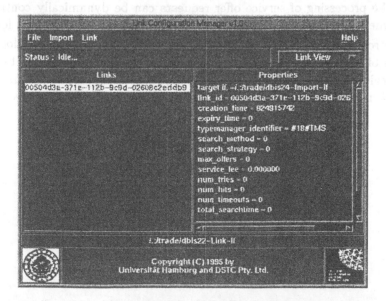

Figure 7: The Link Configuration Manager

request is forwarded to a partner trader. These identifiers are stored by the traders and used to recognise requests that have already been handled. Thus, cyclical requests can be avoided.

- Requests may be forwarded to other partner traders. In this case, the forwarding trader behaves to his cooperation partner in the same way as a simple client.

- Policies, which are passed together with the request, can be used to influence the processing of the request, e.g. concerning the involvement of partner traders or the specification of optimisation criteria.

- The results of subrequests are merged and returned to the immediate client of trader. In this way, the origin of a service offer is transparent for the initiator of the request.

Other implementation aspects as, e.g., performance and memory usage have also been considered in the IWT project, partly by using the DCE thread library. By means of this library *asynchronous remote procedure calls*, which are not directly supported by DCE, could be realized in the extended TRADEr prototype scenario.

5.4 A sample application scenario

In order to gain first experience with the implemented prototype trader cooperation mechanisms described above, an example taxi booking service was realized. Using this simple application, it was also possible to demonstrate how the processing of service offer requests can be dynamically controlled at run-time. For example, requests can be specified to be processed locally or also across trading domain boundaries. Figure 8 shows a sample dialog box by means of which users can automatically select the most appropriate taxi booking service available anywhere by using (location transparently!) either local or remote trader functions interconnected by respective LCM managed external links.

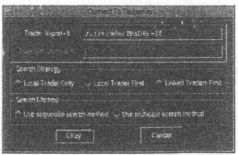

Figure 8: Policy selection using the taxi booking client

225

6 Summary and Outlook

This article gave an overview of concepts, alternatives, and a prototype implementation of advanced trading functions which aim at realizing global, i.e. inter-domain cooperation of local traders. It first addressed problems of centralised service mediation approaches and then introduced as an attractive alternative that of global trader cooperation. The most important core component of such a global trading cooperation mechanism is the *link management* facility. The design and implementation of a prototype for such a component was finally presented in the main section of the paper as developed as part of the "Inter-working of Traders" project, a joint project between the Australian "DSTC" and the German Hamburg University recently.

In general, link management functions enables local traders to extend their service offer space beyond local domain boundaries using protocols to contact remote traders whenever service requests can not be granted locally. All information necessary for that is stored in so called *links* within each trader and covers binding information as well as statistical data to qualify a link and enable an optimised selection of cooperating partners. Example test scenarios using the mentioned prototypes demonstrated the usability of both the proposed trader cooperation concepts and their respective realizations as reported in this paper. In these test scenarios, trader functions developed independently in Brisbane and Hamburg could be connected in an application scenario where an example taxi booking services could be mediated across domain boundaries. This way also first experiences could be made with a trader cooperation mechanism as initially specified (but not tested yet!) in the respective ODP standard draft extension.

Among several yet unsolved problems of a trading link management mechanism is, for example, the (dynamic!) control of requests sent to other traders. Yet, ways have to be found to synchronise subrequests and, for example, stop complete request chains where subrequests exceed resource limits or where the requested number of service offers has been reached. In this context, partial results in *mobile agents* research [MLL96] seem promising, but autonomous request coordination protocols will have to be evaluated as well in the future. Additionally, trader links are still only unidirectional references. It is also yet to be examined which consequences (concerning, e.g., the autonomy of cooperating traders) would arise from changing to explicitly negotiated bidirectional trader links instead.

Acknowledgements

The authors wish to thank their Australian partners in the IWT projects David Barbagallo, Melfyn Lloyd, Kerry Raymond and Andreas Vogel etc. at the *Distributed Systems Technology Centre* (DSTC) in Brisbane for the fruitful and stimulating cooperation which lead to many of the results reported here.

The authors would also like to acknowledge technical support from subsequent joint work in related areas with the GMD *Research Institute for Open Communication Systems* (FOKUS) in Berlin.

References

[BB94]   A. Beitz and M. Bearman. An ODP Trading Service for DCE. In *Proceedings of the First International Workshop on Services in Distributed and Networked Environments (SDNE)*, pages 42–49, Prague, Czech Republic, June 1994. IEEE Computer Society Press.

[BR92]   M. Bearman and K. Raymond. Federating traders: An ODP adventure. In J. de Meer, V. Heymer, and R. Roth, editors, *Open Distributed Processing, Proceedings of the IFIP TC6/WG6.4 International Workshop on Open Distributed Processing, Berlin, 1991*, pages 125–141. Elsevier Science Publishers B.V. (North–Holland), 1992.

[Fou92]   Open Software Foundation. *Introduction to OSF DCE*. Prentice–Hall, Englewood Cliffs, New Jersey, 1992.

[GGL+95]   K. Geihs, H. Gründer, W. Lamersdorf, M. Merz, K. Müller, and A. Puder. Systemunterstützung für offene verteilte Dienstemärkte. In K. Franke, U. Hübner, and W. Kalfa, editors, *Kommunikation in Verteilten Systemen: Neue Länder – Neue Netze – Neue Dienste*, Informatik–Aktuell, pages 445–459. Springer–Verlag, February 1995.

[GMJL96]   F. Griffel, K. Müller-Jones, and W. Lamersdorf. Ein Interoperabilitätskonzept zur komponentenbasierten Software–Entwicklung auf heterogenen Middleware–Plattformen. To be published in Proceedings of GI'96, Klagenfurt, Austria, February 1996.

[KW94]   E. Kovacs and S. Wirag. Trading and distributed application management: An integrated approach. In *Proceedings of the 5th IFIP/IEEE International Workshop on Distributed Systems: Operation and Management*, October 1994.

[LM95]   L. Lima and E. Madeira. A model for federated trader. In *Proceedings of the Third International Conference on Open Distributed Processing (ICODP '95)*, Brisbane, Australia, February 1995.

[LMM95]   W. Lamersdorf, M. Merz, and K. Müller–Jones. Middleware support for open distributed applications. In *Proceedings of the First International Workshop on High Speed Networks and Open Distributed Platforms*, St. Petersburg, Russia, June 1995.

[MLL96]   M. Merz, B. Liberman, and W. Lamersdorf. Interorganizational workflow management with mobile agents in cosm. In *Proceedings of the First International Conference and Exhibition on The Practical Application of Intelligent Agents and Multi-Agent Technology*, 1996.

[MML94a]   M. Merz, K. Müller, and W. Lamersdorf. Service trading and mediation in distributed computing environments. In *Proceedings of the 14th International Conference on Distributed Computing Systems (ICDCS '94)*, pages 450–457. IEEE Computer Society Press, 1994.

[MML94b] K. Müller, M. Merz, and W. Lamersdorf. Der TRADE–Trader: Ein Basisdienst offener verteilter Systeme. In C. Popien and B. Meyer, editors, *Neue Konzepte für die Offene Verteilte Verarbeitung*, pages 35–44. Verlag der Augustinus Buchhandlung, Aachen, September 1994.

[MML95a] K. Müller–Jones, M. Merz, and W. Lamersdorf. Kooperationsanwendungen: Integrierte Vorgangskontrolle und Dienstvermittlung in offenen verteilten Systemen. In F. Huber-Wäschle, H. Schauer, and P. Widmayer, editors, *GISI 95 – Herausforderungen eines globalen Informationsverbundes für die Informatik, Zürich, 1995*, pages 518–525. Springer–Verlag, 1995.

[MML95b] K. Müller–Jones, M. Merz, and W. Lamersdorf. The TRADEr: Integrating trading into DCE. In K. Raymond and L. Armstrong, editors, *Open Distributed Processing: Experiences with distributed environments, Proceedings of the third IFIP TC 6/WG 6.1 international conference on open distributed processing, 1995*, pages 476–487. Chapman & Hall, 1995.

[ODP95] Draft International Standard 13235 – ODP Trading Function. International Organisation for Standardization, International Electrotechnical Commission, May 1995.

[PMGG95] A. Puder, S. Markwitz, G. Gudermann, and K. Geihs. AI–based Trading in Open Distributed Processing. In K. Raymond and L. Armstrong, editors, *Open Distributed Processing: Experiences with distributed environments, Proceedings of the third IFIP TC 6/WG 6.1 international conference on open distributed processing, 1995*, pages 157–169. Chapman & Hall, 1995.

[VBB95] A. Vogel, M. Bearman, and A. Beitz. Enabling interworking of traders. In *Proceedings of the Third International Conference on Open Distributed Processing (ICODP '95)*, Brisbane, Australia, February 1995.

[WB95] A. Waugh and M. Bearman. Designing an ODP Trader Implementation using X.500. In *Proceedings of the Third International Conference on Open Distributed Processing (ICODP '95), Brisbane, Australia*, February 1995.

Analysing Requirements Using ODP

F. Caneschi

FINSIEL - U.A. TECSIEL Pisa

Abstract: This paper describes an ODP-Based approach for the classification of requirements for projects devoted to enterprise systems. The real problem to be faced is not the number of requirements, as they are very often scarce and imprecise, but the fact that the requirements a system designer can get are normally sparse, i.e., they belong to extremely different categories. Many design methodologies try to define a process for analysing requirements, but only seldom is a methodology able to keep track in a proper way of all requirements, show whether and how a particular requirement is satisfied by the proposed solution, show which system's components satisfy which requirements, show how new requirements can fit in a pretty advanced design, and how these new requirements are related to others. This paper claims that a coherent classification schema of these requirements, such as that provided by the ODP Reference Model, can give interesting answers to the problems above. The ODP Reference Model does not claim to define a methodology, not even for a requirement's analysis: yet, a requirement's analysis performed using ODP concepts and terms has shown promising results in a real project that is described in this paper. The analysis is not complete, as the project still is running: yet, it is believed that the results that have been attained already show the usefulness of the approach.

1. INTRODUCTION

When developing architectures for enterprise systems, one difficult initial task is to find your way in the jungle of requirements that pop up since the first day of the project, but keep on coming till the last days (and, sometimes, even later). An additional burden is due to the vagueness of some requirements, and, more, to the fact that you have to demonstrate, better sooner than later, that those very vague requirements are indeed satisfied by your proposal.

At first sight, one could state that the requirement's space is a two dimensional space, as what is shown in Figure 1, where axes represent time (when requirements show up) and vagueness (imprecision of requirements).

System architects tend to like a very small requirement space and, even more, a space that is as close to the origin as possible (few requirements, very precise, all stated at the beginning of the

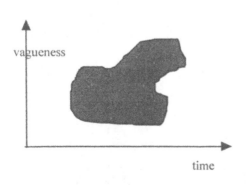

Figure 1. The requirements space

project). However, the following extreme situations can be handled effectively:

1. many vague requirements, but defined at the beginning;

2. few requirements, even if they are vague and stated in different times;

3. many requirements, stated in different times, but very precise.

The last case may often lead to radical changes in the system architecture, or even to impossible situations, but this is normal design life.

Unfortunately, there is another factor that complicates life to the system architects, namely that the requirements you get belong to extremely different categories, i.e., are not generally comparable, and must be handled in different phases of the project and by different people. For example, in a client server environment, a requirement for rapid development time (which can be an early requirement) might lead to a data server solution, but another requirement on security over a geographical network (which could arrive later) might lead to a function server solution. By incidence, every requirement category adds another dimension to the requirement's space. Thus, the real problem is to have means to position requirements in a co-ordinated and integrated way within the architecture one is developing.

Many design methodologies try to define a process for analysing requirements, but only seldom is a methodology able to keep track in a proper way of all requirements, show whether and how a particular requirement is satisfied by the system, show which system's components satisfy which requirements, show how new requirements can (or cannot) fit in a design already on its way.

This paper tells about an ODP-based analysis of requirements for a project aimed at the definition of architectures for spreading services (generally offered by Public Administrations) to the citizens. After a brief introduction of the aims of the project, and of the process followed to get requirements, a flat list of the requirements we gathered is given. Then, the requirements are classified onto categories derived from the ODP viewpoints, with some simplifications, and the implications that requirements bear to the different viewpoint's architectures are shown. Finally, some considerations are drawn on the process that has been followed. It can be anticipated that, although the ODP Reference Model does not claim to define a methodology, not even for a requirement's analysis, yet a requirement's analysis performed using ODP concepts and terms has shown to be successful in a real project. The analysis is not complete, as the project is still running: yet, it is believed that some results have been attained, that show the usefulness of the approach.

2. DISTRIBUTING SERVICES TO CITIZENS

When dealing with distributing services to citizens, three main issues have to be solved, namely:

1. who are the users. In the Finsiel environment, the traditional user is an intermediate user, i.e., the typical front end employee of a Public Administration. On the other hand, the very notion of "spreading services" implies a wider and less specialised user community. This community can be modelled as a set of private citizens (the end users) who consume services by means of either "electronic kiosks" or home computers. According to the type of user, different services may (but not necessarily must) be singled out.

2. what "services" mean. When the user is the intermediate user described above, one is led to the model of the "unified counter"[1]. In this case, services are built based on the application interfaces offered by the various information systems of the administrations, possibly with some added value (e.g. information retrieval services for pointing out the desired information). These added value services can be considered as a bridge toward the second category of users, namely, the unsophisticated users. A real world example comes from a parcel carrier, who set up a web server that allows Internet users to get information on their deliveries (where is the parcel, when is it expected to be delivered, and so on) [Fedex96]. This service soon allowed the company to reduce the number of operators (intermediate users), as a relevant percentage of the end users got the information they needed through the Internet. This shows an example of a service offered to end users that can easily be built on top of services offered to intermediate users.

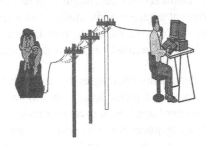

Figure 2. Services diffusion via telephone

---

[1] A unified counter is a single counter with a single operator that is able to satisfy complex requests by accessing a number of different systems. The typical example is a counter where a citizen can obtain all the documents that are necessary for requesting a driving license, even if they are issued by different administrations.

Figure 3. Services diffusion via computer network

3. how services are "distributed" to users. Distribution of services is intended here for the second category of users (the first one representing a limited-size, limited-complexity case of the second one). Two different cases have been singled out. The first one is a traditional, telephone-based service, as depicted in Figure 2. The user calls a centre (named "Call Centre"), where a human operator, or a computer simulation, provides for the requested services. The second one is based on a network access using a browser and a service centre, as depicted in Figure 3. As the two cases can be modelled in the same way, the requirements will be the same, as shown in the next section.

3. IDENTIFYING THE REQUIREMENTS

The definitions of "users", "services" and "distribution" of the previous section are not general definitions: rather, they are bound to the context of the project, and came to us from the commonly used approach of interviewing the foreseen users of the system. A first set of requirements derived from those definitions is:

1. Build services using as a starting base the information (legacy applications and data) already offered by the information systems of the public administrations;

2. simplify, rationalise and standardise access to the services;

3. provide means to build more complex services based on the elementary services described above;

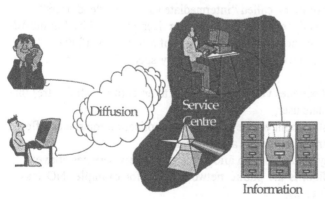

Figure 4. Overall view of the system

4. distribute services using the telephone network (including high speed networks such as ISDN, ATM, ...);

5. take into account that most relevant information is available in legacy systems that must be used, but cannot be accessed directly by the end users. This implies an architectural solution that features one or more server systems that filter accesses to

and information from the legacy systems, and offer the required services.

The resulting architecture is shown in Figure 4, where the information gathered by the legacy systems is filtered and diffused either by a human or by an automaton to the requesting user.

Further interviews gave us further functional and architectural requirements about the structure of the Service Centre system, namely:

1. The legacy applications that provide information should not be modified (not-intrusive approach);
2. access to and location of the legacy systems must be transparent to the Service Centre;
3. legacy systems are connected to the Service Centre by means of heterogeneous networks;
4. legacy systems offer information both via OLTP (transactional) access and via direct access to databases;
5. the "service platform" built in the Service Centre must be independent of the techniques used for diffusing services;
6. service diffusion is based on two paradigms: the so-called "Call Centres" and Internet based systems (e.g. Web servers);
7. in order to avoid problems of software distribution, Java could be used to develop custom solutions.

4. INTEGRATING REQUIREMENTS

What follows is the flat list of all requirements that have been described previously, and is only reported here as a help for reading the next sections:

1. There are two categories of users, called "intermediate users" and "end users";
2. the intermediate user helps the end user to access services provided by Public Administrations. He can access these services by means of a service platform;
3. the end user may access services that are provided by specialised servers via network connections;
4. the end user may request services via telephone calls to an entity (Call Centre) that behaves like an intermediate user;
5. elementary services must be built on the base of the application interfaces offered by the information systems of the public administrations;
6. value added services may be built on top and of the elementary services above;
7. the communication medium is the public network (thus, for example, NO leased lines, NO TV broadcasting, ...);
8. legacy systems must be isolated from end-users by means of specialised servers;
9. specialised servers must feature one or more interface components towards legacy systems. The service diffusion must be based on those interface components;

10. interface components must provide access and location transparency with respect to the legacy applications and data;
11. interface components must be independent of the diffusion techniques;
12. legacy applications should not be modified (not intrusive approach);
13. two components must take care of the diffusion of services: one based on the voice network (Call centre), another one based on data network;
14. the technology to be used for diffusing services on the data network is Internet;
15. some Internet based services can use Java.

All these requirements give constraints on the architectural design of the whole system. One can then basically proceed in either of the two following ways:

a) Try to devise an architecture, or use an already developed solution, then (not necessarily at the end of design) verify that the requirements are satisfied by the proposed solution. If the verification fails, modify the design, then verify again.

b) Start with a fresh mind (from scratch), adopt a general architectural framework, then try to understand which requirement influences which parts of the general design.

We followed this second approach, in the belief that this project could be used as a test bed for the traceability of requirements in all design phases. The following sections illustrate the process we used and the results we gained.

4.1 System architecture and system architectures

It is now common practice[2] to consider the architecture of a system as a set of architectural designs, each of which covering different aspects. We used the same approach to classify in a design-oriented way all requirements. It has to be noted that a single requirement, expressed in different languages, may belong to more than one set, meaning that it can affect more than one architectural design.

What follows describes which implications the various requirements have on the architectural designs that, in our description, are four[3]:

1. Enterprise/Information design, where the domains, the actors, the roles, the information types and the information flows are described;

---

2   At least in the ODP community

3   In actuality, if you use ODP to model your system, you should have five architectural designs, as you should distinguish between Enterprise and Information viewpoints. However, as this paper only deals with the requirements, and as our first analysis did not identify strong Information requirements, for the sake of readability, and to point out the results we got, the Information viewpoint is only present as information flows in the Enterprise analysis of the requirements.

2. Computational design, where computational objects, their interfaces and their interactions are described;
3. Engineering design, where the infrastructure mechanisms that support computational objets are described;
4. Technology design, where the external characteristics of the products used to build the system are described.

The order of the following sections should not lead the reader to the assumption that a cascade methodology had been adopted: rather, we use the same order of viewpoints that is in the ODP standards for the sake of readability.

4.2 Enterprise/Information architecture

Requirements 1, 5 and 8 in section 4 identify three domains to be federated, namely:
1. end users (Service Users);
2. information access servers (Service Providers);
3. legacy applications (Legacy systems).

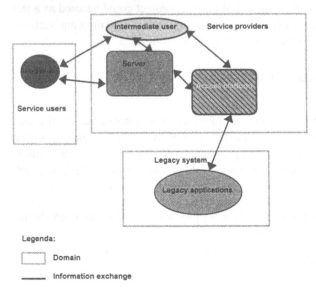

Legenda:

☐ Domain

—— Information exchange

Figure 5. Enterprise design

Table 1 below shows the enterprise objects in the system, their roles, and the information flows (part of the information architecture) that are identified by the requirements. The behaviour of each object is specified in terms of obligations and permissions that, as a whole, identify the policies of the system. The resulting enterprise description is incomplete, as only those objects (and those objects' attributes) clearly identified by the requirements are shown (more objects can be identified in further phases). The information architecture is **very** incomplete, as no indications could be initially drawn from the requirements about information schemata. Numbers (1, 2, and so on) are used to cross-reference the requirements list in section 4.

Object	Role	Obligations	Permissions	Requires info to	Provides info to
Service	Artefact ex-changed between service Provider and service User[3,4].	Based on legacy applications interfaces [5] , or on elementary services built upon legacy applications[6]			
End user[1]	Service user[1]			• Intermediate user[1,4] • Server[3]	• Intermediate user[1,4] • Server[3]
Intermedi-ate user[1]	• Service pro-vider to end user[2] • Access plat-form client[2]			• End user[2] • Access plat-form[2]	• End user[2] • Access plat-form[2]
Server[3]	• Service pro-vider to end user[3] • Service pro-vider to in-termediate user[2,3] • Client of ac-cess platform[8]	Must serve more than one users[3]	May use Java[15]	• End user[3] • Intermediate user[2,3] • Access plat-form[8]	• End user[3] • Intermediate user[2,3] • Access plat-form[8]
Access platform[9]	• Service pro-vider to server[8] • Service pro-vider to in-termediate user[2] • Client of leg-acy appli-cations[8,9,10]	• Create services from appli-cation in-terfaces[5,6] • Cannot modify leg-acy appli-cations[12]		Legacy applica-tions[8,9,10]	• Server[8] • Intermediate user[2]
Legacy ap-plications[5]	Provider of access platform[8,9]	•		Access platform[8,9]	Access platform[8,9]

Table 1. Enterprise objects and information flows

It has to be noted that, to capture the requirements' notion of service, the enterprise term **artefact** has been introduced. This term used to be defined in early versions of the ODP standard, as an enterprise object whose role does not include executing actions, but has been dropped in the final version. We believe that, although the concept of artefact can be defined in terms of already defined concepts (this, in fact, is the reason why it has been dropped), yet it is a useful and general term, that could be introduced in a new Enterprise language standard.

The resulting enterprise design is depicted in Figure 5, where domains, enterprise objects and information flows are represented. Note that the service artefact is not represented in the diagram. We will come back to the domains later, when dealing about interceptors.

4.3 Computational architecture

Aim of a computational design is to identify computational objects and their interfaces at the maximum possible level of detail, such as to identify all those objects that can be distributed, and allow for a clear understanding of the computational needs towards the supporting infrastructure (or, conversely, the infrastructure limitations on the computational objects).

It is assumed that the terms "operational", "stream", "signature" and "behaviour", related to interfaces, are known in their ODP meaning. The reader is, however, referred to [ODP] for the definition of these terms.

Figure 6 shows the provisional computational design that can be derived by the requirements. Again, only those computational objects and interfaces that must be present because of the requirements are indicated. The level of details is the maximum attainable from the requirements, i.e. there are no particular project choices. More computational objects and more interfaces will probably pop out during the project as design choices. As previously, numbers refer to the list of requirements in 4. Interfaces in the diagram are identified by letters (a, b, c, etc.).

The following Table 2 indicates, for each interface, which requirement originated it and which are its characteristics if a requirement specifies them. Behaviour, when specified, is specified in a very informal way, normally by referring to widely known keywords.

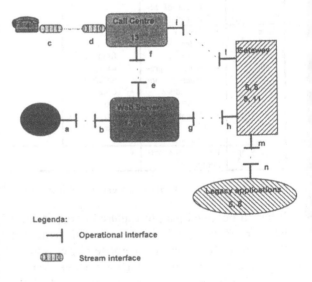

Legenda:

— Operational interface

⫯⫯⫯ Stream interface

Figure 6. Provisional computational architecture

Interface	Requirement	Role	Signature	Behaviour
a	3	Client	HTML[14], Java[15]	Internet Browser[14]
b	13	Server	HTML[14], Java[15]	WWW server[13]
c	4	Client	Voice, tone telephone[4]	
d	13	Server	Voice, tone telephone[4]	
e	4	Server		
f	13	Client		
g	9	Client	CGI[8, 13, 14]	

237

Interface	Requirement	Role	Signature	Behaviour
h	8, 9, 11	Server	CGI[5, 8, 13, 14]	Creates services from legacy information.
i	9	Client		
l	8, 9, 11	Server		Creates services from legacy information.
m	9	Client		
n	5	Server		

Table 2. Computational interfaces

4.3.1 Transparencies

Computational and engineering designs are bound by constraints that one design imposes on the other one. For example, the computational object design can be influenced by the characteristics of an already present (and not modifiable) engineering infrastructure. Conversely, if not modifiable computational objects must be ported in a new infrastructure, this infrastructure should support those functions that the computational objects require.

The ODP concept of **transparencies** is useful to capture these constraints. Requirement 10 underlines two transparencies on the interaction between the gateway and the legacy applications:
1. access transparency, to mask differences in the data representations and interactions mechanisms;
2. location transparencies, to mask addressing mechanisms when an interface is invoked.

These transparencies put requirements on the structure of the communication channels, as explained in 4.4.2.

4.4 Engineering architecture

An engineering architecture includes in one coherent design all functions and components that are needed in a system to support the computational objects and their interactions, in other words, the infrastructure.

Some terms of the engineering language are briefly defined here for the purpose of readability: however, the reader is referred to [ODP] for a complete description and definition of terms.

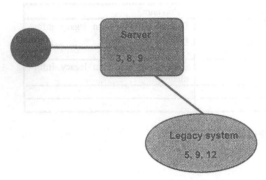

Figure 7. Nodes in the engineering design

The analysis of requirements leads to a first definition of the nodes in the system, which is shown in Figure 7. Nodes roughly correspond to the enterprise domains shown in Figure 5: it has to be noted, however, that a complete set of correspondences among viewpoint designs is to be made as the design of the system is carried on. Again, numbers refer to the list of requirements in 4.

In the drawing, lines represent communication channels between nodes. Before analysing the impact of requirements on the channels, it is worthwhile to look at the internal structure of the nodes. A node can be seen as:

1. A nucleus, which provides and schedules functions;
2. A set of capsules (units of computing and storage);
3. For each capsule, a set of clusters (units of activation and checkpointing).

The following sections deal with the consequences of the requirements listed in 4 on internal structure of the nodes, on nuclei, and on functions. The requirements give no indications on which functions should be available; however, for what stated in 4.4.1, all identified functions will have to be provided by the Server node.

4.4.1 The internal structure of the nodes

If we look at the three nodes in Figure 7:

1. No considerations can be made, neither constraints be imposed, on the node identified as "User", because that is outside the domain of the system. To partially contradict this statement, it is certain that a capsule can be identified in the "User" node, that corresponds to the computational object called "Browser" in Figure 6. This comes from requirement 14, and shows a slight incoherence in the requirements themselves. Objects in this capsule, that we call Browser, communicate with the Server node via a channel that is identified as β in Figure 8.

2. No considerations can be made, neither constraints can be imposed, on the node identified as "Legacy system", due to requirement 12.

3. Inside the "server" node, the following capsules are identified:
   a) WWW server (requirement 13)
   b) Call Centre (requirement 13)
   c) Gateway (requirement 11)

The internal structure of the "server" node is represented in Figure 8, where the capsules listed previously are drawn, together with the communication channels between capsules, that are identified with letters from the Greek alphabet (α, β, γ, etc.). There are no indications from the requirements about the clusters inside capsules. This sub-structuring is thus left to the system's design.

4.4.2 Nuclei

There are no particular requirements on the operating system functions of a node, but it is possible to get indications on the communication channels. Indications can be found for all channels that connect some capsule on the Server node with the outside, i.e. the channels indicated with α, β e γ in Figure 8. A channel, in ODP terms, is a combination of several engineering objects that allow two or more capsules to communicate each other. A channel is made of a **stub**, that allows access transparency, a **binder**, to establish a communication among the interested interfaces, a **protocol**, to steer the information exchange and, when the channel crosses a domain's boundary, an **interceptor**.

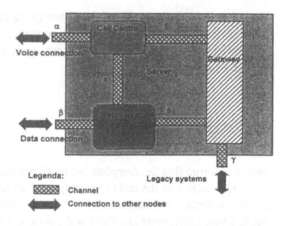

Figure 8. Structure of the server node

When dealing about domains in 4.2 above, we have identified three domains, which indicate both technological and administrative boundaries. The three channels that connect some capsule on the Server node with the outside will thus feature three interceptors. The following Table 3 indicates, for each channel, the characteristics that stubs, binders, protocols and interceptors must have to satisfy the requirements. The characteristics are indicated in a very informal manner (for example, TCP/IP is NOT a Binder, but is used to give an idea of the required binder characteristics). As before, numbers relate to the requirements' list.

Channel	Stub	Binder	Protocol	Interceptor
α		Voice network[4, 7]		Access rights, accounting, billing[4].
β	Must provide HTML support[14]	TCP/IP[14]	HTTP[14]	Access rights, accounting, billing[4].

Channel	Stub	Binder	Protocol	Interceptor
γ	Must provide access transparency[10]	Must provide location transparency[10]	1. 3270 for CICS applications[5] 2. ODBC for database access[5]	Access rights, accounting, billing[4]. Must provide protocol transparency[5].

Table 3. Requirements on communication channels

Note that the characteristics of the interceptors shown in Table 3 are based on the hypothesis that there is a need for access control, accounting and billing when users ask for services. This hypothesis, to be accurate, is not a requirement, rather an anticipation of a requirement.

4.5 Technology architecture

While it is true that the complete list of all products that are present in the system will only be available at the end of the project, the requirements list gives already some indications about the characteristics that some objects that have been identified must exhibit. These indications are listed in the following Table 4. As before, numbers point to the list of requirements.

Objects (architectural description)	Characteristics	Requirement(s)
Web server (Engineering)	Java support	15
Browser (Engineering)	Java support	15
Channel β (Engineering)	TCP/IP and HTTP support	14
Channel γ (Engineering)	3270 and ODBC support	12
Channel α (Engineering)	Voice network support	3
Call Centre (Computational)	Must provide external interface (to be used by Gateway)	4, 5

Table 4. Technology characteristics

4.6 Requirements and architectural designs

The following Table 5 gives a synthetic view of the influence of each requirement on the various architectural designs. Each valid intersection states where the requirement applies.

Requirement	Enterprise / Information	Computational	Engineering	Technology
1	Domains, roles and information flows.			
2	Roles		Node "User"	
3	Service definition. Information flows definition. Provider and user of services. Server obligations.	Browser. Interface a.	Node "user". Node "server".	Voice network support for channel α.
4	Provider and user of services.	Voice object. Interface c. Interface e. Signature of interface c. Signature of interface d.	Binder in channel α. Interceptor in channels α, β and γ.	Interface i must be accessible (not internal).
5	Service Obligations. Access platform obligations.	legacy applications. Signature of interface h. Interface n.	"Node Legacy system". Protocol in channel γ. Interceptor in channel γ.	Interface i must be accessible (not internal).
6	Obligations on access platform.	Gateway.		
7				Communications media for channel α.
8	Role and information flows of server. Role and information flows of access platform. Role and information flows of legacy systems.	Gateway functions. Legacy applications functions. Signature of interface g. Interface h. Signature of interface h. Interface l.	Node "server".	
9	Role and information flows of access platform. Information flows of server Information flows of legacy applications	Gateway functions. Interface g. Interface h. Interface i. Interface l. Interface m.	Node "server". Node "Legacy system".	
10	Role and information flows of access platform. Information flows of legacy applications.	Access transparency. Location transparency.	Stub in channel γ. Binder in channel γ.	
11	Obligations of access platform.	Gateway functions. Interface h. Interface l.	Gateway capsule.	
12			Node "Legacy system". Structure of node "Legacy system".	3270 and ODBC support in channel γ.

Requirement	Enterprise / Information	Computational	Engineering	Technology
13		Call Centre. Interface d. Web server. Interface b. Behaviour of interface b. Interface f. Signature of interface g. Signature of interface h.	WWW server capsule. Call Centre capsule.	
14		Web server functions. Signature and behaviour of interface a. Signature of interface g. Signature of interface h.	Browser capsule. Channel β. Stub in channel β. Binder in channel β. Protocol in channel β.	TCP/IP and HTTP support in channel β.
15	Permissions on the Server	Signature of interface a. Signature of interface b.		Java support in Web server. Java support in browser.

Table 5. Requirements and architectural designs

Table 5 is a useful tool to understand what happens if a requirement changes or when a new requirement is added, as the impact of the modifications on the various architectural designs is immediately evident. As a matter of fact, the list of requirements in 4 was not generated in one shot, rather it was built on a time frame of 3 months. During this time, first drafts of the architecture have been produced, and the impact of the new requirements on the already drafted design was immediately noticeable. This allowed us and our customers to identify the stable set of requirements that we used as starting point for our analysis, and is listed in this paper.

5. CONCLUSIONS

We classified a project's requirements according to the viewpoints defined in the ODP Reference Model [ODP], in order to have a clear view of the implications of those requirements in the system we were designing. This technique was used primarily to have a stable frame for inserting new requirements and, at the same time, to understand the impact of the new requirements that could pop out in the course of the project. The technique we used brought the benefits we expected; additionally, since the initial phases, the classification of requirements in an ODP framework brought in a seamless way a complete and coherent architecture design. The architecture we got, still to be refined in the course of the project, gives already an overall view of what we will deliver. Although the case, from an architectural standpoint, was not complex, we believe that this technique is general enough to be applied to more complex cases, where it can bring the same benefits we experienced in this project.

We did not yet define relationships between the requirements and the correspondences among viewpoint designs, that could be a further step in the analysis. As a matter of fact, we believe that establishing correspondences among viewpoint designs is one of the most important tasks in a project, and could be eased trying to devise which correspondences are already defined or influenced by which requirements.

6. REFERENCES

[Fedex96]   Amy Cortese: Cover Story: SPECIAL REPORT: HERE COMES THE INTRANET Business Week, 26 February 1996

[ODP]   ISO 10746-1, Information Technology - Basic reference model of Open Distributed Processing - Part 1: Overview.

Specifying Multimedia Binding Objects in Z

Richard O. Sinnott and Kenneth J. Turner,
Department of Computing Science,
University of Stirling,
Stirling FK9 4LA,
Scotland.
email: ros || kjt@cs.stir.ac.uk

Abstract

The current standardisation activity of Open Distributed Processing (ODP) has attempted to incorporate multimedia flows of information into its architecture through the idea of stream interfaces. At present the reference model of ODP (ODP-RM) abstracts from the precise nature of the flows of information. As a consequence of this, the ODP-RM only deals with syntactic aspects of stream interfaces and does not require them to satisfy any behavioural considerations. It is shown in this paper how the formal notation Z can be used to reason about these flows of information in a manner that enables behavioural as well as temporal aspects to be considered. The example given to highlight the approach is the ODP concept of a binding object.

Keywords: Z; Open Distributed Processing (ODP); Architectural Semantics; Multimedia.

1 Introduction

The Reference Model of Open Distributed Processing (ODP-RM) is a framework that is being developed to enable standards for distributed systems to be developed in a uniform, consistent and expedient fashion. It is based upon concepts derived from current distributed processing developments and, as far as possible, on the use of formal description techniques to specify the architecture. The ODP-RM itself is based on an *extended* classical object-oriented model where objects are encapsulated entities that interact at interfaces. The term extended is used here to note that as well as the typical object-oriented (RPC-like) paradigm of message passing, ODP also attempts to incorporate more complex message passing phenomenon, namely (multimedia) flows of information.

It is shown in this paper how the formal notation Z can be used to reason about these flows of information in a manner that enables behavioural as well as temporal aspects to be considered. The management and control of these flows of information is also considered. The example given to highlight the approach is the ODP concept of a binding object.

The rest of the paper is structured as follows. Section 2 gives a brief overview of ODP and the ODP-RM and focuses in some detail on the computational viewpoint language of ODP. Section 3 considers aspects concerned with the formalisation of the computational viewpoint language, and in particular at those concepts related to binding of multimedia streams. Section 4 looks at the formalisation of stream and control computational interfaces. Section 5 looks at binding as given by ODP; highlights its weaknesses and proposes extensions to it. Section 6 considers binding objects and the relation between control and stream interfaces. Finally section 7 draws some conclusions from the work.

2 The Reference Model of ODP

The ODP-RM consists of four main parts (documents). Part 1 [5] contains an overview and guide to use of the ODP-RM. Part 2 [6] contains the definition of concepts and gives the framework for description of distributed systems. It also introduces the principles of conformance and the way they may be applied to ODP. In effect Part 2 provides the vocabulary with which distributed systems may be described, reasoned about and developed, *i.e.* it is used as the basis for understanding the concepts contained within Part 3 of the ODP-RM. Part 3 [7] contains the specification of the required characteristics that qualify distributed system as open, *i.e.* constraints to which ODP systems must conform. The main features of Part 3 include the viewpoint languages, conformance issues, functions and transparencies. It is the viewpoint languages that are of concern in this paper, in particular the computational viewpoint. This viewpoint focuses primarily on the functional decomposition of a given ODP system, and on the interworking and portability of ODP functions. It is here that objects interworking with one another are considered in detail. Finally, Part 4 [8, 9] of the ODP-RM contains a formalisation of a subset of the ODP concepts. This formalisation is achieved through "interpreting" each concept in terms of the constructs of a given formal specification language. This work is concerned with ensuring that the reference model for ODP is consistent with itself. It brings formal expression to the semi-formal concepts, *i.e.* concepts written in stylised English, contained within the reference model. It achieves this through interpreting the different concepts in various formal languages. Presently, LOTOS [4], Z [10], ESTELLE [3] and SDL'92 [11] are under consideration. The aim is that it will not be possible to produce incompatible ODP specifications, as was the case with OSI; see [14].

2.1 The Computational Viewpoint Language

The computational viewpoint language is used to consider issues of distribution. Since the approach taken in ODP-RM is an object-oriented one, objects and their interfaces[1] are the fundamental components with which systems are modelled. The computational viewpoint language focuses on the interfaces that computational objects should support. It provides rules that enable interfaces

---

[1]ODP objects may have more than one interface, unlike objects defined in other object models, *e.g.* OMG's CORBA object model.

to be structured correctly, thus permitting meaningful interactions to take place between objects.

Since the ODP-RM is a framework for developing standards, it is not possible to be overly prescriptive with regard to the behaviour of any given object. Rather, objects will in general have different behaviours depending upon the application they are used for. As a result, the ODP-RM addresses only the syntactic aspects associated with the interfaces to given objects, *i.e.* their interface signatures. Various naming rules for operations (and signals and streams) and parameters found in interfaces are given that interfaces must adhere to. Following this type checking is defined — inadequately! — based on interfaces having these syntactic structurings. The consequences of this are that all messages passed to objects will at least have an understood format.

The ODP-RM prescribes three particular types of interface: operational, stream and signal. Operational interfaces may contain announcements and interrogations, and are used to represent object interactions as represented by most message-passing object models. Announcements are used to represent send-only interactions, whilst interrogations are used to represent send and receive interactions. Signal interfaces consist of signals, where a signal may be regarded as the most basic unit of interaction in the computational viewpoint. They may be considered as single, atomic actions between computational objects. Stream interfaces contain multimedia flows of information. The syntactic formalisation in Z of these three types of interface has been shown previously in [13]. In this paper we focus in more detail on stream interfaces.

Paramount to the successful interworking of computational objects is the ODP concept of a binding object. A binding in ODP may loosely be regarded as the composition (synchronisation) of two or more interfaces. A binding object is responsible for, amongst other things, ensuring that a certain level of quality of service is maintained between the interacting objects. The following diagram, figure 1, shows a simplistic system incorporating a binding object between a producer and consumer of multimedia streams.

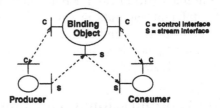

Figure 1: Simplistic Multimedia Binding Object Configuration

The ODP-RM does not prescribe the format of control interfaces, however, it is likely that they will take the form of operational interfaces.

Stream interfaces have associated signatures consisting of flow signatures, where a flow signature contains a name for the flow, the type of the flow and an indication of the causality of the flow. All flow names in a given stream interface must be unique within that interface. The causality of a flow can be either *Producer* or *Consumer*. The issue of typing of flows was abstracted from in [13]. That is, it was simply represented as a basic type in Z. Whilst this enabled a formalisation to be given that satisfied the rules given in [7], it was not a very satisfactory solution. That is, typing of interfaces should ideally be more than simple syntax checking. This is especially so with multimedia flows of information where behavioural and temporal considerations are critical to meaningful interactions.

3 Formalising Aspects of Binding Objects

To formalise a binding object, it is necessary to consider different aspects of that object identified by ODP. For the purpose of this paper, we shall look at stream and control interfaces. These have associated with them an interface signature, a behaviour specification and an environment contract. We shall look at each of these in turn.

3.1 Formalising Syntactic Aspects of Multimedia Streams

The ODP-RM abstracts away from the contents of information flows. As a result, it says very little about binding multimedia streams and how they might be type checked. We shall consider a generic idea of information flow. Here the flow of information is represented by a sequence of *frames* where a frame may be regarded as a particular item in the flow of information. Each frame can be considered as a unit consisting of data (this may be compressed) which we represent by *Data* and a time stamp used for modelling the time at which this particular frame was sent or received. It is also often the case in multimedia flows that particular frames are required for synchronisation, *e.g.* synchronisation of audio with video for example. Therefore we associate a particular *Label* with each frame. This can then be used for selecting a particular frame from the flow as required. From this, we may model a frame as:

$$
\begin{array}{|l}
\hline
\textit{Frame} \underline{} \\
\quad \textit{data} : \textit{Data} \\
\quad \textit{timestamp} : \mathbb{N} \\
\quad \textit{label} : \textit{Label} \\
\hline
\end{array}
$$

It should be noted here that we model time as a natural number as done by [2]. It might well be the case that real (dense) time could be used as in [12], or time intervals [1]. For simplicity here though, we restrict ourselves to discrete time, *i.e.* represented as a natural number.

Information flows have inherent characteristics given by the nature of their flows. For example, flows can be *isochronous* which implies that each frame is sent/received in equal time segments. Alternatively, flows can be *bursty* in nature which implies that the time intervals between successive frames are not necessarily equal. We may thus represent a flow characteristic as:

$$\textit{FlowCharacteristic} ::= \textit{Isoch} \langle\!\langle \mathbb{N} \rangle\!\rangle \mid \textit{Bursty}$$

As stated, interfaces in the computational viewpoint have causalities associated with them, where a causality may loosely be regarded as some notion of expected behaviour. These causalities can be associated with the interface as a whole (operational) or with the individual actions associated with the interfaces (stream). The different causalities may be represented by:

$$Causality ::= Producer \mid Consumer \mid Client \mid Server$$

From this, we may represent a generic multimedia flow as:

$mmFlowType$

$frames : \text{seq } Frame$
$flowChar : FlowCharacteristic$
$rate : \mathbb{N}$

$\forall f_1, f_2 : Frame \mid \langle f_1, f_2 \rangle \text{ in } frames \bullet f_2.timestamp > f_1.timestamp \wedge$
$flowChar = Isoch(rate) \Rightarrow$
$\quad (\forall f_1, f_2 : Frame \mid \langle f_1, f_2 \rangle \text{ in } frames \bullet f_2.timestamp - f_1.timestamp = rate)$
$flowChar = Bursty \Rightarrow$
$\quad (\exists f_1, f_2, f_3 : Frame \mid \langle f_1, f_2 \rangle \text{ in } frames \wedge \langle f_2, f_3 \rangle \text{ in } frames \bullet$
$\quad\quad f_2.timestamp - f_1.timestamp \neq f_3.timestamp - f_2.timestamp)$

This states that a multimedia flow type is given by a sequence of frames with some flow characteristic and temporal ordering. All frames in the sequence have time stamps in ascending order. Isochronous flows have frames separated by equal time intervals, whereas bursty flows may have frames separated by un-equal time intervals.

To formalise stream interfaces, it is necessary to introduce *Name* for things, *e.g.* names of action templates for flows. A flow signature represented as a name, flow type and causality may thus be represented by:

$flowSig$

$fName : Name$
$fType : mmFlowType$
$role : Causality$

$role \in \{Producer, Consumer\}$

Stream interfaces consist of sets of flow signatures. Each flow signature name in a given stream interface signature is required to be uniquely identified. This can be represented as:

$strIntSig$

$flows : \mathbb{P} flowSig$

$\forall fs_1, fs_2 : flowSig \bullet$
$\quad fs_1 \in flows \wedge fs_2 \in flows \wedge fs_1 \neq fs_2 \Rightarrow fs_1.fName \neq fs_2.fName$

This schema describes the syntactic structure of stream interface signatures satisfying the rules given in the ODP-RM. However, it does not prescribe any particular behaviour. Before we look into issues of behaviour and how it affects binding objects, it is necessary to consider control interfaces.

3.2 Formalising Syntactic Aspects of Control Interfaces

Control interfaces are used to manage the flow of information in a given system. ODP does not prescribe the form of control interfaces, however it is very likely that they will be based on operations as opposed to signals or streams. Further, for the sake of simplicity, we shall only consider control interfaces based upon announcements. Operational interfaces including interrogations are considered in more detail in [13].

Announcements may have parameters associated with them. These parameters may be represented by a *Name* and a *TypeIdentifier* used to to represent all types in the system. It should always be possible to determine the type of a parameter in a given system. Thus *param* is introduced as an injective function from names to types.

$$param : Name \rightarrowtail TypeIdentifier$$

It is also useful to introduce sequences of these parameters.

$$paramList == \text{seq } param$$

Announcements consist of a single invocation action, where an invocation action consists of a name for the invocation and the number, name and type of the argument parameters associated with the invocation. An announcement may thus be represented by the following schema:

```
┌─ annSig ─────────────────────────────
  invName : Name
  inArgs : paramList
└──────────────────────────────────────
```

Operational interface signatures consist of sets of announcements and interrogation signatures[2], and the interface as a whole is given a causality: client or server. Naming considerations of the components of the interface are also required. That is, all announcement names in the interface are required to be unique, as are the parameters that are associated with them. This can be represented as:

---

[2]For simplicity, we restrict ourselves to announcements only here.

$ctrIntSig$ _____
$anns$: $\mathbf{P}$ $annSig$
$role$: $Causality$

$role \in \{\,Client, Server\,\}$
$\forall\, as_1, as_2 : annSig;\ p_1, p_2 : param\ \bullet$
$\quad (as_1 \in anns \wedge as_2 \in anns \wedge as_1 \neq as_2 \Rightarrow$
$\qquad as_1.invName \neq as_2.invName) \wedge$
$\quad (as_1 \in anns \wedge \langle p_1 \rangle \text{ in } as_1.inArgs \wedge \langle p_2 \rangle \text{ in } as_1.inArgs) \wedge p_1 \neq p_2 \Rightarrow$
$\qquad first\ p_1 \neq first\ p_2$

This schema describes the syntactic structure of control interfaces satisfying the rules given in the ODP-RM. However, it does not prescribe any particular behaviour. As stated, this is necessarily so since objects will have their own different behaviours generally. It can be said, however, that a behaviour specification consists of a (possibly infinite) set of distinct[3] actions with constraints on their occurrence. These constraints impose a partial ordering on the set of actions. The actions themselves can be *Internal* to the object or observable to the environment, *i.e.* require participation (synchronisation) with the environment.

3.3 An Elementary Notion of Behaviour

In order to consider issues of behaviour in the computational viewpoint, it is necessary to introduce some functions that map action signatures to actions, *i.e.* flow signatures to flow actions, etc. The actions under consideration in this paper are internal actions, flow actions and announcements. These can be represented by a parameterised free type definition such as:

$$action ::= isIntAction \langle\!\langle Internal \rangle\!\rangle \mid isAnnAction \langle\!\langle annSig \rangle\!\rangle \mid isFlowAction \langle\!\langle flowSig \rangle\!\rangle$$

A behaviour specification as a collection of actions with an ordering relation between them may thus be represented by:

$$behspec == \{\, ar : action \leftrightarrow action \mid ar = ar^* \wedge ar \cap ar^\sim = \text{id}\ action \,\}$$

Here a set of relations between actions is being built. These relations are partial orders. That is, the expression $ar_1 = ar_1^*$ states that the relation is equal to its reflexive-transitive closure, which is the same as saying that it is reflexive and transitive. The expression $ar_1 \cap ar_1^\sim = \text{id}\ action$ ensures that the relation is anti-symmetric, *i.e.* no two different actions in the relation are related by the inverse of the relation also. Thus the relation ar is a relation that is transitive, anti-symmetric and reflexive, *i.e.* a partial order.

---

[3] If the actions in a behaviour specification were not distinct then the actual actions associated with an object or interface could be represented by a bag in Z to overcome problems of multiplicity, *e.g.* in recursive behaviour.

3.4 Formalising Aspects of Environment Contracts

Computational interface templates may have environment contracts associated with them. These may be regarded as agreements on the behaviour between the interface and its environment. They may include quality of service constraints such as throughput, delay and jitter, as well as usage and management constraints. We may represent several different types of constraint in Z but restrict ourselves to certain quality of service constraints for simplicity, in particular throughput and maximum delay.

Throughput may be regarded as the number of frames that a producer of a flow wishes to produce, or the number of frames that a consumer wishes to consume. Since we treat time as a natural number, we deal with the number of frames per second. Isochronous flows should have a consistent throughput, whereas bursty flows may have situations where more frames are output (or input) than at other times. In bursty flows it is especially useful to put an upper limit on the maximum throughput of data. Thus throughput may be represented as:

$$
\begin{array}{|l}
maxThru : mmFlowType \rightarrow \mathbb{N} \\
\hline
\forall\, mft : mmFlowType \bullet \\
\quad mft.flowChar = Isoch(mft.rate) \Rightarrow maxThru(mft) = 1 \operatorname{div} mft.rate \wedge \\
\quad mft.flowChar = Bursty \Rightarrow maxThru(mft) = \\
\qquad max\,\{s : \operatorname{seq} Frame;\ f_1, f_2 : Frame \mid s \operatorname{in} mft.frames\ \wedge \\
\qquad f_1 = head\ s \wedge f_2 = last\ s \wedge f_2.timestamp - f_1.timestamp \leq 1 \bullet \#s\}
\end{array}
$$

Here the throughput of isochronous flows is simply represented by the reciprocal of the rate, *i.e.* if the time difference between successive frames was 0.1 seconds then the throughput would be 10. Establishing the throughput of bursty flows is a little more involved however. Here the maximum throughput of a bursty flow is obtained by calculating the maximum subsequence of the flow with a timestamp difference of less than or equal to one second from its first and last elements.

The maximum delay of a multimedia flow may be regarded as the upper limit on the time window at which a frame is expected. For example, a consumer may be able to wait for a certain time for the next frame to arrive. Without considering issues such as buffering[4], this can be represented as:

$$
\begin{array}{|l}
maxDelay : mmFlowType \rightarrow \mathbb{N} \\
\hline
\forall\, mft : mmFlowType \bullet \\
\quad mft.flowChar = Isoch(mft.rate) \Rightarrow maxDelay(mft) = mft.rate\ \wedge \\
\quad mft.flowChar = Bursty \Rightarrow maxDelay(mft) = max\,\{f_1, f_2 : Frame \mid \\
\qquad \langle f_1, f_2 \rangle \operatorname{in} mft.frames \bullet f_2.timestamp - f_1.timestamp\}
\end{array}
$$

For isochronous flows, the maximum delay that a consumer can tolerate without buffering is given by the time difference between two frames. That is, if

---

[4] A considerable simplification.

after this time period the frame is not received, then an error has occurred and some remedying action must be taken, *e.g.* show last frame again. For bursty flows, the maximum delay is given by the maximum time difference between two successive frames in the sequence, *i.e.* if the consumer can consume as fast as the producer can produce, then consumption should be at least as fast as production. We may represent these constraints generally as:

$$Constraints ::= thruPut \langle\langle maxThru \rangle\rangle \mid delay \langle\langle maxDelay \rangle\rangle$$

Thus from this, environment contracts focusing primarily on quality of service constraints may be represented as:

EnvCon _____

qosCons : F *Constraints*

---

4 Computational Interfaces in ODP

Computational interfaces in ODP have associated with them, an interface signature; a behaviour specification and an environment contract. The interfaces under consideration in this paper are control and stream interfaces. We may thus represent control interface templates as:

---
ctrIntTemp _____

ctrSig : *ctrIntSig*
ctrlIntBS : *behspec*
ctrlEnvCon : *EnvCon*

(**let** *annActs* == {*ans* : *annSig* | *ans* ∈ *ctrSig.anns* • *isAnnAction*(*ans*)} •
(**let** *internalActs* == {*ia* : *Internal* |
  isIntAction(*ia*) ∈ dom *ctrlIntBS* ∪ ran *ctrlIntBS* • *isIntAction*(*ia*)} •
(*annActs*, *internalActs*) partition dom *ctrlIntBS* ∪ ran *ctrlIntBS*))

This states that the only actions that can be found in the behaviour specification associated with an operational interface template are either announcements or internal actions.

Stream interface templates may similarly be represented by:

---
strIntTemp _____

strSig : *strIntSig*
strIntBS : *behspec*
strEnvCon : *EnvCon*

(**let** *flowActs* == {*fs* : *flowSig* | *fs* ∈ *strSig.flows* • *isFlowAction*(*fs*)} •
(**let** *otherActs* == {*ia* : *Internal* |
  isIntAction(*ia*) ∈ dom *strIntBS* ∪ ran *strIntBS* • *isIntAction*(*ia*)} •
(*flowActs*, *otherActs*) partition dom *strIntBS* ∪ ran *strIntBS*))

This states that the only actions that can be found in the behaviour specification associated with a stream interface template are either stream actions or internal actions. Computational interfaces represented as streams or control (operational) interfaces generally may thus be represented by:

$$compIntTemp ::= control\langle\!\langle ctrIntTemp\rangle\!\rangle \mid stream\langle\!\langle strIntTemp\rangle\!\rangle$$

5 Binding in ODP

The ODP-RM states that the interfaces supporting computational objects may be bound provided they satisfy certain criteria: they must have complementary signatures, *i.e.* identical apart from causality being reversed. We argue that this is overly restrictive and not prescriptive enough. That is, requiring interfaces to be complementary is too strong as it prohibits interfaces with more behaviours from being bound, *e.g.* a server producing audio and video flows may well be bound to a client of video only if the client has the ability to simply ignore the audio flows as is the case for example with television. Or, a client only invoking a subset of the operations offered by a server interface could not be bound according to these rules. Similarly, requiring flow types to be the same is overly restrictive. It might well be the case that a producer of video flow can be replaced by a producer of audio/video if the consumer can extract the video flow.

The ODP-RM also states nothing about the effect of environment contracts associated with interfaces on the legality of bindings. Thus we propose extending the ODP notion of binding.

5.1 Syntactic Compatibility of Stream Interfaces

One stream interface is syntactically compatible with a second if all of the consumer flows in the first are matched by a producer flow in the second, and all of the consumer flows in the second are matched by producer flows in the first. Here we treat matching as having the same names and same flow types. Ideally we should deal with subtyping issues of multimedia flows. However, generically there are no specific rules since typing depends very much on issues such as compression techniques, etc, *e.g.* an audio/video flow may or may not be a subtype of a video flow. This can be formalised by:

$$strSyntaxOk : strIntSig \leftrightarrow strIntSig$$

$$\forall x, y : strIntSig \mid (x, y) \in strSyntaxOk \bullet$$
$$(\forall ax : flowSig \mid ax \in x.flows \bullet ax.role = Consumer \Rightarrow$$
$$(\exists by : flowSig \mid by \in y.flows \bullet$$
$$by.role = Producer \wedge ax.fType = by.fType \wedge ax.fName = by.fName)) \wedge$$
$$(\forall by : flowSig \mid by \in y.flows \bullet by.role = Consumer \Rightarrow$$
$$(\exists ax : flowSig \mid ax \in x.flows \bullet$$
$$(ax.role = Producer \wedge ax.fType = by.fType \wedge ax.fName = by.fName)))$$

5.2 Syntactic Compatibility of Control Interfaces

A server control interface is syntactically compatible with a client control interface if it provides all of the server operations requested by the client interface, *i.e.* it may have more operations. A client control interface is syntactically compatible with a server control interface if it does not request anything other than those operations in the server control interface. There are subtyping rules associated with the parameters of these operations; however, for simplicity sake we ignore these for now. These rules can be formalised by:

$$ctrSyntaxOk : ctrIntSig \leftrightarrow ctrIntSig$$

$$
\begin{aligned}
&\forall x, y : ctrIntSig \mid (x, y) \in ctrSyntaxOk \bullet \\
&\quad x.role = Client \land y.role = Server \Rightarrow \\
&\quad\quad (\forall ax : annSig \bullet ax \in x.anns \Rightarrow ax \in y.anns) \land \\
&\quad x.role = Server \land y.role = Client \Rightarrow \\
&\quad\quad \neg (\exists by : annSig \bullet by \in y.anns \land by \notin x.anns)
\end{aligned}
$$

5.3 Satisfying Environment Contracts

An environment contract may be deemed as being satisfied when the interface with which it is associated does not exhibit behaviours that contradict it. In our example, we consider maximum throughput and delay of multimedia interfaces. This can be represented as:

$$SatsCons : Constraints \leftrightarrow Constraints$$

$$
\begin{aligned}
&\forall mft_1, mft_2 : mmFlowType; \; c_1, c_2 : Constraints \mid (c_1, c_2) \in SatsCons \bullet \\
&\quad (c_1 = thruPut(mft_1, maxThru(mft_1)) \land c_2 = thruPut(mft_2, maxThru(mft_2)) \land \\
&\quad\quad maxThru(mft_1) \geq maxThru(mft_2)) \land \\
&\quad (c_1 = delay(mft_1, maxDelay(mft_1)) \land c_2 = delay(mft_2, maxDelay(mft_2)) \land \\
&\quad\quad maxDelay(mft_1) \leq maxDelay(mft_2))
\end{aligned}
$$

Here one constraint satisfies another constraint when the flow with which it is associated has a higher or equal throughput and smaller or equal delay. Environment contracts are satisfied when all constraints associated with them are satisfied. This can be represented as:

$$SatsEnvCon : EnvCon \leftrightarrow EnvCon$$

$$
\begin{aligned}
&\forall ec_1, ec_2 : EnvCon \mid (ec_1, ec_2) \in SatsEnvCon \bullet \\
&\quad (\forall qosC_1 : Constraints \mid qosC_1 \in ec_1.qosCons \bullet (\exists qosC_2 : Constraints \bullet \\
&\quad\quad qosC_2 \in ec_2.qosCons \land (qosC_1, qosC_2) \in SatsCons))
\end{aligned}
$$

5.4 Primitive Binding of Interfaces

Primitive binding occurs provided the two interfaces to be bound are syntactically compatible and their environment contracts are satisfied. The result of a primitive binding is a collection of actions with an ordering between them. This ordering is given by the transitive closure of the two partial orderings associated with the behaviour specifications of the interfaces being bound.

$$extPrimBind : compIntTemp \times compIntTemp \twoheadrightarrow (action \leftrightarrow action)$$

$\forall cit_1, cit_2 : compIntTemp; \ str_1, str_2 : strIntTemp; \ strs_1, strs_2 : strIntSig \ |$
$\quad stream(str_1) = cit_1 \wedge stream(str_2) = cit_2 \wedge$
$\quad strs_1 = str_1.strSig \wedge strs_2 = str_2.strSig \bullet$
$\qquad (str_1.strEnvCon, str_2.strEnvCon) \in SatsEnvCon \wedge$
$\qquad (strs_1, strs_2) \in strSyntaxOk \wedge$
$\qquad extPrimBind(cit_1, cit_2) = (str_1.strIntBS \cup str_2.strIntBS)^+ \vee$
$(\forall ctrl_1, ctrl_2 : ctrIntTemp; \ cis_1, cis_2 : ctrIntSig \ |$
$\quad control(ctrl_1) = cit_1 \wedge control(ctrl_2) = cit_2 \wedge$
$\quad cis_1 = ctrl_1.ctrSig \wedge cis_2 = ctrl_2.ctrSig \bullet$
$\qquad (ctrl_1.ctrlEnvCon, ctrl_2.ctrlEnvCon) \in SatsEnvCon \wedge$
$\qquad (cis_1, cis_2) \in ctrSyntaxOk \wedge$
$\qquad extPrimBind(cit_1, cit_2) = (ctrl_1.ctrlIntBS \cup ctrl_2.ctrlIntBS)^+)$

This thus enables interfaces to be bound provided they are syntactically compatible and do not have contradictory environment contracts. To attempt to establish that the two interfaces being bound are semantically compatible would require that the two sets of partial orderings associated with the interface behaviour specifications be known and that they not be contradictory. That is, if (a_1, a_2) were associated with the partial ordering of one interface then (a_2, a_1) would not be associated with the other interface. The actual ordering of two non-contradictory partial orders is then given by their transitive closure. Determining whether partial orderings are contradictory is likely to be problematic in most non-trivial behaviours.

6 Binding Objects and Firing of Actions

A binding object consists of a collection of control and stream interface templates. It will also have some behaviour that relates these interfaces together. This may be simplistically represented as:

$BindingObjectTemplate$
$ctrlInts : \mathbf{F}_1 \ ctrIntTemp$
$strInts : \mathbf{F}_1 \ strIntTemp$
$bs : behspec$

We do not give the precise behaviour specification here, since to do so would require a high level of prescriptivity on specific behaviours. Rather, we highlight the kind of actions that a binding object might have as part of its behaviour specification. Specifically, we consider an announcement for increasing the (isochronous) flow rate of the producer with which it is associated. A faster flow rate may be represented by:

$$FasterFlow : flowSig \leftrightarrow flowSig$$

$$\forall fs_1, fs_2 : flowSig \mid (fs_1, fs_2) \in FasterFlow \bullet$$
$$fs_1.fName = fs_2.fName \wedge fs_1.role = fs_2.role \wedge$$
$$fs_1.fType.rate < fs_2.fType.rate \wedge fs_2.fType.rate \leq maxThru(fs_1.fType)$$

Now the firing of an announcement to increase the flow rate of an isochronous producer may be represented by:

$$
\begin{array}{l}
\underline{\quad FireFasterAnnouncement \quad\rule{5cm}{0pt}} \\
as? : annSig \\
ctrlProd : ctrIntTemp \\
strProd, strProd' : strIntTemp \\
\hline
\exists\, bot : BindingObjectTemplate;\ bci : ctrIntTemp;\ n : Name;\ sis : strIntSig; \\
\quad fs_1, fs_2 : flowSig \mid bci \in bot.ctrlInts \bullet \\
(control(bci), control(ctrlProd)) \in \mathrm{dom}\, extPrimBind \wedge \\
isAnnAction(as?) \in \mathrm{dom}\, bci.ctrlIntBS \cap \mathrm{dom}\, ctrlProd.ctrlIntBS \wedge \\
\{n\} \in \mathrm{dom}\, second\, as?.inArgs \wedge sis = strProd.strSig \wedge \\
fs_1 \in sis.flows \wedge fs_1.fName = n \wedge (fs_1, fs_2) \in FasterFlow \wedge \\
strProd'.strSig = strProd.strSig \wedge \\
strProd'.strEnvCon = strProd.strEnvCon \wedge \\
(\exists\, nbs : behspec \mid \mathrm{dom}\, nbs = \{isFlowAction(fs_2)\} \wedge \\
\quad \mathrm{ran}\, nbs = strProd.strIntBS (\!| \{isFlowAction(fs_1)\} |\!) \bullet \\
\quad strProd'.strIntBS = \{isFlowAction(fs_1)\} \lhd strProd.strIntBS \oplus nbs)
\end{array}
$$

Here the control interface of the producer object must be legally bound to some binding object and the announcement being fired must be in the domain of the behaviour specification of both these objects, *i.e.* it is an action that can be fired at that moment. For simplicity's sake, we do not consider the modifications to the control interface template following the firing of the announcement, or where the frames are being sent, *i.e.* their receipt at the binding object.

Following the occurrence of the announcement, a flow action identified by a parameter in the announcement signature has its rate increased provided the increase does not exceed the maximum as given by the environment contract. The signature and environment contract associated with the stream interface template remain unchanged, but the behaviour specification is modified so that the partial ordering of flow actions in the stream interface has the old flow action replaced by the new faster flow action.

7 Conclusions

This paper has shown how powerful the Z language is for specifying ODP systems. Through the elementary ideas given by set theory and first order predicate logic, complex reasoning about the behaviour of systems can be achieved. The structure of these systems can be specified within the currently existing Z notation, as opposed to extensions to the notation. For reasoning about behaviour Z is perfectly adequate, but for considering issues such as encapsulation and state then it is likely that an object-oriented flavour of Z would be better suited. The modelling of real-time behavioural issues can be dealt with adequately in Z, as opposed to Z used in conjunction with different temporal logics. This includes the continuous real time synchronisation of multimedia such as might be found in lip-synchronisation of audio and video for example.

Aspects of binding objects that have to be considered for distributed interworking of computational objects have been specified. This has extended the basic ODP idea of checking by signature only to include environment contracts and the necessary conditions for behavioural type checking, *i.e.* non-contradictory behaviours.

References

[1] A. Coombes. An interval logic for modelling time in Z. Technical report, Department of Computing Science, University of York, 1990.

[2] N. Delisle and D. Garlan. Formally specifying electronic instruments. *ACM SIGSOFT Eng. Notes*, 14:242–248, 1989.

[3] ISO/IEC. *Information Processing Systems – Open Systems Interconnection – Estelle – A Formal Description Technique Based on an Extended State Transition Model.* ISO/IEC 9074. International Organization for Standardization, Geneva, Switzerland, 1989.

[4] ISO/IEC. *Information Processing Systems – Open Systems Interconnection – LOTOS – A Formal Description Technique Based on the Temporal Ordering of Observational Behaviour.* ISO/IEC 8807. International Organization for Standardization, Geneva, Switzerland, 1989.

[5] ISO/IEC. *Basic Reference Model of ODP – Part 1: Overview and Guide to Use of the Reference Model.* Draft International Standard 10746-1, Draft ITU-T Recommendation X.901. ISO/IEC ITU-T, Geneva, Switzerland, 1995.

[6] ISO/IEC. *Basic Reference Model of ODP – Part 2: Foundations.* International Standard 10746-2, ITU-T X.902. ISO/IEC ITU-T, Geneva, Switzerland, 1995.

[7] ISO/IEC. *Basic Reference Model of ODP – Part 3: Architecture.* International Standard 10746-3, ITU-T X.903. ISO/IEC ITU-T, Geneva, Switzerland, 1995.

[8] ISO/IEC. *Basic Reference Model of ODP – Part 4: Architectural Semantics.* Draft International Standard 10746-4, Draft ITU-T Recommendation X.904. ISO/IEC ITU-T, Geneva, Switzerland, 1995.

[9] ISO/IEC. *Basic Reference Model of ODP – Part 4.1: Architectural Semantics Amendment.* ISO/IEC JTC1/SC21 Working Document N9818. ISO/IEC ITU-T, Geneva, Switzerland, 1995.

[10] ISO/IEC. *Z Notation version 1.2.* ISO/IEC JTC1/SC22/WG19 CD 13568. ISO/IEC, Geneva, Switzerland, August 1995.

[11] ITU-T. *International Consultative Committee on Telegraphy and Telephony – SDL – Specification and Description Language.* CCITT Z.100. International Telecommunications Union, Geneva, Switzerland, 1992.

[12] P. King. A formal specification of signalling system number 7 link layer. Technical Report TR-101, University of Queensland, Key Centre for Software Technology, 1989.

[13] R.O. Sinnott and K.J. Turner. Specifying ODP Computational Objects in Z. In Elie Najm and Jean-Bernard Stefani, editors, *Proceedings of Formal Methods for Open Object-based Distributed Systems*, Paris, France, March 1996.

[14] K. J. Turner. Relating architecture and specification. *Computer Networks and ISDN Systems*, 1996. Accepted for publication in Special Edition on Specification Architecture.

A Generic and Executable Model for the Specification and Validation of Distributed Behaviors.

Dominique Sidou.

Institut Eurécom,
2229 route des crètes, B.P. 193,
06904 SOPHIA ANTIPOLIS CEDEX, France.
email: sidou@eurecom.fr

Abstract. An executable model based approach to validate distributed behavior specifications is presented. Behaviors are simple rewrite rules on data instantiated according to a given information model. They are triggered by events such as operations invoked on computational interfaces. The model is generic in the sense that it does not make any assumption about the information and computation models used, i.e. frameworks such as the OSI Systems Management Architecture, CORBA or SNMP can be adapted. To ensure usability, the execution environment provides for (i) a visual operational semantics of the proposed behavior specification language, and (ii) for dynamic debugging facilities. In addition, a *Scheme* programming environment is shown to be a valuable option to support the implementation, in particular for dynamic debugging purposes.

Keywords : Distributed Behaviors, Data Oriented Executable Specification, Validation, Visual Operational Semantics, Dynamic Debugging, *Scheme*, ODP.

1 Context and Objectives

The paper describes a generic specification and validation framework for distributed behaviors. A special emphasis is put on the genericity and executability of the model, its design and its realization in *Scheme* [4]. Distributed Processing Environments (DPE) have become an available distribution technology to support current and future distributed applications. Satisfactory solutions exist for communication oriented aspects based on protocols, services, and on top Interface Definition Languages (IDL) (e.g. RPC systems, CORBA systems, OSI systems management, SNMP framework). However, behavior aspects are still poorly considered. This inevitably results as inter-working problems between clients and servers. That is the reason why formal approaches are being envisioned, in particular in the ODP framework [16]. First attempts are being made to try to instantiate this framework, e.g. ITU-USG15 [9] work on ODP and TMN information models. Another work of interest is the analysis and design task force [14] launched by the OMG. The proposed model for distributed behaviors aims at a working and usable specification and validation environment. Therefore, the chosen approach for validation is based on executable specifications [8], onto which test cases or scenarios can be exercised. This provides for immediate validation, and can be used directly with the users to confirm that the specification satisfies their initial requirements[1]. Thus as in [20, 1] the objective is quite limited to provide better behavior specifications validated with respect to the informally given original user requirements about a system. As a consequence formal procurement of implementations through proved consecutive refinements steps is not considered. A model oriented approach is used, that typically describes a system in terms of data and operations. Such approaches have also been qualified as Data Oriented Models (DOM) [13], in opposition to Process Oriented Models (POM), i.e. Process Algebraic notations (CCS) or CSP and FSM based approaches. There is, of course, a direct correspondence between DOMs and POMs : both define an abstract machine, i.e. a state and the possible transitions between states. The difference is a matter of presentation. A DOM defines for each action what changes upon state can be expected, whereas, a POM gives for each state what actions are possible. POMs have been used to check properties about the behavior of the whole system (safety and liveness). A DOM seems more adapted to the validation of statements about individual operations, e.g. using *pre* and *post* assertional conditions. However, it is quite simple (and not new [13]) to merge the two approaches, e.g. a DOM with an interleaving semantics. The model advocated follows this approach : it enables to specify guarded action behaviors extended with assertions, that exercise themselves on a notion of Distributed and Shared Memory (DSM). The execution model handles nondeterminism by interleaving the execution of actions. No constraint is imposed about behavior execution contexts. They may include reference(s) to the piece of the DSM concerned with the execution of a behavior. Of course, overlapping can occur which result as potential interference between behaviors. Various notions of execution contexts can be incorporated to the generic kernel by provisioning it with a DSM model and API.

"Ideal" ODP Perspective : The DSM-API corresponds to simple basic primitives to manipulate information objects consistently in regard to the underlying Information Model (IM) used. Information viewpoint languages allows to specify and organize the data in many ways : flat variables, objects, object clusters, relationships. . . . Note that, the DSM-API can be viewed as a notion of interface to information objects. In contrast, at the Computational level signatures of operations are described using interface specification languages. Operation signatures describe the service primitives that are actually invoked from clients to servers in the distributed environment. ODP recommends some degree of separation and

---

[1] In fact, at the point of setting up a first formal specification from the user requirements, executability and prototyping is probably a more usable approach in comparison to e.g. proof systems.

thus different formalisms to be used for information and computation viewpoint specification languages. TINA-C with quasi-GDMO+GRM [18] and ODL [19]; and ITU-SG15 [9] realize such a separation. However, in practice the two issues are often merged in existing formalisms e.g. in GRM + GDMO/ASN.1 and in the SNMP-SMI. In contrast, CORBA-IDL gives only operation signatures, leaving the information model unspecified. Though GDMO allows the specification of information models[2], a given existing GDMO specification may not be complete from the information viewpoint, e.g. there is no guarantee that from an existing GDMO specification all the attributes are there in order to fully specify the behavior of a given action. Therefore, obtaining an information specification may be more complex than just removing from a GDMO specification the computational or any other unwanted aspects.

Towards a Generic and Usable Framework : The approach taken here is to integrate the existing information and interface specification models as-is, and to finalize such specifications according to what would be its projection on the "ideal" ODP perspective. This process may require to separate concerns, to complete unspecified parts.... Integrating GDMO, GRM, IDL as-is brings extraneous work at the beginning to customize the generic model. But on the long run, this provides for a much more usable specification framework. Specifiers/users can write/read specifications close to their universe of discourse. This results as specifications being more easy to write, read and understand than if a general common framework was used with the burden to have to convert, all the time, between concepts of a domain to too general concepts.

Instantiation and validation of the generic model has been done in the context of the Telecommunication Management Network (TMN) [17]. TMN is based on the OSI Systems Management Architecture including GDMO, ASN.1 extended with relationships (GRM) and CMIS/P for communication issues.

Plan of the paper :
1. In section 2 the generic behavior specification template notation is introduced along with its constituent clauses.
2. In section 3 the generic operational semantics is presented, emphasis is put on its visual character because this is a very important factor for the usability of the execution environment.
3. Section 4 presents features about the user environment. The different execution modes are listed. Basic level debugging is presented and hints towards the provision of improved debugging with backtracking are also given.
4. Section 5 describes how the main features of the generic model are realized using *Scheme*.

---

[2] In fact GDMO is a super-set of what is actually needed for an information specification language. That is the reason why ITU-SG15 have defined the GDIO (Guidelines for the Definition of Information Objects) notation and TINA-C have defined the quasi-GDMO+GRM notation.

2 Generic Specification Framework

The generic behavior specification framework is based on Guarded Behaviors. A **Guard** specifies an acceptance condition for a **Behavior Body** to be executed. Both guard and body are clauses of the proposed behavior template notation. This model provides direct support for nondeterministic behavior specifications because at a given step nothing prevents from several guard conditions to be fulfilled. Bodies define rewrite pieces of code on a Distributed Shared Memory (DSM). No assumption is made on the DSM. It can be organized in any suitable way according to the information model used, e.g. flat variables (SNMP-SMI), Objects (OSI-MIM, CORBA) eventually extended with relationships (GRM [12], OMG Relationship COS [15]). Behaviors specify the reaction of the system to the occurrence of an event, i.e. service request from a client, a failure in an equipment. ... In the following the term *trigger* and *event* are used interchangeably. An event is represented in behaviors as a message, this is the reason why the notion of *event-message* is also used below. Event messages typically represent operations that can be invoked at computational object interfaces. Event messages can naturally be sent in behavior bodies thanks to well identified primitives. As one would have noticed, analogy is rather obvious with production systems that can be found in rule based expert systems from the AI field or in Event-Condition-Action (ECA) rules from the active database field [10, 6]. However, goals are not the same because in such domains, the production system is used to support actual operation, management, control. . . applications. Here, an executable specification framework is used to perform validation. As argued by Fuchs in [8], a declarative framework which is exactly what procures a production system is a valuable option for specification executability.

Data Oriented Models : DOMs describe the data in a system and how actions exercise their behaviors onto the data. This is a departure from the process oriented model which have been considered as a conventional choice for executable specifications [3]. In DisCo project [13] the advantages of data versus process oriented models are fully justified. This argumentation is valid at least for functional behavior properties : A DOM avoids thread partitioning, and to determine which thread of control is responsible for which part of the data. Here, the control flow of executed action behaviors is completely driven by data dependencies. Thus maximal nondeterminism is implicitly assumed, and if restrictions with respect to the nondeterminism allowed in the system are to be observed, they have to be given explicitly. Thus what is explicit is the additional constraints (synchronization, atomicity, sequentiality. . .) to observe, this is a better approach from the specification point of view because, in some way, it is minimalist and avoids over-specification. When dealing with functional properties of a distributed system, one is not interested in modeling how object and processes are distributed.

More exactly, one would be interested to make the less assumption as possible about distribution. The advantage is that all the distribution alternatives remain implicitly allowed, so that they remain available to all be legitimately examined at the right place, i.e. when engineering issues are treated.

In contrast, Process Oriented Models (POM) – e.g. Algebraic specifications (Lotos, CCS), CSP and FSM models (SDL, Estelle) – include engineering issues such as behavior and object partitioning among processes. This is necessary to deal with non-functional behavior properties like timing and real time constraints. Thus DOMs and POMs are not to be opposed, they are in fact complementary techniques. DOMs being more abstract are more likely to be used to treat information and computation viewpoint issues. POMs allowing to include behavior properties dependent on the actual distribution of objects are more adapted to deal with engineering issues.

Making Use of Assertions : Finally, the behavior template is extended with **pre** and **post** condition clauses. They are conditions specified just like guards but intended to a different goal, i.e. to check for the correctness of performed executions.

Recap : a behavior template is defined as a tuple with the following clauses : *beh ≡ <label, when, pre, body, post>*. The next section defines more in detail its operational semantics, i.e. how behaviors defined according to this generic template are exercised during execution.

3 Generic Visual Operational Semantics

Because the selected approach for the validation of behavior specifications relies on the execution of test suites and on the observation of their outcome, a good test execution environment is of paramount importance. To this end, two complementary views are provided to give the user a complete description of the whole system's state : the **Object View** and the **Execution View**.

3.1 Object View

The execution model is a data oriented model, into which behaviors can be seen as rewriting rules on a globally available distributed shared memory (DSM). Each time something occurs in a behavior, its eventual effects can be reflected on the underlying DSM. According to the way the DSM is structured, e.g. with objects and relationships, it can be visually represented as a graph. Then any change on this graph can be highlighted to the user which naturally lends to animation.

Figure 1 gives an example of an Object View snapshot[3]. This example is taken from a TMN case study dealing with service provisioning in a generic network infrastructure. This object and relationship graph is instantiated according to TMN information models : GDMO for Managed Objects (drawn as ovals), and GRM for relationships (drawn as rhombuses) and roles (drawn as rectangles). Parts of the object view are hidden because they have been cut. However, they can be restored as needed.

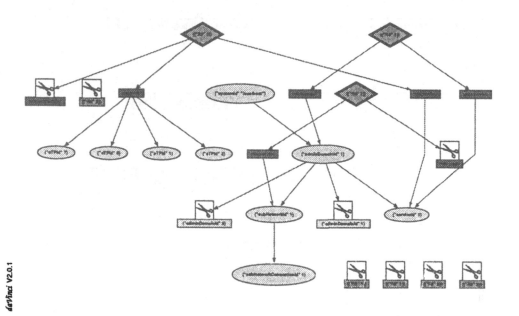

Fig. 1. Object View.

3.2 Execution View

This view is defined by the concept of Behavior Execution Tree (BET), which is itself a tree of Behavior Execution Nodes (BEN). A BEN represents a behavior at a given step of the execution in its body code. In this code, two kinds of primitives can be used to :

- invoke operations on a computational interface, this is done by sending event messages.
- interact with the underlying information objects, this is done by using the DSM-API.

Behaviors may have been defined to model the required reaction of the system to the emission such event messages. This new behaviors being executed define

---

[3] The graph visualization tool *daVinci* [5] is used to provide the object view. It is also used to provide the execution view (see section 3.2).

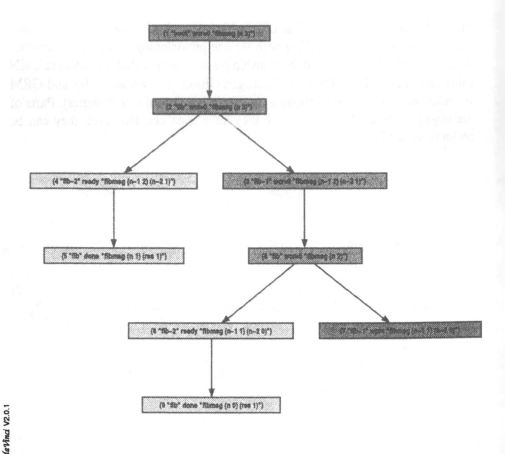

daVinci V2.0.1

Fig. 2. Behavior Execution Tree (Execution View).

new behavior execution nodes that are visually represented as children of the original parent BEN. The BET can be used to provide for a visual description of a complex behavior propagation. It can also be seen as a visual representation of the way the operational semantics of the proposed behavior specification paradigm is exercised. The operational semantics used is based on the interleaving execution model. That is, execution steps of running behaviors can be interleaved in any arbitrary order. Atomic execution steps are defined by behavior body code delimited by interactions with the DSM, i.e. usage of primitives from the DSM-API. Finer grain execution steps are not needed (e.g. at the level of *Scheme* instructions) because it is assumed that behaviors can interfere only on the basis of DSM interactions[4]. Figure 2, gives an example of a behavior execution tree. Each node

---

[4] Note that this assumption is valid only if access to shared behavior variables is limited to the DSM (whatever the way it is implemented). Non careful access within behavior code to global *Scheme* variables can easily violate this assumption.

is documented with a unique identifier accompanied with the label of its corresponding behavior and its state : <i beh-label state ... >. The different values for the BEN state field are explained below. BEN ids can be interpreted as a birth date. This gives an immediate view about how the BET was developed. To get a visual representation, BENs can be labeled and colored differently according to their state. Additional attributes accessible from each BEN can also be added by the user to customize what is actually displayed for each BEN developed. The BET shown in figure 2, illustrates through a toy example how the computation of the value of the Fibonacci function for the integer 3 is being processed. In addition, appendix B gives :

- the corresponding behaviors.
- the unique event message *fibmsg* used to trigger recursive Fibonacci computations.

Note that, this toy example illustrates only control aspects, that is the reason why there is no use of underlying information object accessed through the DSM-API. The different ways into which a BET can be further developed, from a given state, are completely determined by the state of its constituents BENs and their possible individual evolutions. Thus, at this point it is worth to describe more precisely a BEN and its transition diagram. BEN properties, are listed in figure 3.

3.3 BEN Fields

the state field defines the operations that are possible at a given step, i.e. that the user can invoke on the execution node. Its value is one of the list *(ready, wcr=0, wpre, wpost, done)*. A BEN in the *ready* state means that it is ready to execute the next step in its body code. All BENs in this state form the *ready-list* of BENs ready to execute. When the *ready-list* becomes empty, the behavior execution has completed. A terminating state has been reached. Transitions between BEN state values can be described as a finite state machine (see figure 4).

the step field represents the current stage of processing in the behavior body code. It is composed of :

record	Fields
BEN	*<id, state, beh, children, parent, step, wcr=0, bec>*
STEP	*<beh-cont, beh-src-line>*
BEC	*<evt-msg, dsm-context>*
BEH	*<label, when, pre, body, post>*

Fig. 3. Behavior Execution Node Properties.

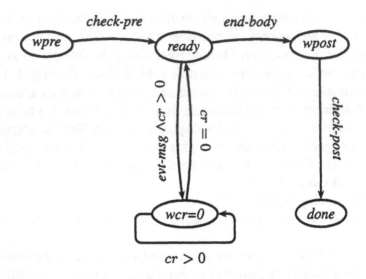

Fig. 4. Behavior Execution Node FSM.

- *beh-src-line* field references to the line number of a behavior source file, thus enabling source level debugging.
- *beh-cont* field is a *Scheme* continuation (see section 5) that is called to resume the execution of this behavior in order to execute its consecutive steps.

the cr field is a decreasing counter. It gives for a BEN that has sent an event message to be propagated, the *child residue*, i.e. the number of child BENs currently being executed and that the (parent) BEN is waiting for completion. As shown on the BEN FSM in figure 4, while $cr > 0$ the parent BEN is not allowed to resume the execution of its body code.

the beh field is the behavior itself that was fetched. It is itself a record with fields values representing internally what has been defined in the behavior clauses using the generic behavior template presented in section 2.

the Behavior Execution Context field (BEC) is a completely opaque data for the generic kernel that is given as argument to each evaluation of behavior clauses. This concerns the guard (*when* clause), *pre*, *body* and *post*. BEC semantics are defined according to the application domain into which one intends to use the generic kernel, e.g. the information and computation model used. From our experience in the TMN context, it is typically composed of :

- *evt-msg* is the message sent that caused this behavior to be fetched. It is, of course, dependent on the services invocation primitives supported by the underlying computational model. So values for this field are out of the scope of the generic model.

- *dsm-context* represents the execution scope of this behavior on the DSM. This field is dependent on the DSM or information model used. This typically references a variable, an object, a group of objects, a relationship or any other data abstraction of interest for a given information model.
- ... any other property required to customize the generic model.

4 Execution Modes and Debugging

The object and execution views are the basis for a powerful debugging tool. The object view enables the user to inspect that the DSM components are assigned with correct values at any execution step. The execution view gives a proper representation of the nondeterminism occurring, i.e. concurrency, choice or unordering along performed executions. Concretely, the user can get a direct feeling of the nondeterminism by seeing all the BENs in the current *ready-list* that are highlighted on the BET. At each step, the user has a full control about which execution branch of the BET should be explored. Other basic debugging features such as trace and breakpoint facilities are also possible.

This enables the following execution modes to be provided :

- The **user driven** mode enables the user to develop the BET as wished. At each step, the user selects the BEN (which belongs to the ready-list) from which its next step is to be executed. In this mode, it is also possible to terminate the execution of a BEN according to one of the policies described below. This is a required feature in order to speed up the development of parts of the BET, e.g. because they are already debugged. ...
- The **random walk** policy enables to develop the BET randomly, and reach one of the possible terminating states.
- The **fixed walk** policy develops the BET according with a fixed strategy, e.g. depth or breath first. This is useful for early stages of debugging, to force the execution to follow always the same path. This avoids to be annoyed by the other problems caused by nondeterminism that one would prefer to fight at a later stage.

Improved Debugging Support : Basic source level debugging support do not prevent from wasting precious debugging time in setting break-points in backward order and re-running the program, or in stepping over the whole execution flow, until the erroneous code is reached. In contrast, an execution backtracking facility in interactive source level debuggers allows users to mirror their though processes while debugging [2]. This enables to work backwards from the location where an error is manifested and determine the conditions under which the error occurred. Such a facility also allows a user to change program characteristics and re-execute from arbitrary points within the program under examination (a "what-if" capability). This very powerful dynamic debugging facility requires two major underlying mechanisms : **control backtracking** and **data backtracking**. Here are given some hints on how such mechanisms could be incorporated to the generic meta-model :

- **Control backtracking** is easy to provide using *Scheme* continuations (see section 5). It is just needed to store the history of steps in each BEN, rather than only the current one. Because each step contains a continuation corresponding to each execution stage in the behavior body, it is possible to go back to any previous execution stage by calling back the corresponding continuation.

- **Data backtracking** is another issue. This requires to be able to restore the DSM states of each behavior execution step. Such a mechanism is totally DSM implementation dependent. If the DSM is implemented on top of database, data backtracking could probably be implemented in terms of transaction processing[5]. If the DSM is directly implemented in the *Scheme* environment, another approach to implement data backtracking is to provide for a data undoing function. However, in order to avoid to re-implement this mechanism for each DSM model, an idea would be provide a generic facility on top of which any form of DSM could be realized. This would enable to define data undoing on the generic storage facility. A notion of generic repository of information based on hash-tables is already being used for the currently used TMN-based instantiation of the generic model. Though not yet implemented, data undoing function should not be too difficult to implement on such generic repositories.

- An execution trace is also needed besides the BET. The backtracking process has to follow this trace in backward direction. This trace can be simply implemented as a stack of BEN identifiers, from which execution steps can be retrieved in backward order.

5 Realization in *Scheme*

Why Scheme *?* It is a simple, clear and sound programming language. Its syntax is reduced to the very necessary and it should not be long to learn (the standard [4] is less that 50 pages). *Scheme* provides the required programming support for behavior coding (control structures, variable notations... that does not have to

---

[5] In effect, a database system offering only a transaction concept is sufficient : Marking a data state is done by starting a new transaction and using a counter for the number of opened transactions. Backtracking is done by aborting a sufficient number of transactions. This works, but in some way the transaction mechanism is abused, since transactions are never committed as long as the behavior propagation is processed.

be reinvented). In addition, if the *Scheme* Library is used [7], facilities such as quantifiers are available. This can be used to simplify the specification of logical expressions (guards, pres and posts).

The Macro System : has been used to define the behavior specification template presented in section 2. *Scheme* provides high level macros that enables to define expressive language extensions and how they are to be expanded to pure *Scheme* code.

Closures or λ-expressions : provide a nice abstraction to store the different pieces of executable specification code present in guards, bodies, pres and posts. All this clauses are expanded and stored as closures (of one argument) in the behavior repository. At evaluation, such closures are called with the current behavior execution context (BEC) as argument. The BEC contains all the relevant information required for the evaluation of such closures.

Behavior Instrumentation : To enable source level debugging behavior instrumentation have to be performed just before behaviors are loaded in the behavior repository of the execution environment. This provides during execution references to the original behavior source code.

Scheme *Continuations :* Though small and simple, *Scheme* provides in the language itself a powerful concept (continuations) and an associated construct (`call-with-current-continuation` often abbreviated as `call/cc`) that enables to set up and store any execution context and the way to go back to this context, by simply calling it as if it was a usual function. Continuations are used to provide the basic control mechanisms needed in order to implement basic debugging support (i.e. stepping and breakpoints). In addition, continuations are extremely useful for implementing a wide variety of advanced control structures, such as complex forms of backtracking. Therefore, they can also be used in the realization of the improved debugging with backtracking support to provide for a straightforward implementation of the control backtracking part. Appendix A gives a quick overview through a simple example on the way continuations are working.

6 Conclusion and Further Issues

The generic behavior specification and validation environment defines a working and usable generic model. It is designed with ODP principles in mind, to allow for a clean distinction between information and computation issues in behavior modeling. The proposed behavior template is based on guarded action behaviors. This is a quite classical approach, and similar constructs have been used for general production systems such as rule based expert systems or ECA-rules in active database systems. Such a declarative framework is also a natural option for executable specifications [8]. In addition, in order to perform validation, the behavior model is enriched with assertions that can be checked along behavior execution paths. This also follows the approach advocated by ITU-SG15 work [9]. This generic behavior model has been first instantiated in the TMN context (GDMO/ASN.1, GRM and CMIS/P) and used in several TMN-based case studies. Work is being done to customize the model towards CORBA based systems. This should prove again more effectively the genericity of the approach. This concerns to reuse and check for the applicability of not only, the specification framework but also, the implemented operational semantics and execution environment.

A further issue is to effectively implement the improved debugging with backtracking facility. This may reveal as a very interesting mechanism to base the support for a powerful problem explanation tool. Though the proposed behavior model can be very useful in order to deliver better distributed behavior specifications (which is in itself a real win), one would contest that the approach is not so formal. In effect, providing another specification language, even equipped with an operational semantics and execution environment, is far from being a sufficient condition towards formality. Without the ability to do some kind of formal reasoning such as analytical proof or exhaustive search, there is little place for actual formality. The executable framework is naturally more oriented towards an exhaustive search approach. In particular, the backtracking facilities can be used to do exhaustive behavior analysis of all behavior execution paths that can be followed for a given test case. This would enable one to highlight all the cases where assertions are violated. And, even if no assertion is violated, it may be interesting to examine all the terminating configurations of the system. May be some of them exhibit unwanted behavior executions. But as usual when exhaustive search is performed in the context of an interleaving execution model, the classical state explosion problem occurs. It is worth to see how well known techniques, e.g. partial order methods [11] could be applied to the generic model considered.

Acknowledgments : The author is indebted to the three anonymous reviewers for their helpful comments and suggestions.

References

1. A CASE Environment for TINA-oriented Applications, 1996. Available at http://andromeda.cselt.stet.it:8080/ace/ACE.html.

2. Hiralal Agrawal, Richard A. DeMillo, and Eugene Spafford. An Execution Backtracking Approach to Program Debugging. Technical Report SERC-TR-22-P, Software Engineering Research Center Purdue University, September 1990.

3. J. P. Briand, M. C. Fehri, L. Logrippo, and A. Obaid. Executing LOTOS Specifications. *Protocol Specification, Testing and Verification VI, IFIP 1987*, pages 73–84, 1987.

4. W. Clinger and J. Rees. *Revised*⁴ Report on the Algorithmic Language Scheme. *ACM Lisp Pointers*, 4(3), 1991. Available at http://www.cs.indiana.edu/scheme-repository/doc/standards/r4rs.ps.gz.

5. The Interactive Graph Visualization System daVinci. Available at http://www.informatik.uni-bremen.de/~inform/forschung/daVinci/daVinci.html.

6. Klaus R. Dittrich, Stella Gatziu, and Andreas Geppert. The Active Database Management System Manifesto: A Rulebase of ADBMS Features. Technical report, University of Zurich, Dept. of Computer Science, 1995. Available at http://www.ifi.unizh.ch/techreports.

7. T.R. Eigenschink, D. Love, and A. Jaffer. SLIB: The Portable Scheme Library, 1994.

8. Norbert E. Fuchs. Specifications are (preferably) executable. Technical Report 92, University of Zurich (CS Dept.), 1992. Available at ftp://ftp.ifi.unizh.ch/pub/techreports/.

9. Management of the Transport Network – Application of the ODP Framework, ITU-T G851-01, 1996.

10. Andreas Geppert, Stella Gatziu, Klaus R. Dittrich, Hans Fritschi, and Anca Vaduva. Architecture and Implementation of the Active Object-Oriented Database Management System SAMOS. Technical report, University of Zurich, Dept. of Computer Science, 1995. Available at http://www.ifi.unizh.ch/techreports.

11. Patrice Godefroid. *Partial-Order Methods for the Verification of Concurrent Systems* – An Approach to the State Exploision Problem. PhD thesis, Université de Liège, Faculté des Sciences Appliquées, 1995. Available at http://www.montefiore.ulg.ac.be/services/verif/papers/thesis.ps.Z.

12. ISO/IEC JTC 1/SC 21, ITU X.725 – Information Technology – Open System Interconnection – Data Management and Open Distributed Processing – Structure of Management Information – Part 7 : General Relationship Model.

13. Hannu-Matti Jarvinen and Reino Kurki-Suonio. DisCo Specification Language: Marriage of Action and Objects. In *Proc. of 11th International Conference on Distributed Computing Systems*, Arlington, Texas, may 1991. IEEE Computer Society Press. Available at http://www.cs.tut.fi/laitos/DisCo/DisCo-english.fm.html.

14. Object Management Group : Object Analysis and Design RFI, 1995. OMG TC Document 95-9-35.

15. OMG Relationship Service Submission, 1994. Revised submission to the Object Services Task Force RFP2 by Bull, Hewlett-Packard, Olivetti, IBM, SNI, and SunSoft. OMG Document 94-05-05, available at http://www.omg.org/docs/1994/94-05-05.ps.

16. Basic Reference Model of ODP – Part 1: Overview and Guide to Use of the Reference Model, ISO 10746-1, ITU X.901.

17. Dominique Sidou, Sandro Mazziotta, and Rolf Eberhardt. TIMS : a TMN-based Information Model Simulator, Principles and Application to a Simple Case Study. In *Sixth International Workshop on Distributed Systems : Operations & Management*, Ottawa - Canada, 1995. IFIP / IEEE. Available at http://www.eurecom.fr/~tims/papers/dsom95-paper.ps.gz.

18. TINA Information Modelling Concepts, 1994. Available at http://www.tinac.com.

19. TINA Object Definition Language (TINA-ODL) Manual, 1995. Available at http://www.tinac.com.

20. User Manual for the IFAD VDM-SL Toolbox, 1996. Available at http://www.ifad.dk/products/toolbox.html.

A Continuations, a Simple Example

The procedure `set-cont-here` sets up and returns a continuation at the following statement from which it is called. As shown below, c1 can be re-called back to redo the three `displays`, c2 for the two last ones and c3 for the last one.

```
scm-prompt> (define (set-cont-here)
               (call-with-current-continuation
                  (lambda (c) c)))
#<unspecified>

scm-prompt> (begin ; this executes the "displays" and sets up the continuations.
               (newline)
               (define c1 (set-cont-here))
               (display "Hi 1!!!") (newline)
               (define c2 (set-cont-here))
               (display "Hi 2!!!") (newline)
               (define c3 (set-cont-here))
               (display "Hi 3!!!") (newline))
Hi 1!!!
Hi 2!!!
Hi 3!!!
```

```
;;; continuations are Scheme objects, whose value can be printed.
;;; This is done here by simply making a list of their values.
;;;
scm-prompt> (list c1 c2 c3)
(#<cont 316 @ 7d390> #<cont 316 @ 77b38> #<cont 316 @ 78070>)

;;; calling back continuation c1
;;;
scm-prompt> (c1 c1)
Hi 1!!!
Hi 2!!!
Hi 3!!!

;;; calling back continuation c2
;;;
scm-prompt> (c2 c2)
Hi 2!!!
Hi 3!!!

;;; calling back continuation c3
;;;
scm-prompt> (c3 c3)
Hi 3!!!

scm-prompt> (quit) ; quitting the scheme interpreter!
```

B Fibonacci Toy Example : Event Messages and Behaviors

```
;;; unique event message used, it contains both n, n-1 and n-2 fields,
;;; and the result.
;;; Behaviors use only the field(s) they are interested in.
;;;
(genrec:define fibmsg n n-1 n-2 res) ; this defines the fibmsg record.

;;; fib behavior.
;;;
(define-behavior "fib"
  (when (and (fibmsg:isa? (msg)) (specified? (fibmsg:n (msg)))))
  (pre)
  (body (cond ((< (fibmsg:n (msg)) 2) (fibmsg:res! (msg) 1))
              (else (let ((becs (msg-send (fibmsg:make2 '(n-1 ,(- (fibmsg:n (msg)) 1))
                                                          '(n-2 ,(- (fibmsg:n (msg)) 2)))))))
                ;; collection of result for fibmsg:n from returned
                ;; fibmsg:n-1 and fibmsg:n-2
                (fibmsg:res! (msg) (+ (val:get becs '(0 msg res))
                                      (val:get becs '(1 msg res)))))))))
  (post))

;;; fib-1 behavior, treats the computation of (fib n-1).
;;;
(define-behavior "fib-1"
  (when (and (fibmsg:isa? (msg)) (specified? (fibmsg:n-1 (msg)))))
  (pre)
  (body (let ((becs (msg-send (fibmsg:make2 '(n ,(fibmsg:n-1 (msg)))))))
          (fibmsg:res! (msg) (val:get becs '(0 msg res)))))
  (post))

;;; fib-2 behavior, treats the computation of (fib n-2).
;;;
(define-behavior "fib-2"
  (when (and (fibmsg:isa? (msg)) (specified? (fibmsg:n-2 (msg)))))
  (pre)
  (body (let ((becs (msg-send (fibmsg:make2 '(n ,(fibmsg:n-2 (msg)))))))
          (fibmsg:res! (msg) (val:get becs '(0 msg res)))))
  (post))
```

```
;;; function to run the process until some intermediate computation state.
;;;
(define (fib:run-example)
  ;; sending to the propagation engine the computation of (Fibonacci 3)
  ;;
  (msg-send (fibmsg:make2 '(n 3)))
  (ben:next 2) (ben:next 2) ; stepping on the BENs.
  (ben:next 4) (ben:next 4)
  (ben:next 5) (ben:next 5) (ben:next 5)
  (ben:next 3) (ben:next 3)
  (ben:next 6) (ben:next 6)
  (ben:next 8) (ben:next 8)
  (ben:next 9) (ben:next 9) (ben:next 9)
  (bet:view)) ; viewing the BET.

;;; calling fib:run-example.
;;;
(fib:run-example)
```

Formal Description and Interpretation of Coordination Protocols for Teamwork

Oliver Frick

Institut für Telematik, Telecooperation Office (TecO)
Universität Karlsruhe, Germany
oli@teco.uni-karlsruhe.de
http://www.teco.uni-karlsruhe.de/~oli

Abstract. With the development of suitable abstractions for distributed computing and the advent of new QoS based multimedia communication services, engineering of teamwork applications is now able to concentrate mainly on the development of coordination issues rather than on communication issues. Coordination regulates the use of communication services by means of a coordination protocol. Coordination protocols today are informally described and their implementation is buried within teamwork applications; neither reuse nor verification by prospected end users is supported. Both aims can be supported when the design of coordination protocols for groupware is based on abstract formal description techniques known from the specification of communication protocols. This approach is demonstrated with a sample SDL specification of a coordination protocol for an application sharing type of teamwork. A design method for coordination protocols is derived from this example. Core design elements of the method are roles that are mapped to states of a state-based specification. This abstract, user-centred description can be transformed to a distributed Java implementation via an intermediate SDL specification.

Keywords: coordination in teamwork, formal protocol specification, SDL, design method for coordination, Java

1 Introduction

As basically every office worker today has a computer on his or her desktop, global end extensive use of computers for teamwork is a vision that is - from an infrastructure point of view - just around the corner. But the development of teamwork applications inherits a number of problems from other areas, namely

- *issues of distributed computing:* an application that supports team members that are geographically dispersed is inherently a distributed application; problems cover the exchange of persistent information objects and the consistent access to shared resources;

- *issues of multi-media communication:* teamwork applications should support user-centred communication by means of audio and video channels; problems here cover transportation of multimedia data streams over networks and their presentation to the end user;

- *issues of multi-user coordination:* coordination support is required whenever the underlying services or individual team members do not behave in a team supporting manner; policies that regulate access to a resource are a typical problem here.

Yet in recent time, the development of suitable abstractions for distributed computing [11] as well as new QoS based multimedia communication services [6] has improved up to a level that the development of teamwork applications will soon mainly deal with the development of coordination service only. However, a special methodology for the development of coordination services is required. Common object oriented design methodologies like OMT [12] are very good at modelling an application from a system point of view or are use case based like [8]. But none of them centres the design of coordination processes around users, e.g., by treating users as first class design objects.

In this paper, we present a step towards a development methodology for teamwork applications by introducing a design method for coordination protocols based on formal specification techniques. To this end, a teamwork model for coordination protocols is introduced. Section 3 gives an experimental SDL specification of a coordination protocol for an application sharing type of teamwork. Based on an analysis of this sample specification, section 4 presents a method for the design of coordination protocols. A 4-level approach is introduced, starting with design artifacts centred around roles that are mapped to states of a state-based specification, going all the way down to a runtime architecture for the interpretation of coordination protocols in a multi-user Java environment.

2   Coordination Model

2.1 Cooperation: Service, Mechanism, Policy and Protocol

Teamwork applications aim to support teams working together, i.e., support teams to *cooperate*. [11] defines cooperation or teamwork as *coordinated communication* where communication is bare and unregulated information exchange and coordination defines the access and ordering rules. According to [2], subject of coordination are shared (and thus limited) and concurrently used resources. Examples for resources are a shared file, a paragraph of a shared document, a multimedia communication channel, or a whole conference. Coordination for a multimedia communication channel for example is required when the social turn-taking coordination protocol know from every day live communication fails due to a long delay on the multimedia channel; a similar example is the coordination breakdown in turn-taking during a transatlantic telephone call on a slow line.

A *cooperation service* is a service view to a cooperative application provided by a cooperation mechanism together with a coordination policy. A *cooperation mecha-*

nism offers means for team communication and interaction; examples are group communication services, shared whiteboards or application sharing services (see section 3.1) and many other services, today often addressed as groupware. Cooperation mechanisms usually offer only very little support for their coordinated use. The rules for coordinated use of a cooperation mechanism are expressed with a *coordination policy*. A coordination policy defines who in the team is allowed to do what and when with the cooperation mechanism, thus defines how the team cooperates and "harmonically works together" [9]. Coordination policies for example define issues of session control or floor control using concepts like an access token or a coordinating chair. Cooperation mechanisms and coordination policies are orthogonal concepts [2]. A cooperation mechanism can be combined with a number of different coordination policies; each combination of cooperation mechanism and coordination policy defines a different cooperation service. A coordination policy is implemented by a *coordination protocol*. A protocol defines the rules and algorithms how individual team members work together and how they are allowed to make use of the underlying cooperation mechanism. Similar to communication services, cooperation can be described taking a service view or taking a protocol view.

2.2 Roles as an Abstraction for Users

Coordination policies and their implementation in coordination protocols are centred around users. Users within a cooperation have certain demands and capabilities or, from a service view, rights and obligations; they are both specific for a particular cooperation and reflect only a fraction of the demands and capabilities of a real user. A user thus plays a *role* within a cooperation that is specific for this cooperation. A role is the appearance of a user for other users within a cooperation. A single user can be enrolled into multiple roles at the same time. Expected behaviour of roles in a cooperation is expressed by

- a number of possible activities performed by or to be initiated from the user enrolled in a particular role

- the right to access defined shared resources.

A cooperation can be defined as the sum of all allowed interactions between all participants enrolled in a role specified for the cooperation. Cooperation takes place whenever operations are initiated and performed by roles. Using a role concept, coordination policies can now be modelled in a user centred way in terms of roles, role rights and obligations, and enrolled users. The coordination rules of a coordination policy defines rules for

- *operation initiation:* which role is allowed to initiate what activity

- *operation execution:* how is an operation performed by a role

- *role change (enrolment, derolment):* when is a user allowed to change his or her role and become a new role with different rights; which activities have to be performed when a role is changed.

3 Using SDL for the Coordination Specification of an Application Sharing Type of Teamwork - an Experiment

According to [2], developing teamwork applications means developing cooperation mechanism that provide the team with basic cooperation and communication tools, and developing coordination policies on top of cooperation mechanisms. This section first introduces a *cooperation mechanism* that supports teamwork providing an application sharing mechanism. Then, an example policy for this mechanism is informally described. Finally, the *coordination protocol* for the sample policy is developed and specified in SDL.

3.1 The Berkom MMC Application Sharing Service

Within the framework of the BERKOM MultiMedia Collaboration service (BERKOM MMC [1]), a number of cooperation mechanisms have been developed that together allow telecooperation in various styles. One of them is an application sharing mechanism provided by the application sharing component (ASC) that can be accessed using the application sharing control protocol (ASCP) [10]. Application sharing is a technique that transparently turns existing single-user applications into multi-user applications following the "What-You-See-Is-What-I-See" (WYSIWIS) paradigm. The right to provide input to an application (i.e., to work with an application) is provided by means of an input token; the participant actively working with an application is a so called "token holder". All other participants (so called "members") can only observe the activities of the token holder on their screen. To provide input to the application, a member has to request the input token which may be passed dynamically to him or her. Members may thus dynamically change their role and become a token holder and vice-versa. The ASCP offers service operations to access and manage the application sharing mechanism. Besides session control operations allowing users to join and leave the application sharing session, most important functionality is provided by the token management operation `ascpChangeControl(user,application)` which initiates the ASC to make `user` the new token holder of `application`; successful completion of this service request is signalled to the coordination protocol by an `ASCP_Input-Control-Changed` event from the ASC.

3.2 A Coordination Protocol for Application Sharing Type Teamwork

The MMC ASC itself is not a teamwork application to be directly used by users. It rather is a cooperation mechanism that has to be completed by a coordination policy before used by a team; the ASC provides no policy on who is allowed to initiate a control change over a shared application. A suitable coordination policy for the ASC mechanism is, e.g., the *timed explicit policy*. This policy represents a mixture between a strict and a loose coordination policy based on a timeout mechanism and introduces a mediating chair as a coordination role. The new policy allows a token holder to work for 10 minutes once an input token has been granted. Within this time limit, all token passing requests have to be explicitly granted by the chair (strict policy). Once a token holder has an input token for more than 10 minutes, every token request is automatically granted to the requester who in turn becomes the token holder and can work with the application for 10 minutes only potentially being disturbed by the chair. The goal of this policy is to allow actively contributing team members (i.e., token holders) to freely develop their ideas for a certain amount of time and on the other hand prevent excessive contribution from a single site (i.e., token possession for a long time).

3.3 Service Specification with SDL

Taking the top-down approach to specify protocols presented in [3], Figure 1 illustrates the SDL service specification of the application sharing service (AS_Service) coordination protocol within the system of a teamwork (AS_Teamwork). The users of the service are located in the environment; they can be considered as individual processes and are not part of the SDL specification. The timed explicit policy takes an arbitrary number of members as longs as at least one member exists, exactly one token holder, and exactly one chair. The users access the service via service access points modelled by channels, sending and receiving signals which represent service primitives (e.g,. UI-REQ-Token, UI-REJ-Token, UI-Grant-Token). A real process in the SDL service specification is mapped to each virtual UI process to explicitly model the interfaces to the users and the number of users supported by the service (i.e. in the example of Figure 1 one chair, one token holder, and at least one member process). The service description AS_Service offers an abstract view of the coordination policy, it just specifies the interface to the service for service users and defines the participants. It does not describe implementation issues of the protocol, nor internal communication (although internal communication is indicated with internal signalroutes).

Fig. 1. SDL system specification for application sharing type of teamwork

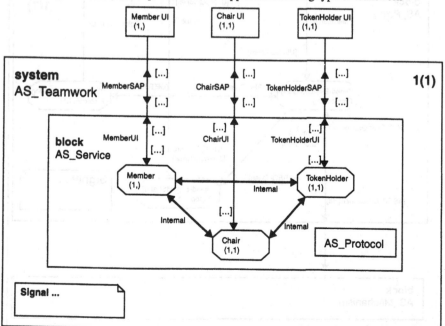

3.4 Service Implementation

The service implementation AS_Protocol has already been introduced into the SDL system design as a substructure substituting the AS_Service block. The AS_Protocol implementation depicted in Figure 2 opens a view to the implementation architecture of the coordination protocol. The AS_Protocol provides its cooperation service by implementing an application sharing policy (block AS_Policy) and by using the MMC application sharing mechanism (block AS_Mechanism). The policy accesses the mechanism using the ASCP protocol. This architecture reflects the general scheme for the design of teamwork application by using existing cooperation mechanisms and augmenting them with coordination policies.

The signals between all involved processes are now specified. The protocol is imple-mented by the same number of processes already defined in Figure 1. But all processes are now implemented by the same process type Timed-ExplicitSharingProtocol. This process type not only specifies the behaviour of all user types involved in the coordina-tion protocol. It also defines the rules for role changes within the scope of the protocol. This is the reason for using one process type for all user types; users have the capabil-ity to change a role within the same process. This design principle will be explained in more detail in the next section.

Fig. 2. SDL specification of the application sharing protocol

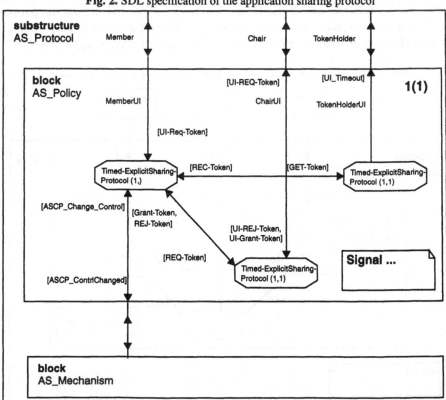

3.5 Coordination Protocol Behaviour Specification

The rules and algorithms of the coordination protocol are finally implemented within the Timed-ExplicitSharingProtocol depicted in Figure 3 and Figure 4. The SDL specification of Figure 3 defines the coordination rules for members requesting and receiving the input token from the token holder. A user without a token is in the "member" state as long as no token management is going on. A token request is performed by sending a UI-Req-Token via a member interface to the AS_Protocol. On receiving the demand, the coordination policy depends on the time the old token holder already holds the token. When the TH_Timeout timer is not active, the reserved period for the token holder has passed and the member sends a GET-Token to the token holder and waits in state "get token". But if TH_Timeout is still active, the members request is to be decided by the chair; a REQ-Token signal is send to the chair and the answer is awaited in state "chair decision". The chair either grants the request with a "Grant-Token" signal which in turn will result in a GET-Token signal to the token holder and the new state "get token". Or the chair may reject the request; on receiving a REJ-Token signal, the coordination rule terminates and the process again gets in the "member" state. Once the member is in the "get token" state, the request is granted and the member receives the token from the current token holder. Having the signal from the token holder, the underlying application sharing mechanism is activated with an ASCP_Change_Control signal to actually perform the control change. On successful control change, the mechanism answers with an ASCP-ContrlChanged signal and the TH_Timeout timer is activated and set to 600 seconds. Finally, the member associated with this process has become the token holder and gets into the "Token Holder" state.

Fig. 3. SDL specification for token passing protocol, token requesters view

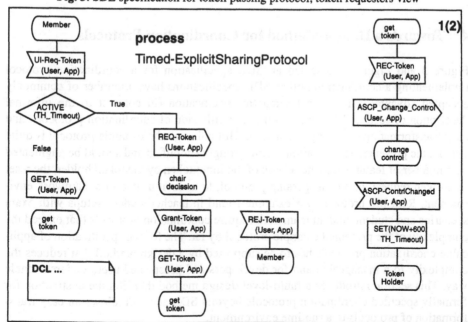

A closer look at the coordination policy and its SDL specification in Figure 3 shows that part 1 of the Timed-ExplicitSharingProtocol is just concerned with rules for users whose processes are in the "member" state, i.e., *users who are in the "member" role*. This part thus describes the capabilities and rights of the "member" role, e.g., the right to get the input token. But most importantly, the protocol also describes the rules of how a process in the "member" state can get to the "token holder" state, i.e., *how a user in the member role can change the role and become a "token holder"*. Figure 4 finally specifies the coordination protocol rules for the token holder and the chair analog to the rules for the member role.

Fig. 4. SDL specification for token passing protocol, chair and token holders view

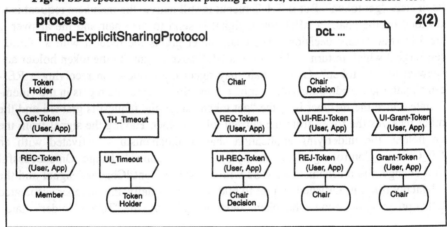

4 Towards a Design Method for Coordination Protocols

Figure 3 and Figure 4 presented an SDL specification for a coordination protocol implementing a coordination policy. SDL specifications have a number of commonly accepted advantages like exact semantic specification (in contrast to the informal description of section 3.2), simulation and verification of coordination protocols, and easy transformation to an implementation. But although the example protocol is quite simple, the presented specification is still strongly simplified and should be augmented by a number of features like the release of the input token by the token holder, the reset of a token request, or a chair passing protocol, to make it usable in a teamwork environment. Real life protocols for example found in teacher-student setups with exam scenarios and student-student teamwork require coordination protocols that exceed the complexity of the presented example protocol by far. The formal specification of applicable coordination protocols has to be supported by a design method that reduces the complexity to a manageable and for developers and prospected users understandable way. This section introduces a multi-level design method that lifts the abstraction for formally specified coordination protocols beyond SDL and still allows an easy transformation of protocols to a runtime environment.

4.1 Level 1: scenario based view to a cooperation service

The first and most abstract level starts the design with scenarios of cooperating users. This level centres around roles as abstractions for users and aims at understanding what kind of users (i.e., what roles) cooperate together. As introduced in section 2, roles represent aspects of users associated with certain capabilities and obligations, reflected by a number of operations a role is able to activate or obliged to perform. This is now modelled by signals a role sends or receives form the cooperation service. The cooperation service under design is specified in level 1 by:

- a set of roles using the coordination service

- the number of instances a particular role may have

- the signals exchanged between a role and the coordination service.

Fig. 5. Level 1: Cooperation scenario for application sharing service

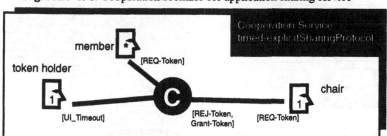

Figure 5 depicts the related design artifact for the application sharing scenario of section 3.2. It shows three roles with the number of allowed instances, the signals between the roles and the coordination service, and an abstract symbol for the coordination service. As level 1 cooperation scenarios only use roles to specify partners of a cooperation, they represent a special variant of Work Scenario Graphs introduced in [7].

4.2 Level 2: role centred behaviour specification

Based on an abstract service specification of level 1, the behaviour of a coordination service, i.e., a coordination protocol, can be specified. An example behaviour specification in SDL was presented in section 3, Figure 6 subsumes the specifications of Figure 3 (right half of Figure 6) and Figure 4 (left half) for an analysis. Taking a roles view, special sections of the behaviour specification can be identified that are related to specific roles (all areas shaded light gray are related to users enrolled in a specific role), i.e., *are only valid when the process associated to a user is in one of the states of the related role*. Although a role may be in intermediate states, a defined state exists that represents the *default state* of the role where the signals representing the obligations and capabilities are received. The default states in Figure 6 are Chair, Member and Token Holder. These observations give a first design guideline:

All states are associated with a certain role; designated states exist that represent the default state of a role. Signals received in the default state represent obligations for roles, signals sent represent capabilities.

This rule motivates designers to think from a users perspective and model coordination protocols around roles, and helps the prospected users to validate their requirements. The design artifact for level 2 specifications depicted in Figure 7 treats roles as first class design elements: a special "state" is introduced that represents the default state of the role where all other role relevant rules originate. Default states are predefined in the member section and can be derived from level 1 roles.

Fig. 6. SDL behaviour specification with roles and enrolment phases

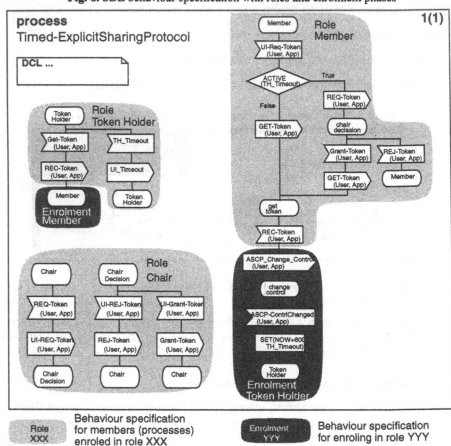

A user may actively participate in a coordination protocol without changing his or her role (for example the role "chair" in Figure 6). But users may as well change their role (e.g., the "token holder" may become a "member"), perform an enrolment process (shaded dark gray in Figure 6) and moves to a new state. A simple enrolment procedure takes place when a token holder becomes a member - no additional actions have to be taken. More complex is the enrolment process for a member to become a token holder: the token has to be received and the underlying sharing service has to be initiated. The activities done in the enrolment process are calls to the cooperation mechanism and are not relevant to the coordination protocol.

285

Following a separation of concern design guideline, enrolment should not have to be modelled within the behaviour specification, as the next design guideline states:

Role changes according to the coordination protocol are modelled with state transitions. Activities in an enrolment process that are not relevant to the coordination protocol should be modelled in separate design artifacts.

The coordination protocol specification on this level thus introduces a special "enrolment macro" depicted in Figure 7 that represent the enrolment process. The exact enrolment process is specified in an enrolment section. With these design guidelines and the level 2 design artifact, behaviour within a cooperation can now be modelled according to the tree types of user activity and behaviour:

1. a user actively participates in teamwork and performs task within the framework of a cooperation mechanism (e.g., working with a shared application). This behaviour is implicitly modelled by the *default role* of a user;
2. a user performs coordination tasks. This behaviour is explicitly modelled by SDL like *coordination rules*;
3. a user changes a role and performs enrolment/derolment activities. This behaviour is expressed by an *enrolment macro*.

Fig. 7. Level 2: role centred behaviour specification (excerpt)

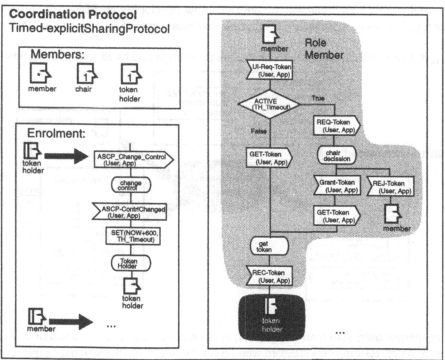

 default role XXX   enrolment macro for role YYY

4.3 Level 3: mapping to SDL specifications

Although design artifacts specified in level 1 and 2 are designed to express role behaviour in a coordination protocol and use specialized design symbols, a mapping to standard SDL specifications is straight forward. The level 1 scenario centred design artifacts presented in Figure 5 contain the same amount of information as the SDL system specification of Figure 1; they can easily be mapped to an SDL service specification as a starting point for an SDL specification of the cooperation service. Main specialization of level 2 artifacts were the use of special state symbols which foster the understanding of the coordination protocol and which can immediately be mapped to states. Substituting enrolment macros should finally result in protocol implementation specifications similar to Figure 3 and Figure 4.

4.4 Level 4: implementation and interpretation

Cooperation between (potentially distributed) users requires that all users act according to the same coordination protocol; if someone does not act according to the agreed policy, a coordination breakdown will occur. Easy distribution of identical copies of the coordination protocol and their interpretation can be achieved by transforming the level 3 SDL specifications to Java [4] code and distributing it via the WWW. As only simple SDL elements were used in the specification phase, the transformation is straight forward and can be based on standard SDL compilation technology using a Java SDL runtime environment; we are right now developing an SDL-to-Java compiler together with a distributed Java runtime environment for SDL using Suns RMI.

Fig. 8. Distributed interpretation of coordination protocols in Java based Web environments

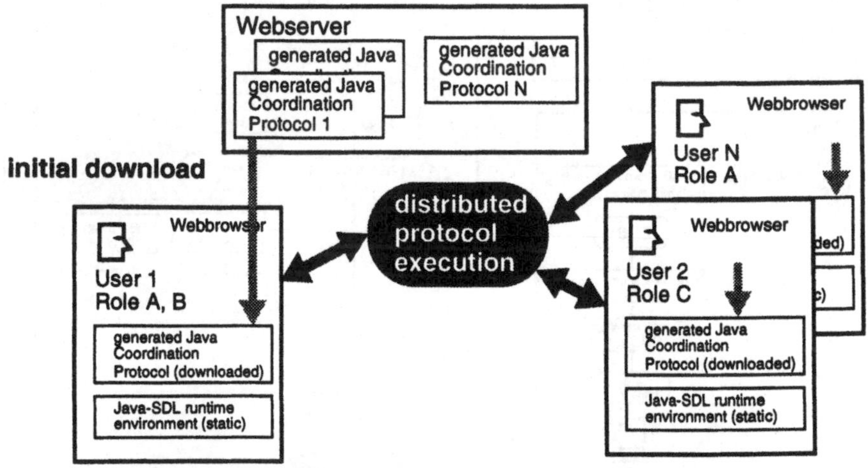

To cooperate, users start their (ubiquitous) Java enhanced web browser and visit a conference server residing on a standard web server. On accessing the web page representing the coordination policy they want to interact, initial cooperation parameters like initial enrolments will have to be specified and the Java code representing the coordination protocol is transparently and identically downloaded to all participants. The

Java code is started and the coordination protocol is executed as a distributed Java application within the web browsers of all participants; no further access to the conference server is required. Figure 8 depicts the runtime architecture for executing coordination protocols compiled to Java.

5 Summary and Conclusion

Cooperative applications are distributed systems where cooperation mechanisms provide means for communication and a coordination policy on top of cooperation mechanisms regulates their concurrent use. A coordination policy is either implicitly provided by a social protocol, or explicitly implemented by a coordination protocol. Coordination protocols are usually informally described and their implementation is buried within a teamwork application. For a better re-use of generic groupware applications and other cooperation mechanisms, coordination protocols have to be separated and specified using formal description techniques.

Using SDL for the specification of coordination protocols is a first step as the example in this paper demonstrated. The general specification approach for service and protocol specification can be done analog to usual specifications of communication systems. The semantics of the coordination policy can be exactly specified and the underlying cooperation mechanism is integrated seamlessly. But real world coordination protocols may become quite complex and an additional methodical support is required. Additionally, the design of coordination protocols for teamwork is a delicate task. To prevent the design of coordination protocols that hinder teams to cooperate efficiently, the design must be centred around the prospected users of the protocol. Badly designed protocols either provide to little coordination, so most effort especially in larger teams goes into repair of coordination breakdowns or additional coordination by establishing a social protocol. Or protocols imply to many rules and limitations on the cooperation, so the co-workers feel massively regulated by the coordination protocol [2] and loose interest in continuing their teamwork. Thus, a design method for formally developing coordination protocols must centre around users and their abstractions within the notion of roles.

Based on this observation, a method for the development of coordination protocols for teamwork was introduced in this paper. Core design elements are roles that are mapped to states of a state-based specification. Using roles to model user behaviour and mapping roles to states enforces user centred design and gives way for more abstract specifications. The method introduces 4 specification levels:

1. an abstract, scenario-centred description focusing on roles and role interfaces,
2. a coordination behaviour specification with roles as first class design elements, enrolment macros and an SDL-like syntax,
3. the mapping of level 1 and level 2 artifacts to SDL descriptions,
4. the transformation of SDL specifications to Java code and the interpretation of coordination protocols in a multi-user Java enhanced Web environment.

The formal specification of coordination protocols according to the presented methodology now opens possibilities for a formal analysis and simulation of a coordination protocol. Abstract specifications of cooperation services as provided by level 1 specifications open a way of integrating these synchronous, small size cooperations into large size workflow style applications using design methods like Scenario Flows [5]. The abstract yet still exact specifications also allows better information exchange between computer scientist who develop teamwork applications, psychologists who provide ethnographic experience for the design of coordination protocols, and users who finally decide whether they will or will not use coordinated teamwork applications.

References

1. M. Altenhofen, J. Dittrich, R. Hammerschmidt, T. Käppner, C. Kruschel, A. Kückens, T. Steinig. The BERKOM Multimedia Collaboration Service. *Proceedings of ACM Multimedia 93*, Anaheim, California, August 1-6, 1993, ACM, 1993, pp. 457-463.

2. H.-P. Dommel and J.J. Garcia-Luna-Aceves. Floor Control for Multimedia Conferencing and Collaboration. To appear in the *ACM Journal on Multimedia Systems*.

3. B. Ferenc, D. Hogrefe, A. Sarma. *SDL with Applications from Protocol Specification*. Prentice Hall, 1991.

4. D. Flanagan. *Java in a Nutshell*. O'Reilly & Associates, Inc., 1996.

5. O. Frick. Multimedia Conferencing Systems as Building Blocks for Complex Cooperative Applications. In M. Mühlhäuser (Ed.) *Proceedings of IFIP Workshop Multimedia System Development*, Springer LNCS, 1996.

6. O. Frick, C. Schmidt. Service Support for Multiuser Multimedia Applications. *In submission*.

7. H.-W. Gellersen, M. Mühlhäuser. Design of Workplace-integrating User Interfaces based on Work Scenario Graphs. In D. Benyon, P. Palanque (Eds.) *Critical Issues in User Interface System Engineering*, Springer Verlag London, 1995.

8. I. Jacobsen. Object-Oriented Software Engineering: A Use Case Driven Approach. *ACM Press/Addison-Wesley, Wokingham, England, 1992*.

9. T. Malone, K. Crowston. What is Coordination Theory and How Can It Help Design Cooperative Work Systems? In *Proceedings ACM CSCW '90*, October 1990.

10. F. Ruge, A. Zehl (Eds.). The BERKOM Multimedia Teleservices Volume II, Multimedia Collaboration. *Internal BERKOM working document*. Release 4.0, May 1996.

11. T. Rüdebusch. *CSCW–Generic Support for Teamwork in Distributed Systems*. Dissertation, University of Karlsruhe, Germany, DUV, Wiesbaden, 1993. (in German)

12. J. Rumbaugh, M. Blaha, W. Premerlani, F. Eddy, W. Lorensen. Object-Oriented Modelling and Design. *Prentice Hall, Engelwood Cliffs, New Jersey, 1991*.

Author Index

Springer-Verlag
and the Environment

We at Springer-Verlag firmly believe that an international science publisher has a special obligation to the environment, and our corporate policies consistently reflect this conviction.

We also expect our business partners – paper mills, printers, packaging manufacturers, etc. – to commit themselves to using environmentally friendly materials and production processes.

The paper in this book is made from low- or no-chlorine pulp and is acid free, in conformance with international standards for paper permanency.

Lecture Notes in Computer Science

For information about Vols. 1–1083

please contact your bookseller or Springer-Verlag